Philip W. Blood

Putin's War, Russian Genocide
Essays about the First Year of the War in Ukraine

With contributions by Chris Bellamy, Philip W. Blood, Dustin Du Cane, Roger Cirillo

Edited by Philip W. Blood

Philip W. Blood

PUTIN'S WAR, RUSSIAN GENOCIDE
Essays about the First Year of the War in Ukraine

With contributions by Chris Bellamy, Philip W. Blood, Dustin Du Cane, Roger Cirillo

Edited by Philip W. Blood

Bibliografische Information der Deutschen Nationalbibliothek
Die Deutsche Nationalbibliothek verzeichnet diese Publikation in der Deutschen Nationalbibliografie; detaillierte bibliografische Daten sind im Internet über http://dnb.d-nb.de abrufbar.

Bibliographic information published by the Deutsche Nationalbibliothek
Die Deutsche Nationalbibliothek lists this publication in the Deutsche Nationalbibliografie; detailed bibliographic data are available in the Internet at http://dnb.d-nb.de.

ISBN-13: 978-3-8382-1833-5
© *ibidem*-Verlag, Stuttgart 2023
Alle Rechte vorbehalten

Das Werk einschließlich aller seiner Teile ist urheberrechtlich geschützt. Jede Verwertung außerhalb der engen Grenzen des Urheberrechtsgesetzes ist ohne Zustimmung des Verlages unzulässig und strafbar. Dies gilt insbesondere für Vervielfältigungen, Übersetzungen, Mikroverfilmungen und elektronische Speicherformen sowie die Einspeicherung und Verarbeitung in elektronischen Systemen.

All rights reserved. No part of this publication may be reproduced, stored in or introduced into a retrieval system, or transmitted, in any form, or by any means (electronic, mechanical, photocopying, recording or otherwise) without the prior written permission of the publisher. Any person who does any unauthorized act in relation to this publication may be liable to criminal prosecution and civil claims for damages.

Printed in the EU

CONTENTS

REFERENCE MAPS 9
   UKRAINE 2022 9
   UKRAINE INVASION MAP 24 FEBRUARY 2022 10
   UKRAINE SITUATION MAP APRIL 2023 11

PREFACE 13
EDITOR'S NOTE 15

THE FIRST YEAR OF THE WAR IN UKRAINE 17
   Dr Philip W. Blood (editor, military & holocaust historian) 19
   Dr Roger Cirillo (retired armoured cavalry, Lieutenant
   Colonel US army, military author, and editor) 25
   Professor Chris Bellamy (professor emeritus Greenwich, UK,
   visiting fellow Pembroke college, Oxford, military historian
   and editor) 28
   Dustin Du Cane (lawyer) 31

**1. MILITARY HISTORY, SOCIAL MEDIA, AND
WAR CRIMES**
Philip W. Blood 35
   War crimes and public media 38
   Coming to terms with the past 47
   Russian war Crimes and Putin's War 54
   The verdict of history 59

2. COLD WAR MEMORIES FROM EUROPE'S PAST
Roger Cirillo 63
   Reflections of a Cold War soldier 67
   Western European Security, NATO and the US commitment
   to Europe 70
   NATO's forward defence strategy 72
   Flexible response shapes NATO strategic thinking 74
   Escalation: from conventional forces to nuclear weapons 75
   The use of chemical/biological weapons fall within nuclear
   escalation 76
   From battlefield nuclear weapons to all-out nuclear war 78
   The long-forgotten unwritten rules and protocols 79
   NATO and Warsaw Pact forces generated a war morality 81

    The US military's attitude towards Europe and NATO............ 83
    NATO's Article 5 84
    Warsaw Pact nations joined NATO 85
    The costs of the military–industrial complex............................ 86
    Impressions of Russian military capability................................ 86
    Ongoing Operations to End of Year One. 87

3. HYBRID AND NON-LINEAR WARFARE IN RUSSIAN STRATEGIC THINKING
Chris Bellamy 91
    Prologue: of little green men.. 91
    The science of future war 97
    Science fiction and visions of future war 104
    'Hybrid war': plus ça change? 108
    The Russian denial 117
    Trojan horses — Afghanistan, 1979.. 119
    Trojan horses — Czechoslovakia, 1968.. 121
    Trojan horses? Hungary 1956 129
    'Revolutionierungspolitik' and 'myatezhevoyna': the gradual evolution of 'non-linear' techniques, 1914–2014......... 132
    Reflexive control and cybernetics: the key to modern Russian non-linear war.. 144
    The cyber dimension 155
    Conclusion.. 163

4. 'NO PLAN SURVIVES CONTACT WITH THE ENEMY'
Chris Bellamy **169**
    The build-up to war: First encircle 171
    The naval build-up 184
    Having encircled, then strike the head … 192
    Ukraine's Stalingrad: Mariupol 204
    Conclusion: from non-linear to linear.. 218

5. STRATEGY IN THE AGE OF GLOBAL WAR
Philip W. Blood... **225**
    Strategy and the path to global war... 227
    The shifting sands of global strategies.. 236
    Putin and NATO - an intractable confrontation....................... 243
    Putin and the Russian population... 250
    Strategic humanitarianism and the case for an European army 259

6. PUTIN'S WAR, RUSSIAN GENOCIDE
Philip W. Blood **275**
Putin's terror 276
Putin's special military operation—Russian security warfare 284
Putin's genocide: holocaust by bombardment 292
The case of the individual perpetrator 301
Post-mortems of social media and genocide 311

7. CRIMES, WAR, AND GENOCIDE
Dustin Du Cane **317**
A genocide lawyer is born.. 318
Towards the Holocaust.. 321
The Holocaust and the law.. 335
Genocide codified... 347
Justice for Genocide.. 354

8. RUSSIAN LAW OF WAR
Dustin Du Cane **381**
Knowing the law... 382
Applying the law 386
Memory in law 412

9. REALKRIEG IN WARTIME
Philip W. Blood **423**
Ripping yarns: culture wars and gaming strategy.......... 426
The Anaconda Plan One Year On 435
The western quandary 443

REFLECTIONS **446**
Philip W. Blood.. 446
Dustin Du Cane 449
Chris Bellamy... 454
Roger Cirillo 461

Also by

Chris Bellamy, *Absolute War: Soviet Russia in the Second World War; a Modern History* (London: Pan Books, 2009).

Chris Bellamy, *The Future of Land Warfare* (London: Croom Helm, 1987).

Chris Bellamy, *Red God of War: Soviet Artillery and Rocket Forces*, 1st ed (London; Washington: Elmsford, N.Y., U.S.A: Brassey's Defence Publishers; Orders, Pergamon Press, 1986).

Philip W. Blood, *Hitler's Bandit Hunters: The SS and the Nazi Occupation of Europe,* (Virginia: Potomac, 2006).

Philip W. Blood, *Birds of Prey: Hitler's Luftwaffe, Ordinary Soldiers, and the Holocaust in Poland* (Stuttgart: ibidem Verlag, 2021).

Roger Cirillo, *The Campaigns of World War II: Ardennes-Alsace - War College Series* (U. S. Army Center For Military History, 2015).

Roger Cirillo, Series Editor, John Nelson Rickard, ed., *Advance and Destroy: Patton as Commander in the Bulge,* American Warriors (Lexington: University Press of Kentucky, 2011).

REFERENCE MAPS

UKRAINE 2022

Map of Ukraine 2023 via CIA The World Factbook August 31 2023 In public domain via https://www.cia.gov/the-world-factbook/countries/ukraine/map/[1]

---

[1] US government products are public domain. No claim made on these images.

UKRAINE INVASION MAP 24 FEBRUARY 2022

Jomini of the West @JominiW Map of Ukrainian Theater on 24 February 2022
Used with explicit author permission. Jomini is Major Ivan Torres, US Army - Strategic Planner US Army Center of Military History.[2] All rights reserved.
Original at https://twitter.com/JominiW/status/1497419233940094981

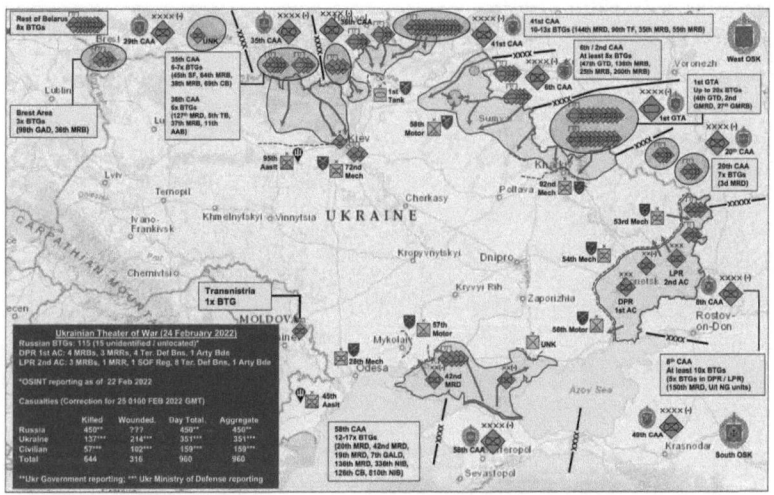

---

[2] For all references to JominiW and Major Torres—'The views expressed are those of the author and do not reflect the official policy or position of the US Army, Department of Defense or the US Government.'

UKRAINE SITUATION MAP APRIL 2023

Jomini of the West @JominiW map of Ukrainian Theater on April 7, 2023
Used with explicit author permission.[3] All rights reserved.
Original at https://twitter.com/JominiW/status/1644436075526463488

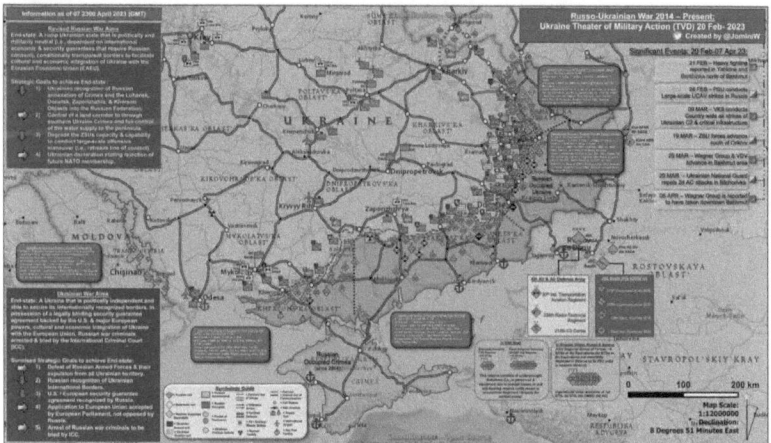

---

[3] As in footnote 2.

PREFACE

This book is the result of a collaborative project started in May 2022. We would like to express our gratitude to those individuals who have assisted the authors. Markus Faulkner, senior lecturer at King's College, London University, and a naval historian, offered invaluable advice and contributed content related to naval operations in the Black Sea from April to July 2022. Markus is on Twitter @NavalHistWar. US Army Colonel (Retired) Douglas Macgregor provided the editor with a paper on the alternative interpretation into the direction of the war. Dr. Ian Garner, an expert on Russian culture and war propaganda, generously shared source materials, including materials from Putin's archive, with the editor. He also published: *Z Generation: Into the Heart of Russia's Fascist Youth* in July 2023; we wish him continued success. Ian is also on Twitter @irgarner.

Paul Six, MA, a solicitor advocate, reviewed sections of the manuscript and provided legal opinions for the editor. He also served as an external reader for the manuscript in the summer of 2022. You can find Paul on Twitter under the handle @SixVpf. The publisher and authors extend their appreciation to US Army Major Ivan Torres, a Strategic Planner at the US Army Center of Military History, also known as *The Jomini of the West* (Twitter - @JominiW, views expressed are his own), for granting permission to use his maps in the manuscript. Ben Skipper assumed the role of art adviser. He runs the Adjutant's Lounge, a platform that hosted some of the content and ideas underpinning this book. Ben's podcasts are available online, and you can connect with him on Twitter @WriteBenSkipper. On behalf of the authors, we would like to extend our heartfelt thanks to our publisher, Ibidem-Verlag in Hannover, in particular Christian Schön and Jessica Haunschild.

Philip W. Blood (Editor)
Aachen, June 2023

EDITOR'S NOTE

This collection of essays was compiled by independent authors. The essays retain their personal style, critical analysis, and findings. They have contributed to the book in their capacity as experts of their field and do not represent any organisations or institutions.

This book was revised and edited several times during the writing process and afterwards in manuscript form. All efforts were made to secure accurate translations, to ensure the correct citations for sources, and to check for the usual everyday errors that arise from writing and compiling a work of diversity. Any errors, mistakes or miss-citations are editorial errors and were not intentional. If practical, we will endeavour to correct any omissions or errors in subsequent editions.

Dr. Philip W. Blood, editor.
26 September 2023

THE FIRST YEAR OF THE WAR IN UKRAINE

On 24 February 2022, Vladimir Putin ordered the invasion of Ukraine. He declared a 'special military operation', expecting a quick victory. The Ukrainian army countered with a spirited defence that foiled his political aims. Putin's special operation descended into a brutal slogging match of massacres. The horror of Bucha, rapes, looting, and the mass kidnap of children were discovered in the wake of Russian retreats. Reversals shattered Russia's army, forcing Putin to unleash his bandit hordes — Chechen thugs and pardoned murderers of the Wagner Group. Russia's artillery, the God of War, continued to hammer Ukrainian culture, cities, and civilians. Mariupol was devastated in the turmoil of mechanised genocide. In the first year, western experts filled social media with analogies of irrelevant wars and false predictions of Ukraine's progress. The authors of this volume have challenged institutional orthodoxy and pushed back against this outpouring of social media. They identified a chilling narrative of existential warfare and the struggle for survival.

Modern warfare is complex yet retains fundamental traits common to all wars. Throughout the ages, the military-political-economic power complex has developed weapons, raised armies, and set state policy. From the socio-cultural undercurrents there have always been the soldiers, the casualties, and the bystanders of war. This is common to all armies since antiquity. Since 1945, with the end of the age of total war, the power complexes became increasingly sophisticated and remote from societies. The modern professional armies and their modern societies were separated by new technology, societal change, and public attitudes. At one time military service was wrapped in codes of duty, honour, and sacrifice. Once societies abandoned national conscription, a significant gap emerged between the professional soldier community and wider society. Increasingly soldiers believed their 'sacrifice' to the nation was no longer appreciated, while civil society pushed back against military socioeconomics. After the end of the Cold War societies drew breath and prepared for a new less violent age. Wars in faraway places — Vietnam, the Middle East and Afghanistan — had proven deeply unpopular among the general public. After 1989 societies became war averse, even when the civil war in Yugoslavia turned into ethnic-cleansing and genocide. UN peace-keeping forces grasped a moment of public approval, as NATO air power was criticised. War and genocide had returned to Europe, but western societies wanted to avoid war — the west was war exhausted. The War on Terror that followed the 9-11 atrocities captured the sense of public outrage but over-interpreted the scale of jingoism. Anti-war protests in major western cities reflected war-aversion. Meanwhile in Russia, war became a tool for holding the empire together, and internal violence was orchestrated for a national policy that advances an authoritarian regime. War in Russian culture, through Putin's politicisation of the Soviet Union's victory in the Great Patriotic War (1941-45), weaponised nostalgia for a lost greatness and amplified by fantasies of making Russia great once again.

During the writing of this book, we recognised the emerging tragedy of modern war — that lethal combination of genocide and war — which renders conventional analysis highly unpredictable. *Putin's War, Russian Genocide* reflects on the west's response to the Ukraine-Russia war since February 2022 and presents a counter to how social media has separately classified the war from the genocide. The war has exposed the demise of the traditional power complex that once functioned in the defence and security of the nation. Security and defence are remote from democratic processes and barely raised in public discourse. Political parties laud Ukraine's defence and the supply of arms but are reluctant to engage the public in the prospect of a call to arms. The remoteness of security in public discourse has encouraged western governments to allow their national armed forces to become run-down and military stockpiles to become emptied. The bewilderment of the western public at NATO's reluctance to be drawn into Ukraine, which contrasted with the heavy bombing of Yugoslavia in the 1990s, has made it harder in the future for political leaders to raise defence in public.

Long after the Yugoslavian civil war; regardless of the presiding human rights legislation, international courts, and genocide mandates of the UN, few perpetrators faced justice, and the politics of violence has still not been assuaged. In Grozny in 1999, Putin unleased Russian military forces in the perpetration of crimes against humanity, imposed mass destruction and carried out acts of genocide. Since March 2022 Russian soldiers, with government approval, have been prosecuting genocide. Meanwhile, western societies have generally remained reluctant to contemplate war.

The Authors of this book concluded their essays in May/June 2023, in a one-year collaborative project. Each essay can be read as a self-contained piece of writing with specific bibliographic footnotes. The collective aim was to examine the war's first year before it became mired in myths and memory. The entire focus of the book is on that first year, which was documented in the media but with nagging uncertainties. The war continues with indications of a prolonged conflict. The range of essays include the impact of historical writing on social media, the legacy of the Cold War, Hybrid and Non-Linear warfare, Putin's special military operation, crimes during war, war-related genocide, the Russian army's conduct, the rules and laws of war, and the global future of warfare. The authors acknowledge that the war has become an unpredictable routine within everyday life, marking a significant shift in the trajectory of European history.

Dr Philip W. Blood
(editor, military & holocaust historian)

Navigating the tumultuous waters of a war in real-time poses an immense challenge for any historian. Let's begin with a general impression of Putin's war, followed by a concise glimpse into the themes of my essays within this volume.

In this particular conflict, anticipation had preceded the outbreak of hostilities, as events in the preceding year had exacerbated superpower tensions, especially with the contentious developments on the Polish-Belarus border. While I wasn't taken aback by

Putin's pre-emptive strike against Ukraine, I found myself perplexed by the Russian Army's sluggish performance and NATO's failure to impose a no-fly zone over Ukraine. The initial expectations of a swift Russian victory over the Ukrainian forces were quickly shattered by the shocking brutality of Putin's resort to genocide. However, it wasn't just Russia's underwhelming military performance that raised concerns. There was a stark warning for NATO forces, which had seen significant reductions in their military capabilities due to short-sighted policy decisions. These reductions across military establishments and weapon stockpiles reflected more than just complacency; they hinted at a politicized disarmament process obscured from public view. The rise of populist politics had expedited the decline in military power as a core state function, leading to the hollowing out of security institutions and a general indifference to defence preparedness. The question yet to be answered is who or what was expected to fill the defence void in the event of war? It's evident that the west relied on NATO and the USA, while depleting the very forces needed to carry NATO successfully through a war — thus raising the question: who was deluding who? This contradiction left a profound impression of the West's political self-delusion.

The spectre of war has hung over Europe for more than a year, without any sign of a functioning European Army or clear evidence of a European vision for strategic defence. Europe's history was riddled with recurrent conflicts fought over the same battlefields, leaving deep scars that never truly healed. The devastation of European cities during World War II, exemplified by the destruction of Dresden, had fostered a genuine pacifist sentiment. However, in November 1991, urban destruction returned to Europe with the devastation of Vukovar, marking the beginning of a decade of bitter conflicts. Sarajevo endured a prolonged siege, while Srebrenica witnessed a tragic humanitarian catastrophe. The events of Mariupol in April 2022, were believed to have surpassed Vukovar in terms of destruction, reducing a once-vibrant city to a lifeless ruin.

In this ongoing war, memorials to past conflicts have been shattered or vandalized, reflecting the turmoil and destruction that has engulfed the region. The town of Trostianets, for instance, bore witness to two wars, with heavy bombardments reducing it to ruins, leaving only a T-34 tank from the Great Patriotic War as a sombre reminder of the past. Russian artillery's deliberate targeting of civilian communities amounted to nothing short of genocide, deviating from the typical collateral damage seen in conventional warfare. Ukrainian culture, cities, and people were being mercilessly ground into rubble. Putin's "mechanized genocide" was not only inflicting unspeakable suffering on the Ukrainian people but also allowing Russia to maintain control of the strategic initiative. In contrast, the West adopted an uncertain strategic stance, neither fully committing to war nor embracing peace—more like the depleted arsenal of a disappearing democracy profiting from the plight of Ukraine. In 2022, Europe had regressed into a climate of war, endangering its cultural heritage. Putin's readiness to turn European cities into wastelands demanded decisive action to safeguard Europe's civilization. Putin has shown he is quite prepared to put European cities to the torch—he and Russia must be stopped for the sake of Europe's civilisation.

In my contributions to this volume, I explored three overarching themes emerging from Putin's 2022 invasion. These themes encompassed the use of security warfare in Russian strategic thinking, the perpetration of genocide by the Russian army during military operations, and the West's response to the war through social media.

Historically, operational security in military campaigns had often been relegated to a secondary role. My research, drawing from the study of Nazi occupation security, introduced the concept of "security warfare," representing a form of warfare driven solely by modern interpretations of national security. This spectrum of "security warfare" encompassed colonization, decolonization, counter-revolution, occupation, and various forms of counterinsurgency—often the military euphemisms for controlling, securing, and sometimes killing civilians. Identifying the political purpose behind "security warfare" in Hitler's campaigns revealed its relevance to other authoritarian regimes.¹ During the Cold War, Western governments experimented with these methods, applying a less genocidal form of security warfare during decolonization insurgencies, the Vietnam War, and the War on Terror, albeit with limited success. Putin's "special military operation" drew parallels with the strategy of an Anaconda Plan—a security warfare strategy aiming to encircle Ukraine within its borders, applying constriction through bombardment, and the prosecution of military operations at points along the entire Russian-Ukraine frontier. Thus, Putin's operation was not an unprecedented phenomenon in the annals of warfare. My essay *Putin's War Russian Genocide* delves into this perspective.

Genocide emerged as a second key theme in my contributions, focusing on the politics of violence within warfare. The human tragedy in Putin's invasion escalated rapidly with deliberate attacks on civilian communities, far more sinister than typical collateral casualties. It was essential to dispute the armchair generals on social media who generally ignored the genocide or those military experts who argue millions of people must first be slaughtered before the declaration of a genocide. Other pundits have also claimed the war was not real but imagined, or that it represented a form of hyper-realism, or a postmodern construction of war laced with fact and fiction. My essay on genocide refutes all these unrealistic interpretations of the war.

Putin's Russia has routinely incorporated war crimes in its military operations since 1999. My research of security warfare helped demonstrate that Putin's resort to genocide was a calculated part of the Russian general staff's pre-planning, rather than a hasty decision during the invasion. My research was extended to examining small-unit actions within military occupations, demonstrating how advanced GIS mapping and forensic analysis could isolate and identify genocide concealed within conventional military operations. The findings highlighted the actions of individual soldiers willing to commit killings during patrols, epitomizing the practice

---

[1]   Philip W. Blood, *Hitler's Bandit Hunters: The SS and the Nazi Occupation of Europe*, (Virginia: Potomac, 2006).

of "shoot first, ask questions later".[2] In the essays for this book, I referred to specific cases of war crimes investigations in recent conflicts, including the former Yugoslavia, Iraq, and Afghanistan, to explain why Putin expected brutal behaviour from his soldiers. Consequently, I contend Putin's war in Ukraine is a case of genocidal security warfare. The essays *Military History, Social Media, and War Crimes* and *Putin's War Russian Genocide* delve into these pressing issues.

Lastly, there is a third subject—the media's role in the war. Specifically, from the perspective of an academic historian I reflect on the perplexing responses from the Western world, especially on social media platforms. In the early weeks of the invasion, social media became inundated with discussions related to the war, encompassing a wide range of claims, historical analogies, and predictions. Western reporting increasingly relied on Ukrainian sources for content, while the unregulated nature of social media allowed unverified claims to proliferate. In theory, the war should have been framed as a clash between Russian might and Ukrainian resilience. In that context, the Russians would be perceived as employing their considerable firepower, long frontiers, and numerous frontier penetrations to stretch the Ukrainian defenders thin. Whereas the Ukrainian resistance might have adopted a hit-and-run strategy, continually harassing the enemy whenever an opportunity arose. Rather than framing the conflict as a clash between Russian might and Ukrainian resilience, the war became depicted as a David and Goliath contest.

By contrast, early into the war, those substantive strategic imperatives were set aside by overly optimistic predictions of future Ukrainian victory. Military experts from a number of military academies across Europe, observed the Ukrainian army adopt an operational stance of trading the Russians punch-for-punch, rather than taking a more nuanced strategic approach. A French advisor (name withheld) informed me there was no evidence of strategic thinking in Ukrainian operations. This confidence to confront the invasion

---

[2] Philip W. Blood, Birds of Prey: Hitler's Luftwaffe, Ordinary Soldiers, and the Holocaust in Poland, (Stuttgart: Ibidem-Verlag, 2021).

head on was heightened in the portrayal of Russia as a Cold War relic, a former superpower led by an ineffectual cadre of aging and senile leaders, and a military organisation incapable of sound defence or attack. This sentiment became particularly prominent during the Ukrainian offensive in autumn 2022 when both experts and pundits conveyed hopes for success. When this offensive ultimately faltered, analysis remained scant, replaced instead by aspirations for future campaigns.

The war has had far-reaching consequences largely as a result of the reporting in social media. Western political leaders have lost their focus on the war and public support for Ukraine is waning. A notable case in point was how war reporting has eroded the credibility of British counterinsurgency doctrine and its associated force structures, which had been actively politicised by the UK government up to 2022. This contrasted with the United States. Caught off guard by the invasion and seeking breathing space to establish a response, the USA beat the drums of war, but ordered NATO to assume the role of a concerned but powerless observer. European nations, including energy-dependent countries like Germany, found themselves ill-prepared to confront Putin. They lacked a coherent security strategy, the operational structures, or the necessary forces to put up robust defence. Safe in comfort of NATO's article five, of collective defence, and the nuclear arsenal, western strategy involved sanctions against Russia and massive financial-weapons support for Ukraine. There is no evidence that NATO strategy is working — indeed it could be argued that the west is losing the war to save western peace and posterity.

In just six months since the war's outset, Western politicians were revealing just how out of touch they were with the realities of modern warfare. Many resorted to slogans to mask their inadequate leadership. Putin treated Western leaders as if they were mere paper tigers, and they, in response exposed their frailty. To simplify and contextualise this incoherence within the politics of war and the growing sense of detachment from the reality of war, I coined the term *RealKrieg*. While *Realpolitik* once epitomized realism and pragmatism in politics, *Realkrieg* signifies the West's illusions about war juxtaposed with disjointed defence policies. The Western defence and security posture has taken on a surreal quality, fostering misguided beliefs that cost-focused budgeting can still yield military prowess—this arrogance toward war still prevails in the West. For a more comprehensive exploration of this topic, I invite you to delve into the essay titled *RealKrieg in Wartime*, which delves into these intricacies about the war in social media.

Dr Roger Cirillo

(retired armoured cavalry, Lieutenant Colonel US army, military author, and editor)

A soldier's military opinions invariably are informed by a triple sectored analysis: strategy, operations, and tactics. Having lived the first half of my life in military schools, operational readiness or planning jobs, and unit field assignments, this methodology sticks out as the way to probe military events. Putin's unwanted war in Ukraine has tumbled into this model.

The strategy of Russia, seeking to isolate Ukraine from NATO membership is understandable. The West's policy since the Clinton Administration is one of crowding NATO surrogates onto Russia's borders and along their pathways to European commerce. Thus, this move by Russia against Ukraine was neither unprovoked nor unexpected. Putin as the legatee of the Soviet Union's central political mantle, the head of Russia, has repeatedly said "Nyet" to NATO's expansion, and the arming and training of former Soviet nations by NATO, which has crossed all the political red lines expressed diplomatically. Action was to be expected, and perhaps courted, by certain NATO powers.

Remembering my teenage experience living near a Strategic Air Command base during the Cuban missile crisis, the day the bombers all flew away to dispersed airfields to prepare for a possible nuclear war, has come forward from that past with a foreboding worry. The similarity is haunting. The idea that nations could simply sit by and watch their nearby neighbours converted into lily pad launching sites for nuclear tipped missiles or drone sites from a hostile political entity, is strategically not an event that can be ignored. Russia has reacted to that threat. NATO's economic attempts to marginalize and sequester Russia have failed. Instead, Russia thrives with new Asian and South Asian markets. Its armed forces show no evidence of ruin or defeat. Militarily trying to move Ukraine into an Article 5 guarantee of defence by the collective NATO nations, is not a status Russia will accept.

NATO urged a non-negotiating stance for Ukraine and has armed and has acted as a proxy ally in providing satellite and drone intelligence, active targeting, and an endless supply of munitions, vehicles, weapons and "contractors" to operate complex systems. Essentially, NATO is actively at war with Russia. It is relying upon its own nuclear capability to deter Russia from responding militarily despite the fact that Russians have been killed by NATO directed weapons. NATO has dared Russia to defend itself.

Anyone familiar with information warfare will recognize that the press blackout on criticism, the lack of neutral battlefield reporting and the lack of critical discussion in the press that the war has evoked, is not indicative of a democracy at peace. Russia has been delayed by mud and the unwillingness of Putin to launch a final offensive, but tactically, the war has been a disaster not for the Russians, but for the Ukrainians whose human losses cannot be replaced. Strategically, the war appears to be an impasse, which will be settled by which power outlasts the other.

Operationally, the multi-pronged Russian invasion from different sides of the geography of Ukraine using friendly or oneself owned terrain looked familiar to one whose planning experience dealt with NATO's own defensive stance to Warsaw Pact threats. Russia's operational design matched the geography, but Ukraine has done nothing more than attempt to fight every incursion, substituting tactics for an operational plan. Russian Mobile armoured divisions proceeding on convergent axes centred on roads and against major population and economic centres seemed both rational and predictable. What was new was the abandonment of echelons of units attacking to destroy its enemy in depth using the Billy goat attack tactics framed for a cold war encounter. A far different unit organization, and a methodical, low tempo operation was launched, whose intent was neither to destroy Ukraine nor to conquer it. It was specifically aimed at the systematic writing down of Ukrainian forces, most probably to encourage an early ceasefire.

Operationally, the Russians have shown no haste, and have been content to accept a favourable exchange ratio in return for a longer period of commitment. Nor has their cost in fuel and support for mobile operations increased as the relatively stable front has easily accommodated the high rates of fire seen by Russian tube and missile artillery which have been able to achieve high execution against enemy moves without the necessity of large terrain moves. Russia's "Fires Offensive" doesn't need to manoeuvre or gain ground to be effective.

Ukraine at Bakhmut, has acted like France at Verdun, shovelling in fresh levies to be churned over by concentrated firepower for terrain that is not contested by ground elements, but solely by artillery and missile concentrations. The Red Army may have faltered in its early advances, but only in a manner of adjusting its long term aims. It appears to be fighting not for destruction of Ukraine and its army, but in attempting to force a political settlement. This has proven to be a synchronous fit for Russian operations and tactics, while Ukraine has no operational options and tactically have bled themselves white attempting to recover every lost meter of ground for no benefit at all.

Ukraine is fighting a tactical war, having lost both masses of vehicles and trained leaders to execute a large-scale counteroffensive. Meanwhile, Russia has tuned up its force with hundreds of thousands of fresh trained troops, still awaiting commitment as the "fires only" tactic still plays out. There is no evidence that Russia has suffered tactical defeat, it merely has continued attrition as a shaping exercise before it decides to move on hard ground to seize large areas it doesn't want to hold, but which will be necessary for it to bring the war to end.

Currently, the West plays a strategy game, ignoring the required operational and tactical problems they are facing. The West has brought this war onto the Ukrainian people by pressuring Ukraine not to discuss neutrality or any guarantees regarding NATO, but instead wants Ukraine to play a Domino Theory in reverse, with containment being replaced by an ever-increasing number of NATO nations seeking to cordon off and marginalize Russia.

NATO's strategy, operations, and tactics have not put the Russia Bear back into his cave, and it appears that this war is being perpetuated like Spain in 1936, with both sides being supported by others. The threat of the Russian Bear had disappeared in 1991. NATO's policies in the past decades, has awakened a threat that did not need to reappear.

NATO has reignited the Cold War and is pushing towards a long-term opposition to a country whose past moves in Crimea and Ukraine have been defensive to block NATO expansionism, not to reassemble an unsupportable new USSR with countries who are neither politically nor emotionally attuned to being part of Russia. Eastern Europe begs to be a political neutral zone, one in which the west and the Russians can live in peace, not in perpetual mistrust and war.

Professor Chris Bellamy
(professor emeritus Greenwich, UK, visiting fellow Pembroke college, Oxford, military historian and editor)

My observations are conditioned by much of a life spent studying Russian military history, theory and practice and their interrelationship. My first essay covers the theory and the historical precedents, which are many, and the second relates them to events in Ukraine since 2014. As a former artilleryman, I long ago noticed that the Russians had a tradition of excellence in this arm and my first book, published in 1987, Red God of War, became unexpectedly relevant 35 years later when the full-scale conventional war in Ukraine erupted. The old Russian reliance on artillery and firepower resurfaced. However, the norms for using artillery fire to achieve predicted levels of destruction, calculated according to mathematical formulae detailed in that Cold-War era book, had always appeared unsustainable. As one of my fellow gunners observed, 'you'd need a conveyor belt going back to the factory'. In the first year of the war in Ukraine that has appeared to be right.

The official Russian definition of 'Military Doctrine' is 'a state-accepted system of views on the character of future war for a given (specific) time'. The Russians have a long pedigree of analysing the nature of future war going back to at least 1877. The methodology for my research was simple. Analyse everything, I could find that the Russians wrote about the character of 'future' war, or, sometimes, 'contemporary warfare', and then compare that with what actually happened. I have used this again.

When Russia annexed Crimea in 2014, I have to confess that my sympathies were partly with the Russians. Historically Crimea has been Russian since Catherine the Great and has a vastly important place in the Russian heart. However, in the ensuing years my view changed, particularly with Russian support for the breakaway communities in Donetsk and Luhansk. My personal view is that had the Russians just taken Crimea — they might just have got away with it. Foolishly, however, they did not stop there.

My two full essays relate to military theory and practice as they affect the first year of the Ukrainian war. There is an important proviso: that whereas Russian military theory has always been formidably scientific and framed in excruciatingly intellectual and abstruse fashion, Russian military practice has been crude and brutal. The first essay covers the evolution of the Russian doctrine — and I believe it is that — of 'non-linear' or hybrid war. Endless ink, megabytes and hot air have been expended on the various names for holistic warfare involving not just bullets, shells, and bombs but also energy, food, raw materials, media and so on. We in the west have given this the adjective 'hybrid' and the Russians 'non-linear'. After 2013 there were numerous references to 'Russia's new art of war in Europecon, as detailed in my first essay. There has also been an argument as to what to call the concept — which is neither 'new', nor peculiarly Russian, The Russians were themselves the target for non-linear warfare when the Germans brought Lenin in the 'sealed train' to Russia in 1917 to foment the Bolshevik Revolution and overthrow the Provisional Government. My first essay includes a graphic showing how the various strands of Russian involvement with 'hybrid' or 'non—linear' war have converged over the past century plus. Much printer's ink, megabytes and endless hot air have, again, been wasted on whether the ideas in Gerasimov's 2013 articles should be called the 'Gerasimov Doctrine', or not. I believe these arguments are a waste of time. If the Chief of the General Staff signs articles with his name on, that is, for me, a 'state-accepted system of views on the character of future war'. Therefore, to me, it is 'Doctrine'.

One of Gerasimov's most interesting observations was that in a future operation the ratio of 'non-linear' to 'linear' effort would be four-to one. Putin obviously hoped the 'linear' component would be far less than that. Gerasimov could conceivably argue that in terms of time alone, the eight years from 2014 to 2022 would relate to a sustained conventional effort of, at most, two years. As noted in my second essay, even that would be hard to argue. And, after one year, time is running out.

In my second essay I recount the events of the first year of the 'non - linear' war which form the framework for allegations of war crimes, crimes against humanity and, more widely, genocide. With something of a maritime background, I also cover the war at sea, which has been relatively neglected in reporting which focusses, understandably, on land and the air above. But many of the Russian missiles have been fired from the sea and Ukraine has inflicted catastrophic losses on the Black Sea Fleet. Even more relevant to the wider context is the Russian blockade of Ukraine which has turned the war into a global issue, hampering Ukrainian grain and sunflower oil exports and also exports of nitrates for fertiliser. The blockade has therefore made food prices soar in Africa and the Middle East, affecting food security in the developing world. The Black Sea initiative signed between Turkey, Ukraine and Russia under UN auspices in July 2022 promised to alleviate this situation, but its implementation has proved problematic. The war has indeed reflected what Mark Galeotti has called 'the weaponisation of everything'.

Dustin Du Cane
(lawyer)

My contribution to the book was to bring general legal expertise and analysis of Russian law. I have contributed two essays, which explain the complicated subject of international criminal law and how it pertains to the war in Ukraine. The law of war was extended to include atrocities committed by ordinary soldiers with some reference to legal and moral precedents for the 21st century. There is a fundamental problem methodising law to historical writing, this comes party from how International criminal law is treated by news corporations and social media. Many news programmes fail to engage with the understanding and meaning of law. This causes confusion and public misunderstandings of both the concepts and the regulation of law. The reader must face a simple legal rule: soldiers mustn't kill civilians; but to administer justice, trials can be hideously complex in even for qualified lawyers.

The legal essays in this book examine these complicated concepts. Their format is not framed in professional jurisprudence but for readers with an interest in the laws of war and genocide. The essays place examples before the reader of breaches of law set against the international criminal laws and codes. The purpose of these essays is highly functional, directed toward context and content. This differs from the usual esotericism found in legal journal, working papers and blogs which function entirely for the legal profession and the schools of law.

The essay on the laws of war, genocide, and crimes against humanity (essentially about International Humanitarian Law) presents an abridged and general introduction to the history of International Humanitarian Legislation (IHL). This essay concentrates on Raphael Lemkin, the person who defined the meaning of genocide, both as a definable crime and as a framework for legislation. He was a Polish lawyer, born in a part of current Belarus (then Poland), to a Jewish family, educated in Lviv, current Ukraine (then Poland: Lwów) and was one of the first to classify Holodomor as an act of genocide perpetrated against Ukrainians, then part of the

Soviet Union. He wanted to ensure 'never again' never happened again, regardless of whether to Jews, Ukrainians, or Armenians. Criminal liability mechanisms for breaches of IHL from both the past and present day are discussed in some detail. This essay represents a snapshot of the academic writing about IHL, which could easily fill a large book.

My essay on Russian laws of war adopts a dialectic approach to how laws differ from western law, how it is taught in Russia, why it's not taught to soldiers and how it has been ignored or indeed subverted by Putin's war in Ukraine. This essay represents an overview of the fundamental legal challenges facing experts at this time because it endeavours to explain why soldiers, generals, and politicians, from all nations, commit crimes in war. However, the central focus will reflect on Russian history and the law. Contemporary Russian propaganda is also scrutinised within the nexus of laws against inciting genocide, 'fake news' and genocidal incitement by journalists and media pundits. Russian sources are linked and referenced. This essay has had to rely on numerous footnotes, which facilitate references to lists of Russian crimes, breaches of Russian and Ukrainian law, and contemplating the absence of law.

Since my role in this book is that of a legal advocate, I have accepted all sources including Wikipedia, which may come as a surprise to readers. Including Wiki references in footnotes illustrates to the reader how much legal content and evidence is placed on that website and to illustrate how far it is accepted as a platform for legal opinion. The references are valuable primary and secondary source material. For example, an abridged list of alleged Russian war crimes in Ukraine is most readily available in Wikipedia. Journal papers cited here were useful, but this is war is unravelling daily, and faster than legal scholars can contemplate appropriate responses within the existing laws or the preparation of new legislation. In addition, there are newspapers, magazines, and active blog posts within the references, referring to crimes and abuses. Time will determine whether the allegations become crimes. Twitter is a primary source, where those voluntary statements on social media, are made by Russian diplomats with genocidal intent.

I studied at Warsaw University at a time when the current

International Criminal Court chief judge, Piotr Hofmański, lectured on criminal law procedure (not my supervisor), I was living at the same nearby address as Rafael Lemkin practiced at, and I passed the bar in Warsaw, where I still practise with various tangential interests much like early Lemkin.

1. MILITARY HISTORY, SOCIAL MEDIA, AND WAR CRIMES

Philip W. Blood

In April 2022, Vladimir Putin's illegal invasion of Ukraine was in full swing. Reports of Russian massacres and rapes were dominating the headlines. During the troubles a popular writer posted a tweet that attempted to draw parallels between Russian actions in 1945 and those in 2022:

> We now know that in territories even briefly occupied by Russian troops there was rape, looting, random killings, assaults on schools and hospitals. This is what the Red Army did in central Europe in 1944-45, and apparently nothing has changed.[1]

Does history simply judge nothing has changed, or are there deeper dimensions at play? Vladimir Putin has consistently adapted his propaganda tactics, shifting between portraying himself as a crusader against the West and as a victim of Western aggression. His messages, while nuanced, consistently serve the same purpose, as he leverages Russian history as a political weapon to justify his oppressive regimes. Since the invasion of Ukraine, Putin has strategically manipulated social media to depict a menacing image of a Russian horde descending upon Europe with war and barbarism. Rather than denying allegations of crimes, Putin and Russian media have amplified accounts of massacres, sexual assaults, and genocide. Paradoxically, though unintended by Applebaum, Putin capitalized on Western fears of the 'Russian horde' and exploited it for his terror His politics of violence hinge on extreme war imagery and the glorification of genocidal warfare to instil fear in his

---

[1] Anne Applebaum (@anneapplebaum), Tweet, 3 April 2022, https://twitter.co m/anneapplebaum/status/1510427182149033991 (accessed 7 October 2022).

adversaries. Regrettably, Applebaum's tweet failed to stimulate a broader discourse within military history circles regarding wartime sexual violence. Right-wing populists in the West, including politicians, writers, and media figures, have accused Russia of crimes, but Putin adeptly fans the flames of outrage to intensify the terror in his strategies. The conflict in Ukraine had already devolved into extreme violence on the battlefield and was fostering deep political divisions in the West, where concerns of a return to barbarism sent ripples across Europe. Overcoming this fear of war among Europeans remains a strategic challenge for those advocating for a proactive stance against Russia.

While it may seem that we understand the unfolding situation in Ukraine, the reality is that few in the West have a comprehensive grasp of the true events transpiring there. This knowledge gap parallels our understanding of military history, particularly regarding the mass rapes and massacres that occurred at the end of World War II. We often assume these acts, committed after the Nazis surrendered on May 8/9, 1945, were war crimes, but the intricacies of why these crimes constitute acts of murder and sexual violence within civilian legal codes remain relatively obscure. The widespread rapes were, in fact, crimes against humanity. The major powers turned a blind eye to the wartime violence, perpetuating self-deception by ignoring its persistence long after the war had ended. The conclusion of the war left a strange imprint, with an aura of victor's exceptionalism. While all nations acknowledged German guilt for racial extermination and genocide, they conveniently overlooked the Western Allies' use of unrestricted bombing on German civilians and the Soviet Union's encouragement of massacres and mass rapes. In 1945, few nations could claim the moral high ground.

Eighty years later, these unresolved wartime crimes continue to hinder lasting peace and reconciliation across Europe, as witnessed in Ukraine and previously in the former Yugoslavia. In the West, the rise of populist governments has further complicated matters, as they have propagated a narrative of cultural exceptionalism, emphasizing the victory over Nazism while downplaying the more troublesome aspects of history. For historians, transcending the limitations of military history necessitates looking beyond the battlefields and delving into the complex aftermath. To understand the challenges faced by societies deeply scarred by extreme violence, a more open-minded and coherent engagement with history is imperative. Scholars must grapple with the question of why military history has been reluctant to delve into the examination of war crimes. This reluctance partly explains why Western analyses of Putin's war in Ukraine have thus far been ill-informed and poorly judged. This presents a conundrum for academic history as it strives to come to terms with the genocidal realities of the ongoing conflict in Ukraine.

This essay delves into how the West has portrayed Red Army crimes in television and literature and examines the repercussions on the reporting of the ongoing war in Ukraine through social media. The central question it aims to tackle is why popular Western writers tend to exaggerate crimes as unique to Russians while largely disregarding similar crimes committed by Allied soldiers. The essay also raises concerns about the failure of military history, strategic studies, and war studies to adequately address the aspects of extreme violence, war crimes, massacres, rapes, and genocide within the study of military operations. This issue stems from the Western analysts' tendency to commodify war and strategy. It's essential to recognize that claims of national exceptionalism can be highly profitable in popular military history and revealing uncomfortable truths can impact profits.

In contrast, Russia, particularly since Putin's rise to power, has seen the politicization of war nostalgia. While accounts of Red Army rapes are known, they are not typically treated as insidious war crimes or cases of postwar sexual violence. In Anglo-American military history, accounts of these rapes have not yielded valuable historical insights, despite an abundance of books by popular writers and documentaries on public television featuring interviews with the victims. Readers and viewers often gain little understanding of why these crimes occurred or their significance within the Russian military culture. Curiously, there are no comparable accounts of mass rapes committed by Allied soldiers in the Western theatre in 1944/5. Putin, on the other hand, has exploited Red Army crimes for his political agenda, using them to instil fear of war among Western adversaries, which is a vital component of his war strategy. In some ways, he has accurately gauged the reluctance toward war among Europeans. By glorifying the Red Army as a symbol of Russia's martial prowess and endorsing massacres and mass rapes in Ukraine, Putin has harnessed history to amplify his strategic goals. This situation presents scholars with a complex challenge, where history is manipulated for political gain in the West, while Putin exploits history for terror and the restoration of the Russian empire. Meanwhile, the history of the rapes remains clouded, with uncertainty over who sanctioned such behaviour and why.

War crimes and public media

'You have paid dearly for Leningrad', admonished a Red Army soldier. On 2 May 1945, Berlin surrendered, and the Red Army celebrated. The walls of the old Reichstag buildings were daubed in graffiti by euphoric Russian soldiers.[2] They had fought and won one of the most vicious battles in history and wanted to record their presence, their survival, and their victory.[3] They had come from as far as Baku, Moscow, or Smolensk; others announced their presence by scrawling 'we are from Kharkiv'. Another soldier recorded a small part of his war: '[W]e defended Odesa, Stalingrad, came to Berlin.' An officer wrote: '[F]rom Moscow to Berlin, Major Yakovlev.' Karen Felix, a guide at the Bundestag, made it her business to find out who the soldiers were and located Boris Zolotarevsky. He was a teenager serving in the Red Army during the battle and recalled everyone being drunk on victory.[4] In 1947, the Soviet commandant of Berlin ordered the graffiti to be cleansed, the obscene

---

[2] 'Art at the German Bundestag', Bundestag, n.d., https://www.bundestag.deresource/blob/394562/e9b7fac699d80e1d5e2ec78813d15e62/flyer_graffiti-data.pdf (accessed 20 September 2022).

[3] 'Graffiti', Rio Wang blog, n.d., http://riowang.blogspot.com/2010/05/graffiti.html (accessed 20 September 2022).

[4] 'Ich war hier—Здесь был Die Graffitis im Reichstagsgebäude', BPB, 6 August 2018, https://www.bpb.de/system/files/dokument_pdf/bpb__Leseprobe__Felix_3872-1.pdf (Accessed 20 September 2022).

remarks scrubbed and more ideologically appropriate slogans added.[5] During the 1990s restoration of the building, the German government decided to incorporate the remaining graffiti as a lesson from history in Norman Foster's conceptual design for the Bundestag as a 'living museum'.[6] The parallels between Berlin 1945 and Ukraine 2022 tease historians, but scholars should remain wary to as yet undisclosed evidence. Hidden away in one alcove of the Bundestag is an example of the obscene graffiti that survived the cleansing — 'I fuck Hitler in the arse' — an echo of the soldiers' thirst for revenge and the frenzy of sexual violence which was widespread at the end of the Nazi-Soviet war. The Red Army was a federal institution composed of Russians, Belarusians, Ukrainians, Moldavians, Cossacks, Poles and many more. Can we reasonably assume that only the Russian soldiers committed the rapes?

In Britain and America, Purnell's History of the Second World War was hugely popular in the 1960s and '70s. This was a weekly magazine, eight volumes in total, that published articles from veterans, serving soldiers and scholars, contributing to an anthology about the war. Despite its popular appearance, the publisher and editors worked in cooperation with the Imperial War Museum, and it was greatly influential in the production of television documentaries. Long before social media, those involved in such projects knew how popular their products were through feedback from BBC polls and high street sales. How they exploited that feedback partly explained why the earliest English-language accounts of the battle barely mentioned the crimes. In 1966, former Red Army Major General Ivan Parotkin contributed an article about the battle for the weekly magazine.[7] He had participated in the battle but did not mention any crimes. In Britain, the primary interest for the public was the death of Hitler and the end of his regime. Professor Alan

---

[5] 'Soviet Soldiers' Graffiti on Reichstag Open to Public', *Astana Times*, 13 May 2014, https://astanatimes.com/2014/05/soviet-soldiers-graffiti-reichstag-open-public (accessed 20 September 2022).

[6] Norman Foster, Frederick Baker, Deborah E. Lipstadt, *The Reichstag Graffiti* (Berlin: Jovis, 2003).

[7] Ivan V. Parotkin, 'Berlin: The Battle', in *Purnell's History of the Second World War*, vol. 6, no. 86 (London: Phoebus Publishing, 1966), pp. 2391–408.

Bullock's article gave an account of Hitler's end and followed Parotkin's piece. Two years later, Earl Ziemke wrote Purnell's battle book on the battle. His only reference to the crimes was to relativise rape to the ruin of Berlin, 'rape had become an unnecessarily strenuous way of attaining something that in a war torn almost starving city hundreds of women were willing to provide on professional or semi-professional terms'.[8] In the 1960s, such publications attracted widespread public readership and for a time met the growing demand for informed content.

The television age shaped the 1970s, nourishing a huge demand for historical content. Typical was the World at War documentary series, which introduced a sharper narrative to the public. On 3 April 1974, Christa Ronke, a teenager in Berlin at the time, disclosed on British television that she had been raped. In a segment of less than thirty seconds, she explained how the first Russian soldiers to arrive were very kind, 'but the next Russians were quite different. One of them raped me and the other inhabitants in the house.' Ronke's disclosure was a remarkable moment in British television history but was too brief to have any lasting impact. The episode moved swiftly on. Friedrich Luft, a music critic residing in Berlin, recalled how the first Russian soldiers were very businesslike and professional. He indirectly referred to the rapes but not in detail.[9]

In 1976, Marcel Ophüls released a documentary film, *Nicht Schuldig? The Memory of Justice*.[10] Restored in 2015, this masterpiece of oral history engaged with the surviving Nazi war criminals from the Nuremburg Tribunals, the prosecutors, and a selection of the victims. Ostensibly, the film was broadly based upon Telford Taylor's, *Nuremburg and Vietnam: an American Tragedy* (1970), but the director also engaged with young Germans, old Nazis and

---

[8] Earl F. Ziemke. *Battle for Berlin: End of the Third Reich* (London: Macdonald, 1968). pp. 147–9.

[9] ITV, *World at War*, episode 21, 'Nemesis', 1974. See also Richard Holmes, *The World at War: The Landmark Oral History* (London: Ebury, 2007), e-copy, pp. 651, 653.

[10] Marcel Ophüls had previously directed *The Sorrow and the Pity* (1969), about the Nazi occupation of France.

confronted the issues raised during the trials. There were two short vignettes. The first concerned the sensitive question of the Katyn Massacre—which the Soviet Union denied and insisted was a German crime. Then near the end of part one, during the filming of the Berlin wall on the former Potsdamer Platz overlook platform, an unnamed woman interrupted them talk about memories of the area. Ophüls asked: 'Did you see the Russians when they came?' She said 'yes' and added that she was treated 'as everyone else. I was raped.' He asked, 'you were raped by the Russians?' 'Yes of course,' she replied, 'there was no place to hide.' Ophüls asked her if it was a terrible experience and the woman replied, 'yes, but not all that terrible.' He asked if, 'there are worse things in life' and she said 'yes, definitely.' Unscripted, unprepared, their conversation was brief and uncomfortable, leaving a number of unanswered questions.

Nine years later, the Cold War tensions in Berlin had increased. The veteran broadcaster Charles Wheeler narrated a BBC Timewatch episode that examined the battle. Wheeler was a British soldier in Berlin in July 1945 and had seen the Red Army at first hand. Lothar Loewe, a Hitler Youth member in the city, claimed 'there was a lot of raping going on'. He remembered the vicious street fighting during the day and women screaming all night long from the rapes. A German veteran, Major Wilke, informed Wheeler that the German soldiers were fighting to protect German women and girls. Wheeler observed that at the time of the battle Berlin had become 'a city of women' as Loewe mentioned the 'millions' of civilians. Hannah Neskmann (phonetic spelling), a nineteen-year-old during the battle, was hiding in a shelter in her parents' home. She heard Russian soldiers ransack the house. Later she recalled watching an old man pulling a cart with his dead wife and daughter; they had been raped multiple times. She also mentioned a neighbour's wife of about fifty years of age whom the Russians tried to rape. She and her husband put up such resistance that the Russians shot them both. Wolfgang Leonhard, a former city official, explained that the 'drunkenness and especially ... the rapes' were a major problem for the socialist administration of the city. German communists, he remembered, were horrified at the behaviour of the Red Army.

Leonhard also claimed Red Army politruks were very worried about the long-term costs of the rapes—a cost they described in terms of 'political roubles'.[11]

Following the collapse of the Soviet Union, historians began re-examining Soviet crimes from within the Russian archives. Norman Naimark compiled an important history of the first years of the Russian occupation of Germany. His explanation of the motives for the rapes was more than acts of revenge for Nazi crimes. Naimark attributed male behaviour, in particular binge drinking, and Asian cultures, with complex attitudes to rape and sexual violence, as also responsible.[12] During the same period, television documentaries granted more time for witnesses to explain their memories. In September 1997, the memory of the mass rapes reached its most horrific in the recollections of Waltraud Reski. She was a schoolgirl from Demmin in 1945. Demmin is a small town in Mecklenburg-Western Pomerania by the River Peene. During the retreat, the German Army had destroyed the bridges, and though this delayed the arrival of the Red Army until 30 April 1945, Demmin was ultimately given up without any fighting. This didn't assuage the Red Army soldiers, who in a frenzy of sexual violence conducted mass rapes and executions. Reski's mother was traumatised after being raped upwards of twenty times and became 'an entirely different person'. More than 900 people in Demmin committed suicide, many women who had been raped drowned themselves in the local river, and only her grandmother saved her family from that fate.[13] If there was no heavy fighting and the war had ended, then the reason for the mass rapes went beyond revenge, raising questions over whether the Red Army had lost the ability to control its soldiers.

Two years later, Gerda Steinke recalled her experience for yet another BBC documentary. She was a teenager in Berlin and was hiding in an air raid bunker when she saw her first Russian— 'a huge Mongolian with a machine-gun, who took all their valuables'.

---

[11] BBC, *Timewatch*, 'Battle of Berlin', May 1985, narrated by Charles Wheeler.
[12] Norman M. Naimark, *The Russians in Germany: A History of the Soviet Zone 1945-1949*, (Cambridge: Belknap Press, 1995).
[13] BBC, *Nazis: A Warning from History*, 'Fighting to the End', episode 6, 1994.

Later, her sister-in-law arrived, having been raped several times; she was almost killed by her parents, who committed suicide afterwards. The focus then turned to Vladlen Anchishkin, a veteran of 1st Ukrainian Front, who confessed to killing captured Germans after the surrender. They were SS soldiers and had opened fire while retreating. He and his comrades led the prisoners down to a basement, where they were killed. Before the camera, Anchishkin described the building where the killings took place, the sharpness of the knife, how he killed the men and how they died. He explained why he felt justified in carrying out this act of revenge: '[F]or years you hunted me. You killed hundreds of my friends and comrades. … You were allowed to do all this, and I am not?' He added: '[T]hey were out to get me. Why else would they shoot at me when the war was over?' He was asked: 'Don't you think it was a war crime?' He replied: '[N]o I don't. Otherwise, I wouldn't have done it. Don't look at me as if I were a criminal. It was a long time ago.' With such a precise recall of detail, it was perhaps surprising that he was not asked for his opinion about the rapes.[14]

In 2002, Alexander Popov, a Soviet officer of the 5th Shock Army, described the euphoria of victory to Antony Beevor during a BBC documentary. 'Russian soldiers fought thousands of bloody kilometres, from Stalingrad to Berlin,' he said, adding: 'Thousands of bloody kilometres, you tell me how we felt at the end of the war.' For the vanquished in the battle, the documentary turned to Magda Fintrop, a nineteen-year-old at the time. She recalled how 'it happened very quickly, lots of small Russians with slitty eyes from Mongolia hungrily shouting Frau, Frau! Then one really brutal man grabbed me and raped me.' The documentary's attention returned to Popov for an explanation: '[T]here was strict orders, there shouldn't be any looting or violence towards civilians; after all they weren't guilty of anything. These orders were carried out 100 per cent.' The documentary noted that the claims of mass rapes by the Red Army had always been denied by officials from both regimes in Russia, where the subject had remained taboo. The documentary summarised the rapes as being partly revenge and partly the

---

[14] BBC, *War of the Century*, 'Nemesis', episode 4, October 1999.

Russian way of war. The rapes included victims of Nazism, of women in concentration camps and prisons, highlighting the frenzy of sexual violence. In conclusion, the documentary claimed 2 million rapes, mostly German women, and 150,000 rapes in Berlin.[15]

In 2005, Ronke once again appeared on British television. She explained that nobody talked about the rapes for years afterwards and that only 'now' could she talk about her experience. During the battle, Ronke was fifteen years old, and she recalled the first wave of Russians as being correctly behaved. During the second wave, soldiers led her outside. Her mother tried to intervene but was pushed back. She was then taken upstairs, and when she tried to resist, the soldier pointed his revolver at her and raped her. She added the drunken soldiers were the worse and would howl Frau komm! She appeared reconciled to the view that the women were the prize because of German behaviour in the east. Leonhard was again interviewed about the rapes. He now claimed the Red Army officers told him not to make a fuss about raping because 'the German women want it'. Leonhard said he had witnessed German women remove their clothes when a Russian soldier approached because they were deeply traumatised and reacting like automatons.[16] The documentary stated that 100,000 women were raped in Berlin but added that the actual numbers remain unknown. However, the documentary went on to refer to rapes in the western theatre, which was treated as a taboo subject. In the Stuttgart area, French soldiers committed a sexual rampage. Weeks later, many women discovered they were pregnant; some tried to carry out abortions themselves, while others committed suicide. Although abortion was still illegal in Germany, the doctors began to perform abortions.[17]

From the 1980s, scholars began dedicated research into

---

[15] BBC, *Timewatch*, 'Battle of Berlin', 2002, narrated by Antony Beevor, refer to Vimeo

[16] Chris Bellamy, *Absolute War* (London: Pan, 2007), argued that the Soviet political officers had condoned and 'legally sanctioned' the rapes.

[17] BBC, *After the War*, 'Conquering Germany', Diverse Productions, 2005.

genocide, but questions of sexual violence remained an awkward subject.[18] In the wake of the resurgence of genocide and sexual violence in the former Yugoslavia and Rwanda during the 1990s, research into the politics of violence and genocide was accelerated.[19] This scholarship encouraged the wider study of gender and war within military history and other disciplines.[20] By the first decade of the twenty-first century, a historiography of Allied sex crimes in the West was also beginning to emerge.[21] By the second decade, European women were no longer being depicted in the literature as prizes of war, booty or victims. However, the legacy from the years of 'silence' about Soviet crimes could stir serious questions over the nature of the war, especially in the West. The publication of accounts of rapes in the West has often received off-hand criticism and absolute denial, but Miriam Gebhardt's examination of mass rapes, at the end of the war, was deeply uncomfortable research. She used Berlin 1945 as a start point to trace the progression of Goebbels' propaganda. On 21 October 1944, the Red Army made a breakthrough south of Königsberg at Nemmersdorf in East Prussia. They occupied the village of 700 residents for forty-eight hours before a German counterattack forced them back. The Nazis used this brief occupation to stage a propaganda stunt, claiming the barbaric Red Army had committed war crimes, murder, and rapes. The massacre at Nemmersdorf remains disputed, but it represented that moment when the Nazis began to push project fear on to the German public.[22] Goebbels' project fear had been validated by Russian soldiers' behaviour, and the horror became lodged in public memory.

---

[18] Dan Stone (ed.), *The Historiography of Genocide* (Basingstoke: Palgrave, 2008).
[19] Beverly Allen, *Rape Warfare: The Hidden Genocide in Bosnia–Herzegovina and Croatia* (Minneapolis: University of Minnesota Press, 1996).
[20] Dagmar Herzog, *Brutality and Desire: War and Society in Europe's Twentieth Century* (Basingstoke: Palgrave, 2011). Sara Meger, *Rape, Loot, Pillage: The Political Economy of Sexual Violence in Armed Conflict* (New York: Oxford University Press, 2016).
[21] Giles MacDonogh, *After the Reich* (London: John Murray, 2007); William I. Hitchcock, *The Bitter Road to Freedom* (New York: Free Press, 2008).
[22] Miriam Gebhardt, *Crimes Unspoken: The Rape of German Women at the End of the Second World War* (Cambridge: Polity, 2017).

Gebhardt went further spotlighting the crimes of the Western armies in 1944–5. She observed: 'The women violated by GIs, British and French soldiers, ... [were] punished with contempt.' Her research found few examples of British crimes, but there was a case in Soltau on 17 April 1945.[23] Gebhardt referred to the late Clive Emsley's opinion that the total absence of British records was in itself suspicious. Yet, in a conference on policing and occupation, held at the Open University in 2002, Emsley claimed the police held files of women raped by British soldiers as well as reports of British women who had fraternised with Germans during the occupation of the Channel Islands. Years later, Emsley published an account of a British Army chaplain who was aware of mass rapes.[24] Accounts of sexual violence circulated in the 1990s, especially at the fiftieth anniversaries of the war, but discussions with veterans mostly resulted in only vague recollections. In 2013, Sean Longden found evidence of many British soldiers having committed rapes that were reported to the military police but argued the number of cases did not compare with the Red Army.[25]

The painful public disclosure by Ronke, in 1974, had been met with silence because it was too uncomfortable for the time. It passed by without comment, and few recalled the clip at the time, but today the account is lodged in public memory due to the popularity of the TV series. The more important question is why a popular author like Beevor should claim in a BBC documentary 'that the Battle of Berlin had never been told from the view of the ordinary Russian soldier nor has it been told from the point of view of the revenge they took on the population of Berlin when they captured it.'[26] A remarkable claim given the subject has been in the British public domain since 1974 and in Germany since the 1950s. More importantly, why was the same rigour of investigation not applied to

---

[23] Ibid., pp. 13–14.
[24] Clive Emsley, *Soldier, Sailor, Beggarman, Thief: Crime and the British Armed Services since 1914*, (Oxford: Oxford University Press, 2013).
[25] Sean Longden, *To The Victor The Spoils*, (New York: Little Brown, 2013).
[26] BBC, *Timewatch*, 'Battle of Berlin', 2002, narrated by Antony Beevor, refer to Vimeo

his other books about the war in the west and in particular in regard to the behaviour of Allied soldiers? Putin took a swipe at this trend when he criticised 'cynical falsifications of World War II history, escalating Russophobia, praising traitors, mocking their victims' memory and crossing out the courage of those who won victory through suffering'.[27] There is hypocrisy directed toward Russian behaviour, at the same time as the fervent denials of the west's political and military crimes in Iraq and Afghanistan.

Coming to terms with the past

On 9 May 2022, during the early months of the war in Ukraine, Moscow hosted the commemorations for the victory parade in the Great Patriotic War—the defeat of Nazi Germany. A solitary T-34 tank, bearing a Red Army victory banner and sporting old battle emblems, drove through Red Square. The tank commander saluted Putin and the Russian general staff, but it was the Red Army veterans, proudly wearing their war medals, who projected the memories of the Soviet past. The T-34 was followed by mobile ballistic missiles, those atomic dinosaurs of the Cold War, ramming home the propaganda message of the continuity of military power and Russia might. There was no sign of modernising reconstruction, no evidence of a shift from the mindset that had ruled Russia throughout the Twentieth Century, and no effort at reconciliation with the victims of the Red Army or coming to terms with an extremely violent past or recognising Russia's uncertain path in a genocidal future. The history of war has shaped European culture, but the story of Russian crimes during the age of total war has remained a political question rather than a series of legal cases that never faced justice. The history of Russian war crimes and atrocities in the Twentieth Century is primarily a history of the Red Army and is unique in modern European memory because the Red Army was never dissolved after the end of the Cold War. In some cases, the rapists justified the mass rapes and massacres as a punishment for the crimes

---

[27] 'Victory Parade on Red Square', President of Russia, 9 May 2022, http://en.kremlin.ru/events/president/transcripts/68366 (accessed 20 September 2022).

of the Nazis—but trading crimes is not how modern societies function if justice and reconciliation are to prevail.

The contrasting politics of violence between Russian/Soviet and German/Nazi with hard evidence reveals they were never the same. Nazi Germany created extremist institutions to administer and perpetrate racial extermination on an industrial scale. Russia expounded extreme violence through everyday military culture and perpetrated genocide through the standard operating procedures of military discipline. These differences have always troubled scholars since such comparisons raise questions about modernity, human progress or ongoing primitive traits, and the quest for civilisation, but also understanding how military forces function. Was Soviet Russia less modern than Nazi Germany, was the Red Army a primitive horde, and were the Germans more civilised because of Goethe or Beethoven and social sophistication? The trajectories to extreme violence and genocide were different, Nazi Germany adopted, and adapted, national hierarchies to institutionalise violence that paved the way to genocide. The Red Army was borne in the politics of violence of the Bolshevik revolution to be the guardian of the regime rather than as the defender of the nation. Extreme violence was a unifying cultural trait that determined its behaviour in war or security. Ironically, it was the liberation of Nazi extermination camps that served to cloak the growing barbaric reputation of the Red Army as it advanced through central Europe. It is remarkable that after 1945 Soviet Russia brutally oppressed Eastern Europe and committed ethnic cleansing, and yet that story is barely known in the west. The Red Army crimes in Germany and Eastern Europe represent an unhealed scar in European culture and yet without the Red Army, a federal army of nations[28], Nazi Germany could never have been defeated—this is a conundrum for historians.

What is the real purpose behind Russia's genocide and who is the real target of Putin's war? The general research of massacres, rapes and genocide had broken into the centre ground of historical

---

[28] Alexander Hill, *The Red Army and the Second World War*, (Cambridge: Cambridge University, 2017).

discourse by the late 1990s. In the introduction to a collective history of massacres, Mark Levene almost foreshadowed 2022 when he wrote: 'The news is awash with bloody massacre.' Back then he referred to Rwanda, Burundi, Algeria and Srebenica, all different countries, today he would refer to Ukraine and the Russian massacres in Bucha, Mariupol, and Bakhmut. In seeking to define a term of reference, Levene argued that 'all massacre is violence, but not all violence is massacre', but the simplicity of such an argument is undermined by the war in Ukraine. He identified certain traits in massacres that materialised through history: the use of primitive hunting measures refined to suit circumstances, the eternal questions of civilisation, the structure of societies that generated social group anxieties, the identification and isolation of social outcasts, and the impact of culture and social conditioning that led to massacres. In regard to the Ukraine, we must consider the crimes as deliberate acts and germane to Putin's strategy. Levene pondered that with time, modernity might bring about the end of massacres. He argued that military forces, in regard to the state's 'monopoly of violence', had once been a safeguard against massacres. Revolutions had removed those safeguards as armies perpetrated crimes against their own citizens in the name of the regimes they were sworn to protect. Post-revolutionary regimes were beset by violent opposition and the regimes often responded with massacres. Levene noted western civilisation's complacency of self-righteousness was punctured in 1972, in Londonderry, when British soldiers shot and killed Irish civil rights protesters.[29] In the Ukraine, Russian forces are killing, raping, and looting indiscriminately—this has been a shock for the west—but they are deliberate to Putin's strategy and critical to his regime of terror.

Although some of his argument is flawed, Levene augured a deeper concern about massacres that has since been proven by Putin's war. In a sense, Levene helps us understand that not all massacres are genocidal, but some massacres signal the onset of an existential war. Levene was less convincing in his assessment of

---

[29] Mark Levene & Penny Roberts (ed.), *The Massacre in History*, (Oxford: Berghahn, 1999), pp. 1-38.

massacre by modern technology. He pondered whether aerial warfare might cause a massacre from the air, where the remoteness of the perpetrators from the victims would be significant. Although Levene could recognise face-to-face killing was at one time central to massacres in history, he was less confident with the notion of the remote machinery driven massacres. Although one lesson from modern warfare has been the increase in the remoteness between perpetrators and victims, Levene was troubled by remoteness and the separation of the perpetrator and the victim. Historically, in modern warfare, the killing of civilians during remote bombardments was usually treated as collateral casualties. In Putin's war, Russian artillery and missiles have used advanced technology to zero-in on civilian targets. Putin's war has introduced mechanised genocide and remote massacres to conventional warfare.[30]

Rape and massacres were not unique to the Red Army—digressing here for one moment. In graphic detail, Iris Chang estimated there were upwards of 80,000 rapes in Nanking, perpetrated by the Japanese army in 1937, and concluded it was 'one of the greatest mass rapes in world history.'[31] Chang dubbed the massacre of Nanking a 'forgotten Holocaust, questioning why the world knew of Auschwitz and Hitler's Holocaust but Nanking was forgotten. She cited Susan Brownmiller, who argued that Nanking was only surpassed in wartime rape by the sexual violence of Pakistani soldiers against Bengali women in 1971 that surpassed the numbers of rapes in former Yugoslavia.[32] Chang explained that the extent of the rapes included children, killed afterwards, and that this often preceded the killing of entire families. She focused upon Japan's denial of the crimes and in particular Japanese academia's

---

[30] Philip Blood, 'From God of War to Putin's Hammer', Substack newsletter, *Fallout* (blog), 24 March 2022, https://fallout.substack.com/p/from-god-of-war-to-putin-s-hammer. Also '(PDF) From the God of War to Putin's Hammer: Explaining Why Mechanised Genocide Features in the Russian Way of War | Philip W Blood - Academia.Edu', accessed 1 August 2023, https://www.academia.edu/74240183/From_the_God_of_War_to_Putins_Hammer_Explaining_why_Mechanised_Genocide_features_in_the_Russian_Way_of_War

[31] Iris Chang, *The Rape of Nanking*, (USA, Basic Books, 1997), p.89.

[32] Susan Brownmillar, *Against Our Will: Men, Women and Rape*, (New York: Simon & Shuster, 1975)

deliberate cover-up of the story. Japanese academics alleged the female victims of rape were prostitutes or sex workers. Chang concluded that, 'The Rape of Nanking was only one incident in a long saga of Japanese barbarism during nine years of war.'[33] The book received considerable criticism mostly because it wasn't scholarly in style or structure.

Years before Chang published, Ian Buruma a popular writer examined the memories of war in Germany and Japan. He noted that a Japanese historian had argued the massacres were not systematic, but chaotic following a tough battle against stiff Chinese resistance. Buruma questioned whether crimes committed six weeks after the fighting still constituted hard fighting. He also recognised the deeply polarised and binary opinions of the two interpretations of the massacre in Japanese politics — the revisionists who denied the crimes and the left activists who advocate public discussion to prevent a resurgence of Japanese imperialism.[34] Buruma cited a Japanese politician who denied the massacres as a Holocaust and argued that Japan must confront its own history otherwise 'aliens' would propagandise the story which would cause the Japanese people to lose a sense of their own history. In Buruma's opinion, this was another form of identity politics. Years later a scholar, the late Callum MacDonald formulated an explanation to why the Japanese army officers used rape. He claimed it was a reward for soldiers after a harsh battle. Rape, he argued, was about power and used as a means to subjugate and humiliate defeated nations. He also noted that 'rape was a means of punishing a society' and served the same function for the Red Army in Germany in 1945.[35] Cutting across cultures, it took a period of time and work to build a functional comparison of Japanese army crimes in Nanking with Red Army crimes in Germany. The elephant in the room is that most rape is committed by men but not all men are rapists. The

---

[33] Chang, ibid, p.215.
[34] Ian Buruma, *Wages of Guilt*, (London: Vintage, 1995), pp.119-123.
[35] Callum MacDonald, 'Kill All, Burn All, Loot All': The Nanking Massacre of December 1937 and Japanese Policy in China', in Mark Levene & Penny Roberts (ed.), *The Massacre in History*, (Oxford: Berghahn, 1999), pp-223-246.

primary cause of the Red Army rapes was the male soldiers. Male cultures extend to soldiering, where bonding and comradeship extend to killing. Violence, sexual or otherwise, is often described as bloodlust or sexual lust. Sexual crimes and violence against women are social crimes that happen in civil society. The sanction for the mass rapes was political, binge drinking, and other cultural traits facilitated the crimes, but the primary purpose was both to impose terror and control the army.[36] However, the most sinister aspect of the crimes was the rape of children, as young as 5 and their murder. The egregious unknown is whether sexual violence was endemic within the Soviet Union and if it continued against children.

Russo-Soviet history is littered with massacres, rapes, and genocide, which flowed from revolution although there are grounds for suggesting they had threads to an older past. Michael Mann referred to the Red Terror, that followed the Bolshevik revolution in 1917, to open his examination of Stalinism. He thought the civil war heightened the state's resort to military power and the para-militarism of the Bolsheviks. Eventually 'militarism began to colour party rhetoric' as the reds perpetrated widespread killing of enemies of the state and transformed Bolshevism into war communism. The Bolsheviks conducted a war against Ukrainians and Cossacks, but not as ethnic enemies. They were viewed as class enemies, the natural allies of Tsarism and the old social order—feudal aristocrats and the bourgeoisie etc.—but typically dehumanised as 'parasites' or 'leeches'. Subsequent radicalisation of Soviet politruks after the civil war, and the radicalisation of 'Socialism in One Country' led to the collectivisation and social engineering of the Soviet Union that had genocidal consequences. The violent reaction against Sovietisation measures led the former Bolsheviks to perpetrate successive waves of extreme violence and enforced starvation. The treadmill of violence increased as perpetrators and victims refused to compromise. The level of violence further radicalised Stalin's regime and its security forces as the gulag system became fully operational. The Kulaks (rich peasants) were vilified and became the hate figures of the regime. Atrocities mounted and famine brought

---

[36] Catherine Merridale, *Ivan's War*, (London: Faber and Faber, 2005).

mass deaths of more than eight million, as the Stalinist terror was unleashed on the Ukraine. There were cases of 're-Russifying' Ukrainian cities and 'pastoralising' Ukraine society. By June 1941 when the Nazis invaded Soviet Russia, Russian society had experienced a continuity of violence of almost twenty-four years. Regardless of the existential war with Germany, Stalin continued to prosecute violent social engineering including against territories ravaged by the German occupiers.[37] By 1945, Soviet society had been militarised.[38] It's not a leap of faith, therefore, to believe Stalin had sanctioned the massacres and rapes — verbally — to placate the loyalty of the Red Army in safeguarding his regime.

Since coming to power, Putin has strenuously pushed back at the portrayal of the Second World War in western literature. Putin took the cultural symbolism of the Great Patriotic War, which is the pride of the Russian people's sacrifice in the defeat of Nazism and used it for his political ends. All history is political, but Putin has wielded history like a battle axe to fell his critics. After 2014, and the Crimea crisis, Putin's response to western interpretations of the Second World War noticeably hardened. He accused the Polish foreign minister, in 1939, of colluding with Hitler. In 2019 he declared it was 'our sacred duty is to protect the real heroes' meaning Russia's soldiers, civilians, and the national sacrifice. In 2020, during the commemoration of the seventy-fifth anniversary of the liberation of Auschwitz, Russia, Poland, and Ukraine were locked in a memory war.[39] This rhetoric was woven into Putin's political aims and his war-talk, since the invasion of Ukraine. Putin has embraced all the Red Army's deeds (victories and crime) and Soviet totalitarianism to portray an exceptionalism in Russian war-making, to heighten the fears of war within the western public mindset. This is partly explains why Putin encourages the Russian army to commit massacres and rapes — he's safeguarding his regime, distorting

---

[37] Michael Mann, *The Dark Side of Democracy: Explaining Ethnic Cleansing*, (Cambridge: Cambridge University Press, 2005), pp.321-330.
[38] Richard Overy, *The Dictators: Hitler's Germany, Stalin's Russia*, (London: Penguin Books, 2005), p.539.
[39] Marlene Laurelle, *Is Russia Fascist? Unravelling Propaganda East and West*, (Cornell: Cornell University Press, 2021).

history, but trashing his army—in other words like Stalin but the inverse of Stalinist terror.

Russian war Crimes and Putin's War

Soviet and Red Army crimes were endemic in the existential struggle with Nazi Germany. In one sense there were few options for Russians in the face of Hitler's war of extermination, but there were still choices and not all Germans were massacred by all Russians. One reason for the social conditioning for killing and rape was the Soviet system. As Michael Mann has observed, it was a revolutionary system that became defined by militarism and mass killing. The Soviet system, through the Red Army, had brutalised the soldiery. The soldier's sacrifice to Mother Russia was absolute and to the death. We often assume that the Russian soldier was brutalised by Hitler's war, but the Soviet system contributed to this process by holding its soldiers in isolation until unleashed on the battlefield. The Soviet military's socialisation process had benefits in waging aggressive war, which became difficult to control when the army was operating outside the battlefield.

Amir Weiner found that the Soviet system operated at peak efficiency within the limits of Total War. The system was equally efficient at producing tens of thousands of tanks and killing tens of thousands of its own soldiers. At the same time, the traditions of the Russo-Soviet way of war expounded the collective over the individual in warfare. Not unusual for modern armies, except the Red Army institutionalised mass sacrifice in its operations. Weiner observed that for a long time the rapes of German women were a taboo subject in Russia. However, the collective system facilitated the rapes. Weiner cited a Soviet veteran, Leonid Rabichev who recalled, 'women, mothers and daughters, lie right and left along the highway, and a crackling armada of men with pants pulled down in front of each of them.' Several accounts refer to Stalin's dismissal of the rapes as 'boys having fun'. Weiner concluded that the regime had encouraged the rapes and the rapes continued until two years after the war ended. Mass abortions continued into 1948 when finally, the Red Army was ordered into barracks and away from civilian society. Weiner noted that some officers believed the rapes represented rank-and-file justice, while others claimed the German women understood they were the prize for the soldiers' victory, while others claimed the bourgeois appearance of German women inflamed the soldiers. Weiner decided the Soviet system offered 'its citizens something to die for, and a lot to kill for.'[40] The rapes are not a closed history, there is a more complex interpretation lingering, which demands further research.

The west placed great faith in the Nuremburg War Crimes Tribunals that took place after the Second World War. The tribunal partly redefined Anglo-American laws of war, but western literature has written the Soviet Union's participation out of the tribunal's history and rode back the traditions of Just War to the western dogma of war.[41] It can be stated, that the concepts of humanitarianism which underpin the western way of war, but that was based upon a postwar judgement by the allies of how they fought their war. This faith in the tribunals is cited in explaining America's wars for democracy. Typical is Samuel Moyn's recent work on America's wars. In May 2022, he joined a podcast conference and reiterated his opinion that the tribunals were progressive in the judgement of war. However, there is another interpretation of the tribunals' progress.

During the later tribunals, the allied (mostly American) officials and the public alike began to share a disquiet that justice was not being served. Afterwards there was a common concern over the efficacy of such proceedings. This was partly caused by the prosecutors, who believed the public were losing interest against the tidal wave of documentary evidence presented in the tribunals and partly from how the media reported the proceedings.[42] Rebecca

---

[40] Amir Weiner, 'Something to die for, a lot to Kill For: the Soviet System and the Barbarisation of Warfare 1939-1945, in George Kassimeris (ed.), *The Barbarisation of Warfare*, (London: Hurst, 2006), pp.101-125.

[41] Francine Hirsch, *Soviet Judgment At Nuremberg: A New History of the International Military Tribunal after World War II*, (Oxford: Oxford University Press, 2020).

[42] Telford Taylor, *The Anatomy of the Nuremberg Trials*, (London: Bloomsbury, 1993).

West, a court reporter at the time, wrote of the mind-numbing dullness of the proceedings. Telford Taylor, the US prosecutor, in an effort to restore the reputation of the tribunals, decided to introduce Nazi turncoats and victims to bring first-person testimony to stimulate tensions within the proceedings.[43] The tribunal became newsworthy again, but the quality of the evidence was questionable, and the proceedings lost some of their legal gravitas. The accounts of mass rapes by allied and Red Army soldiers reached the Nazi defendants and were used as mitigating testimony in final defence statements. In one case the defendant conflated the Soviet atrocities with the allied bombing of Dresden and the starvation of civilians in displacement camps.[44] These changes remained a deep concern for some former Nuremberg prosecutors' long after the war.[45]

In 2003, a sociologist estimated that 14,000 European women were raped by American soldiers in 1942-5. J. Robert Lilley described how sexual violence was a tool of genocide, a form of revenge but more seriously an element of military culture.[46] The English language edition unaccountably was taken out of print. In 2005, Richard Drayton referred to Lilly's book and explained why in 2003 it was removed from print after 9-11 but was then re-published in French. He cited a report in *Time Magazine* from September 1945, which claimed both the US and British armies had done their 'share of looting and raping'. Drayton warned that the West's ethical stance and patriotic myths could be seen as a blank cheque to 'bomb, maim and imprison'. He observed that 1945 had acquired a mythical status in both the West and in Putin's Russia, where it was 'a key political resource'.[47]

---

[43] https://www.academia.edu/43099548/Turncoat_expert_or_fraud_Erich_von_dem_Bach_Zelewski_s_evidence_during_the_Nuremberg_war_crimes_process

[44] Imperial War Museum (London), Nuremberg Tribunals, Einsatzgruppen Case IV, final testimony of Oswald Pohl, p.8013.

[45] Following discussions in 1996 with former Squadron Leader Peter Calvocoressi, author of *Nuremburg: The Facts, the Law and the Consequences*, (London: Chatto and Windus, 1947).

[46] J. Robert Lilly, *Taken by Force: Rape and American GIs in Europe during World War II* (Basingstoke: Palgrave, 2003).

[47] 'An Ethical Blank Cheque', *The Guardian*, 10 May 2005, https://www.theguardian.com/politics/2005/may/10/foreignpolicy.usa (accessed 20 September 2022).

During an RUSI conference in 2002, Steve Crawshaw from Human Rights Watch raised the issues of 1945, 'when our great ally in the fight against Hitler swept through Eastern Europe'. Crawshaw referred to Beevor's book to summarise how the Red Army had raped on an 'extraordinary scale'. He reflected: 'At the time, the Western Allies did not interfere because it was not quite proper to talk of such matters, together with the fact that we needed those Russians.' He omitted that many of the crimes of murder and rape were committed after the war was over. He observed the Soviet regime encouraged ordinary soldiers to rape German women, while the West had few moral qualms about this behaviour and 'we still have whispers of tacit understanding ...'[48] The problem we face as scholars: if mass rapes by the Red Army were symptomatic of annihilation warfare in the east, how should we explain the rapes by Allied soldiers in the west?

The discomfort of confronting war crimes and sexual violence carried out by Allied soldiers is in direct contrast to how the West has portrayed Russia's annihilation warfare in Putin's war in Ukraine. This has wider implications for Putin's war and any Western involvement in a future war. When we ask why official histories in the West had covered up Soviet crimes for so long, we might assume it was to cloak a similar problem of sexual violence among Western armies. Several right-wing righters and a segment of German society still argue the Nuremberg War Crimes Tribunals was an extension of 'victors' justice', which can have dire consequences when fascism is once again on the rise across Europe. The tribunals ignored the Soviet Union's crimes in Poland in 1940 while it was still an ally of Nazism (1939-41), as in the case of the Katyn massacre. While the failure of the Red Army to support the Warsaw Uprising (1944) remain symbolic acts of oppression to those nations 'occupied' by the Soviet Union during the Cold War.

Given the direction of Putin's illegal war, had there been more willingness for genuine reconciliation and a more open and shared memory of the true nature of the war after the Soviet collapse,

---

[48] Steve Crawshaw, 'Military Activities and Human Rights', in Patrick Mileham (ed.), *War and Morality*, RUSI, Whitehall Paper 61 (London: RUSI, 2004), p. 130.

would Russia's war in Ukraine have taken a genocidal turn? The West's constant vilification of the Red Army, as the bearer of war crimes like a latter-day Mongol horde, has to a certain extent backfired. US and NATO war-making, since 1990, has attracted accusations of war crimes and even genocide, which Putin has dubbed western hypocrisy. In a speech to the Russian people on the first day of the invasion, Putin accused 'Western colleagues' of serious abuses of international law, specifically in Iraq and Syria and in the 'illegal use of military power against Libya'.[49] The test of biased or exception history is how the rest of the world judges Russia and the West. Long term, western hypocrisy might explain why many non-aligned or former colonial countries have taken sides with Russia.

In 2020, Putin blamed the United States and the UK for pushing the German people towards war in 1939, adding that it was Western capital that financed Hitler's rearmament and supported the far-right movements in Europe. He also stated: 'Stalin and his entourage, indeed, deserve many legitimate accusations. We remember the crimes committed by the regime against its own people and the horror of mass repressions.' However, Putin's interpretation of 1945 completely ignored the Red Army's crimes and extolled the fighting power and virtues of the Soviet legacy.[50] Putin exploits Soviet history for his politics. He spotlights the reputation of the Red Army to fuel his project fear against the West. Putin pushes memories of the Red Army and calculated threats to use nuclear weapons to intimidate the Western public into an anti-war or an indifference to the war. This is old-school psychological warfare, which has been quite effective since there are also concerns over Putin's general sanity and his tinkering with global war.

---

[49] 'Address by the President of the Russian Federation', President of Russia, 24 February 2022, http://en.kremlin.ru/events/president/transcripts/67843 (accessed 20 September 2022).

[50] '75th Anniversary of the Great Victory: Shared Responsibility to History and Our Future', President of Russia, 19 June 2020, http://en.kremlin.ru/events/president/news/63527 (accessed 20 September 2022).

The verdict of history

The crimes committed by the Red Army have been widely known for over six decades, while those of the Russian Army have garnered headlines since 1990. Does this indicate a pervasive culture of extreme violence within the Russian military? Several essays in this book aims to address this question. They also examine the global implications of Putin's 'special military operation' and elucidate how he has weaponized history. It is imperative that Putin does not succeed in turning the history of this war into a pillar of his reign of terror. While we should consider whether criminal behaviour is ingrained in the Russian Army's culture or if war crimes are the synergy from Putin's politics and strategy, the more pressing issue is to discern the trajectory of Putin's war-making. Russia once again stands at the apex of European history and remains an authoritarian security state functioning as a semi-corporate militarised state. The deliberate decision to resort to genocide early in the war was a calculated political move aimed at extending the regime's reign of terror with strategic menace. Confronting past crimes necessitates confronting Putin's weaponized ideology, which also involve unravelling decades of fabricated history employed to foster Russian unity through apolitical agenda grounded in nostalgia and nationalism. Fake history has proven to be a useful tool in Putin's extreme politics of violence, which he manipulates to control opponents in Europe.

As an illustration, on May 9, 2022, during the national celebrations of victory in the Great Patriotic War, Putin met with the father of Vladimir Zhoga. He was an army officer killed while commanding the Sparta Battalion in the Donbas in 2022. Putin posthumously awarded him the Star of the Hero of Russia. His father was encouraged to laud his grandfather, a Red Army veteran who served as a sergeant of artillery and concluded his war in *Königsberg*. Notably, the choice of a relative from the artillery and the use of *Königsberg* instead of its current name, Kaliningrad, deserve attention. This award went largely unnoticed in the West, as did Putin's final words: '[O]ur men are fighting courageously, heroically, and professionally.'[51] Though not explicitly stated, this statement carried the veiled threat aimed at European cities, suggested by the reference to *Königsberg* (rather than Kaliningrad), the mention of artillery (their weapon of choice), and the allusion to the Red Army's historical reputation.

Was Applebaum correct to claim the Soviet Union and Putin's Russia are the same? Since Putin's invasion, Russian atrocities have escalated dramatically. The shift in propaganda, from portraying Russia as a crusader against the West to casting it as a victim of Western aggression, has mirrored the evolving nature of the conflict—from war crimes to acts of genocide and terror. It's crucial to emphasize that Putin's crimes should not be equated with the actions of the Red Army during the Second World War. A closer examination of Russian atrocities in Chechnya during the late 1990s provides deeper insights into Putin's character than merely studying the crimes of the Red Army. It also underscores the urgent need to stop Putin for the sake of Ukraine, Europe, and civilization as a whole. Applebaum's tweet raised heads about the more important issue of the continuing massacres, rapes, and genocide.

The horrifying massacres in Bucha in March 2022 began with sporadic incidents and the deliberate use of heavy bombardment to obliterate civilian communities. A meticulous forensic investigation of these crimes will uncover evidence of rape, child abduction and indoctrination, genital mutilation of prisoners of war, forced extraditions, mass deportations, shootings, and deliberate attacks on civilians. These Russian crimes serve as a psychological tactic woven into the fabric of military operations, sustaining a level of violence aimed at discouraging Western intervention. Putin's strategic plan for Ukraine's extermination becomes evident through this systematic resort to criminal acts from the outset. It's not just a threat to Ukraine but also a declaration of intent against the West.

This approach to warfare is crafted from the memory of an older Russian way of conducting warfare, with the purpose of

---

[51] 'Meeting with Father of Hero of Russia Vladimir Zhoga', President of Russia, 9 May 2022, http://en.kremlin.ru/events/president/transcripts/68369 (accessed 20 September 2022).

compensating for the massive reduction in fighting power since the fall of the Soviet Union. A sign of Putin's vulnerability is his reliance on old reputations to galvanise his regime. It's a calculated strategy, akin to a *maskirovka* — a camouflage of Russia's true power and his political objectives. Sadly, the West to have fallen for the ruse, allowing Putin to maintain the strategic advantage. Putin's use of genocide as a strategy becomes evident in his willingness to showcase evidence for maximum coverage on global social media platforms. However, his methods may well backfire in the long run if the Russian people believe, they have become the unwitting pawns of Putin's ambitions.

Putin's orchestration of war crimes and the pursuit of aggressive annihilation warfare aims to spread fear and resurrect the spectre of barbarism in Europe. Putin's ultimate goal was to weaken NATO and European powers from within, exploiting latent fears across Europe of war as symbolised in Dresden, Berlin, Srebrenica, and Grozny. The reluctance of Western publics to engage in war has limited the actions of governments and politicians, reflecting the human condition when faced with impending catastrophe. In this age of global conflict, Europeans must confront and remember war, as their history and longevity can no longer be taken for granted.

2. COLD WAR MEMORIES FROM EUROPE'S PAST

Roger Cirillo

In 1982, Gwynne Dyer broadcast a documentary about the nature of modern war. In the opening episode to War, a six-part series, Dyer explained:

> Wars always had a high price in money, misery and lives, but we shouldn't fool ourselves. We have gone on fighting wars all down our history because we were willing to pay the price. Now the price is getting totally out of control and still we don't know how to stop.[1]

Dyer, a Canadian journalist, was approached by the National Film Board of Canada to create the mini-series. The peace movement had protested the threat of nuclear war, generated by the Cold War, and the series was moulded in part by an anti-war agenda. This was anti-war but contextualised to the rhetoric of the historical necessity for war in human progress as well as in eradicating vile and malicious regimes. In episode 5, 'Keeping the Old Game Alive: Conventional War', Dyer examined the nature of Cold War confrontation. This episode opened with clips of the human suffering in war. The Pentagon had allowed Dyer to interview and record NATO forces, and the USSR had granted some access to interview a Red Army strategist. Dyer opened the episode by stating 'peace is an ideal we deduced from the fact that there have been intervals between wars'. Dyer condensed 200 years of military history into Blenheim, Leipzig, the Great War, bombing Dresden, down to the Iron Curtain as the future frontline in the next war. He reflected on NATO and the Warsaw Pact as the latest in a long history of military alliances and remarked that major wars in Europe had erupted

---

[1] *War*, National Film Board of Canada, 1982.

every fifty years. The episode included an interview with Colonel John Sherman Crow, the regimental commander of the US 11th Armoured Cavalry Regiment. He explained 'his' troops would be 'scouting', and once the major enemy formations were detected, 'then we will kill them'. Scouting, watching, monitoring, those were the basic daily work routines of patrolling the 'frontline'.

With echoes from the film Apocalypse Now (1979), the episode took to the air, for an operational perspective, flying in Cobra helicopters from the 11th US Armoured Cavalry Regiment. The constant state of alert meant small events were magnified, as explained by US Sergeant Major Emerson. Colonel Crow interjected to explain there were two missions—enemy surveillance and preparing for war. The sense of officialdom, of US Army efficiency, was palpable. To counter the American perspective, Red Army General Rair Simonyan, a Soviet military strategist, explained that the Soviet Union was not about to attack anyone, but if attacked, they would inflict a devastating retaliation. Dyer stood by 'the wall' to explain there were 3 million soldiers and 20,000 tanks and aircraft of the Warsaw Pact forces and in 'the West' more than 2 million soldiers and 10,000 tanks and aircraft. Dyer discussed how those forces structures were comparable to the last large-scale war in Europe that had cost 40 million dead and destroyed most cities on the European continent but added 'that was without nuclear weapons'. Thus, to avoid nuclear war, the concept of conventional war was created to explain war without atomic weapons. The narrative turned back to helicopters with troops on manoeuvres, which Dyer dubbed 'dress rehearsals'. Both sides intended these dress rehearsals to project power and aggression. Crow explained that the Soviets would be highly motorised, 'armoured, very volatile, chaotic, ruthless, mechanised attack'. They would ride tanks and armoured personnel carriers into war, supported with chemical weapons, large artillery concentrations and bombardments, and an extensive screen of air power. Turning to an official Soviet film about military manoeuvres, Dyer compared the content to a bad war film from the 1950s that almost parodied Crow's observations. The Soviets, Dyer explained, had more conventional forces, mostly cheap, working and durable, to fit their mission. That mission was to carry the fight over the border, rapidly preventing war from being fought on Warsaw Pact terrain. This meant a war of waves of men forced into a high-speed drive—a capability to deliver a powerful punch with the weight of force behind it.

Joseph Luns, NATO secretary general, agreed the Soviet Union had no intention of attacking Western Europe, mostly because the leadership had fought in the last war, but they had the capability. Intentions change, explained Luns, who used the analogy of Neville Chamberlain's 'peace in our time' to illustrate why caution was necessary when confronting Soviet capability. To assuage the West Germans about the Soviet capability, NATO had devised forward defence, to counter the Red Army's penetration. Bundeswehr General von Senger, NATO-general Central Europe, explained his mission to defend Western Europe as far forward as possible — the inner German border or the Czech–German border. Dyer explained that forward defence was not a coherent military strategy, but for political reasons it was necessary to form a defensive corridor along the east–west frontier. To the Soviets, however, forward defence was not defensive but an aggressive doctrine. Retired British General Sir John Hackett, a former NATO commander, argued the Soviets were not stupid, that NATO had no aggressive plans, but nor had they created the plans for a defence in-depth. He added that all linear defences break down eventually when faced with overwhelming forces, which inevitably meant the deployment of battlefield nuclear missiles. Dyer added that Soviet superiority in conventional forces was the legacy of the Second World War, and history was shaping military doctrines and strategies.

The Fulda Gap was imagined as turned into the biggest battlefield in history, with forces funnelled by the terrain into killing zones. Dyer revealed that predictions about the next wars are often wrong, mostly because advances in technology change the shape of war. The view that the Cold War would be like the Second World War with chemical weapons was an illusion. Europeans, and especially Germans, believed it was a 'house of cards'. Nuclear weapons had in many ways undermined and rendered redundant the military profession, regardless of nation, but still the Western military establishments thrived. Images of paratroops in wargames introduced a segment about an operational manoeuvre as the camera followed British armoured troops—'in war without consequences'. In modern war, the troops would be expected to fight for up to eighty hours with the widespread use of amphetamines. Each modern tank cost $3 million, in 1980, vastly raising combat capability over the older generations of tanks, and their power would 'empty the battlefield'. Combat aircraft were regarded as the cutting edge of technology, though they were delicate, costly and took a long time to build. An F-15 Eagle was a potent weapon, but they cost $23 million each and took eighteen months to build. Another problem facing Cold War strategists of war was what happened after there were no more conventional forces/weapons. Dyer introduced chemical weapons; his graphic descriptions of lingering death punctuated with the horrendous symptoms. Amoretta Hoeber, a US defence analyst, tried to rationalise the horrified response to chemical weapons, which she attributed to a timeless human reaction to the 'age of witches'. Decontamination became the watchword, as the expectation of cleaning depended upon a vast supply of readily available water. Medical services carried Oxene tablets, a prophylaxis against chemical attacks, and Atropine to cope with casualties on the battlefield. Civilians in this story were entirely unprotected from chemical warfare, with casualties expected to reach to the millions, even before nuclear weapons.

Time and survival in modern war was set in minutes. In a wargame, escalation to nuclear war took a matter of days. Again, Dyer raised the issue of what happens when conventional forces run out of weapons? NATO adopted the flexible response strategy, the threat to use nuclear weapons. General von Senger explained there was no pre-planned escalation to nuclear weapons use. He explained a ladder of escalation: 'This would be very much against our flexible response', which meant 'the enemy faces an incalculable risk, it might even be that we use nuclear weapons from the outset, as a political decision ...' He argued the military was prepared 'to do it'. General Simoyan replied that the first use of nuclear weapons would trigger the other side to use nuclear weapons, leading to general nuclear war—'the dialectic of war'. He added that all modern forces were structured around nuclear weapons. Hackett added that trying to control nuclear war, after first use, was fantasy; they mustn't be used.

Forty-two years after Dyer's War and episode 5, one member of the 11th US Armoured Cavalry Regiment, from 1980, is still active in military history. Retired US Army Lt Col Roger Cirillo, PhD has taught soldiers and civilians military history ranging from the Great War to the conflicts of the 1990s. For this book, he was prepared to provide an oral history, to serve as an aide memoire of how the Cold War was expected to be conducted and represent a contrast to Dyer's anti-war broadcast. This short segment is the forgotten piece in the jigsaw of Putin's war. The Cold War defined Western relations with the Soviet Union for forty-four years. The legacy of that period still exerts pressure on Russia, Ukraine, Europeans, NATO members and the United States. During the Cold War, protocols of understanding to reduce confrontation were agreed by both sides. Both sides renounced aggressive war, but both sides armed aggressively. The Cold War was a dichotomy for history, where violence was limited but terror was heightened, through propaganda and psychological threats. The bastions of the Cold War took years to build, but the entire edifice was undermined and dismantled in days. The Cold War ended so quickly that both sets of 'belligerents' were unable to grapple with the realities.[2]

Reflections of a Cold War soldier

In 1976, I was a professional officer in the US Army. After four years' service and duty in the 3d Armoured Cavalry Regiment in Texas and as a staff officer in both a divisional Cavalry Squadron and a Brigade Staff in Korea, I was a Captain and attended the Armor Advanced Course. This course had recently added the Army's updated Doctrine from the controversial FM 100-5 Operations manual outlining the Active Defence, and its family of "71" series manuals for the Company Team and Battalion Task Forces. The Cavalry Troop-to-Regiment manual was also revamped, to incorporate new

---

[2] Information and text contributed by the editor, Dr. Philip Blood.

organizations and air cavalry for a European type battlefield.

More than two thirds of the curriculum consisted of tactics, which was heavily weighted with the "applicatory method," using map exercises, command post exercises, and tactical exercises without troops (TEWTs) along with both live fire and an extended field exercise with tanks, and helicopters. The Armor School faculty was heavily salted with Vietnam Combat veterans, and among the Allied officers attending the course were veterans of the 1971 Indo-Pakistan War and both Egyptian and Jordanian officers that had fought on the opposite side of the war against our Israeli exchange officer. One of the German exchange faculty, had been in the Afrika Corps at Alamein. These men added their experience and comments to tactical instruction.

This proved an exceptional preparation for my assignment to the 11th Armoured Cavalry Regiment in Fulda, Germany. Virtually everything in the course was immediately applicable.[3] Fulda is about 90km from Frankfurt, in a narrow waist of West Germany, guarding the approaches to the Rhine known as the Fulda Gap.[4] In peacetime, the 11th patrolled the interzonal border along 185km of fenced boundary line. In time of war, the Regiment was expected to serve as the Corps Covering Force after being augmented with five Squadron/Battalion Task Forces, on the forward edge of V Corps Defence.

Initially, I served as the squadron plans officer for the First Squadron and was responsible for drafting all squadron plans for the General Defence Plan mission. I also acted as the operations officer in the forward command post on exercises. I assumed command of Troop B, in November 1978, taking command of 215

---

[3] One large table-top computer exercise featured the defense of the "Hunfeld Bowl," along Highway 84, rearward of my designated General Defence Plan (GDP) designated war position for the Cavalry Troop I commanded from 1978-1980. See "Reflections of the B Troop Commander," in *Fulda Gap*.

[4] The actual Fulda Gap is the low ground following the Kinzig River valley, between the Vogelsberg and Hohe Rohn mountains. The wider, flatter approach north of the Vogelsburgs, the "Hessian Corridor," is linked with it in military terms, and is often mistaken as part of the "Gap." The Gap is the shortest way from East Germany to Frankfurt, and then the Rhine river, though the Hessian corridor is both a larger and more suitable mobile avenue.

officers and men and forty-three combat vehicles, including twelve tanks.[5] In 1980, I returned to the States for a two-year assignment in the Reserve Officers' Training Corps. From 1982 to 1985, I was a military history instructor at the staff college while also receiving the staff college diploma. In 1985, I returned to Germany, serving in the 3rd Armoured Division, as a brigade staff officer and as executive officer of the Divisional Cavalry Squadron. In 1987, I was assigned as a corps-level war plans officer at NATO's Central Army Group with the primary responsibility for oversight and coordination of the V Corps' war plan. With five years' service in V Corps, I was intimately familiar with both the ground and character of V Corps' defence.

The 8 national corps comprising Allied Forces, Central Europe, were backed by two Allied Tactical Air Forces. Each was expected to fight its own battles within defined sectors based on a concept that integrated and shaped everything as a joint battle. The priorities of air sorties, both for offensive attacks on Warsaw Pact airpower and against ground interdiction targets, were based on the joint campaign picture of the Allied commander, Central Europe, and his Air Commander-in-Chief. Corps had plans to extend their strikes of missiles and artillery deep into the enemy rear as part of an overarching campaign plan. I worked towards harmonising V Corps planning within the wider brief. I became a team member and later chief of the wargaming team that carried out analytical war gaming at the SHAPE Technical Centre at Scheveningen, The Hague, on a periodic temporary duty basis. We gamed various war scenarios based on expected probabilities and later provided key data to the diplomats negotiating the Conventional Forces Europe Reduction Treaty. After the reunification of the two Germanies, NATO had not replaced its Emergency War Plan prior to the end of my tour, and operated in a vacuum defined by preserving NATO country borders which included the newly reunited Germany. In 1990, after promotion to lieutenant colonel, I served for a year in the

---

[5] My assigned battle position and plan is discussed in detail in Fulda Gap: Battlefield of the Cold War Alliances. Dieter Kruger and Volker Bausch editors. Lexington Books, 2018, pp. 113-144. "The Battle for Highway 84."

office of the Commander-in-Chief, US Army, Europe, as his special assistant and personal staff officer. In nine years in Europe, I was directly involved in operations, planning and command of troops for a period of seven years, all under NATO operational command, including three years specifically on a NATO operational staff whose responsibilities solely dealt with the operational command of NATO forces in wartime. I was directly involved with planning for the emergency war contingencies of NATO and participated frequently in war games and operational exercises that rehearsed NATO's emergency missions from Division, Corps, Army Group and Theatre level. Three years were served on the combined staff of US, German and Canadian officers at CENTAG, and I worked with British, Netherlands, Belgian and French officers concerning various NATO plans. Based on this experience, I offer several insights into how the West deterred Soviet Russia.

Western European Security, NATO and the US commitment to Europe

US troops had been in Germany since 1944. The US Army of Occupation continued until 1955, and later as part of NATO. For thirty-five years, America's major overseas commitment was to the security of Western Europe. This played heavily on US Army organisation but also on training and operational doctrine. Nearly every theoretical war exercise employed in training in Army Service schools from the officer basic course through to the staff college, used European maps and featured scenarios where US forces had been assigned. Realistic enemy scenarios using Russian lookalike 'Threat Forces' were portrayed as opponents. Prior to assignment in both the 11th Cavalry, and later 3d Armoured Division, I had already 'defended and counterattacked' a number of times in the 'Fulda Gap' east of Frankfurt and was intimately familiar with the geography and military duties of forces there.

At its peak, the United States had more than 300,000 troops in Europe comprising more than five divisions. The US Air Force based hundreds of jet aircraft in Belgium, Germany, France and

Italy, as well as the United Kingdom. During the first decade of the Cold War, the Strategic Air Command based and rotated nuclear bomb carrying Medium Bombers in both North Africa and the United Kingdom. The US Sixth Fleet plied Mediterranean waters, and US submarines and carrier groups sailed the Atlantic and northern waters. All three services held nuclear weapons stores in the European theatre. The United States was fully committed to defend Europe, including through the use of nuclear weapons on order, and practised these measures constantly to maintain an unrelenting high state of readiness as both a deterrent and a defence in emergencies.

The US Army was committed to the ground defence mission and was the largest, most visible and ever-present element of all US forces. Additional to the forces on the ground, the army maintained six division 'sets' of equipment in a high state of maintenance and operational readiness for US troops that could be flown to Europe immediately, giving more than a 100 per cent increase in combat ready forces in less than two weeks. Reinforcements from the reserves and National Guard would be sent by sea in the month that followed a full mobilisation. This posture was no idle threat or a paper plan for use in diplomatic discussions.

Every Reserve/Guard unit had a preassigned wartime mission, and its leaders were familiar with our plans. Their own peacetime exercises were modelled on their wartime assignments, and many of their officers attended the same branch and staff college courses that used Europe as its centrepiece for theoretical training. The Army never relented in its training on European missions even during the Vietnam War, which focused more than half of the army's effort in South East Asia. During the Vietnam war, Army service schools still retained a large percentage of its instruction and map exercises focusing on the defence of Europe.

Following the creation of an all-volunteer force from its previous state as a draft army, the US Army rewrote its manuals and reoriented its total combat readiness programme towards a possible conventional or nuclear war in Europe. New models of tanks, personnel carriers, artillery, helicopters, missiles and support vehicles were created for primary use on European battlefields. Implicit in this effort was that the army would be a coalition force acting under NATO operational command. The army conducted RE-FORGER exercises in the 1970s and '80s. The Return of Forces to Europe exercises practised the actual shipment of a full corps of two-plus divisions by rapid sea and airlift, which on arrival conducted a full field training exercise near its actual wartime terrain. These exercises rarely involved fewer than 50,000 men and 700 tanks. An in-place NATO corps usually provided its opponent during the field training exercise portion of a REFORGER. This provided a large, in place cadre of experienced commanders, staff officers, and non-commissioned officers already experienced both in the reinforcement process, as well as the immediate integration into a European battle environment, from the "dead start" of mobilization and deployment.

NATO's forward defence strategy

The NATO Emergency Deployment Plan of the late 1950s and '60s featured a delay action forward of the Rhine River, behind which NATO would mount its main defence. This included the newly created Bundeswehr, the West German Army. It was generally held that NATO, including the French Army, could hold on to the Rhine but that to restore the original boundaries of West Germany and the Netherlands, tactical nuclear weapons would be used in support of the counteroffensive, which could only occur after the reinforcement of NATO by US-based forces, and the full mobilisation of every NATO partner. Even at full mobilisation, NATO would be outnumbered more than two or three to one in most sectors and about three to one in tanks. Massive failure on the ground would not only prompt NATO to order deployment of tactical nuclear weapons to stabilise the situation, but the threat of massive nuclear exchanges also existed. It was generally held that the employment of tactical nuclear weapons would be uncontrollable in an endless tit for tat exchange, and full-scale massive nuclear war would result.

With the growth and equipping of the twelve divisions of the

Bundeswehr, European diplomatic pressure encouraged NATO to add more conventional capabilities to avoid a nuclear exchange, as well as to 'defend forward' of the Rhine River. This placed forward the "theoretical trigger line" for the threat of 'first use' of nuclear weapons by NATO to halt a Warsaw Pact offensive.

This raised the threshold of nuclear use until the armies added a new generation of modern conventional weapons that far outpaced the capabilities of Second World War-type tanks, artillery and carriers that formed the bulk of NATO's ground forces. The exit of France's forces from the military alliance, not the political treaty of NATO, forced the forward defence to materialise. The French, however maintained active liaison with NATO military forces, and the French First Army was committed to reinforce NATO in emergency. They maintained a headquarters section co-located with Central Army Group and participated in CENTAG war exercises. In time of war, the French Army would serve under the Commander-in-Chief, Allied Forces Central Europe, and most likely due to its peace locations, be assigned to CENTAG as its reserve.

New tactics and a greater understanding of the effects of modern weapons came from the October 1973 war based on the successful defence of the Sinai and Golan Heights by Israeli forces using US-type equipment against Arab-manned Soviet equipment. This further encouraged NATO to push its main dispositions far forward, especially in the American corps. This required a more robust and advanced intelligence system based on satellites and communications intelligence that would give a two-week warning window to NATO of a full Warsaw Pact mobilisation. In the US sectors, the creation of a heavy armoured covering force for deployment forward of the main forces placed units of the two Armoured Cavalry Regiments virtually at the interzonal border where they would defend, not conduct the traditional delay backwards. The addition of highly precise Pershing II missiles to replace the older 1950s systems would add both reach and accuracy to hitting the enemy advance in depth at its logistical nodes. The augmentation of air force tactical A-10 tank killer aircraft and missile-carrying helicopters further added greater firepower to the robust conventional defence.

By the 1980s and with the introduction of the advanced M-1 tanks, Apache helicopters, multiple rocket launchers, fire-finder anti-artillery radars and a new family of advanced munitions, the forward conventional defence especially in the US-dominated Central Army Group was considered both possible and a greater deterrent. The upgrade of the German forces' equipment with Leopard tanks and the British with Challenger tanks paralleled the new US efforts. The United States added a forward deployed armoured brigade to the Northern Army Group and intended to deploy a full attack helicopter brigade to balance NATO's conventional capabilities. The collapse of the Soviet Union witnessed a distinct quality advantage being held by NATO over its Warsaw Pact counterparts. The forward defence and upgrade to highly capable, survivable conventional weapons raised the nuclear threshold by negating the Soviet quantitative advantage in the early stages of a conventional conflict and caused both a redesign of Soviet forces and upgrade in equipment that was beginning at the end of the Cold War.

Flexible response shapes NATO strategic thinking

The important issue to understand in this subject was that tactical doctrine changed in the US forces, and that had a parallel change in NATO concepts. The original defence of the 1950s and 1960s was informed by Second World War experience in using both position and mobile defence tactics. This was heavily influenced by the size of the NATO frontage, and the space and time ratios considered by deployment and a mass attack of Second World War 'front proportions' by the Warsaw Pact. By the mid- and late 1970s, the Americans had embraced active defence, which like its First World War model of German tactics in 1918, permitted movement to shoot 'and counterattack by fire' and exploit the unevenness of terrain, enemy advances and local success. The introduction of the 'operational level' in the 1980s refined this to the 'Deep Battle' to deal with multiple echelons. NATO accepted this as the FOFA defence, or the Follow on Forces attack. While the Europeans insisted on semantic changes to the deep battle concept, this accentuated the need for interdiction of the following echelons to permit those in the battle line to fight, while extending the battle in depth into the enemy's rear. This favoured transferring as much of the battle in time to the enemy rear. The adoption of multiple rocket launch artillery, jet-boosted artillery shells, extensive deployment of missile-armed helicopters and the use of aerial radars (AWACS) to predict locations of enemy echelons for targeting meant this concept became more technically possible to execute and orchestrate fires, manoeuvre and air.

The complete adoption of these ideas drove forward the technical capabilities of the NATO forces, with US forces leading in modernisation, followed by the Germans, British and others in turn. While CENTAG had oriented itself to this type of battle, NORTHAG, the British, German, Dutch and Belgian force, was forced by its slower advancing technology to continue in a Second World War view of the mobile defence, pivoting on an extensive barrier and flooding plan in certain seasons. NATO's lack of homogeneity of force capabilities was paralleled in the Warsaw Pact by the most capable Group Soviet Forces Germany force, and then the Polish, Czech and East German armies all using older equipment, and wedded to the older, less flexible forms of operations. The Cold War bankrupted Russia, and its satellites disappeared with the dissolution of the Soviet Empire, ending this military conundrum for everyone.

Escalation: from conventional forces to nuclear weapons

Discussions with retired Soviet officers under the sponsorship of the now defunct Parallel History Project for the Cold War NATO and Warsaw Pact revealed interesting concepts often unknown or misunderstood in the West. While the Warsaw Pact held both a robust battlefield nuclear and chemical stockage and capability, the Soviets had long learned that this was never advantageous to use, especially as their frequently gamed and replanned 'Seven Days to the Rhine' exercises had shown. If the Soviets' weapons of mass destruction would blow a hole in the NATO conventional defence, the mere rush to the Rhine proved theoretically impossible due to radiation, gas-polluted areas and the destruction of paths, bridges and clear areas both for manoeuvre and forward displacement of troops and logistics stores. The Russians feared not only NATO retaliation but the fact that radioactivity carried by the eastward prevailing winds would engulf Russia after about two weeks. Moreover, NATO's stated and practised (in exercises) policy of response to weapons of mass destruction (i.e. chemical, biological or radiological weapons) would incur a response by NATO's use of tactical nuclear weapons. This would theoretically offset any advantage gained by using 'nukes and gas' and threaten the build-up of follow-on echelons of forces. The theoretical threshold of massive response would be lowered perilously, and total nuclear war would be nearly inevitable, preventable only by halting and withdrawal and immediate armistice. Thoughtful Soviet analysts therefore predicted stalemate, or nuclear war. Successful conventional war for the Warsaw Pact was theoretically impossible. [6]

The use of chemical/biological weapons fall within nuclear escalation

The Soviets were aware of NATO's order of battle in complete detail, and possible plans were not only known but viewed for what they were, defensive plans. The Soviets did not fear a NATO assault after 1980. Their own attack plans were viewed as necessary as pre-emptive contingencies in case of a massive political change. The Soviet theoretical mindset of attacking any possible attacker first was more than a slogan, as it underlay all planning during the 1980s. To the Soviets, the pre-emptive offensive was primarily a defensive

---

[6] Army Magazine. *"The Cold War in Perspective."* Maj. Gen. Neil Creighton and Lt. Col. Roger Cirillo. July, 2006. Volume 56, No. 7, pp. 57-62; and especially, *War Plans and Alliances in the Cold War. Threat Perceptions in the East and West.* (Vojtech Mastny et. al. editors). CSS Studies in Security and International Relations, 2013, passim.

strategy. Group Soviet Forces Germany represented the power of this capability. The upgrade of weapons did concern the Soviets. The deployment of longer-range and precise battlefield weapons, like the Pershing II missile, meant the unwritten rule that battlefield systems should not be able to target any capital, Brussels, Paris, London or Washington for the West, and Prague, Warsaw and Moscow in the East, had been broken.

This meant that tactical nuclear weapons could reach the political centres of all the main Warsaw Pact players on the Central Front. This was the major fear raised during the ABLE ARCHER Exercise in 1983. This signal was less well perceived in the West. As was revealed to the author in these discussions, the Soviets did not perceive the ability to confine tactical nuclear weapons to a supporting role, and that first use by either side would prompt retaliation, and the scaling of their use would be impossible as one side gained significant military advantages. Use would always incur response, and inevitable first use of massive retaliation would have to follow unless surrender or armistice was immediately agreed to. [7]

After the Ussuri River incident in 1969, the Soviet Army viewed China as the most immediate threat to Russian territory. The thirty-year existence of NATO as a defensive shield was both believable and quantitatively likely in the 1980s. Nor did the Soviets ever discover any offensive NATO plans as such were forbidden by agreement within NATO. While they were fully conversant with the Single Integrated Operational Plan for general nuclear war as rehearsed by the US Strategic Air Command and the American Polaris submarine fleet, the Soviets, who had more variable 'scenarios' for total war, were confident that only failed diplomacy would change the stand-off in Europe. The Warsaw Pact had several different ground 'scenarios' for conventional conflict, but these were held by them to be in response to our 'defensive plans'. The likelihood that we could mount an offensive on their soil due to our smaller forces held both sides in check regardless of what the militaries of either side could theorise.

---

[7] Army Magazine, ibid. War Plans and Alliances, passim.

From battlefield nuclear weapons to all-out nuclear war

Both the NATO and Warsaw Pact armies did not consider general nuclear war within their missions, though the air forces, no doubt, kept back aircraft for nuclear strike missions if ordered. NATO forces had the general war forces within their air forces and navies, primarily in submarines. The armies had tactical nuclear weapons and chemical capabilities to different degrees. The primary mission of both ground forces was to destroy the ground force of their opponents. The forward defence strategy of NATO essentially relegated the battleground to the area between the interzonal borders and the Rhine, regardless of whatever distant objectives the Warsaw Pact may have held. The depth of the Warsaw Pact battlefield could be extended to the borders of the Soviet Union by both aircraft and battlefield missiles, but the area nearest the interzonal boundary of the East and West was always considered the most crucial by both sides.

In a war, the failure to hold its forward sector implied either total war or surrender by NATO. If deeply penetrated, NATO had two choices in such a case: either the limited use of tactical weapons to force the enemy to halt, or total nuclear response. The release of tactical weapons was practised annually from every level from Brussels to the nuclear-capable force headquarters, but no modern game ever played out total war at the NATO level, though US wargaming of nuclear war is known to have taken place, primarily for targeting purposes. The basic General Defence Plan for NATO existed to meet a Warsaw Pact attack; it did not factor the prevention of civilian casualties as a priority of planning except within the realm of possible humane action but never in forfeit of military advantage. Plans to evacuate civilians from the forward areas upon 'Simple Alert' could be exercised, but the primary need to man defences was paramount. This reflected the firm belief that a failed defence would lower the nuclear threshold for employing tactical nuclear weapons.

The long-forgotten unwritten rules and protocols

A total conventional surprise attack was viewed as militarily impossible because huge forces were necessary to gain their operational objectives, though it was theoretically possible to phase an attack during their annual manoeuvres, which would give very little warning to the covering forces and would prompt a request for immediate use of tactical nuclear weapons. This would require the political will to risk total destruction for the achievement of local military gain. War is a political act, and the willingness to survive versus the possibility of fighting to the death is a decision made not by the masses but by the political elites of the countries involved. Just as the Japanese Emperor's decision to surrender, as opposed to the military's will to fight to the death, was exercised at the end of the Second World War, the ability of NATO's representatives to vote unanimously in Brussels was always a theoretical vote 'yes' and incorporated in operational exercises triggering a nuclear riposte. This may have played out differently in an actual engagement. The reality of large civilian deaths in the fighting zone was always high, but the large death toll of a nuclear spasm war was viewed by humane men as too high to permit even the occasion of making such war possible. This deterrence did eventuate, and no war was launched, though many believe without nuclear weapons a conventional war would have been begun by Stalin.

NATO's plans and exercises were carefully scripted and had to be approved by the NATO military committee in Brussels for exercises above corps (national level), and all NATO exercises followed a similar scenario from 'Simple Alert to Defence'. No offensive planning for crossing the interzonal border by ground forces was permitted at any level. Air planning for interdiction did not apply to this. Nuclear planning was considered to be top secret or higher and very closely controlled. Plans for such were not generally known and were not conducted by NATO-earmarked forces. Two types of exercises existed: headquarters exercises, which may be with or without full complements of troops, or headquarters exercises using computer-based troops and forces, with an identifiable result requiring decisions and plans to exercise the staff functions and decision processes at multiple levels. Large-scale field training exercises of corps or divisions were held by national armies annually to train units in their capabilities using scenarios that paralleled their wartime tasks. Exercises were never considered to posit a strategy or provide firm strategic conclusions.

NATO annually exercised their headquarters in several corps and army group headquarters to practise command and control, air–ground coordination and planning, and to exercise the logistical staffs. A separate NATO exercise staff provided a 'standard enemy' complete with plan, enemy forces based on actual formations, and one capable of internal command and control using known enemy doctrine and Warsaw Pact 'norms' for movement, artillery, air support and logistics and movement tables was always included in NATO headquarters exercises. These exercises normally started mid-way in a war to provide maximum problem solving and were always scripted to end after a specified number of days of battle. A completely separate exercise using the actual members of the NATO committee in Brussels that would approve the release of nuclear weapons was exercised, until the Supreme Commander, also a player, was impelled to ask for nuclear release with a series of targets already prepared for authorisation. The fact that Ronald Reagan and his counterparts chose to play in ABLE ARCHER 83, which was one such exercise, prompted a Soviet nuclear alert. Never before or since has a head of state played directly in a NATO exercise.

None of these exercises were merely 'make work'. Technical lessons were noted and procedures adapted, additional resources were provided when necessary, and plans and procedures were amended when required. Exercises provided both experience and insight into problems that were likely to arise. Repetitive exercises ensured that new personnel met their counterparts, that teamwork was developed, that commanders and staffs learnt the full extent of their responsibilities and were then forced to adapt to realistic situations driven by the data produced by computer-generated losses and movements. These were training exercises. Lessons learnt were those in staff and procedural coordination. Operational lessons were not drawn concerning actual war plans, even though these plans were exercised within the scenarios.

As general nuclear war was not within the realm of military decisions at NATO, though it could be advised by the very highest commanders, the moral and physical questions of waging such a war, though remaining unspoken, and were generally not thought of by military players. While my Soviet counterpart informed me that Soviet exercises were run using a large release of tactical nuclear weapons, these always proved both the impossibility of controlling damage that would prohibit regular tactical manoeuvres and that no real advantage was seen in using large numbers of tactical nuclear warheads. [8]

The Soviets did have one actual nuclear exercise, before above-ground testing was banned, using a unit to "attack through the still hot nuclear target area". Heavy casualties resulted. The United States did have tests of small tactical nuclear weapons near dug-in troops in the 1950s, though no manoeuvres were conducted over hot areas. These were to gain confidence in the small-yield atomic cannon then being fielded. While some medical effects have been noted over the years, this programme was discontinued, and the actual deployment of the atomic cannon was made superfluous by the creation of low-yield smaller nuclear cannon shells for guns as small as 155mm. These were standard in NATO from the 1970s onward, though the United States kept control of the ammunition, which was issued to nuclear-capable artillery units, including those of our allies, only on order from Brussels and through a special secure coded system for nuclear release.

NATO and Warsaw Pact forces generated a war morality

While the morality and policy for general war are topics for national war colleges, the tactical-level schooling of any army did not discuss these issues, as policy is followed, not created at junior levels.

---

[8] This discussion took place in Stockholm, during the Parallel History meeting, whose edited transcript is reproduced in *Cold War Plans and Alliances*.

The authority for the use of nuclear weapons was in civilian hands even in the old Soviet Union. While soldiers and airmen do the targeting, these are based on civilian guidance and the civilian national decision authority. I met with Stavka officers in the early 2000s and discovered how much the Soviets knew of NATO plans and capabilities, though it is difficult to prove what they knew until their archives are opened. [9]

One thing is certain: Soviet combat units would have been given very narrow specific plans confined only to their own sectors. These plans would have been followed with no leeway given to flank manoeuvre out of sector, or the ability to improvise. Units behind them would have followed the same route and plan with additional information added for a deeper objective. This system permitted no retreat, no failures. Apart from advanced detachments and reconnaissance units, this conveyor belt of men and equipment would continue forward until expended. The Soviet soldier expected detailed tasks and considered it his duty to perform and serve his unit. The larger and wider task was the business of higher headquarters, and secrecy was accepted as normal to include the deeper purpose or mission of his unit.

While Western armies consider it their right to know as much as possible so as to chew over the plans at the next higher level, this is a Western trait needed to encourage initiative and flexibility. History shows that Soviet command could be creative, flexible and achieve surprise and accomplish much through improvisation, but that is not how the Soviet planning process and training normally worked. There is little reason to believe that Soviet generals gave their subordinates much leeway in exercises, but the initial wave of any attack was believed to have been given wide latitude in achieving surprise and would then obtain fire dominance by sheer weight of numbers. Russian artillery was known to be concentrated with heavier tube numbers allocated on key avenues of approach in their plans. This fire was scheduled initially to lift from objective to objective, but additional fires would be available on targets of opportunity. Russian artillery and attack aviation were our greatest

---

[9] Ibid. these meetings took place in both Stockholm and in Bodo, Norway.

threats. The primary duty of the echelon commander would be to press forward on successful axes and to bypass obstacles and stay behind forces on the thrusts that were halted by combat. Within sector, the head of the 'snake' would always press forward, with its body and tail following as full units in marching echelon.

The US military's attitude towards Europe and NATO

NATO had very good information about the Warsaw Pact, and information programmes existed to ensure that soldiers understood their reason for serving in NATO. Information both classified and unclassified was available for use not only in planning but in training. US officers received manuals on Soviet equipment and doctrine, and this information was always incorporated in training. At higher levels, more detailed information on enemy order of battle, unit locations and training trends was known. At battalion level and higher, it was usually known exactly which enemy units were ticketed for your sector based on locations, distances and the latest 'appreciation' of what logical tasks were required by the enemy to accomplish their missions. Enemy missions by distant objectives were theorised by terrain and location, using standard enemy doctrinal norms.

For example, in our sector in the 11th Cavalry, we faced the five divisions of the Eighth Guards Army, which was backed by the four or more divisions of First Guards Tank Army, which we believed to be the operational manoeuvre group tasked to seize objectives on the Rhine. [10]

The US V Corps was tasked to destroy both Guards Armies in succession as they appeared. The Americans were always confident in their being able to accomplish the mission as well as the resulting conventional outcome of a war. This was especially true in the mid-

---

[10] Our assessment was that Eighth Guards would affect a penetration to press the Fulda Gap, while First Guards tank would develop the Hessian Corridor as its major axis, thus splitting V Corps from III German corps, to penetrate to the Rhine after Eighth Guards had dealt with the northernmost forces in V Corps.

to late 1980s as the Army was fully equipped with the latest weapons. New capabilities caused significant changes in the earlier plans for the defence, giving the forwardmost units more capacity and permitting the shift of reserves to deal with the second echelon, which was expected to be attacked while in depth by long-range accurate battlefield rockets and missiles. As the Soviets were known to have added heliborne troops to their airborne units to infiltrate the rear, the concept of fighting three simultaneous battles in depth from the depth of the enemy's echeloned move to our own rear was considered both a normal and achievable contingency.

NATO expected that the Warsaw Pact at highest level had very good information on us and our plans. Not only was our order of battle an open book due to signposted units, phone books listing units and the usual shoulder patches, but we knew that the Stasi was exceptionally adept at gathering information. The KGB did not operate easily or in numbers in West Germany, but the Stasi did net large loads of information. It has been identified on the internet that the Stasi had a copy of our corps plan; its reproduction in German translation is available through the National Security Archive. Other plans were no doubt acquired through espionage, and the frequent 'terrain walking' of battle positions where commanders briefed their commanders on site of their planned battles were no doubt both noted and carefully sorted by Stasi plants acting as farmers and locals.

NATO's Article 5

Article 5 is a Cold War artefact.[11] Its adoption was guaranteed to stop the Russians from taking only one piece of terrain and to assure the Europeans that the Americans would not abandon them to being conquered in consideration of no nuclear weapons used on US soil. This was always a sore point, that US forces might ask for nukes to be used in Europe and have the leeway of not having them used against US targets. The fact that the United States manned

---

[11] Article 5 states that an attack on one NATO nation is considered an attack on all of NATO.

most of the German front and the British the northern front was a guarantee also to Europeans that Britain would fight as a continental force. The several hundred thousand American dependents were also not only a guarantee that America would fight, but could almost be considered a hostage to the thought of 'not using' nuclear weapons in Europe. The use of tactical nuclear weapons was really a Soviet call. If they used chemicals that we considered a weapon of mass destruction, we would respond with tactical nukes. This was significant as about 20 to 30 per cent of their artillery stocks at one time were estimated to be chemical weaponry. This percentage may have dropped in the 1980's, as NATO became more vocal about responding to Chemical Warfare by nuclear strikes.

Warsaw Pact nations joined NATO

The United States aided the Russians secretly during their retrograde by removing their left behind chemical stores and shipping them to Kwajalein to the disposal by burning site for chemicals that we have there. This was done during the spring of 1991. In the late 1980s, NATO forces knew that Group Soviet Forces Germany had discipline and morale issues, which the Russians of course did not deal lightly with. They also knew the Eastern pact nations, especially the Poles, were disloyal to the Warsaw Pact and not trustworthy in their ideas. NATO was convinced the East Germans were very disciplined, less so the Czechs, with the Poles at the bottom. In a war, Poland might just sit, as the Pope and others made inroads into their communist roots. I met a Polish general who had lost a father in the Katyn massacre and was put in a penal battalion on the eastern front. He survived to become a Major General and Polish chief of staff of the Warsaw Pact headquarters. I also met the head of the Czech Army, quite young, and a still convinced communist. He denied any missions in the Cold War for his army. I recall they were set to pass through Austria in the event of war.

The costs of the military-industrial complex

NATO did not overspend on defence, though each country maintained differing levels of authorised men and equipment, with the United States and Germany providing the bulk of troops, equipment and airplanes. NATO Nations pledged to spend a certain GDP percentage, with the Americans probably spending double or triple the minimum to maintain back-up units and capabilities in the United States. In the 1980s, the European allies began to lag both in capabilities and money spent while the United States replaced and modernised all its foreign-based forces and maintained all units at full or higher strength.

The first lag in American commitment began with the transfer of units from Europe to the Persian Gulf. These units in almost every case didn't return to duty in NATO but were permanently reassigned to the United States, and some units were inactivated. The American Armed Forces suffered a 30-plus per cent reduction within a year of the end of the 1991 Gulf War. US Army Europe had nearly 200,000 troops in 1990 and was reduced to 90,000 plus and eventually to 60,000 by 2000. With the break-up of the Soviet Union, European support for NATO has waned, though it must be noted that NATO forces volunteered to serve in Afghanistan after the 2001 9-11 attack on the United States. This was under Article 5 of the NATO treaty that considers an attack on one NATO country an attack on all, though this interpretation is exceptional to the original treaty as no attack occurred in the normal NATO area of responsibility and NATO did not fight in the previous Vietnam War where America's participation was voluntary.

Impressions of Russian military capability

The Soviets had severe economic issues, and I was in the Central Army Group headquarters when the wall came down. There was no warning, and the Russians were ordered to sit and do nothing. After that, the Russian bear seemed demoralised. On 24 April 2015, the 11th Cavalry Regiment's veterans met old Eastern German border guards from the opposite side to the US Army camp Alpha also called Point Alfa. We walked a 'joint patrol' under the old guard towers and past our wire. The West had won, that was definitive. Driving all the way to Leipzig convinced me of how primitive the living conditions were in the East. Looking from the tower at Observation-Post Alfa at night during the Cold War, the sparse lights of East Germany had always been a strong indication of the poverty and backwardness. By 2015, this had changed significantly. Observing the end gave one pause to comprehend what had been done. By holding out against Communism, East Germany became free and reunited and the Warsaw Pact crumbled. There was a euphoria for a new world.

Ongoing Operations to End of Year One.

While it is impossible to accurately judge ongoing operations as both the Ukraine and Russia are engaged in active information warfare operations, painting their own situations to suit their ends, some impressions can be gained. Despite what appears to be a miscalculation by the Russians in sizing their force at the war's onset, the Russians have displayed both competence and subtlety in their use of long range fires, targeting by drones and satellites, and the lack of echeloned fighting techniques in their attacks. They have not been drawn into extensive fighting over terrain, but have replied by counter fires and precision strikes to any Ukrainian bid to hold ground or to counterattack to regain lost terrain. Only limited objective attacks, designed as gaining "fire bait," have been launched in the past nine months.

The Russians began what appeared to be a conventional attack, but far different in one major aspect than those we expected to be used against NATO in the Central Battle, i.e. the battle for Northwest Europe. Russian units were not committed in Echelon, as a jackhammer to expend units on penetration, breakthrough, and deep penetration far into the operational depth of the enemy, and to pass on to the economic and political depth of the country. Instead, units were spread using a more flexible and capable battle group at battalion level, both to engage and continue operations forward. Artillery, the true 'Red God of War,' was retained not only for preparation fires, but for the attrition battle to be fought against manoeuvre units.

Russian attacks were slow to close and overrun units, showing a regard for keeping their own casualties low, and also for limiting damage to Ukrainian villages and towns except to that which was needed to fight Ukrainian units, and not break the will of the Ukrainian people. Extensive fires were used targeted by both drones and satellites. Reconnaissance by fire or simply forward movement was abandoned to fight orchestrated actions, piling massive firepower and gradual moves to eat through the crust of the defence. This resulted in almost a "bite and hold" method reminiscent of the battles of World War I, while limited objectives were seized, and massive counterfire was used to break up counterattacks, which is where the prime killing of the defence occurred.

This subtlety in method caused most Western Analysts to claim Russia's Army had failed, and this was supported by NATO information warfare text releases claiming horrific losses and total dissolution of Russia's attack capability. After three months of attrition, Russia withdrew her main forces for regeneration, reinforcement and training, while employing Chechen and Wagner Group forces to continue to develop local situations for the main opportunity of creating fire targets for Russian guns and missiles, and continuing the attrition of the Ukrainian regular and reserve army. Russia mobilized and total refit plus significantly reinforced its forces by the end of 2022. During this period, the Ukrainian main force had been attritted heavily as it continually fought both to hold and regain terrain, a major military cost to its forces. Russian losses appear to be as little as one fifth to a quarter as much as those lost by the Ukrainians whose trained army is far smaller.

Russia has committed forces in a slowly building offensive, aimed first at the total destruction by attrition of Ukraine's fighters, and maximizing their advantages in electronic warfare, targeting, and long range precision fires by both tube artillery and rockets. As Zelensky has determined to hold every inch of ground, this favours the Russian fires tactic as Ukrainian forces the positions like

Bakhmut which are simply huge target areas in which their army has been drawn onto targeted ground and are ground up with no sustainable unit survival rates, much in the manner in which French units had been ground up for no favourable exchange rate at Verdun or Dien Bien Phu. Russian losses are minimized to that which opposing artillery can produce, which is less than a tenth the firing capability of the Russians, whose supply of tubes and shells has not been affected by shortages.

Clearly, the Russians are using politically sensitive areas as bait to destroy increasing numbers of Ukrainian men and equipment while risking little itself. As Russia has committed its late model T-90 models of tanks plus late model carriers, the Russians are waiting to bleed the enemy further before launching a determined long range ground push. While losing the advantage of frozen ground and a winter offensive, the attrition has stepped up regardless of the methodical advance tactic adopted.

Despite NATO help, Ukraine is being bled to death on the battlefield. To end the war, Russia might inevitably surround and take Kiev and Odessa and the area east of the Dnepr, but at this writing Ukraine's army is being regenerated with poorly trained conscripts of both sexes, either too young or too old to make adequate front line troops. Once these levies are expended, a decision must be made to either sue for armistice or to fight to the end.

This is not the type war envisioned by NATO in the Cold War, but it is a battle brought on in large part by NATO advice and technical support. Consistent counterattacks to the extent of self-immolation were a NATO response to holding terrain forward to prevent nuclear war in the hopes that the enemy would stop. NATO resolve was always trumpeted as its greatest strength. Never tested in the Cold War, this policy seems to be bleeding Ukraine dry.

One Russian truism has remained from its history. Massive fires and persistent operations favour the larger Army, especially one with large manpower reserves. Adapting from massive offensives to a limited objective supported by heavy fires was always the British solution in the latter part of World War I and in Montgomery's campaigns in Northwest Europe. Both were done to minimize losses and to use metal, not bodies, to achieve a long-term strategy.

It is remarkable that the Russian Army found on the battlefield, is far more sophisticated, and less bloody minded, than the one envisioned that we would be found in Europe during the Cold War. It is also most likely to win under the current conditions of the battlefield at the end of Year One.

To summarize, as this is written, the Russians have appeared to fight by using mass fires, and have not fought over built-up areas except to attack by fire, any Ukrainian forces defending in numbers. This type of attrition war favours the one with the most fire, and appears that Russia has fired up to ten rounds of artillery or missiles for every one launched by Ukraine. It is definitely a strategy of inflicting large attrition over time, a type strategy never considered during the Cold War.

I believe that NATO is a North Atlantic alliance and should not have induced the Eastern European former Soviet republics to be part of it. This poses an existential threat to Russia and has justified new Cold War. Just as the United States refused to countenance a Russian missile presence in Cuba in October, 1962, Russia refused such a possibility in the Crimea at the mouth of the Black Sea. Historically, Russians are paranoid about their borders, and Polish nationalism and the excesses of other former republics should not be given cover as a military dependency of the Western Alliance. These countries should claim NEUTRAL status. The Russians will respect that. An enlarged NATO is both unnecessary and dangerous to itself. The American people are not willing to die for one of the 'stans' or any other republic that is not a traditional ally and extending the protection of Article 5 to these nations is a questionable practice. American military assistance to Ukraine is the cause of certain American elites.

3. HYBRID AND NON-LINEAR WARFARE IN RUSSIAN STRATEGIC THINKING

Chris Bellamy

Prologue: of little green men

On 27 February 2014, Ukrainian People's Deputy Petro Poroshenko, shortly to become Ukrainian president, flew to Simferopol, the capital of Crimea (see Figure 1). Cracks had opened up in Ukraine between people who looked westward, towards the European Union and NATO, and those, mostly in the east and Crimea, who looked towards Moscow. Ukraine's Parliament had tasked Poroshenko with holding talks with the leader of the Crimean Autonomous Republic to stabilise the situation on the peninsula, which, while part of Ukraine, was about to elope with an old flame, Russia.

Crimea had been part of Ukraine since 1954, when Nikita Khrushchev (1894-1971) gave it to the then Ukrainian Soviet Socialist Republic as a thank-you for being his power base. Because Ukraine was then one of the fifteen republics that made up the Soviet Union, it did not matter much. But with the break-up of the Soviet Union in 1991, Ukraine became an independent country. Its government started looking towards the European Union and NATO. The western parts of Ukraine had until 1939 been part of Poland, and some, before 1918, had been part of the Austro-Hungarian Empire. So the city of L'viv (Ukrainian) had been Soviet Russian L'vov, Polish Lwów and Austro-Hungarian Lemberg. Russia saw the swing towards the West as a threat to its protective belt in the 'near abroad', keeping NATO at a distance. Even worse, other areas within the Russian Republic itself might get the same idea.

Even more important, however, was that coruscating diamond in the Russian imperial crown: the Crimean Peninsula (See Figure 1). Crimea had a largely Russian population, and Sevastopol was still home to the Russian Black Sea Fleet, which shared bases on a lease system with newly independent Ukraine. The Russian Black Sea Fleet was one of just four fleets opening Russia's windows on the world, along with the Baltic, Northern and Pacific. Sevastopol — from the Greek 'Magnificent City' — is a critical geostrategic harbour. Around 1780, when Russia's greatest general, Aleksandr Suvorov, first espied its deep inlet, protected from the sea and surrounded by high ground, he said there was nowhere else in the entire Black Sea 'where the fleet and its personnel could be more conveniently and securely stationed'.[1]

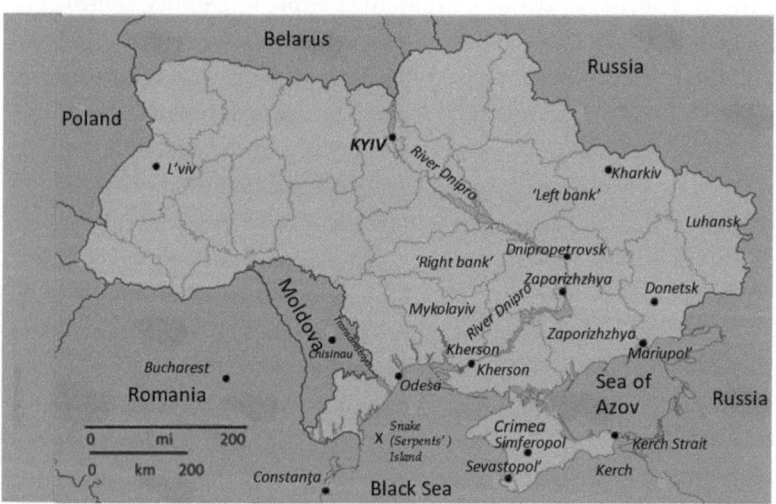

Figure 1 - Map of Ukraine 2023 via CIA The World Factbook August 31, 2023. In public domain via https://www.cia.gov/the-world-factbook/countries/ukraine/map/

Sevastopol holds a cardinal place in the Russian heart and soul. Two terrible sieges had cost Russia blood, tears and sweat, to an

---

[1] "Imperiia: 1783: The Founding of Sevastopol', Imperiia: a spatial history of the Russian Empire, accessed 3 August 2023, https://scalar.fas.harvard.edu/imperiia/1783-the-founding-of-sevastopol.

unimaginable degree: the siege by French, British, Italians and Turks in the 1853–6 'Eastern' or 'Crimean' War; and that by the Germans, Romanians and Italians from October 1941 to July 1942 in the 1941–5 Great Patriotic War.[2] The former was documented by none other than Count Leo Tolstoy, a young artillery officer. His Sevastopol Sketches (1855), journalistic reporting disguised as fiction to frustrate the censors, provided graphic and bloody material for scenes in his later masterpiece War and Peace (1869).[3] The Russians played on this sentiment as part of the justification for the 2014 re-annexation of Crimea, for which they were understandably condemned.[4]

As the crisis deepened, Poroshenko had been told that Simferopol airport was already blocked by troops and others sporting civilian clothes. He decided to go anyway.

He was accosted by protesters as he left the airport, but they backed off when he came within range of TV cameras. He was taken by car to the Crimean Supreme Council Headquarters to meet the chairman, Viktor Konstantinov. He got within 400 metres and then got out to walk. Poroshenko revealed what happened two years later, in 2016, when speaking on oath as a witness at the trial of former Ukrainian President Viktor Yanukovych. Yanukovych had disappeared from Kyiv on 22 February 2014 before resurfacing in Russia on the very day of Poroshenko's mission to Crimea, 27 February. Giving evidence two years later, Poroshenko said:

> I personally witnessed that it [Crimean Supreme Council HQ] had been

---

[2] Chris Bellamy, Absolute War: Soviet Russia in the Second World War; a Modern History (London: Pan Books, 2009), p.458.

[3] Leo Tolstoy and David McDuff, The Sebastopol Sketches, Penguin Classics (Harmondsworth, Middlesex, England; New York, N.Y., U.S.A: Penguin Books, 1986).

[4] The Russian 'myth' about Sevastopol had been under attack for some time, even before 2014. See Serhii Plokhy, 'The City of Glory: Sevastopol in Russian Historical Mythology', Journal of Contemporary History 35, no. 3 (July 2000), pp. 369–83. For a more recent and remarkably even-handed perspective, see Aleksei Erkhov, 'The Other Side of a Myth', Al-Sabah op-ed, 2 April 2018, https://www.dailysabah.com/op-ed/2018/04/03/the-other-side-of-a-myth (accessed 19 September 2018).

closed. It had not been working, it had been cordoned off by 'little green men' — servicemen of the Russian regular forces, and a chain of men sporting camouflaged clothing, the ones who called themselves 'Crimean self-defence', but were coordinated by officers of the Russian special services. There came a command to block me off, surround me, and use the means of physical influence. I attempted to not let them do that. My attempt to get into the Crimean Supreme Council building was blocked by those individuals, including the Russian military.[5]

Poroshenko had no doubt that these were Russian troops. The first accounts of 'green men' seem to refer to the Russian forces already emplaced in Crimea, such as the marines from the Russian naval base at Sevastopol. But we know that in February 2014 the 3rd Guards Spetsnaz Brigade of Russia's Main Military Intelligence Directorate (Glavnoye Razvedivatel'noye Uptravleniye; GRU) were deployed 'for the protection of strategic facilities in Crimea ... until the full stabilization of the situation in Ukraine'.[6]

Two days later, on 1 March, exiled President Yanukovych asked Russia to use military forces 'to establish legitimacy, peace, law and order, stability and defending the people of Ukraine'. On the same day, Russian President Vladimir Putin requested and received authorisation from the Russian Parliament (Duma) to deploy Russian troops to Ukraine. By the end of the following day, the Russians had taken full control of the Crimean Peninsula.

But the Russian troops, wearing green uniforms and with Russian military equipment, including sophisticated radios able to send encrypted signals, and riding in Russian vehicles with Russian number plates, were already in Crimea. Some had already been based there as part of the Russian presence, notably the 810th Naval Infantry (Marine) Brigade, part of the Black Sea Fleet, but the 3rd Guards Spetsnaz Brigade had been inserted in February. They had

---

5   'Poroshenko Says Personally Saw "Little Green Men" on Crimea Visit in 2014, There Was "Threat to Life"', UNIAN, 21 February 2018, https://www.unian.info/politics/10015997-poroshenko-says-personally-saw-little-green-men-on-crimea-visit-in-2014-there-was-threat-to-life.html (accessed 30 August 2018).

6   John R. Haines, 'How, Why, and When Russia Will Deploy Little Green Men — and Why the US Cannot', Foreign Policy Research Institute, 9 March 2016, https://www.fpri.org/article/2016/03/how-why-and-when-russia-will-deploy-little-green-men-and-why-the-us-cannot (accessed 30 August 2018).

been deployed before Putin obtained authorisation from the Russian Duma to intervene, not that such a decision would have mattered much. In old-fashioned terms, they had been deployed well before the commencement of 'war'.

The phrase 'little green men' was first used in connection with Crimea in late February, even before the overt Russian takeover. Crimean citizens, whether pro-Ukrainian or pro-Russian, noticed strange soldiers wearing green uniforms without any identifying insignia. The soldiers were reluctant to talk — although they did talk to the locals, they were utterly taciturn with foreign journalists. 'Little green men' thus referred to their uniform colour and their mystery. One commentator noted similarities with the British Monarch's Guards at Buckingham Palace: say nothing, and do not react.[7]

Once the presence of Spetsnaz on the streets was clear, the locals subtly changed the nickname. From zelënye chelovechki, 'little green men', to zelënye lyudishki, 'little green people',[8] probably because it became clear that some of the Russian troops were women. The well-equipped and heavily armoured 'local militia', whom most people agree were Russian troops, were not easily identifiable by gender. However, one of the photographs showed a soldier wearing white nail varnish. It was a woman. That could well explain the locals' subtle transmission of 'little green men' to 'little green people'.[9]

It was dangerous to talk in such terms, either in Russia or within the Russian communities in Ukraine. It was taboo to refer to the use of the Russian military garrison already in Crimea, or its reinforcement by some 550 Special Forces' troops. The 'little green

---

[7] Comment in 'Russia's Little Green Men Enter Ukraine: Russian Roulette in Ukraine', YouTube, 3 March 2014, https://www.youtube.com/watch?v=TNKsLl K52ss (accessed 12 September 2022).

[8] Some commentators ascribed the change from 'chelovechki' to 'lyudishki' as 'green men' to 'little green men', but this is wrong. *Chelovechek* means 'little man'. The plural of *chelovek*—'man'—is *lyudi*—'people'.

[9] I am grateful to Professor Caroline Kennedy, professor of war studies, for this astute observation, which I had missed, at a presentation to the University of Hull, in 2013.

men' — or 'people' — therefore quickly also became known as 'polite people' (vezhlivye lyudi) as they were perceived to have behaved peacefully with little practical interference in the residents' daily lives. That term had, however, been used for special forces before, as early as 2015.¹⁰ Spin doctors were sent from Moscow to Crimea to reinforce this message.¹¹ The diminutive chelovechki was a deliberate translation of the 1940s and 1950s Americanism 'little green men',*¹² referring to space aliens and fantastical stories of alien encounters and flying saucers. As one Russian commentated: 'It conveys an ironic sense, something that in any case cannot be trusted, a knowingly false report.'¹³ I was first alerted to the term by an article in the Financial Times. 'Green men' referred to the unattributable troops. *¹⁴ The local militia, wearing bits of Russian military clothing that can be bought in any military shop, and are often worn by huntsmen and bought as 'army surplus', were given away by their scruffiness, often wearing trainers. But the 'green men', or, later, 'green people', wore smart Russian military uniforms, albeit without insignia, carried the latest Russian equipment, including sophisticated encrypted radios, and rode in Russian vehicles. The first giveaway was that they were wearing proper boots, which all matched. Many of them were also wearing knee protectors, which can, admittedly, also be bought in DIY and gardening shops but, given their uniformity, suggested they were expecting to scurry through buildings on their knees. Common sense said they were

---

10   See Vladmiri Kvachkov, *Spetsnaz Rossii, Vexhliviyw lyudi (Russian Spetsnaz. Polite people)*, Moscow, Algoritm, 2015)

11   However, Haines translates 'зелёные человечки'/*zelyonye chelovechki* (Russian) and 'зелені чоловічки'/*zeleni cholovichki* (Ukrainian) as 'green men', whereas it means 'little green men'. The '-ch-' is still a diminutive.

12   Mindy Weisberger, 'Why Do We Imagine Aliens as "Little Green Men"?', Live Science, 12 July 2016,https://www.livescience.com/55370-why-are-aliens-littl e-green-men.html (accessed 30 August 2018).

13   Alexander Anichkin, 'Zelenyye Chelovechki' (Little green men), Tetradki (Notebooks) blog, 13 March 2014, https://european-book-review.blogspot.co m/2014/03/little-green-men.html (accessed 30 August 2018).

14   Sam Jones, 'Ukraine: Russia's New Art of War; Nato Has Struggled to Counter Moscow's Tactics in Conflict Where Traditional Might Is Only a Part', *Financial Times*, 28 August 2014,http://www.ft.com/cms/s/2/ea5e82fa-2e0c-11e4-b760 -00144feabdc0.html#axzz3ID2mwpHQ (accessed 12 September 2022).

regular Russian Army or even Spetsnaz troops.

After some initial uncertainty, I became convinced that these were regular Russian troops when doing an interview for the TV channel Al Jazeera English early in March 2014. Just before I went on, Al Jazeera carried a report from one of its teams in Crimea that had stumbled on a derelict building and site where 'green men' had been based. They found empty ration packs marked 'Armed forces of the Russian Federation. Not for sale.' That was the final giveaway. At the time, I reflected that the British Army would not have been as sloppy or careless and would have buried the incriminating evidence, as we always did on exercise.

The science of future war

The media and the commentators seized on the 'little green men', or 'people', story and ran with it. Some almost immediately saw it, as the Financial Times (FT) put it, as 'Russia's new art of war.'[15] This essay will conclude that it was neither 'new' nor peculiarly Russian. The 'new art of war' view had been underlined and reinforced by two publications in the first quarter of 2013. These articles had clearly set out the blueprint for future warfare as the Russians saw it. But the FT had taken the brief snapshot, not the film or its antecedents.

The publications—one article and the transcript of a speech—were by Valeriy Gerasimov, the chief of the Russian general staff. The more easily available one, which most analysts used, was in the Russian Military-Industrial Courier, with an ostentatiously scientific and obscurantist title: 'The Value of Science in Forecasting'.[16] However, the other, the text of Gerasimov's address to the Academy of Military Sciences, appeared in the first 2013 edition of its quarterly journal. Hence it appeared at much the same time and

---

[15] Ibid.

[16] Valeriy Gerasimov, 'Tsennost' nauki v predvidenii' (The value of science in forecasting), *Voyenno-Promyshlenny Kur'er* (Military-industrial courier), 27 February 2013 (accessed 1 September 2018).

was probably more important.[17]

Most analysts, including the current one, homed in on the Military-Industrial Courier article, quite possibly because it was easier to get hold of. In his excellent 2018 study, Russian Hybrid Warfare, Ofer Fridman sounded a cautionary tone, saying that Gerasimov was simply explaining his views on the operational environment and the nature of future war, not proposing a new Russian way of warfare or military doctrine.[18]

This author is not so sure. If the chief of the general staff puts his name to an article about the nature of future war, that is significant. It is military doctrine, which the Russians define as 'a state-accepted system of views on the character of future war for a given (specific) time'.[19] In this context, General Gerasimov, the chief of the general staff, equivalent to the British chief of defence staff, writing about future war, is the state. Furthermore, the article's 'scientific' style and profile, as well as its content, instantly signalled that this was a significant statement on military doctrine. It had all the hallmarks of Russian and Soviet pronouncements on the character of future war going back to the nineteenth century.[20]

In the Military-Industrial Courier article, Gerasimov described the lessons of the 'Arab Spring', the wave of demonstrations and

---

[17] Valeriy Gerasimov, 'Principal Trends in the Development of the Forms and Methods of Employing Armed Forces and Current Tasks of Military Science Regarding Their Improvement' *Vestnik Akademii Voyennykh Nauk* (*VAVN*) 1, no. 42 (2013), p. 24.

[18] Ofer Fridman, *Russian Hybrid Warfare: Resurgence and Politicisation* (London: Hurst, 2018). Also published online by Oxford University Press in February 2019 (www.oxfordscholarship.com/view/10.1093/oso/9780190877378.001.0001 (accessed 12 September 2022)) citing Charles Bartles, 'Getting Gerasimov Right', *Military Review* 96 (2016), p. 31.

[19] Defined in *Sovetskaya voyennaya entsiklopedia* (*SVE*) (Soviet military encyclopaedia), vol. 3 (1977), p. 223, a definition repeated by Marshal Nikolay V. Ogarkov, *Vsegda v gotovnosti k zashchite otchestva* (Always in readiness to defend the motherland) (Moscow: Voynizda, 1982), p. 53.

[20] See my '"Catastrophes to Come ...": Russian and Soviet Visions of Future War, 1866 to the Present', in Ljubica Erickson and Mark Erickson (eds.), *Russia: War, Peace and Diplomacy; Essays in Honour of John Erickson* (London: Weidenfeld & Nicolson, 2005), pp. 20–40, 301–8 A summary of my PhD thesis 'The Russian and Soviet View of the Military-Technical Character of Future War 1877–2017' (University of Edinburgh, 1991).

protests—violent and non-violent—riots, coups, foreign interventions and civil wars in North Africa and the Middle East that began with the Tunisian Revolution on 18 December 2010. But then he went on:

> The role of non-military means in achieving political and strategic targets has grown, which in a number of cases significantly surpass force of arms in their effectiveness. The essence of the methods of conflict lies in the widespread use of political, economic, informational, humanitarian and other non-military means, carried out with the utilisation of the protest potential of the population. All this permits military means to have a covert character, including information warfare and the action of Special Operations Forces. Frequently the open use of force will have the appearance of peace support operations and crisis management, and will only move to that stage to achieve final success in the conflict.[21]

The actions in Crimea and the east of mainland Ukraine certainly used the 'protest potential of the population'. Ethnic Russians, speaking Russian, who opposed the westward-looking Kyiv government teamed up with Russian forces to fight Ukrainian troops.

Gerasimov's article featured a table contrasting traditional 'forms and means' of warfare with new ones. Traditionally, military action started after strategic deployment—which could therefore be detected. It involved the frontal collision of powerful force groupings and the destruction of personnel and weapons, and the successive seizure of phase lines and territory. Military operations took place on land, at sea and in the air, controlled through a hierarchical command structure. In the new warfare, military action by groups of forces begins in peacetime. That was exactly what happened in Crimea, with Poroshenko seeing Russian troops on 27 February, two days before the Russian Duma authorised military action. Most significantly, although some analysts missed it,[22] the 'new' warfare would involve 'highly manoeuvrist contactless military action by

---

[21] Gerasimov, 'Value of Science'.
[22] Bettina Renz and Hanna Smith, 'Russia and Hybrid Warfare: Going beyond the Label', Aleksanteri Papers 1/2016, p. 6, http://vnk.fi/en/government-s-analys is-assessment-and-research-activities . They say that the term 'hybrid' does not appear in the article, but it does, as *mezhvidovoy*.

hybrid [mezhvidovykh] groups of forces'.[23] Russian forces inserted 'for the protection of strategic facilities in Crimea ... until the full stabilization of the situation in Ukraine' could, at a pinch, be categorised as undertaking 'Peace Support Operations'. (PSO) Although the term 'hybrid' (here, literally 'inter-species') does not occur in the text, it is clear in the table, translated here (Figure 2).[24]

Traditional forms and means	New forms and means
• Military action starts after strategic deployment • Frontal collision of powerful force groupings with ground forces as the basis • Destruction of personnel and weapons with the successive seizure of phase lines and areas with the aim of seizing territory • Defeat of the enemy, destruction of his economic potential and conquest of his territory • Conduct of military operations on land, in the air and at sea • Direction of military forces through a strictly hierarchical command structure.	• Military action by groups of forces begins in peacetime • Highly manoeuvrist military action by hybrid (*mezhvidovye*) groups of forces (see explanation in text) • Reduction of the military-economic potential of the [target] state by the neutralisation of critical national infrastructure in a short time • Massed use of high precision ('smart') weapons (*Vysoko Tochnye Orushiya* (*VTO*), widespread use of special forces (*spetsial'nye voyska*) and weapons based on new physical principles and participation of civil-military component in military action. • Simultaneous action against enemy forces and targets throughout the entire depth of his territory • Simultaneous action in all physical dimensions and in cyberspace (*informatsionnoye prostranstvo*) • Use of asymmetric and indirect action • Direction of forces and means in a single informational space.

Figure 2. - 'Changes in the Character of Armed Struggle: attaining political targets.[25]'

Most importantly, General Gerasimov noted that non-military

---

[23] See table 'Changes in the Character of Armed Struggle: Attaining Political Targets', on page 3 (of 7). *Tseley* might also be translated as 'aims', but 'targets' is more literal.

[24] Ibid., translated by the author.

[25] Original source: *Military-Industrial Courier*, 27 February 2013. p. 3 of 7. Translated by the author.

measures in operations were used over military operations by a ratio of four to one.²⁶

Gerasimov's Academy of Military Sciences (AVN) speech covered the same ground and made the same key points:

- wars are no longer declared;
- 'colour revolutions' — mass popular demonstrations undermining national governing institutions — can occur quickly;
- the protest potential of the population could be mobilised;
- Peace Support Operations and 'crisis regulation' could be used to conceal overt military deployments;
- the principal form of contact between opponents would be 'non-contact' or remote engagement, as information technology had reduced the spatial and temporal distances between them. As a result, the three levels of military art — strategy, operational art and tactics — were becoming blurred together, and there would be no operational pauses or no man's land between combatants;
- the use of Special Forces, no-fly zones, blockades and private military companies were all becoming more prevalent.

Gerasimov referred to 'New Type War' -'voyna novogo tipa' and appears to- have been the first to use the expression that is the preferred Russian term at the time of writing.²⁷

The Russians subsequently denied categorically that they had a concept of 'hybrid warfare', the Western version of which they refer to using the English-derived term gibridny. Gerasimov, as noted, had originally used a Russian biological term, mezhvidovoy, literally 'inter-species', for the same thing. But that was a one-off.

---

26 As perceptively noted by Timothy Thomas, 'Russia's Military Strategy and Ukraine: Indirect, Asymmetric — and Putin-Led', *The Journal of Slavic Military Studies* 28, no. 3 (2015), pp. 445–61, https://www.tandfonline.com/doi/abs/10.1080/13518046.2015.1061819?needAccess=true& (accessed 16 February 2019). See the section on reflexive control later in the essay.

27 Gerasimov, 'Principal Trends ...', *VAVN* 1, no. 42 (2013), pp. 24–9. Analysed by Timothy L. Thomas, 'The Evolving Nature of Russia's Way of War', *Military Review* (July–August 2017), pp. 34–42, at pp. 35–6.

The next significant article appeared in the long-established and prestigious journal Voyennaya Mysl' (Military thought) in October 2014. Written by Lt Gen. S. A. Bogdanov and Colonel S. G. Chekinov, it referred to 'new-generation warfare', a term that has since disappeared, at least from the open source literature.[28] The article concludes that 'information superiority and anticipatory operations will be the main ingredients of success in new-generation wars'.[29] There is nothing new about hitting the enemy first, and preferably when he is not looking, but new-generation weaponry makes it easier, as long as you move first, and essential. The authors noted the potential of robotics, which, for example, could conduct reconnaissance, coordinate operations of different arms and services, repair weapons, build defences, destroy enemy weapons and equipment—the potential for killing people is always morally and ethically controversial—and clear mines and decontaminate areas.[30]

'New Type Warfare'—voyna novogo tipa—came back eighteen months later, in a speech to the AVN in early 2015. Whereas Bogdanov and Chekinov focused on the influence of new-generation weapons on 'new-generation warfare', Lt Gen. (later Col-Gen.) Andrey V. Kartapolov added to the mix by re-emphasising asymmetric methods—non-standard forms and methods—as a way of levelling the enemy's technological superiority.[31] As usual, Kartapolov accuses the Americans of doing this, using 'hybrid methods that include information-psychological effects including indirect actions that consist of covert activities directed towards igniting internal problems in an opponent's population and the use of so-

---

[28] S. G. Chekinov and S. A. Bogdanov, 'On the Character and Content of Wars of a New Generation', *Voyennaya Mysl'* (Military thought) 10 (2013), pp. 13–24. Comment is Thomas, 'Evolving Nature', pp. 37–8.
[29] Chekinov and Bogdanov, 'On the Character and Content', p. 24.
[30] Ibid., pp. 17–22 cited in Thomas, 'Evolving Nature', p. 38.
[31] Lt Gen. Andrey V. Kartapolov, 'Uroki voyennykh konfliktov, perspektivy razvitiya stredstv sposobov ikh vedeniya: Pryamye I nepryamye deystviya v sovremennykh mezhdunarodnykh konfliktakh' (Lessons of military conflicts and prospects for the development of resources and methods for conducting them: Direct and indirect actions in contemporary international conflicts), *Vestnik Academii Voyennykh Nauk* (*VAVN*) (Journal of the Academy of Military Sciences) 2 (2015), p. 35, cited in Thomas, 'Evolving Nature', p. 39.

called "third forces".'[32] In fact, this is exactly what the Russians did so effectively in Ukraine. Kartapolov summarises how a 'New-Type War' (it should be noted that that new-type war does involve shifting to classical methods of waging war) might be conducted in a useful graphic, reproduced as Figure 3.

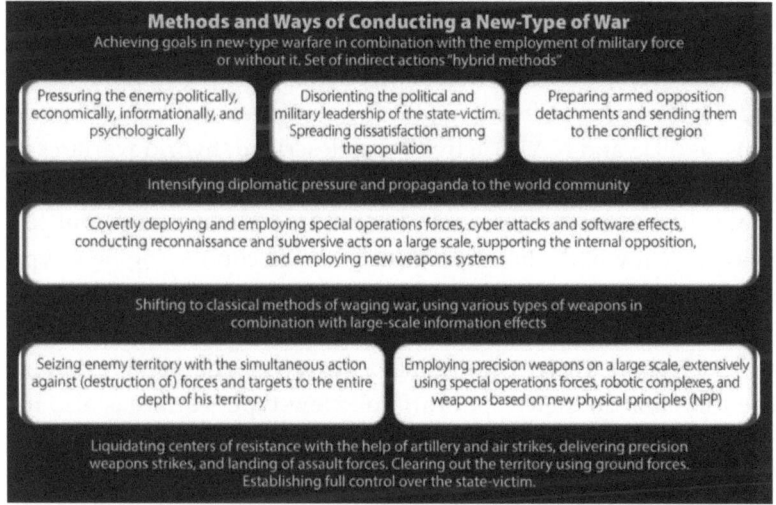

Figure 3. - Method and Ways of Conducting a New-Type of War. Graphic from Andrey V Kartapolov's 'Lessons of Military Conflicts and prospects...' *VAVN* 2/2015, p. 35, translated by Dr Harold Orenstein and reproduced from *Military Review*, July-August 2017, p. 40. *Military Review* content produced by Army University Press is in the public domain as an US government product.

In particular, Kartapolov, or whoever wrote the article for him,[33] noted that

> non-standard forms and methods are being developed for the employment of our Armed Forces, which will make it possible to level the enemy's technological superiority ... For this the features of the preparation and conduct of new-type warfare are being fully used, and 'asymmetric' methods of

---

[32] Andrey V. Kartapolov, 'Lessons of Military Conflicts', *VAVN* 2 (2015), p. 29, cited and analysed in Thomas, 'Evolving Nature', pp. 39–40.

[33] It was once said of the former Chief of the General Staff Marshal Nikolai Ogarkov (1917–94) that 'on mnogo pisal' - 'he wrote a lot'. 'No', a Soviet general told the author in 1988, 'on mnogo *pod*pisal'- 'he *signed* a lot'.

confronting the enemy are being developed.³⁴

The phrase 'non-standard methods' echoes another term that had emanated from outside the professional military, nelineynaya voyna, as we shall see shortly. For the Russians, 'hybrid' (gibridny) warfare is what other people try to do to them.³⁵

At the time of writing, it is not clear how much Russian thinking has evolved since 2015. In March 2017, Gerasimov made another speech at the AVN that showed little change from his views in 2015. It is notable, however, that he characterised 'hybrid operations' as a US and NATO activity and described 'hybrid warfare' as a term promoted by the mass media, claiming that 'its use as an established term is, at present, premature'. He also said that the Russian Army had 'shown skill [in Syria] in conducting new-type warfare'.³⁶ And he confirmed that 'hybrid warfare' was something to be 'unleashed against Russia and its allies'.³⁷

So 'hybrid warfare' (gibridnaya voyna) is what the West does. The Russians do 'new-type warfare'. New-type warfare is also referred to as 'non-linear warfare' (nelineynaya voina), a term that has wider implications and was apparently coined by President Putin's highly talented advisor Vladislav Surkov, originally from the worlds of art and theatre.³⁸

Science fiction and visions of future war

Surkov was born on 21 September 1964 as Aslambek Andarbekovich Dudayev in the Chechen-Ingush Autonomous Republic.

---

[34] Kartapolov, 'Lessons of Military Conflicts', p. 35, cited in Thomas, 'Evolving Nature', p. 39.

[35] See Thomas, 'Evolving Nature', pp. 35–6.

[36] Valeriy Gerasimov, 'Contemporary Warfare and Current Issues for the Defense of the Country', speech to Academy of Military Sciences, March 2017, trans. Harold Orenstein, Foreword by Timothy Thomas, *Military Review* (November–December 2017), pp. 22–7, at p. 23.

[37] Ibid., Gerasimov's words, p. 27.

[38] See the brilliant film *Nonlinear Warfare: A New System of Political Control* (2014) by Adam Curtis, YouTube, 31 December 2014, https://www.youtube.com/watch?v=tyop0d30UqQ (accessed 3 September 2018).

He is believed to be a distant relation of Dzhokhar Dudayev (1944–96), the Soviet Air Force general who became leader of the Chechen independence movement and was killed by a Russian air strike, apparently targeted on his mobile phone.[39] Aslambek Dudayev later changed his name to Vladimir Surkov, dropped out of university and was called up for the army. He was an aspiring artist and began training to be a theatre director but was expelled from art school after a fistfight.[40] He became a bodyguard to post-Soviet Russia's richest oligarch, Mikhail Khodorkovskiy, who recognised his talents and promoted him to head his advertising and PR department. And then, in 1999 — after lucrative jobs in business and banking, after building the empire and shaping the image of Russia's richest man — Surkov was brought on to Boris Yeltsin's presidential staff, where he helped launch his chosen successor, Vladimir Putin, into the presidency. He was deputy chief of the Russian presidential administration from 1999 to 2011, deputy prime minister for economic modernisation from 2011 to 2013, and then became personal advisor to President Putin. He is a talented writer, particularly of science fiction under the pseudonym Natan Dubovitskiy. In that sense, he fits the mould of much Russian 'future war' writing, where 'fiction' was used a discreet cover for discussion of potential future operations and science fiction for longer-term developments.[41]

---

[39] 'Surkov makes Kremlin comeback', *The Moscow Times*. 22 September 2013.

[40] Whitney Milam, 'Who Is Vladislav Surkov?', Medium, 14 July 2018, https://medium.com/@wmilam/the-theater-director-who-is-vladislav-surkov-9dd8a15e0efb (accessed 8 November 2018).

[41] In the 1880s and 1890s, two 'fictional' works appeared as the prospect of war with the United Kingdom, the greatest naval power of the time, loomed. Vice Admiral A. K. Belomor wrote *Rokovaya voyna 18?? Goda (Otdeleniye ottiski iz zhurnala 'Russkogo sudokhodstvo*) (The fatal war of 18?? (Extracts from the journal 'Russian seaborne trade')) (St Petersburg: R. Golika Press, 1899). This provided startling and accurate predictions of what would happen in the First World War. The other is *Kreyser 'Russkaya Nadezhda'* (The cruiser *Russian Hope*) (St Petersburg: S. S. Lyubavin, 1887) by one 'A. K.', whom I have been unable to identify, but who might possibly be Belomor as well. More far-sighted and superb science fiction is Aleksei Tolstoy, *Giperboloid Inzhenera Garina* (Engineer Garin's 'Hyperboloid' (death-ray)) (Moscow: Sovetskiy pisatel', 1939). Translated into English as *The Garin Death-Ray* (1955). The latter ends with a denouement worthy of a James Bond film in which Garin, as a non-state actor, is attacked on his

By an interesting coincidence—and therefore probably not coincidence—Dubovitsky (i.e. Surkov) published a chilling short story called Without Sky in May 2014.[42] It is full of allusions to a new kind of war that was largely silent, unlike the wars of the past, apart from the occasional screams of casualties in the few manned aircraft, although most were uncrewed. The term non-linear appears here, only three months after the Gerasimov article:

> This was the first non-linear war [*nelineynaya voyna*]. In the primitive wars of the nineteenth, twentieth, and other middle centuries, the fight was usually between two sides: two nations or two temporary alliances. But now, four coalitions collided, and it wasn't two against two, or three against one. It was all against all.
> And what coalitions they were! Not like the earlier ones. It was a rare state that etered the coalition intact. What happened was some provinces took one side, some took the other, and some individual city, or generation, or sex, or professional society of the same state—took a third side. And then they could switch places, cross into any camp you like, sometimes during battle.

The goals of those in conflict were quite varied. Each had his own, so to speak: the seizing of disputed pieces of territory; the forced establishment of a new religion; higher ratings or rates; the testing of new military rays and airships; the final ban on separating people into male and female, since sexual differentiation undermines the unity of the nation; and so forth.

The simple-hearted commanders of the past strove for victory. Now they did not act so stupidly. That is, some, of course, still clung to the old habits and tried to exhume from the archives old slogans of the type: victory will be ours. It worked in some places, but basically, war was now understood as a process, more exactly, part of a process, its acute phase, but maybe not the most important.[43]

---

private island by the US Navy and blows the eight warships of the American squadron into the air (English edn, p. 285).

[42] First published as an annex to the magazine *Russkiy Pion'er* (Russian pioneer) 46 (May 2014). *.Bez neba* First published as an annex to the magazine *Russkiy Pion'er* (Russian pioneer) 46 (May 2014).*Without Sky* by Natan Dubovitsky [as in original], , http://www.bewilderingstories.com/issue582/without_sky.htm l (accessed 8 November 2018).

[43] *Without Sky* by Natan Dubovitsky [as in original], p. 2, http://www.bewilderin gstories.com/issue582/without_sky.html (accessed 8 November 2018).

The parallels with Gerasimov's official, 'non-fiction' description of future warfare, published just three months before Surkov's science-fiction work, are striking and easy to plot. The last sentence in the extract above describes the military phase as just 'part of a process, its acute phase, but maybe not the most important'. That mirrors Gerasimov's statement that the 'process' will 'only move to that stage to achieve final success in the conflict'. The second and third paragraphs describe many of the conflicts in this book. Fragmented states, parts of which align against other parts, and often in alliance, overt or covert, with neighbouring states. Bosnia, Ukraine/Crimea and Syria are all good examples.

In World War V, Without Sky's 'author' (narrator), whose parents are killed in a silent bombing raid, mostly by drones, when he is six, suffers brain damage. When he awakes, he can only see in two dimensions, black and white. There are no subtleties, and he shows disdain towards those who can see in three dimensions and numerous shades of grey. The last three paragraphs are an allusion to the world of 'fake news' and disinformation in which we now live:

> If it was only that we didn't see the sky above our village, that would be nothing, but our very thoughts lost the concept of height. We became two-dimensional. We understood only 'yes' and 'no', only 'black' and 'white'. There was no ambiguity, no half-tones, no saving graces. We did not know how to lie ...
>
> We ... prepared a revolt of the simple, two-dimensionals against the complex and sly, against those who do not answer 'yes' or 'no', who do not say 'white' or 'black', who know some third word, many, many third words, empty, deceptive, confusing the way, obscuring the truth. In these shadows and spider webs, in these false complexities, hide and multiply all the villainies of the world. They are the House of Satan. That's where they make bombs and money, saying: 'Here's money for the good of the honest; here are bombs for the defense of love.'
>
> We will come tomorrow. We will conquer or perish. There is no third way.[44]

The short story is both a promotion and an implied criticism of hybrid-warfare techniques. It came from Putin's right-hand man, and

---

[44] Ibid., p. 4.

just three months after an absolutely classic Russian 'future-war' prescription, signed if not entirely written by the chief of the general staff. It complements Gerasimov's article perfectly. And coming from Putin's advisor, the term 'non-linear' must be considered the preferred Russian term for 'hybrid warfare'.

'Hybrid war': plus ça change?

'Hybrid warfare', in a general sense, is therefore not new. As Williamson Murray and Peter Mansoor observed in their edited volume Hybrid Warfare (2012), 'complex opponents' had been using 'hybrid forces' for centuries.[45] Perhaps the most obvious example is Wellington's use of Spanish 'guerrillas' in concert with regular British, Spanish and Portuguese forces in the Peninsular War, the origin of the term now used for any irregular combatant. So, to some extent, was Mikhail Kutuzov's 'scorched earth' policy in Russia in 1812, and the Cossacks' harrying of the withdrawing Grande Armée. The Russian use of partisans in the occupied Soviet Union in the Second World War, controlled from and supplied by the NKVD in Moscow, working in concert and coordinated with the Red Army, was also obviously 'hybrid'.

There has been an extensive debate about whether the Russians practise 'hybrid warfare'. Most experts agree that 'gibridnaya voyna' is Western in origin and that the Russians use it to describe what the West is trying to do to them. Mark Galeotti, an authority on Soviet and Russian military, strategic and geopolitical thinking, said in a November 2018 article that two kinds of hybrid warfare have been 'unhelpfully intertwined in Western thinking'.*[46]

The first and more conventional type of Russian 'hybrid' or 'non-linear war' involves a shooting war using the latest and best technology and techniques, preceded by a phase of political

---

[45] Williamson Murray and Peter R. Mansoor (eds), *Hybrid Warfare: Fighting Complex Opponents from the Ancient World to the Present* (Cambridge: Cambridge University Press, 2012).

[46] Mark Galeotti, '(Mis)Understanding Russia's Two "Hybrid Wars"', Eurozine, 29 November 2018, https://www.eurozine.com/misunderstanding-russias-two-hybrid-wars (accessed 7 March 2019).

destabilisation, as in Crimea and Ukraine.

The second has arisen because of Moscow's weakness vis-à-vis the West. Russia has therefore adopted a strategy that targets the West's unity and will to act, using a variety of non-military means. It is a political war that Moscow is waging against the West, in the hope not of preparing the ground for an invasion, but rather of dividing, demoralizing and distracting it enough that it cannot resist as the Kremlin asserts its claims to what it considers its rightful role as a great power, not least including a sphere of influence over most of the post-Soviet states of Eurasia.[47]

As noted, the term 'hybrid' applied to warfare is Western in origin. Early references to 'hybrid opponents' are largely indistinguishable from those of a century before to 'small wars' and fighting what Charles Callwell, writing in 1896, termed 'savages and semi-civilised races'.[48] 'Small wars' were not necessarily small in terms of scale, but the term was used to refer to 'all campaigns other than those where both the opposing sides consisted of regular troops'.[49]

That definition stood for a century, and the 1940 US Marine Corps Small Wars Manual was republished in 1990 as a recommended guide to what were by then called 'low intensity conflicts'.[50] It has been re-published repeatedly since.[51] It is therefore not surprising that the earliest work on modern Russian hybrid warfare was produced under the auspices of the US Marines and at

---

[47] Ibid.
[48] Charles E. Callwell, *English: Book Presenting Valuable Contribution on the Subject of Small Wars by C. E. Callwell.*, 1906, 1906, United States Army Command and General Staff College, https://commons.wikimedia.org/wiki/File:Small_Wars_-_Their_principles_and_practice_(C._E._Callwell).pdf.
[49] Ibid. And Galeotti, *Misunderstanding*.
[50] US Marine Corps, *Small Wars Manual 1940* (Washington, DC: US Government Printing Office, 1940, reprinted as FMRP 12-15, 1990), Foreword by Maj. Gen. M. P. Caulfield, deputy commander warfighting. The first edition had appeared in 1935, https://archive.org/details/UsmcSmallWarsManual1940Reprinted1990/page/n1 PCN 140 121500 00 (accessed 12 September 2022).
[51] US Marine Corps *Small Wars Manual*, republished paperback by Pavilion Press 2005, republished 1 October 2007 by Skyhorse Publishing, and numerous other editions.

the Naval Postgraduate School at Monterey, California, as we shall also see under 'Reflexive Control', below. In 2002, Major William J. Nemeth, US Marines, completed a master's thesis entitled 'Future War and Chechnya: A Case for Hybrid Warfare'.[52] It was not so much the war as the threat that was hybrid. Nemeth wrote of Chechnya as a 'hybrid society', a 'pre-state' society characterised by the extended family, resentment against state control, a common enemy—Russia—a pervasive religion—Sufi Islam—and personal pride, honour and vengeance.[53] Writing a century before that Chechen war, Callwell would have recognised all the same characteristics in the societies that caused the British such trouble. A Russian Spetsnaz soldier told this author, who was reporting on that conflict: 'The Chechens are the fiercest, cruellest people in the world. By day they are men, but by night, they are werewolves.'[54]

The term 'hybrid war' came into widespread use due to the activities of Hezbollah—the Lebanon-based Shi'a Islamist political party and militant group—during the Second Lebanon War of 2006.[55] As such, it conformed to the definition of a hybrid opponent, but Hezbollah also possessed advanced military technology from Syria, Iran and China. At the time of writing, it is probably the most powerful non-state actor in the world, with armed forces comparable to those of many Arab states. On 14 July 2006, an Israeli corvette, the INS Hanit, was 10 nautical miles off Beirut when it was hit below the waterline, was set on fire and four crew were killed. However it stayed afloat and managed to limp back to Ashdod.

---

[52] William J. Nemeth, 'Future War and Chechnya: A Case for Hybrid Warfare' (MA thesis, Naval Postgraduate School, Monterey, California, 2002). See also Frank Hoffman and James Mattis, 'Future Warfare: The Rise of Hybrid Warfare', *Naval Institute Proceedings* 132 (November 2005).

[53] Nemeth, 'Future War and Chechnya', pp. 4, 31.

[54] Spetsnaz soldier to the author and Anatol Lieven in the Post and Telegraph Office, Vladikavkaz, shortly after the recapture of the Presidential Palace in Grozny on 19 January 1995. The Spetsnaz troops had gone to the Vladikavkaz PTT, in pro-Russian territory and some way from the action, in order to call their families to let them know they were OK.

[55] See Fridman, 'The Birth of "Hybrid Warfare"', in Fridman, *Russian Hybrid Warfare*, pp. 31–45. Hezbollah/ Hezbullah or Hizbullah, Arabic Ḥizb Allāh ("Party of God"),

Although the Israeli warship had advanced anti-missile defences, it seems they were switched off. There had been some warnings that Hezbollah might have anti-ship missiles, but they had not percolated down to the ships.

The US analyst Frank Hoffman found that the conflicts in Afghanistan, the former Yugoslavia and Chechnya all had 'hybrid' elements, including the combination of conventional and irregular tactics, terrorism and criminal activity. But the Second Lebanon War was the most comprehensive prototype, and Hezbollah 'the clearest example of a modern Hybrid challenger'.[56] Conventional and irregular forces were combined with the use of low-tech rockets, uncrewed aerial vehicles, cruise missiles and advanced surveillance equipment with an information campaign that exploited and multiplied their effect. Most importantly, perhaps, this was coordinated at the strategic, operational and tactical levels simultaneously.[57] This is presumably what Gerasimov meant when he wrote of 'direction of forces and means in a single informational space', in the table at Figure 3.

Hoffman's contribution to the debate was immensely important, and 'hybrid' was a handy way of summarising the way that different modes of warfare were in the process of amalgamating with each other, though the combinations could take an infinite variety of forms.[58] In that sense, it is like a 'cocktail'. The subsequent development of the term in the United States, in particular, lies beyond the scope of this study,[59] but mention must be made of a book by two US majors, Timothy McCulloh and Richard Johnson of the

---

[56] Frank Hoffman *Conflict in the 21st Century: The Rise of Hybrid Warfare* (Arlington, VA: Potomac Institute for Policy Studies, 2007), p. 35, cited in Fridman, *Russian Hybrid Warfare*, pp. 34–5. See also Hoffman, 'Hybrid Threats: Reconceptualising the Evolving Character of Modern Conflict', *Strategic Forum* 240 (April 2009).

[57] Fridman, *Russian Hybrid Warfare*, pp. 35–6, summarising Hoffman, '"Hybrid Threats": Neither Omnipotent nor Unbeatable', *Orbis* 54, no. 3 (2010); Conflict in the 21st Century, 'Hybrid Warfare and Challenges', *Joint Force Quarterly* 52 (2009); 'Preparing for Hybrid Wars', *Marine Corps Gazette* 91, no. 3 (2007), pp. 57–61.

[58] Fridman, *Russian Hybrid Warfare*, p. 37.

[59] Fridman covers it, and the multifarious sources, in 'The Birth of "Hybrid Warfare"', pp. 31–45 and the seventy-five references on pp. 183–7.

School of Advanced Military Studies at Fort Leavenworth in 2013.[60] McCulloh deals with the theory and Johnson more with the practice.

In formulating seven principles to describe hybrid war, the authors draw heavily on the Russian and Soviet partisan experience:

- The composition capabilities and effects of a hybrid force are unique to the temporal, geographical, sociocultural and historical setting. This applies to Hezbollah, drawing on the large Shi'a population in Lebanon and on Syrian and Iranian support. In the case of Russia, terrain, space and communist ideology were all cardinal to the effect of the partisan movements in the First World War, Civil War and Great Patriotic War.
- The existence of a specific ideology. In Lebanon, the Iranian Revolution provided ideological underpinning. In Russia, communism did.
- A perceived existential threat from a potential adversary 'drives the hybrid force to abandon conventional military wisdom to achieve long-term survival'. For Hezbollah, it is Israel; for the Russians, it was Nazi Germany, and, now, the perception of encirclement by a stronger West.
- The asymmetry between hybrid forces and a stronger potential adversary will make the former seek ways of offsetting the latter's advantage.
- A hybrid force contains conventional and unconventional elements.
- Hybrid forces impose a war of attrition on their adversaries both physically and psychologically.[61]

'Hybrid warfare' is therefore only 'new' in the sense of the means

---

[60] Timothy McCulloh and Richard Johnson, 'Hybrid Warfare' (JSOU Report 13-4) (Joint Special Operations University Press, MacDill Air Force Base, 2013). Republished by CreateSpace Independent Publishing Platform, 9 August 2017.

[61] Ibid., pp. 16–17, 21–3, 30–2, summarised in Fridman, *Russian Hybrid Warfare*, pp. 39–40.

for its implementation, and the term has its critics.[62] However, it is a handy way of summarising the multifarious aspects of modern conflict and the growing interaction between 'true' or traditional symmetric military operations, and all kinds of others. The former involve armies, navies and air forces clashing with those of a clearly defined and identifiable enemy. In asymmetric conflict, guerrilla forces or terrorists may clash with regular forces, usually armies, or with each other. Hybrid warfare goes wider, embracing space-on-space, information warfare, cyber-warfare, deception, intelligence and espionage. It usually describes a strategy that combines conventional military force, irregular informational and economic warfare and, now, cyber-warfare tactics. But it can go even wider than that. In 2008, the US Army chief of staff defined a hybrid threat as an adversary that incorporates 'diverse and dynamic combinations of conventional, irregular, terrorist and criminal capabilities'.[63] The introduction of the criminal element adds a further dimension, although Western democracies usually define terrorists as criminals, too:

'Linear' conflicts involve the methodical progression of a planned strategy by opposing sides, whereas non-linear conflict is the simultaneous deployment of multiple, complementary military and non-military warfare tactics. A nonlinear war is fought when a state employs conventional and irregular military forces in conjunction with psychological (terrorist and organized criminal), economic, political, and cyber assaults. Confusion and disorder ensue when weaponized information exacerbates the perception of insecurity in the populace as political, social, and cultural identities are pitted against one another. The resultant blurring of fact and fiction and consequent confusion divides influential interest groups and powerful political organizations by exploiting identity politics and allegiances. Nonlinear warfare tactics also act as a deterrent

---

[62] Damien Van Puyvelde, 'Hybrid War: Does It Even Exist?', NATO, 7 May 2015, https://www.nato.int/docu/review/2015/also-in-2015/hybrid-modern-futu re-warfare-russia-ukraine/en/index.htm (accessed 12 September 2022).

[63] Brian P. Fleming, 'Hybrid Threat Concept: Contemporary War, Military Planning and the Advent of Unrestricted Operational Art', US Army Command and General Staff College, August 2015.

towards a more powerful ally of the besieged state.[64]

So a hybrid war takes place on three distinct battlefields: the conventional battlefield, the indigenous population of the conflict zone, and the international community.[65] The cyber-dimension encompasses or overlaps with all three. The middle battlefield, the indigenous population, is often the most important and reflects Rupert Smith's concept of 'war amongst the people'.[66]

However, the Ukraine conflict also had profound international implications stretching back to the Cold War. On the international stage, Ukrainian pride and sensibilities notwithstanding, the key obstacle and objection to Russia taking Crimea back was the December 1994 Budapest Memorandum on Security Assurances. Following the break-up of the Soviet Union, the new sovereign state of Ukraine found itself in possession of the world's third largest nuclear arsenal. Two other former Soviet republics, Belarus and Kazakhstan, also had Soviet nukes. On 5 December 1994, at a meeting of the Organization for Security and Co-operation in Europe (OSCE) in Budapest, three identical political agreements were signed: one by the United States, United Kingdom, Russia and Ukraine, and two others by France and China. Ukraine agreed to eliminate the strategic missiles, missile silos and bombers on its territory and transfer the 1,900 nuclear warheads to Russia, the successor state to the Soviet Union, for disassembly, in exchange for security guarantees. The first three guarantees were that the United States, the UK and Russia all agreed to respect Belarusian, Kazakh and Ukrainian independence and sovereignty and the existing borders; refrain from the threat or use of force against those three countries; and to refrain from using economic pressure on them in order

---

[64] Joshua Ball, 'What Is Hybrid Warfare?', Global Security Review, 10 June 2019, https://globalsecurityreview.com/hybrid-and-non-linear-warfare-systematically-erases-the-divide-between-war-peace (accessed 12 September 2022).

[65] Alex Deep, 'Hybrid War: Old Concept, New Techniques', Small Wars Journal, 3 February 2015, http://smallwarsjournal.com/jrnl/art/hybrid-war-old-concept-new-techniques (accessed 12 September 2022), citing John McCuen, 'Hybrid Wars', *Military Review* 88, no. 2 (March/April 2008), p. 107.

[66] Rupert Smith, *The Utility of Force: The Art of War in the Modern World* (London: Allen Lane, 2005), pp. 1–3.

to influence their politics. The critical phrase is in the first: 'Respect existing borders.' However far back Russia's claim to Crimea ran, the fact was that it had not respected 'existing borders'.[67] However, NATO countries are not immune from criticism either. When Germany was reunified in 1990, and into 1991, there had been a cascade of assurances from Western heads of state and foreign secretaries promising Mikhail Gorbachev that NATO would not expand 'one inch eastwards'.[68] Nearly thirty years on, with NATO just 140 kilometres from St Petersburg, those broken promises make the Russians' use of illusion and denial look rather tame.

Surkov's use of trompe l'oeil—'to fool the eye'—reflects what artists have done for millennia. An artist, as Surkov obviously is, creates a fake flat world, whether on a wall, a canvas or a piece of paper. The image, fake and flat, is nevertheless recognised by the human (though not, for example, by a cat). The human creative intelligence still recognises it as three-dimensional and therefore representing reality. However, the recent Russian use of 'hybrid' or non-linear warfare, except in terms of the channels available, though evolved, is definitely also not 'new'. Surkov's references to a two-dimensional world in Without Sky perhaps allude to this visual deception. Throughout history, military deception has mirrored that used by the artist, or by the conjurer. Deceive the onlooker with a convincing image or deception and, in the case of the conjurer, deflect their attention at the critical moment.[69]

---

[67] Steven Pifer, 'The Budapest Memorandum and U.S. Obligations', Brookings, 4 December 2014, https://www.brookings.edu/blog/up-front/2014/12/04/the-budapest-memorandum-and-u-s-obligations (accessed 27 September 2018).

[68] National Security Archive, George Washington University, 'NATO Expansion: What Gorbachev Heard', 12 December 2017, https://nsarchive.gwu.edu/briefing-book/russia-programs/2017-12-12/nato-expansion-what-gorbachev-heard-western-leaders-early (accessed 16 March 2019). This particular phrase is from CIA Director Robert Gates. This is a superb collection of thirty US, Soviet, German, British and French documents.

[69] The most famous example is the British Jasper Maskelyne (1902–73), a society conjurer in 1930s London from a conjuring family, who was then employed by Gen. Sir Archibald Wavell, from 1940, as an officer in the Royal Engineers, to create elaborate deceptions. These included 'moving' Alexandria harbour and inducing the Germans to bomb the fake harbour three times. See https://www.magictricks.com/war-magician.htm (accessed 17 January 2019). There can be

As part of the perception game, the aggressor in 'hybrid' or 'non-linear' war also seeks to avoid attribution and, therefore, possible retribution. Hence the 'little green men'. Who are they? Where are they from? Who sent them? Are they really 'locals'? No-one will say.

Many people immediately thought such tactics marked a 'revolution' in warfare. But as we shall see, they did not. Most striking, certainly in the case of Crimea, was the overall strategic objective, which was very traditional: a strategic peninsula with a superb harbour commanding the Black Sea, and thus a key factor in Russia's access to the wider world. The inevitable comparison made was, perhaps, atavistic, with Russia's own Greek and Byzantine past and mindset.

Inserting Special Forces, commandos, pathfinders or saboteurs behind enemy defences prior to more conventional operations is as old as recorded warfare. The obvious example on which several cartoonists opposed to the Russian operation drew in 2014 was the wooden horse of Troy. A 'humanitarian convoy' at the end of August attracted particular opprobrium and satire.[70]

---

no doubt that he exaggerated his own role, for which, significantly, he received no official recognition, but his story is intriguing. David Fisher, *The War Magician: The Man Who Conjured Victory in the Desert* (New York: McCann, 1983, republished London: Corgi, 1985 and Weidenfeld & Nicolson, 2004). The similarity between Maskelyne's surname and the Russian *maskirovka*, meaning 'deception' or 'camouflage', appears to be coincidental.

[70] See, for example, 'Russian "Humanitarian" Convoy to Ukraine a Trojan Horse Full of Weapons', People and Places, 28 August 2014, peopleus.blogspot.com/2014/08/russian-convoy-to-ukraine-trojan-horse.html (accessed 12 September 2022). Moscow insisted that the 280 trucks contained only aid for Ukraine. The convoy had left the Russian city of Voronezh bound for the Russian region of Belgorod. Kiev intended to halt the convoy before inspecting its contents. The West feared it contained military equipment, but that was denied by Putin's officials. A military radar truck seen on video near the convoy added to suspicion. Critics of the convoy ruthlessly satirised the 'aid' on social media, and the International Red Cross requested more information about the aid convoy to support Russian claims, which appeared to tally with Gerasimov's February 2013 statement about using 'humanitarian aid'. See also, for example, 'Is European Radical Right-Wing Camp a Trojan Horse of Moscow?', Ground Report, 24 December 2014, https://www.groundreport.com/is-european-radical-right-wing-camp-a-trojan-horse-of-moscow (accessed 12 September 2022). The cartoon shows a Russian-flagged Trojan horse labelled 'humanitarian aid'

The Russian denial

The Russian operations against Ukraine were widely categorised as 'hybrid warfare'. The Russians denied that they had a concept of hybrid warfare or practised it and instead blamed it on the Americans. What appears to have been the categoric Russian denial and riposte came the following year, 2015, with a book by Andrew (Endryu) Korybko called Hybrid Wars: The Indirect Adaptive Approach to Regime Change.[71] It was reviewed by the Diplomatic Academy of Russia and released with the assistance of the Peoples' Friendship University of Russia, where Korybko is a member of the Expert Council for the Institute of Strategic Research and Predictions. It therefore appears to bear the imprimatur of the Russian state. The English-language publicity for the book gives his name as 'Andrew'. The title uses the English-derived word gibridny— 'hybrid'. Korybko argues that the United States, and not Russia, spearheaded the use of hybrid wars, and that it is irresponsible to call Russia's alleged involvement in the Ukrainian Crisis a 'hybrid war'. He argues that the United States is far ahead of any other country in practising this new method of warfare. Hybrid wars, as he labels them, are when the United States combines its colour revolution and unconventional warfare strategies to create a 'toolkit' for carrying out regime change in target states. When a colour revolution attempt fails, as in Syria in 2011, the fall-back plan is to roll out an unconventional war that builds directly upon the former's social infrastructure and organising methods. In the case of Euromaidan in Ukraine, Korybko cites Western news sources such as Newsweek, the Guardian and Reuters to argue that in the days immediately prior to the coup's successful completion, Western Ukraine was in full-scale rebellion against the central government, setting the stage for an unconventional Syrian-esque war in the heart of Eastern Europe. Had it not been for the sudden overthrow

---

carrying missiles towards a castle labelled Donetsk (the mainly pro-Russian Eastern Ukrainian region).

71 Endryu (Andrew) Korybko, *Gibridnye voyny: Nepryamoy adaptivny podkhod k smaene rezhimov* (Hybrid wars: The indirect adaptive approach to regime change) (Moscow: Institute for Strategic Studies and Predictions, 2015).

of President Yanukovych, the United States was prepared to take the country down the path of the Syrian scenario, which would have been its second full-fledged application of hybrid warfare.

The final part of Korybko's book forecasts where such wars may next occur. He introduces the concept of the 'Colour Arc', a contiguous line of states stretching from Hungary to Kyrgyzstan where the waging of hybrid wars would most seriously damage Russia's national interests. This approach analyses the colour revolutions through a geopolitical prism. This is suggested as a means to understand the United States' evolved approach to regime change and the physical and geopolitical forms it may take in coming years.

Published in August 2015, Hybrid War was Korybko's first book, following a couple of articles published earlier, in February and May 2015.[72] Gerasimov's military-scientific article in February 2013, Surkov's science-fiction story of May 2014 and Korybko's international relations analysis of August 2015 could be seen as related. The concept of a 'Colour Arc' embracing colour revolutions ties in with Gerasimov's focus on the Arab Spring. The idea of such an 'arc' reflects long-standing historic Russian fears of encirclement, and the perceived threat from adjacent countries shuffling off Russian dominance and ideology reflects Soviet experience, as we shall see in following sections.

Since 2013, the terminology has evolved rapidly: in 2013, Gerasimov could talk of 'inter-species' groups of forces; in 2014, Surkov talked of 'non-linear' war instead; and by 2015, Korybko was using 'hybrid war', taken directly from Western usage, and saying it was an American nostrum.

---

[72] Andrew Korybko, 'Lead from Behind: How Unipolarity Is Adapting to Multipolarity', Sputnik News, 2 February 2015, http://sputniknews.com/columnists/20150129/1017517136.html Korybko, 'Hybrid Wars: The Indirect Adaptive Approach to Regime Change', Institute for Strategic Studies and Predictions, Moscow, 2015, http://orientalreview.org/wp-content/ uploads/2015/08/AK-Hybrid-Wars-updated.pdf (accessed 12 September 2022); Korybko, 'Democratic Security in Macedonia: Between Brussels and Moscow', *Oriental Review*, 25 May 2015, http://orientalreview.org/2015/05/25/democratic-security-in-macedonia-between-brussels-and-moscow (accessed 12 September 2022).

Trojan horses — Afghanistan, 1979

At the time of writing, in 2022 - 23, the political situation and UK relations with Russia bore a striking similarity with the period after Christmas 1979, when the Soviet Union invaded Afghanistan. Subsequently, Prime Minister Margaret Thatcher suspended nearly all dialogue with the then Soviet Union. At the time of writing, some forty years on, it seems those times have returned.

But there are many more similarities between Russia's 'non-linear' or 'hybrid' war in Crimea and Ukraine in 2014 and its invasion of Afghanistan over Christmas 1979. Gerasimov said that the 'new' warfare involved deployment of forces before the outbreak of open hostilities. The same thing happened in Afghanistan, though not, initially, at Soviet instigation.

By mid-1979, the often-turbulent state of Afghanistan was in crisis. The president, Nur Mohammad Taraki (15 July 1917 — 8 October 1979), had taken power on 1 May 1978 after the Saur Revolution. He was greatly assisted by Hafizullah Amin, who subsequently murdered him. This established a Marxist state, headed by Taraki. President Taraki signed a twenty-year Treaty of Friendship with the Soviet Union on 5 December 1978 that greatly expanded Soviet aid to his regime.

However, many of Taraki's reforms, inspired by his pro-Soviet leanings, including women's education and encouraging men to cut off their beards, were unpopular in traditional Afghan society. He asked for Soviet intervention to help but was refused. On 17 or 18 March 1979, as the crisis deepened, Taraki spoke to Soviet Premier (Brezhnev's deputy) Aleksey Kosygin (1904–80). Taraki's suggestion would not have been unfamiliar to Surkov or Putin:

We ask that you render practical and technical assistance involving people in arms. Why can't the Soviet Union send Uzbeks, Tajiks and Turkmen in civilian clothing? No one will recognize them. We want you to send them. They can drive tanks and because we have all these nationalities in Afghanistan. Let them don Afghan costume, Afghan badges and then nobody will recognize them as foreigners ... I suggest that you place Afghan markings on your tanks and aircraft and then no one will know. Your troops could advance from the direction of Kushka and the Direction of Kabul. In our view no-one will be any the wiser. They will think these are Government troops.[73]

The thinking is clear. There must be no attribution and, therefore, no potential retribution by the international community. The international community was the other key player. This had all the hallmarks of hybrid or non-linear war.

Oddly, the Russians were slightly reluctant to accede to Taraki's request, and this comes through from the sources. However, they quickly acted on it. In April 1979, the Main Intelligence Directorate of the Soviet Ministry of Defence, the GRU, gave an order. It would create a special-purpose battalion (SPB)(BON — Batal'yon Osobogo Naznacheniya) based in Tashkent. The SPB would consist of Tajiks, Uzbeks and Turkmens, who were ethnically and linguistically similar to Afghan nationals immediately across the border in Afghanistan. The 154th Separate Spetsnaz ('Special Forces' — Spetsial'nogo Naznacheniya; hence 'Spetsnaz') Detachment, known as the 'Muslim battalion', comprising 500 soldiers under Major Khalbayev.[74] Spetsnaz units normally operate under the auspices of the GRU and not the former KGB or its Russian successors, the Federal Security Agency (FSB) or the External Intelligence Service (SVR). The former could be compared to the British MI5 (domestic intelligence and counter-espionage) and the latter to MI6 — foreign intelligence. But the 'sister services', as they refer to themselves, keep in very close touch. GRU is military intelligence and therefore equates most closely to the British Defence Intelligence Staff or DIS.

On 6 December, the Politburo endorsed a proposal by KGB head Yuri Andropov (1914–84) and Chief of the General Staff Marshal Nikolai Ogarkov (1917–94) to send the GRU Spetsnaz 'Muslim battalion' to Kabul. Andropov later succeeded Brezhnev as leader of the Soviet Union in 1982. The Muslim battalion was airlifted from

---

[73] Transcript of conversation between Nur Mohammad Taraki and Premier Kosygin on 17 or 18 March 1979, Cold War International History Project, Woodrow Wilson International Center for Scholars, 2002. Cited in Ali Ahmad Jalali, *A Military History of Afghanistan: From the Great Game to the Global War on Terror* (Lawrence: Kansas University Press, 2017), p. 360.

[74] Jalali, *Military History of Afghanistan*, pp. 361, 365.

its camp in Uzbekistan to the Soviet airbase at Bagram and thence to Amin's presidential palace. There, they killed him and acted, effectively, as the 'forward detachment' of the invasion. And they looked, for all intents and purposes, like Afghan national troops.[75]

In 1979, the Soviet Union was therefore implementing 'hybrid' or 'non-linear' warfare in a recognisable way, including a Trojan horse: the deployment of soldiers of the same ethnic background as the target state, dressed in that state's uniforms and marked with its insignia. So, as Taraki implied or certainly recognised before his untimely death, there would be no attribution and, therefore, the chances of foreign retribution were minimised. And the Russians got it. And, clearly, still do.

Trojan horses — Czechoslovakia, 1968

However, Afghanistan was not the first time the Soviet Union had waged hybrid or non-linear warfare on a target state in full view of the international community. In 1968, a year of widespread political revolution and student unrest, Czechoslovakia (now the Czech Republic and Slovakia) erupted in protest against the Soviet domination of Eastern Europe.

After ousting a Stalinist president, the country's new communist leader, Alexander Dubček (1921–92), abolished government censorship and ushered in a free press. Thus began the 'Prague Spring'. Dubček attempted to create 'socialism with a human face'. In the context of the prevailing riots and unrest throughout much of Western Europe, particularly in France, and general unrest among the younger 'sixties' generation, the situation in Czechoslovakia attracted particular attention in the West. It also looked threatening from Moscow. The so-called 'Prague Spring', which bequeathed its name to the 'Arab Spring' forty-two years later, was a danger to Soviet hegemony in Eastern Europe, the 'near abroad'.

The Soviet intelligence services had long been waging a 'cold war' against the West. It had started long before, not long after the

---

[75] Ibid., p. 365.

November 1917 Russian Revolution, with the infiltration of intelligence agencies and, indeed, governments in the United States, the UK, France, Nazi Germany, the Federal Republic of Germany and Italy.[76]

However, the prelude to the invasion of Czechoslovakia in 1968, Soviet Operation 'Progress', was also a clear example of 'hybrid' or 'non-linear' war.[77] And, again, it started well before the overt initiation of hostilities. Operation Progress had two aims: to undermine the reform movement in Czechoslovakia and prepare the way for Operation 'Moldau', also known as Operation 'Danube', the full-scale invasion by five Warsaw Pact countries. These were the Soviet Union, Bulgaria, Hungary, East Germany and Poland. On the night of 20–21 August 1968, about a quarter of a million troops with 2,000 tanks attacked. The foreign Warsaw Pact presence later rose to half a million. Ironically, perhaps, the invasion of Czechoslovakia prompted KGB officer Vasiliy Mitrokhin to copy the files that provide the basis for what follows, although the full collection covers the KGB and its predecessors, the MVD, NKVD, NKGB and Cheka back to 1917. Mitrokhin initially tried to pass the files to the Americans in Riga in 1992, but they were not interested. So, seeing the Union Flag fluttering above the British embassy, he passed them to the British instead, which is how they ended up in Cambridge.[78]

In Czechoslovakia in 1968, as in Hungary in 1956, Andropov's plan was based on a combination of deception — what we now call 'fake news' — and conventional military power. It was 'hybrid war'. A cardinal component was the so-called 'illegals' — Soviet agents

---

[76] The most accessible account is Christopher Andrew and Vasili Mitrokhin, *The Mitrokhin Archive: The KGB in Europe and the West* (London: Penguin, 2000).

[77] Ibid. Author used original typescript online, 'The Sword and the Shield: The Mitrokhin Archive and the Secret History of the KGB', https://archive.org/stream/TheSwordAndTheShield-TheMitrokhinArchiveAndTheSecretHistoryOfTheKGB/The+Sword+and+the+Shield+-+The+Mitrokhin+Archive+and+the+Secret+History+of+the+KGB_djvu.txt (accessed 12 September 2022).

[78] Cambridge University's Churchill Archive Centre has opened nineteen of the Mitrokhin archive's thirty-three volumes to the public. They are Russian-language versions of Vasiliy Mitrokhin's notes; the original manuscripts and notebooks remain closed.

posing as Western foreigners — controlled by KGB Department 'S'.[79] Their use in Czechoslovakia marked a major innovation in the KGB's use of 'illegals'. Previously, they had mainly been sent to the West, not into Warsaw Pact countries.[80] But Czechoslovakia was in danger of slipping away from the Soviet fold, and special measures were used.

In March 1968, five months before the eventual August invasion, Andropov, the head of the KGB from 1967 to 1982, ordered that by 12 May some fifteen of the first twenty 'illegals' should be in place in Czechoslovakia. The Soviet Union had used illegals before, to recruit other agents or ensnare seditious and disloyal inhabitants of Warsaw Pact countries. However, this was by far their most extensive deployment yet and greatly exceeded their use in Western countries. There is a clear link between Czechoslovakia in 1968 and Afghanistan in 1979, as Andropov was head of the KGB for both. In passing, we might note that the Soviet and Russian habit of keeping senior people in post for a long time, as opposed to catapulting them to the top and retiring them a few years later, can be useful in playing a 'long game' in international relations, security and strategy. According to Mitrokhin, at least five of the agents, and probably another two, posed as West Germans. There were also three alleged Austrians, and three bogus British. There was also one surrogate Swiss, one alleged Lebanese and one masquerading as a Mexican.

Deception and disinformation are always the basis of war, as Sun Tzu said in the fourth century BC.[81] But surely the traditional terms 'deception' and 'mis- (or dis-) information' are just what we

---

[79] Andrew and Mitrokhin, *Mitrokhin Archive*.
[80] Ibid.
[81] Sun Tzu, *The Art of War* (probably 400–320 BCE), trans. and ed. Samuel B. Griffith (Oxford: Oxford University Press, 1963), p. 1. Sun Tzu (or Sun Pin, or Sun Wu) may have taken references from earlier commentators, but this author believes, based on evidence cited by the scholarly US Marine Samuel B. Griffith, who produced what in this author's view is the definitive edited translation for a DPhil at Oxford, that he is right and that it dates from the fourth century BCE. Griffith's conclusion is based on the author's (or authors') mentions of chariots and crossbows, then in use in China, and not of cavalry, which came in later, around 320 BCE.

now call 'fake news'? In Czechoslovakia, as in Afghanistan and Crimea and Ukraine more recently, they were also pivotal.[82] 'Hybrid warfare' is all about deception. But warfare certainly evolves, albeit gradually, as Cyril Falls said.

An intricate and subtle game of disinformation, bluff and counter-bluff began. On 1 May 1968, Soviet Premier Aleksey Kosygin berated his Czech opposite number, Oldrich Cernic. He said that 'agents and saboteurs' disguised as Western tourists had been able to penetrate Czechoslovakia because of poor border security. This was absolutely true, but Kosygin did not say — although he obviously knew it — that all these 'agents and saboteurs' with Western passports, from bogus British to masquerading Mexicans, were in fact KGB agents. On the same day, agent 'Gromov', none other than Vasiliy Gordievskiy who defected to the British in 1972, and agent 'Guryev', Valentin Gutin, attempted to kidnap two key members of the Czech Prague Spring movement. They were to be persuaded that they were in danger and 'exfiltrated' in a car with diplomatic number plates to East Germany. If they proved reluctant, they were to be subdued using 'special substances'. The episode was a miserable failure, but it has all the hallmarks of Russian practices before and certainly ever since.[83]

While the Soviet attempts to undermine the Prague Spring and to target its most prominent leaders were conducted in traditional, cloak-and-dagger fashion, however, a still more ambitious deception — 'fake news', again — was implemented. It was Operation 'Khodoki' — 'Go-betweens'. 'Khodoki' was to fabricate evidence of a conspiracy by anti-Soviet Czechs and by Western intelligence services to overthrow the Czech communist government and therefore to justify Soviet intervention. Posing as sympathetic Westerners, the 'illegals' tried to persuade editors and journalists to publish or broadcast attacks on the Soviet Union. But it went deeper. They also tried to persuade key Czech organisations including K-231, a group of political prisoners formerly jailed by the communists, to accept aid from a fictitious underground organisation supplied with arms

---

[82] Andrew and Mitrokhin, *Mitrokhin Archive*.
[83] Ibid.

by the West.[84]

Josef Houska, the chief of the Czech state security force StB (Státní bezpečnost), was told of the plan and agreed to cooperate with the KGB.[85] By mid-July, as part of Operation Khodoki, the 'illegals' had succeeded in planting evidence of preparations for an armed coup. On 19 July, Pravda reported that a secret cache of US weapons had been found near the West German border. These had allegedly been smuggled into Czechoslovakia by 'revenge seekers' and 'enemies of the old order'. The Soviet authorities, Pravda claimed, had also obtained a copy of a secret American plan to overthrow the Prague government. The press throughout the Soviet bloc followed up on the Pravda story, which was based on real finds of weapons labelled 'made in USA' hidden all over Czechoslovakia. At the same time, information was fed to the StB implicating the counter-Soviet movements, especially K-231, in an anti-Soviet conspiracy with Western intelligence services.[86]

The Soviet Politburo met to consider its next step in the crisis on the same day as the first Pravda report of secret arms caches, 19 July 1968. Soviet Communist Party General Secretary Leonid Brezhnev (1906–82)[87] – effectively head of state, as general secretary from Khrushchev's ouster in 1964 to his death in 1982 – began by proposing a final meeting with the Czech leadership to try to reach a negotiated settlement. Andropov, head of the KGB, wanted 'extreme measures' – invasion – immediately. He argued that the Czech rebels were on their last legs and fighting to survive and that this was the time to defeat them. Andrei Gromyko, the foreign minister, probably reflected the majority view that a meeting with the Czech leadership was merely a necessary prelude to invasion. The

---

[84] Ibid.

[85] StB was the plain-clothes communist secret police force from 1945 to 1990. It dealt with any activity that could possibly be considered anti-state or Western-influenced. Christopher Andrew and Vasili Mitrokhin, *The Sword and the Shield: The Mitrokhin Archive and the Secret History of the KGB* (New York: Basic Books, 1999).

[86] Ibid., Chapter 15.

[87] A Soviet metallurgical engineer, but actually Ukrainian, born in 1906, in Kamianske, Ukraine. Initially trained in land management and then as a metallurgist.

Czech–Soviet meeting took place on the Czech border between 29 July and 1 August. The Czech StB had discovered that although the arms caches contained genuine Second World War US arms, they were in Soviet-made packaging. Other evidence linking Czech movements with Western secret services was also found to have been fabricated. The StB also uncovered a KGB plan to murder the Soviet wives of senior Czech officials and blame it on nationalist 'counter-revolutionary' elements. However, the Khodoki 'illegals', already in place, remained undetected.[88]

At a meeting in Moscow on 18 August, the Soviet Union and its four most reliable Warsaw Pact allies, Bulgaria, East Germany, Hungary and Poland, agreed on the final invasion plan. East Germany's participation was cancelled at the last minute because the Russians thought that it would provoke much stronger resistance from the Czechs, following their experience in the Second World War. The remaining four countries' forces crossed the border at about 11 p.m. on 20 August. The invasion was extremely well planned and coordinated. Simultaneously with the border crossing by ground forces, a Soviet airborne forces (VDV) division captured Prague's Ruzyne International Airport (now Prague Václav Havel Airport) in the early hours of the invasion. It began with a special Aeroflot flight from Moscow carrying more than 100 agents in civilian clothes. They quickly secured the airport and prepared the way for a huge airlift, in which An-12 transport aircraft unloaded VDV troops equipped with artillery and light tanks.

The Czechs had not prepared to meet an invasion because they did not think the Soviet Union would invade. The Czech government and security forces were divided between supporters of Dubček's reforms and pro-Soviet opponents. Dubček ordered his people not to resist, although some, mostly civilians, did. The Czech forces therefore put up virtually no resistance, although some 137 Czechs and Slovaks were killed and hundreds wounded in attacks on the Soviet forces. Dubček was arrested and taken to Moscow along with several of his colleagues. Dubček and most of the reformers were returned to Prague on 27 August, and Dubček

---

[88] Andrew and Mitrokhin, *Sword and the Shield*, Chapter 15.

retained his post as the party's first secretary until he was forced to resign in April 1969.

The invasion of Czechoslovakia also played out on the international stage. Andropov had been playing up fears of the United States sponsoring an armed coup, which was clearly fictitious. But in fact the Americans were just not interested. The United States and NATO essentially turned a blind eye to the evolving situation in Czechoslovakia. While the Soviet Union was worried that it might lose an ally to the west, exactly the same situation as with Afghanistan in 1979 and between Russia and Ukraine in 2014, the United States did not want it. President Lyndon B. Johnson had already involved the United States in the Vietnam War and was unlikely to get support for a potential conflict in Czechoslovakia, particularly during the 1968 'summer of love'. And rather than risk nuclear war, which could conceivably result from a US–Soviet clash, he wanted to pursue the Strategic Arms Limitation Treaty, SALT, with Moscow. He needed a willing partner in Moscow in order to reach such an agreement, and he did not want to throw that away for Czechoslovakia. After all, as UK Prime Minister Neville Chamberlain had notoriously said thirty years before, it was 'a quarrel in a faraway country between people of whom we know nothing'.[89] Chamberlain, for all his faults, had added: 'It seems still more impossible that a quarrel which has already been settled in principle should be the subject of war.' That is also apposite. It had been settled in principle in 1968 as well. Czechoslovakia was not worth nuclear war.

For these reasons, the United States made it clear that it would not intervene on behalf of the Prague Spring, giving the USSR carte blanche to do what it wanted. A meeting of the UN Security Council (UNSC) was called on the night of the invasion. Canada, Denmark, France, Paraguay, the United Kingdom and the United States all requested the meeting. The following afternoon, the council met to hear the Czechoslovak ambassador to the UNSC, Jan Mužík, denounce the invasion. The Soviet ambassador to the United Nations, Jacov Malik, insisted the Warsaw Pact actions were those of

---

[89] *The Times*, 28 September 1938, p. 10. Reporting broadcast of 27 September 1938.

'fraternal assistance' against 'antisocial forces'. The next day, several countries put forward a resolution condemning the intervention and calling for immediate withdrawal.

The Soviet Union, which, as a member of the 'Permanent Five', the ultimate victors of the Second World War (the United States, the UK, the Soviet Union, France and China), could veto any UNSC motion, played for time. Ten UNSC members, some members of the 'Permanent Five', others of the 'Temporary Ten', supported the motion. Algeria, India and Pakistan abstained. The USSR, a Permanent Five member with veto power, and Hungary, a Soviet ally, opposed it. Canadian delegates immediately introduced another motion asking for a UN representative to travel to Prague and work for the release of the imprisoned Czechoslovak leaders. Malik, the Soviet ambassador, accused Western countries of hypocrisy, asking 'who drowned the fields, villages, and cities of Vietnam in blood?' He had a point. By 26 August, another vote had not taken place, but a new Czechoslovak representative, now, obviously, pro-Soviet, requested the whole issue be removed from the council's agenda.

However, the United States was not in a strong moral position given its strategy in Vietnam at the time. Although its representatives insisted that Warsaw Pact aggression against an independent sovereign state was unjustifiable, President Johnson had recently been responsible for the overthrow of the government of the Dominican Republic. The UN had determined that the latter was an issue to be worked out by the Organization of American States (OAS) and therefore not subject to UN input. The OAS accepted adherence to Marxism–Leninism as an armed attack justifying self-defence by the United States. The Americans were therefore on shaky ground, given Soviet claims of armed conspiracies against its East European order in Czechoslovakia. But more of a blow to the Americans on the international stage was the widespread international view, and also that gaining ground in the United States, that, as summarised in a crushing line from UN Secretary-General U-Thant, that 'if Russians were bombing and napalming the villages of Czechoslovakia, he [the OAS representative] might be more vocal in his denunciation'.⁹⁰

Trojan horses? Hungary 1956

So far, we have traced characteristics of non-linear war back to Czechoslovakia in 1968. That naturally focuses attention on the Soviet invasion of Hungary in November 1956. The first link is Andropov, who was the head of the KGB during the invasions of Czechoslovakia in 1968 and Afghanistan in 1979. From 1954, he was Soviet ambassador to Hungary and played a key role in persuading an initially reluctant Khrushchev to intervene militarily in 1956. The Warsaw Treaty Organisation (Warsaw Pact) had only been created the previous year, in response to the creation of NATO in 1949 and the European Coal and Steel community — the precursor of the EU — in 1948. Unlike Czechoslovakia, the Hungarian intervention only involved Soviet forces, plus, naturally, within the country itself, pro-former-government Hungarian forces and the state security police (Államvédelmi Hatóság; the ÁVH). Marshal Georgiy Zhukov had initially opposed the intervention, and his arch-rival, Marshal Ivan Koniev, commanded the operation, codenamed vikhr' — Whirlwind. The five Soviet divisions stationed in Hungary before 23 October were augmented to seventeen.⁹¹

At first sight, Hungary shows few 'non-linear' aspects, but Andropov's role and experience were crucial. The leader of the Hungarian revolution, Imre Nagy (1896–1958), heard of more Soviet troops crossing the border on 1 November. Andropov assured him that the Soviet Union would not invade, which was untrue. The Hungarian cabinet declared Hungary's neutrality, withdrew from

---

⁹⁰ 'If Russians were bombing and napalming the villages of Czechoslovakia, he might be more vocal in his denunciation.' U-Thant, cited in Thomas M. Franck, *Nation against Nation: What Happened to the U.N. Dream and What the U.S. Can Do about It* (New York: Oxford University Press, 1985).

⁹¹ 'Hungarian Revolution 1956', *Encyclopaedia Britannica*, last updated 7 September 2022, https://www.britannica.com/event/Hungarian-Revolution-1956 (accessed 12 September 2022). For chapters on the Hungarian Revolution of 1956 and related issues, see Jenő Györkei, Alexandr Kirov and Miklos Horvath (eds), *Soviet Military Intervention in Hungary, 1956* (New York: Central European University Press, 1999). p. 350.

the Warsaw Pact and requested assistance from foreign diplomats in Budapest and the UN to defend them. Ambassador Andropov was asked to inform his government that Hungary would begin negotiations on the removal of Soviet forces immediately. Andropov duly arranged 'negotiations' on Soviet withdrawal at the Soviet Military Command at Tököl, near Budapest, on 3 November. At around midnight that evening, the KGB arrested the Hungarian delegation; the next day, the Soviet Army again attacked Budapest. At 05.20 the next morning, Nagy broadcast his last thirty-five-second message.[92] He sought refuge in the Yugoslav embassy but was arrested outside it. He was secretly put on trial and executed two years later. The Soviet Union successfully imposed a news blackout, which helped hamper reaction by the international community at a time when other permanent members of the UN Security Council — the United States, Britain and France — were preoccupied with the Suez Crisis. The first Soviet report of the invasion came a full twenty-four hours after those in Western media. Nagy's former colleague and designated replacement, János Kádár, had been flown secretly from Moscow to the city of Szolnok, 60 miles south-east of the capital, and took power with Moscow's backing.[93]

Besides the inevitable use of deceit, subterfuge and secrecy, the Hungarian operation formed the foundation for the subsequent evolution of non-linear operations through Andropov's own experience. In Russian and Soviet history, the role of personality may outweigh that of process. As Christopher Andrew observed:

> As Soviet Ambassador in Budapest ... he had watched in horror from the windows of his embassy as officers of the hated Hungarian security service were strung up from lampposts. Andropov remained haunted for the rest of his life by the speed with which an apparently all-powerful Communist one-party state begun to topple. When other Communist regimes later seemed at risk — in Prague in 1968, in Kabul in 1979, in Warsaw in 1981, he was convinced that, as in Budapest in 1956, only armed force could ensure

---

[92] Andrew and Mitrokhin, *The Sword and the Shield*, Chapter 15; 'Soviets Put a Brutal End to Hungarian Revolution', History, 24 November 2009, https://www.history.com/this-day-in-history/soviets-put-brutal-end-to-hungarian-revolution (accessed 12 September 2022).

[93] Andrew and Mitrokhin *The Sword and the Shield* Ibid.

their survival.[94]

Afghanistan and Czechoslovakia certainly included most of the features of 'hybrid' or, as the Russians prefer to call it, 'non-linear' war. The most striking is perhaps the equivalent of 'little green men': the 154th Spetsnaz Muslim battalion of Tajiks, Turkmens and Uzbeks inserted into Afghanistan wearing Afghan uniforms, and native speakers of the local languages in 1979. They were therefore indistinguishable from local Afghan troops and therefore 'unattributable'. And the GRU or KGB agents — maybe both — in civilian clothes on an Aeroflot flight into Prague on the night of 20 August 1968, who quickly seized the airport and opened the way for the landing of Soviet airborne forces. They were initially unattributable, with two consequences: first, uncertainty about their identities and purpose added to confusion; second, without clear attribution, there could be no retribution.

In both the preceding cases, as also with Ukraine in 2014, the hybrid war was fought in three theatres: the indigenous population of the conflict zone, the international community and, finally, the conventional battlefield.

In all three cases, the war was eventually fought in a conventional way but with prior insertion, 'before the outbreak of hostilities', as Gerasimov said in 2013. The earlier two saw the insertion of the 154th Spetsnaz 'Muslim' battalion into Afghanistan in 1979. And the unprecedented number of 'illegals' masquerading as Westerners, attempts to foment mysterious foreign plots and the 100 plain-clothes GRU and KGB agents on an Aeroflot flight into Czechoslovakia in August 1968. Both those earlier campaigns also depended on covert operations to divert the attention of the target state's government, its people and the international community away from Russia's and the Soviet Union's real intent, just like Russia and its assault on Ukraine in 2014. As with Ukraine and Crimea in 2014, the battleground in both the earlier cases was primarily internal: mobilising the 'protest potential' of the population. The examples above — Ukraine, Afghanistan and Czechoslovakia — were

---

[94] Andrew and Mitrokhin, *Mitrokhin Archive*. This is not the same book as *The Sword and the Shield* (refs. 50, 51, 53, 57).

all waged against a current or former ally. So, maybe, 'hybrid' or 'non-linear' warfare against a new target—not a former member of the Soviet Union or of the Warsaw Pact—would mark a departure or an extension.

'Revolutionierungspolitik' and 'myatezhevoyna': the gradual evolution of 'non-linear' techniques, 1914–2014

The author has noted the lessons learned by the USSR from Russia after 1917, and by the new Russia from the USSR after 1991. Geographic, environmental, geopolitical and geostrategic forces apply across eleven time zones, whatever the political complexion of the regime currently in power. There is also a strong element of personal continuity. Andropov, as noted above, was ambassador to Hungary in 1956 and head of the KGB for both Czechoslovakia and Afghanistan.

As head of the KGB, Andropov must have had dealings with Putin, who joined that elite service in 1975. Whether young Putin was a protégé is unclear, but he certainly admired Andropov and has modelled many of his ideas on his former boss.[95] In Putin's memoirs (2000), he indicates that he sees the security services as a critical force in reforming society, believes that restructuring the armed services can be assisted and facilitated by security professionals, and that the power of his office and of services can reduce corruption as practised by regional bosses and business oligarchs.[96] Stalin, Peter the Great and Ivan the Terrible would all have agreed.

As often happens with nations fighting 'wars', a state's adoption of new techniques may owe much to being a victim of their success. A good example is the British adoption of paratroops, an idea they had previously dismissed after the successful, if costly,

---

[95] Robert W Pringle, 'Putin: The New Andropov?', *International Journal of Intelligence and CounterIntelligence* 14 (2001), pp. 545–58, https://www.tandfonline.com/doi/abs/10.1080/08850600152617155? (accessed 12 September 2022).

[96] Ibid., p. 545.

German capture of Crete in 1941. There is no doubt that the success of the 7 November 1917 (25 October Old Style) Bolshevik Revolution owed much to German efforts to undermine Russia as a formidable Allied power in the Great War. Germany targeted the imperial Russian regime before the 3 March (23 February Old Style) Revolution and, more particularly and specifically, the Provisional Government between then and November.[97] This was the famous 'sealed train' episode, familiar to all students of European, Russian, Soviet and later Russian history, when the Germans smuggled Vladimir Ilych Ulyanov, aka Lenin, from exile in Switzerland through Germany, to Sweden and then on the Finland Station in Petrograd (formerly and now, again, St Petersburg). The aim was to destabilise Russia as a major and significant combatant in the Great War.

According to Richard Pipes' history, relying on numbers from the German Marxist economist Eduard Bernstein (1850–1932), the German government sent 'more than 50 million deutsche marks in gold' from 1917 to 1918 to help the Bolsheviks seize and keep power. In 1917, that was 9 million US dollars, equivalent to 173 million US dollars today. That was a big investment, but, in terms of the 'political target', to use Gerasimov's words, to help end Russian involvement in the First World War, it paid off.[98] The German foreign secretary at the time of Lenin's passage, Richard von Kühlmann (1873–1948), either came up with the plan or at least approved the idea of letting Lenin pass through German territory to return to Russia. The 'sealed train' that took Lenin from Switzerland to Petrograd via Sweden, carrying some of that money with him, was an example of 'non-linear' war.[99] There was nothing

---

[97] By the twentieth century, the Old (Julian) calendar had slipped thirteen days behind the New (Gregorian) calendar. After the revolution, the Bolsheviks adopted the 'New' (Western, Gregorian, system). Therefore the 'February Revolution' took place in March and the 'Great October Socialist Revolution' in November.

[98] Richard Pipes, *The Russian Revolution* (New York: Vintage, Random House, 1991).

[99] See, for example, Sean Mcmeekin, 'Was Lenin a German Agent?', *New York Times*, 29 June 2017, https://www.nytimes.com/2017/06/19/opinion/was-lenin-a-german-agent.html (accessed 26 January 2019). Some sources – e.g. 'Did the Germans Purposefully Arrange to Send Lenin to Russia to Start a

particularly new about a German plot, or anyone else's, to undermine an enemy government in wartime. The Germans even coined a word for this specific type of influence operation: 'Revolutionierungspolitik' or 'policy of revolutionising'.[100] It included supporting secession by nationalist minorities from the Russian Empire and existed before 1917 but was given a second wind by the February (March) Revolution.[101] Some 5 million marks were authorised on 3 April.[102] These figures support Pipes' assertion.

Until the Bolsheviks seized power on 7 November, the scope for the Germans to fund the Bolshevik movement was limited. It was only once the Bolsheviks seized power that a concerted propaganda campaign using posters, leaflets and Pravda could begin to convert a largely rural population to the narrowly based party.[103]

The impact of the German 'non-linear' campaign on Russia's withdrawal from the war must therefore be treated with caution. Rumours that the German-born tsarina was a German spy were already widespread. At the beginning of 1914, British Military Attaché Alfred Knox, whose diary is one of the few key sources in

---

Revolution? (https://history.stackexchange.com/questions/14608/did-the-germans-purposefully-arrange-to-send-lenin-to-russia-to-start-a-revoluti (accessed 12 September 2022)) — allege that Lenin had 'ten million dollars' with him on the train, although that seems unlikely. See also 'Who Funded the Bolsheviks' Rise to Power in Russia?', https://www.quora.com/Who-funded-the-Bolsheviks-ri
se-to-power-in-Russia (accessed 12 September 2022), and George Katkov, 'German Foreign Office Documents on Financial Support to the Bolsheviks in 1917', *International Affairs (Royal Institute of International Affairs 1944–)* 32, no. 2 (April 1956), pp. 181–9, https://www.jstor.org/stable/2625787?seq=1#page_scan_ta
b_contents (accessed 26 January 2019).

[100] Irina Novikova, 'The Provisional Government and Finland: Russian Democracy and Finnish Nationalism in Search of Peaceful Coexistence', in Jane Burbank, Mark von Hagen and Anatoly Renev (eds), *Russian Empire: Space, People, Power* (Bloomington: Indiana University Press, 2008), pp. 398–421, at p. 414. The work is available online at http://rusasww1.ru/view_post.php?id=262 (accessed 26 January 2019). In note 77, Novikova cites Manfred Menger, *Die Finnlandspolitik des deutschen Imperialismus, 1917–1918* (Berlin: Akademie-Verlag, 1974), p. 55 and a despatch from state secretary (effectively a permanent secretary) in the German Ministry of Foreign Affairs Arthur Zimmerman of 15 March 1917.

[101] Ibid.

[102] Ibid.

[103] Martin Ebon, *The Soviet Propaganda Machine* (New York: McGraw-Hill, 1987).

English,[104] had reported that the Russian Army was 'sound at heart'. With hindsight, he then added:

> [T]here can be no doubt that if the national fabric had held together or, even granted the [March 1917] Revolution, a man had been forthcoming who was man enough to protect the troops from pacifist propaganda, the Russian army would have gained fresh laurels in the campaigns of 1917, and in all human probability would have exercised a pressure which would have made possible an Allied victory by the end of the year.[105]

Knox did not ascribe the collapse of the Russian military effort entirely or even significantly to German hybrid war, noting that 'the Russians, like ourselves during the war were inclined to attribute the result of their own shortcomings to the machinations of the enemy'. There was, for example, no evidence that German intrigue had anything to do with the Kornilov affair, the attempted military coup by the Commander-in-Chief of the Russian Army, General Lavr Kornilov from 27–30 August (O.S., 10–13 September N.S.) 1917, against Aleksandr Kerenskiy's Provisional Government.[106] On 12 October, he reported a Russian colonel saying that 'if Bolshevism winds up all along the line in the rear it is doubtful if the men will remain in the trenches'. Bolshevik agitators were working hard to disintegrate the army but were more successful in the navy, whose more technically adept personnel tended to come from the urban proletariat. The disintegration of the armed forces and the understandable sympathy felt by soldiers for rioting civilians can also be attributed to war-weariness. As Alexander Shlyapnikov (1885–1937) recalled in his 1923 memoirs, one of the best accounts by a communist agitator: 'Every worker had a vague idea that inside those grey greatcoats, soldiers' hearts were beating in time with his own wishes. The task of the proletariat for 1917 was to

---

[104] Later Maj.-Gen. Sir Alfred Knox, *With the Russian Army: Being Chiefly Extracts from the Diary of a Military Attaché*, vol. 1 (London: Hutchinson, 1921), Digitised in 2007 by the Internet Archive, http://www.archivearchive.org/details/withrussianarmy101knoxuoft; vol. 2 (New York: Dutton and Company, 1921), digitised in 2015 by Internet Archive, https://archive.org/details/withrussianarmy02alfr

[105] Ibid., vol. 2, p. 552.

[106] Ibid., vol. 2, p. 691.

draw the army into a revolutionary front against the tsar [sic], the landlords, the bourgeoisie and the war.'[107] The effect of the German investment would come later. Knox summed up the situation in Petrograd, where the Bolshevik Revolution started as a 'handful of fanatics' who had 'seduced by money, wine and promises the armed workmen, the sailors and a small part of the garrison'.[108]

The German policy of Revolutionierungspolitik to assist revolutionary movements in Russia and elsewhere during the First World War was much the same as Gerasimov's 'mobilising the protest potential of the population'. In Russia, it was money well spent and far more successful than, for example, in Ireland. But the communists in Russia had been working on overthrowing the tsarist regime since 1903. The goal of the Communist Party of the USSR was a world federation of Soviet socialist republics to be established through the strategy and tactics of world revolution. Historically, its strategy has been divided into three phases. From 1903 to the March Revolution of 1917, the immediate objective was the overthrow of tsarism. In the second phase, from March to November 1917, it was the overthrow of the bourgeois Provisional Government in Russia and withdrawal from the 'imperialist' war that Alexander Kerensky's government still supported. In the third phase, after the November Revolution, it was to consolidate the socialist dictatorship in one country, where it could be used as a powerful lever to overthrow imperialism in all countries and open the epoch of world revolution.

Therefore, after 1918, and after the 'thin, cold, insubstantial conflict in the realms of Dis', [109] the communists became the government. In this strategy, the chief reserves of the revolutionary

---

[107] Alexander Shlyapnikov, 'On the Eve of 1917', January 1923, https://www.bolshevik.info/on-the-eve-of-1918/all-pages.htm (accessed 29 January 2019).
[108] Knox, *With the Russian Army*, vol. 2, p. 723.
[109] Winston S. Churchill, *The World Crisis*, vol. 4, *1918–1928: The Aftermath* (1931) (London: Bloomsbury Academic, 2015), Chapter 12, 'The Russian Civil War', p. 232. The numbering of the volumes varies with the edition and, rather confusingly, in the Thornton Butterworth 1931 edition, vol. 4, *The Aftermath*, precedes the final volume — 5 or 6, depending on the edition, covering the war on the Eastern Front. *The Aftermath* covers the war's long shadow including the Russian revolutions, the Russian Civil War and the Irish partition.

army were considered to be the masses in highly industrialised countries and the native populations in colonial and dependent lands. According to Bruce C. Hopper's seminal article of July 1941, written close to the time, 'throughout any one phase the strategy remains fairly constant in its principles; it changes only as the revolution moves from one phase to the next'.[110] Tactics, on the other hand, change repeatedly within any given phase, according to whether the revolutionary tide is ebbing or flowing, advancing or receding. Its instruments in conducting its external relations are two—the Narkomindel (Foreign Office), used to maintain formal relations with other states and to promote peace during the period of building Socialism in Russia; and the Comintern (Communist International), used to promote class war everywhere outside Russia, to convert imperialist war into civil war, and to further the cause of world revolution.[111]

Comintern—also known as the Third International—was founded in 1919 and finally dissolved in 1943. Its aim was 'struggle by all available means, including armed force, for the overthrow of the international bourgeoisie and the creation of an international Soviet republic as a transition stage to the complete abolition of the state'.

After about 1928, the policy of 'socialism in one country' came to predominate, and while the communist movements in other countries continued to receive Soviet support, they found themselves increasingly isolated.[112]

The key organisation in 'mobilising the protest potential of the population', to use Gerasimov's 2013 term, was the OMS—Otdel mezhdunarodnoy svyazi—'International Liaison Department',

---

[110] Bruce C. Hopper, 'Narkomindel and Comintern: Instruments of World Revolution', *Foreign Affairs*, July 1941, https://www.foreignaffairs.com/articles/russian-federation/1941-07-01/narkomindel-and-comintern (accessed 19 February 2019).

[111] Ibid.

[112] Jane de Gras (ed.), *The Communist International 1919–1943: Documents Selected and Edited by Jane de Gras*, vol. 3, *1929–1943* (London: Royal Institute of International Affairs, 1964), https://www.marxists.org/history/international/comintern/documents/volume3-1929-1943.pdf (accessed 19 February 2019).

founded at the Third Comintern Congress in 1921 and dissolved in 1939. It has also been translated as the 'Illegal Liaison Section' and 'Foreign Liaison Department'.[113] The OMS was the Comintern's department for the coordination of subversive and conspiratorial activities. Some of its functions overlapped with those of the main Soviet intelligence agencies, the OGPU and GRU, whose agents were sometimes assigned to the Comintern. But the OMS maintained its own set of operations and had its own representative on the central committees of each Communist Party abroad.[114]

In 1924, direction of the OMS was transferred to the GRU and to the Joint State Political Directorate, OGPU. The latter was the successor to the Cheka and predecessor to the NKVD, MGB and KGB. Between 1919 and 1922, people frequently moved back and forth between the Razvedupr and Comintern.[115] For the rest of the interwar period, the Soviet Armed Forces used the Comintern, especially the OMS, primarily for agent support and as a source of recruits for its own purposes. After 1927, agents of the OMS usually acted as liaisons between the Comintern and military intelligence (the GRU).

Therefore, by the end of the 1920s and certainly by the mid-1930s, Soviet efforts to mobilise world revolution through OMS were gradually subsumed into more traditional intelligence operations, which had a strong military and strategic focus. This was perhaps the first clear example of the confluence and complementarity of non-linear and linear warfare in Russia, as shown graphically in Figures 5.

More promising targets for 'mobilising the protest potential of the population' potentially existed overseas, in Western states' colonial empires. Foreign relations were central to the political imagination of the Bolsheviks and to their actual political behaviour from the day they seized power, even during the era of 'socialism

---

[113] Nigel West, *Mask: MI5's Penetration of the Communist Party of Great Britain* (London: Routledge, 2007).

[114] Thomas L. Sakmyster, *Red Conspirator: J. Peters and the American Communist Underground* (Urbana: University of Illinois Press, 2011), pp. 37–8, 40, 62–3.

[115] Raymond W. Leonard, *Secret Soldiers of the Revolution: Soviet Military Intelligence, 1918–1933* (Westport: Greenwood Publishing, 1999), pp. 16–18.

in one country'. Party and Comintern congresses began with an assessment of the international situation and Russia's world position.[116] The Communist International was founded at a time when the Bolsheviks believed that the sparks of revolutionary conflagration would jump from Russia to Germany in the immediate future and the blaze they ignited then sweep through Europe. In the months that followed, Lenin concluded from the defeats of the revolutions in Berlin, Munich and Budapest that 'the vanguard of the working class' had been won over to revolutionary socialism, but that additional effort would be required 'to awaken the dormant masses'. He also concluded that the successes of the October Revolution in Russia demonstrated the means by which that task was to be achieved. However, he was wrong.[117]

The alternative strategy was fairly obvious. As Jon Jacobson observed:

> Those who made the Russian Revolution turned to Asia as they lost confidence in revolution in Europe. After the defeat of proletarian revolutions on the Continent in 1919, the Bolsheviks, switching targets 180 degrees, promoted anticolonial rebellions in Asia. Lenin's theses on the colonial question at the Second Comintern Congress, the convocation of the Baku Congress of the Peoples of the East, and revolutionary involvement in Islamic Asia followed. Later, after the abortive 1923 revolution in Germany, an increasingly bolshevized Comintern turned eastward a second time and channelled resources toward China. In both instances the revolution in Asia was supported to redress an unfavourable correlation of forces in Europe. Promoting revolution in 'the East' compensated strategically for defeats in 'the West'.[118]

Although British–Russian rivalry in Asia had abated with the 1907 British–Russian agreement, the 'Russian' — now 'Soviet' — threat re-emerged. In 1918, a percipient David Lloyd George noted that the Turks, whose empire was to be split up under the 1916 Sykes–Picot agreement, were unlikely 'ever to be dangerous to our interests in

---

[116] Jon Jacobson, *When the Soviet Union Entered World Politics* (Berkeley: University of California Press, 1994), p. 7, https://publishing.cdlib.org/ucpressebooks/view?docId=ft009nb0bb&chunk.id=d0e1758&toc.id=d0e1758&brand=ucpress (accessed 12 September 2022).

[117] Ibid., Chapter 2, p. 33.

[118] Ibid., Chapter 5, p. 106.

the East'. Russia, however, 'if in the future she became regenerated, might be so'.[119]

Perhaps the most imaginative example of attempting to 'mobilise the protest potential of the population' was Comintern's plan to recruit black people in the United States and to create a breakaway Afro-American state.[120] Starting in the 1920s, the Soviet Union made a concerted effort to turn disaffected African-Americans from the party of Lincoln to the party of Lenin. During the early 1920s, a black communist called Cyril Briggs advanced a plan for a 'colored autonomous state' in sparsely settled western states like Nevada. Comintern approved a $300,000 fund for propaganda purposes in black America, and key African American leaders and communist sympathisers were invited to Russia to be wooed by Lenin and other Soviet officials inside the Kremlin. Those plans began in earnest in 1928, when the Comintern declared there would be 'self-determination in the Black Belt'.[121] Ultimately, Comintern's efforts proved counter-productive, as the communist association undermined what many Americans saw as a more legitimate civil rights movement, and as more Afro-Americans joined the middle classes. The Soviet Communist Party ended its campaign for black self-determination in 1958.[122]

During the fourteen years of Comintern's existence, no party affiliated with it succeeded in seizing power in Europe, Asia, Africa or the Americas. But Comintern had some successes. In the 1923–7 period, it advised and assisted a revolution of national liberation and unification in China. In the 1930s, it coordinated the sympathies of the European and American left—trade unionists and intellectuals, communists and non-communists alike—for the Soviet Union, for its effort to build socialism and for the struggle against fascism. The 1936–9 Spanish Civil War, where the Soviet Union

---

[119] UK National Archives, War Cabinet Minutes, CAB/23/6, cited in John Silverlight, *The Victors' Dilemma* (London: Barrie & Jenkins, 1970), p. 97.
[120] Sean Braswell, 'When the Soviet Union Tried to Woo Black America', OZY, 18 February 2017, https://www.ozy.com/flashback/when-the-soviet-union-tried-to-woo-black-america/62517 (accessed 16 February 2019).
[121] Ibid.
[122] Ibid.

armed and advised the Republican side, was arguably a 'hybrid war' as well as a proxy war. Three types of states became communist. The first were Russia and China. The second were invaded by Soviet forces—Georgia in 1920, Poland, Hungary, Czechoslovakia, East Germany from 1944 and North Korea in 1945. The third—Cuba and Mozambique, for example—eschewed the capitalist world system and sought help from existing communist states to escape domination by the major colonising powers. The Comintern was part of all three patterns. Parties associated with the Comintern produced the leaders who took power in the states of Eastern Europe from 1944 to 1948, in communist China in 1949 and in Cuba in 1959. 'In these ways', Jacobsen wrote, 'the movement organized by the Communist International did have a significant impact on twentieth-century world politics.'[123]

But besides the German use of Revolutionierungspolitik to overthrow the tsarist regime and then Kerensky's republic, and the lessons the Soviet Union learned from it and applied throughout its existence, there was another tributary that fed in after the Soviet Union collapsed. This was the contribution of the White Russian émigré Yevgeny Messner (1891–1974). Messner, of Russian-German descent, had joined the Imperial Russian Army in 1912 and rose rapidly through the ranks. By early 1917, as a divisional chief of staff, he was acutely aware of the disintegration of the army due to revolutionary propaganda. His division was demobilised in March 1918, by which time he had been through 1,000 days of battles and received twelve medals including the Cross of St George. He then joined the Whites and became the last chief of staff of the Kornilov division of General Wrangel's White Russian army. He left Russia in November 1920 on board one of the last ships to evacuate the defeated Whites.[124]

Messner moved to Belgrade, capital of the new state of

---

[123] Jacobson, *When the Soviet Union Entered World Politics*, pp. 32–3.
[124] Fridman, 'Reading Evgeny Messner', in Fridman, *Russian Hybrid Warfare*, pp. 73, 50–1. See also Adam Klus, '*Myatezh Voina*: The Russian Grandfather of Western Hybrid Warfare', Small Wars Journal, 2016, https://smallwarsjournal.com/jrnl/art/myatezh-voina-the-russian-grandfather-of-western-hybrid-warfare (accessed 10 March 2019).

Yugoslavia, which was perhaps the most prominent in openly welcoming and using the pool of Russian émigré talent.[125] In the 1920s and 1930s, Messner produced numerous articles on military theory and tactics. In 1931, he was appointed a lecturer in the Belgrade branch of the Higher Military Science courses established by another Russian officer, the White General Nikolai Golovin (1875–1944). Virulently anti-communist, Messner continued to lecture under the German military occupation of Serbia and then supported the formation of the Russian Liberation Army set up by captured Soviet Lt Gen. Andrey Vlasov (1900–46), which fought under the Germans against the Soviets. Messner was lucky that the 1st Russian National Army, in which, by 1945, he was head of the propaganda department, surrendered in Liechtenstein, which refused to extradite Russians who had fought with the Germans. He and his wife emigrated to Argentina in 1947, where he produced his principal works on hybrid war or, as he called it, 'myatezhevoyna' — 'subversion war'. He died in Argentina in 1974.[126]

As Messner was anti-communist and had collaborated with the Germans, his work, published in Russian-language journals in South America, could not have been acknowledged, let alone incorporated into official military thinking in the Soviet period. However, after the Soviet Union dissolved in 1991, the work of this patriotic Russian became accessible and acceptable. Most of Messner's thinking about myatezhevoyna[127] can be found in: Lik sovremennoy voyny (The face of modern war) from 1959, Myatezh: Imya tret'yey vsemirnoy voyny (Subversion: The name of the third worldwide war) from 1960, and Vsemirnaya myatezhevoyna (The worldwide subversion war), from 1971.[128]

---

[125] Others included the United States, where the aviation genius Igor Sikorskiy moved from designing the world's first four-engine heavy bomber for tsarist Russia to helicopters for the United States.

[126] Fridman, *Russian Hybrid Warfare*, pp. 51–2.

[127] Sometimes translated as 'mutiny war', but this is wrong because a mutiny, in the sense of a revolt against military authority, is a *bunt*. A *myatezh* is a rebellion, insurrection or insurgency. See Fridman, *Russian Hybrid Warfare*, p. 66.

[128] All three books were published by the South American Division of the N. N. Golovin Institute for the Study of the Problems of War and Peace.

Messner was writing in the context of the Cold War and correctly identified the Soviet attempts to support 'national liberation movements' and undermine Western colonial governments and Western societies identified in the previous section. In 1959, he had written that 'it is easier to degrade a state rather than conquer it by arms'.[129] As soon as the Soviet Union dissolved, his work—which was, helpfully, in Russian—became the subject of great interest in Russia. In 1994, two officers observed that 'by rejecting the exclusive role of Marxism as the solely true teaching that explains the nature and character of war we … need to clarify … the scientific basis of … our views on war as a special societal condition'.[130] In other words, imperial Russian and émigré military thinking was back in business. Ironically, while Messner had been writing about the threat of worldwide 'subversion war' sponsored by the Soviet Union and, to a lesser extent, China, the post-Soviet Russians now thought that the West had undermined the Soviet Union in exactly the same way.

Starting in 1994, Aleksandr Savinkin, who, as a colonel in 1988, had been the first to press for military reform, published a string of edited books on the contribution of Russian émigrés to military thought and their relevance to modern Russian requirements. 'The spiritual revival of the military today', he wrote, 'is impossible without studying and understanding the patriotic and military thinking of the Russian émigrés, the ideas of the White [movement] and its traditions.'[131]

Messner's 'subversion war' originally referred to what the Soviet Union had been trying to do. The Russians now saw in it the

---

[129] Messner, *Lik Sovremennoy voyny*, p. 7.

[130] V. Solov'ev and A. Dremkov, 'Yeshchë raz o predmete I strukturevoyennoy nauki' (One more time on the content and structure of military science), *Voyennaya mysl'* 9 (1994), pp. 34–5. Cited in Fridman, *Russian Hybrid Warfare*, p. 71.

[131] Aleksandr Savinkin, 'Zashchita Rossii' (The defence of Russia), in *Russkoy zarubezh'ye: Gosudarstvennaya-patrioticheskaya I voyennaya mysl'* (The Russian abroad: State-patriotic and military thought) (Moscow: Humanitarian Academy of the Armed Forces, 1994), p. 8. This and the other works edited by Savinkin are listed in full in Fridman, *Russian Hybrid Warfare*, Chapter 3, p. 192, note 108. The works were published initially by the Humanitarian Academy of the Armed Forces (1994), then by the Military University (1995–2007).

cause of their defeat in the Cold War. But Messner's revival was also helped by the fact that myatezhevoyna corresponded perfectly to what post-Soviet Russia needed now. It needed an asymmetric and non-linear strategy to offset what it saw as overwhelming Western superiority, with NATO expansion and the potential encirclement of Russia. Myatezhevoyna offered a way to deal with the defection of the ring of countries in the near abroad — the other former Soviet republics. Writing in 1959, Messner had described all the characteristics of 'hybrid', 'new-type' or 'non-linear' war noted earlier in the chapter:

The traditional military objective — the enemy's army — has been dispersed into people at war; the traditional geographic objective — the capital — has become one of many [surrogate] capitals ... there is one final goal, but there are also many intermediate ones, and they are in different fields: military, diplomatic, socio-political and physiological.[132]

This reads very much like Gerasimov and Kartapolov. Given the attention Messner received in Russia from 1994 onwards, twenty years after his death, he and myatezhevoyna must bear some responsibility for the evolution of aspects of 'new-type', 'non-linear' or 'hybrid' war. Messner had put his finger on it, and the post-Soviet Russians got it. Messner's work and, crucially, its recognition in post-Soviet Russia, were, in this author's view, a most important tributary feeding in to that very broad 'non-linear warfare' river.

Reflexive control and cybernetics: the key to modern Russian non-linear war

The Russian theory of non-linear war originated fifty years ago, in the 1950s and '60s, and was being analysed in the West by 1986. In 2015, Timothy Thomas explicitly noted the progeny of the 'new' non-linear strategy[133] to which he and others had referred in many

---

[132] Messner, *Lik sovremennoy voyny*, p. 18, translated by Fridman in *Russian Hybrid Warfare*, p. 70.
[133] Thomas, 'Russia's Military Strategy and Ukraine', pp. 445–61.

earlier articles.¹³⁴ The 2015 article detailed how Russia's military strategy had evolved and how it may have been applied in Ukraine. It examined both traditional and contemporary elements of strategy, with a particular focus on the effect of President Putin's competitive logic and the general staff's reliance on non-military methods of thought. Thomas focused on the concept of reflexive control. He said reflexive control had been used as a propaganda method during the Ukraine intervention to exert informational and psychological influence on Russia's domestic and international audiences. More than a decade before, in 2004, Thomas had explicitly examined Russia's use of 'reflexive control' and noted that it had been around in the Soviet Union and Russia for nearly forty years. The theory had both military and civilian uses. His 2004 article described both the theory and practice of reflexive control, focusing on recent developments. By then, he said, the concept's meaning was close to the US concept of perception management.¹³⁵ The Russian phrase 'refleklsivnoye upraveniye' or 'refleksivny kontrol'' now primarily refers to 'reflexive practice' in an educational or personnel management context. Nevertheless, given its widespread application in Western analysis, and the absence of a suitable replacement, reflexive control will be used here. Reflexive control also has a lot in common with what NATO calls 'influence operations'.¹³⁶

Following the initial, post-2014 excitement about Russia's 'new art of war', which was neither 'new' nor exclusively 'Russian', authoritative comment guided by scholarship swiftly returned. This included recognition of reflexive control as a key component of Russian non-linear warfare. The key analysts were Timothy Thomas, of the US Army Command and Staff College Foreign

---

¹³⁴ See also Timothy Thomas, 'Russia's Reflexive Control Theory and the Military', *Journal of Slavic Military Studies* 17 (2004), pp. 237–56, https://www.rit.edu/~w-cmmc/literature/Thomas_2004.pdf (accessed 16 February 2019).

¹³⁵ Ibid., p. 237.

¹³⁶ Flemming Splidsboel Hansen, 'Russian Influence Operations: Trying to Get What You Want', DIIS Policy Brief, 30 October 2018, https://www.diis.dk/en/research/russian-influence-operations (accessed 18 March 2019).

Military Studies Office in Fort Leavenworth, Kansas;[137] Keir Giles of the NATO Defense College in Rome;[138] James Sherr, of the UK Royal Institute of International Affairs (Chatham House), in London;[139] Andrew Monaghan, then also at Chatham House;[140] and Major Christian Kamphuis of the Dutch Army, writing in the NATO journal Militaire Spectator in 2018.*[141] Major Kamphuis noted that reflexive control had originated half a century before and its connexion with the long-established and highly competent Russian tradition of maskirovka, which can either mean camouflage, in the physical sense, or deception.[142]

This is a description of 'new-type warfare', moving from covert and political action to military action in the final stage. In that same year, 1986, the US Naval Postgraduate School published a study of

---

[137] See also Timothy Thomas, 'The Evolution of Russian Military Thought: Integrating Hybrid, New-Generation and New-Type Thinking', *Journal of Slavic Military Studies* 29, no. 4 (2016), http://www.tandfonline.com/doi/abs/10.1080/13 518046.2016.1232541 (accessed 13 September 2022), and Timothy L. Thomas, *Kremlin Kontrol: Russia's Political-Military Reality* (Fort Leavenworth, KS: Foreign Military Studies Office, 2017).

[138] Keir Giles, James Sherr and Anthony Seaboyer, 'Russian Reflexive Control', Defence Research and Development Canada, October 2018, https://www.researc hgate.net/publication/328562833_Russian_Reflexive_Control (accessed 11 March 2019).

[139] See also James Sherr, 'Ukraine's Fightback Has Surprised the Kremlin | Chatham House – International Affairs Think Tank', 1 August 2014, https://w ww.chathamhouse.org/publications/the-world-today/2014-08/ukraines-figh tback-has-surprised-kremlin. (accessed 10 October 2023)

[140] Andrew Monaghan, 'Putin's Way of War: The "War" in Russia's "Hybrid Warfare"', *Parameters: Journal of the US Army War College* (Winter 2016), https:// ssi.armywarcollege.edu/pubs/parameters/issues/Winter_2015-16/9_Monaghan.pdf (accessed 5 January 2019).

[141] Major C. Kamphuis, 'Reflexive Control: The Relevance of a 50-Year-Old Russian Theory Regarding Perception Control', *Militaire Spectator* 187, no. 6 (2018), pp. 323–39,https://www.militairespectator.nl/sites/default/files/uitgaven/i nhoudsopgave/Militaire%20Spectator%206-2018%20Kamphuis.pdf (accessed 16 March 2019).

[142] Ibid., citing Tom Clancy, *Red Storm Rising* (New York: Putnam's Sons, 1986, republished London: HarperCollins, 1993), p. 44. Emphasis of *maskirovka* is added.

reflexive control.[143] During the 1950s, there was an upsurge of interest in scientific decision-making in the Soviet Union, linked with increased automation in technology and industry and the emergence of computers. This coincided with the emergence of cybernetics, the science of complex, dynamic systems in the West. Initially, cybernetics was rejected as non-Marxist, but by 1956 the Soviet Cybernetics Institute had been established and the science became accepted, while, ironically, it went into decline in the West. The Russians were particularly impressed by the work of the Englishman W. Ross Ashby (1903–72), who was not so highly regarded in the West.[144]

In the Soviet Union, cybernetics was initially developed at the First Computer Centre of the Soviet Defence Ministry. The main man was Vladimir A. Lefebvre, born in Leningrad in 1936. He was a mathematician working in a section of the department developing algorithms for the automation of computers under a Colonel Tkachenko. Lefebvre later became a prolific author and moved to the United States, where he worked as a mathematical psychologist at the University of California, Irvine.[145] He created equations that help predict the large-scale consequences of individual actions.

In 1963, Lefebvre proposed a different approach to the problem from the game theory methods being used by the other scientists. He suggested using a modelling system comprising three sub-systems: a unit to simulate one's own decisions, one to simulate the adversary's decisions, and one to adjudicate. In response to criticism, he came up with reflexive control, whereby one influenced the adversary's information channels and shifted the flow of information to make the adversary make what, to them, seemed an

---

[143] Diane Chotikul, 'The Soviet Theory of Reflexive Control in Historical and Psychocultural Perspective: A Preliminary Study' (Monterey, CA: US Naval Postgraduate School, July 1986), https://calhoun.nps.edu/bitstream/handle/10945/30190/soviettheoryofre00chot.pdf?sequence=1 (accessed 12 September 2022).

[144] Ibid., p. 84.

[145] In 2010, for example, he published a paper entitled 'Modeling the Behavior of Terrorist Groups with the Theory of Reflexive Games', *Progress in Biophysics and Molecular Biology* 131 (June 2017), https://www.researchgate.net/scientific-contributions/2034094747_Vladimir_A_Lefebvre (accessed 12 September 2022).

'optimal' decision but that was in fact optimal to the opposing side.[146]

In 1967, Lefebvre was, perhaps rather extraordinarily, allowed to publish an unclassified book, Conflicting Structures.[147] In it, Lefebvre introduced two new concepts: that of a reflexive system — a system that has an image of the self — and that of reflexive control (conveying a basis for making the decision that is advantageous to the side conducting the reflexive control). Both concepts have since become firmly established in modern theories of decision-making. The book contains the author's model of the universe as a reflexive system (Janus-Cosmology) as well as the description of a device that turns fears into reality through reflexive control, constructed by the author for the purpose of experimental study. In addition, the author also explains how to use reflexive control over processes of reflexive control.

Lefebvre's work clearly had great relevance to the Soviet military and security services, and in 1968 a KGB agent named Panov published a classified report on Lefebvre's work. According to Diane Chotikul, who wrote the 1986 Naval Postgraduate School report, it was rumoured — she does not say by whom — that the KGB organised its own laboratory for reflexive studies.[148] She met Lefebvre at the Naval Postgraduate School on 12 September 1984. Lefebvre himself said that reflexive control became a classified subject shortly after the publication of Panov's report. Military interest heightened with the publication of K. V. Tarakanov's book Mathematics and Armed Combat in 1974[149] and V. V. Druzhinin and D. S.

---

[146] Lefebvre's own account of his work at this time is in his chapter 'Second Order Cybernetics in the Soviet Union and the West', in Robert Trappl (ed.), *Power, Autonomy, Utopia: New Approaches toward Complex Systems* (New York: Springer-Verlag US, 1986), pp. 123–31.

[147] English translation: Vladimir A. Lefebvre, *Conflicting Structures* (New York: Leaf and Oaks Publishers, 2015).

[148] Chotikul, 'Soviet Theory of Reflexive Control', p. 89.

[149] K. V. Tarakanov, *Matematika I vooruzhennaya bor'ba* (Mathematics and armed combat) (Moscow: Voyenizdat, 1974; translated by US Air Force (FTD-ID(RS)T-0577-79) (AD-8043718), 15 August 1979).

Kontorov's Problems of Military Systems Engineering in 1976.[150] These officers all claimed that reflexive control was used extensively in teaching, diplomatic and administrative activities, as well as in military affairs. As well as its obvious utility in making the enemy do what you want, it was also useful for troop control and leadership training. Chotikul's study includes a helpful diagram illustrating the development of reflexive control in the Soviet military and security world, reproduced here as Figure 4.[151]

---

[150] V. A. Druzhinin and D. S. Kontorov, *Voprosy voyennoy sistemotekhniki* (Problems of military systems engineering) (Moscow: Voyenizdat, 1976). See also Druzhinin and Kontorov, *Ideya, algoritm, resheniye* (Concept, algorithm, decision) (Moscow: Voyenizdat, 1972; translation Washington, DC: US Government Printing Office, 1975), and *Konfliktnaya Radiolokatsia* (Conflicting radar detection) (Moscow: Radio i Svyaz, 1982).

[151] Chotikul, 'Soviet Theory of Reflexive Control', p. 91. Diagram reproduced as far as possible in similar format to the original.

Figure 4. - Based on from Diane Chotikul's Figure 17, The chronological development of formalized reflexive control theory. Author's translation. Redrawn by author.

The diagram clearly shows the origins of the concept in Military Unit 01168, a secret military unit established in 1954 and involved in early military computer development.[152] Of particular interest are Lefebvre's works Conflicting Structures and The Algebra of Conflict.[153]

Chotikul's perceptive analysis reflects Western analysts' awareness of the Soviet concept of reflexive control by 1986. The current author first encountered it two years later, while studying at the University of Edinburgh. The late Professor John Erickson explained that it was about making the enemy do what you wanted him to do, not just think what you wanted him to think.[154] He was right. Moving on to 2004, Tim Thomas explicitly stated that reflexive control differs from any known Western concept because it is about controlling perception, and not about managing perception. Managing perception, and not controlling perception, is the essence of Western perception management within the context of information warfare.[155] In his important 2004 article, Thomas cited the work of several Russian authors: Major Generals N. I. Turko and M. D. Ionov, Colonel S. S. Leonenko, S. A. Komov, and Captain First Rank — Navy — F. Chausov.[156]

Ionov wrote several articles on the subject of reflexive control in Voyennaya mysl'. When he began writing, in the 1970s, the term 'reflexive control' was not listed in any Soviet military

---

[152] Yakov Fet, 'Norbert Wiener in Moscow', *SORUCOM: Proceedings of the 2014 Third International Conference on Computer Technology in Russia and the Former Soviet Union, 13–17 October 2014* (Massachusetts: IEEE Computer Society, 2014), pp. 194–5.

[153] V. A. Lefebvre, *Algebra konflikta* (Moscow, 1968) (translation available by G. L. Smolyan, National Technical Information Service, US Department of Commerce, 1971).

[154] Conversation with Professor John Erickson, Edinburgh Conversations, December 1988.

[155] Giles, *Handbook of Russian Information Warfare*, p. 19.

[156] Timothy Thomas, 'Russia's Reflexive Control Theory and the Military', *Journal of Slavic Military Studies* 17 (2004), pp. 243–9.

encyclopaedia and, therefore, people were disinclined to listen to him. Therefore, in many of his initial articles, Ionov simply spoke about 'control of the enemy' rather than 'reflexive control'. Ionov noted that the objective of reflexive control is to force an enemy into making objective decisions that lead to their defeat by influencing or controlling their decision-making process. So, control over the enemy is realised by undertaking a series of measures, related by time, aim and place, which force enemy decision-makers to abandon their original plan, make disadvantageous decisions or react incorrectly.[157]

Komov set out key elements of reflexive control that reflect traditional Russian maskirovka and also subsequent elements of 'hybrid', 'non-linear' or 'new-type war':[158]

- Distraction: create a real or imaginary threat to the enemy's flank or rear during the preparatory stages of combat operations, forcing him to adapt his plans.
- Overload (of information): frequently send large amounts of conflicting information.
- Paralysis: create the perception of an unexpected threat to a vital interest or weak spot.
- Exhaustion: compel the enemy to undertake useless operations, forcing him to enter combat with reduced resources.
- Deception: force the enemy to relocate assets in reaction to an imaginary threat during the preparatory stages of combat.
- Division: convince actors to operate in opposition to coalition interests.
- Pacification: convince the enemy that pre-planned operational training is occurring rather than preparations for combat operations.
- Deterrence: create the perception of superiority.
- Provocation: force the enemy to take action advantageous to

---

[157] Ibid., pp. 243–5.
[158] Ibid., pp. 248–9, citing S. A. Komov, 'About Methods and Forms of Conducting Information Warfare', *Military Thought* (English edn) 4 (July–August 1997), pp. 18–22.

one's own side.
- Suggestion: offer information that affects the enemy legally, morally, ideologically or in other areas.
- Pressure: offer information that discredits the enemy's commanders and/or government in the eyes of the population.

Charles Blandy of the UK Defence Academy at Shrivenham later offered the following summary of reflexive control. Having established the 'target', he wrote,

> the military mind works backwards from the selected objective to its present position. Subsidiary goals are identified for achieving the objective. The Soviet and Russian General Staffs over a long period of time have studied the application of reflexive control theory both for deception and disinformation purposes in order to influence and control an enemy's decision making processes ... Control of an opponent's decision is achieved by means of providing him with the grounds by which he is able logically to derive his own decision, but one that is predetermined by the other side. This can be achieved:
> - By applying the pressure of force.
> - By assisting the opponent's formulation of an appreciation of the initial situation.
> - By shaping the opponent's objectives.
> - By shaping the opponent's decision making algorithm.
> - By the choice of critical decision making moment.[159]

There appears to be little to distinguish the half-century-old theory and practice of reflexive control from many elements of 'hybrid', 'non-linear' or 'new-type' warfare.

The Soviet Union's blockade of Berlin from 24 June 1948 to 12 May 1949 is a very good example of economic sanctions and blockade as a tool of non-linear war. The post-war division of Germany into sectors roughly corresponding to Allied troop advances had left Berlin 160 kilometres inside the Soviet-occupied sector. Stalin wanted a weak Germany and, expecting the Western allies to withdraw, planned to create a Germany that was both Soviet and

---

[159] C. W. Blandy, *Provocation, Deception, Entrapment: The Russo-Georgian Five Day War*, Defence Academy of the United Kingdom, Advanced Research and Assessment Group 09/01 (Shrivenham: Defence Academy, 2009).

communist.¹⁶⁰ But the Western Allies started rebuilding western Germany in their own image. The trigger for the Soviet use of non-linear tactics was financial. The Allies introduced the new Deutsche Mark, frustrating Soviet plans to keep western Germany weak. The Soviets responded by delaying and then blocking US, British and French access to the sectors of Berlin under their control by road, rail and canal. The Soviets offered to end the blockade if the newly introduced Deutsche Mark was withdrawn from West Berlin. Two days later, the Western Allies and Britain's Commonwealth partners—Canada, Australia, New Zealand and South Africa—began the Berlin airlift, using the three air corridors into the city that had earlier been agreed with the Soviets. It was the first battle honour for the newly created United States Air Force. Before 1946, it had been the US Army Air Force.

The Berlin airlift is highly instructive for delicate management of non-linear war. The Soviets did not disrupt it for fear this might lead to open conflict, even though they far outnumbered the Allies in Germany and especially Berlin. However, it failed to achieve its objectives. By the spring of 1949, the airlift was clearly succeeding, and by April it was delivering more cargo than had previously been transported into the city by rail. On 12 May 1949, the USSR lifted the blockade.

Since 1949, the Soviet Union and Russia have more often been the victims of sanctions than users. The US boycott of the 1980 Moscow Olympics in response to the 1979 Soviet invasion of Afghanistan, accompanied by economic sanctions, is one example. The following year, 1981, more sanctions were imposed following Soviet pressure on Poland to suppress the Solidarity movement. In 1974, US President Gerald Ford signed off trade restrictions against the Soviet Union and other communist countries in a measure known as the Jackson–Vanik amendment for its congressional sponsors. The issue was the right of certain people, especially Jews, to

---

¹⁶⁰ See Michael Laird, 'Wars Averted: Chanak 1922, Burma 1945–47, Berlin 1948', *The Journal of Strategic Studies* 19 (1996), pp. 343–64; Roger Gene Miller, *To Save a City: The Berlin Airlift 1948–1949* (College Station: Texas A. & M. University Press, 2000), p. 13.

emigrate from the Soviet Union. Nearly four decades passed before President Barack Obama lifted those restrictions on 14 December 2012. Yet at the same time, new restrictions on certain Russians believed to be human rights violators entering the United States, the so-called Magnitsky Act, were brought in.[161]

After Russia seized Crimea in February 2014, many countries, including the United States and the members of the EU, imposed sanctions against Russian businesses and officials from Russia and Ukraine. Russia responded with its own sanctions against a number of countries, including a total ban on food imports from the EU, the United States, Norway, Canada and Australia. These imports were worth about 1.5 billion euros a year. The Russians also imposed travel bans on some eighty-nine named individuals from those countries and other politicians and officials.[162]

When the Turkish Air Force shot down a Russian Su-24 bomber on the Syrian–Turkish border in November 2015, Russia responded by banning the import of Turkish fruit and vegetables, poultry and salt, the sale of package holidays in Turkey for Russians and contracts with Turkish firms in Russia for construction projects. Later, Russian pressure on Ukraine has continued with more targeted sanctions against Ukrainian individuals and legal entities. On 1 November, 2018 Russia imposed 'special economic measures' on 322 Ukrainian individuals and sixty-eight companies. On Christmas Day, 2018, a further 200 individuals and legal entities were added to the list.[163]

Therefore, although sanctions, whether economic or personal, do not feature much in Russian discussion of non-linear warfare, they clearly have a potential role. In the case of Ukraine, they were

---

[161] Greg Myre, 'U.S. Sanctions against Russia Never Go Away: They Just Evolve', National Public Radio, 21 July 2017, https://www.npr.org/2017/07/21/538086476/u-s-sanctions-against-russia-never-go-away-they-just-evolve?t=1552900644994 (accessed 18 March 2019).

[162] See Nikolaj Nielsen, 'Russia Imposes Retaliatory Sanctions on EU', EU Observer, Brussels, 7 August 2014, https://euobserver.com/foreign/125205 (accessed 18 March 2019).

[163] Radio Free Europe/Radio Liberty, 'Russia Expands Targeted Sanctions against Ukraine', 25 December 2018, http://www.rferl.org/a/russia-expands-sanctions-ukraine/29675861.html (accessed 18 March 2019).

clearly part of the hybrid warfare that since before the current crisis first became public in 2014 with the illegal annexation of Crimea, the eight-year conflict in Luhansk and Donetsk and the 2022 full scale war.

The cyber dimension

Given the long evolution of a 'non-linear' strategy in parallel with 'black' or 'grey' operations against perceived traitors, what is new about recent Russian operations using Trojan horses and other related means? This author believes not much. The only really new development is so-called cyber-war—computer network operations (CNO) and other activities in cyberspace, and the separate but related issue of Artificial Intelligence (AI).

The Russians do not talk about 'cyber-war'. It is not a separate function or domain and is not a Russian concept. It is a subset of 'information warfare'—informatsionnaya voyna or informatsionnoye protivoborstvo. When they translate the term literally, it refers to Western terminology and Western concepts.[164] Just as gibridnaya voyna also refers to Western terminology and practice.

The Russians refer to 'information space' rather than 'cyberspace', and it embraces not only the virtual world but also the human one—effectively the cognitive domain. Information warfare includes the use of traditional media for fake news. A probable recent example was the release in January 2019 of the details of 4,000 Latvians allegedly used as KGB informers during the Soviet period. The KGB left so-called 'Cheka files', named after its precursor but two, when Latvia became independent and the KGB left its Riga headquarters in August 1991. Piles of documents and a partly destroyed Delta electronic database were seized by the Latvian authorities. They were closed for eighteen years but then released.

---

[164] Keir Giles, *Handbook of Russian Information Warfare* (Rome: NATO Fellowship Monograph, Research Division, NATO Defense College, November 2016), pp. 1-8. See also Keir Giles and Andrew Monaghan, 'Legality in Cyberspace: An Adversary Vie', US Army War College Strategic Studies Institute, March 2014, http://www.strategicstudiesinstitute.army.mil/pubs/ display.cfm?pubID=1193 (accessed 23 February 2019).

Some of those named admitted working for the KGB and informing on neighbours, but others were shocked, denied working for the agency and said they would go to court to clear their names.[165] Vita Zelče, a historian at the University of Latvia, said 'what are these files? A real historical record, or a strange Soviet disinformation operation? We just don't know.'[166] Whatever the answer, the records date from the Soviet period and could reflect KGB exaggeration and over-enthusiasm. But any such find could now be exploited by Russia to discredit influential citizens of target states.

The closest the Russians get to separating CNO from the use of traditional media and other information activities, including academic conferences, is the division of information warfare into two types, as explained in 2004 by Vladimir Kvachkov, a former GRU officer:

- information-psychological warfare (to affect armed forces personnel and the population) conducted under conditions of natural competition, that is, permanently; and
- information technology warfare (to affect technical systems which receive, collect, process and transmit information), conducted during [and, we might add, in the run-up to] wars and armed conflicts.[167]

By now, the reader will recognise similarities with the Russian emphasis on the permanent state of confrontation and the end of clear states of 'war' and 'peace' and Gerasimov's table stating that action begins 'in peacetime' (see figure 3). The second type of information warfare, 'information technology warfare', does not map directly

---

[165] Andrew Higgins, 'Disbelief at Latvia's KGB List', *New York Times*, 21 January 2019, pp. 1, 5.
[166] Ibid., p. 5.
[167] Vladimir Krachkov, *Spetsnaz Rossii* (Russia's special purpose forces) (Moscow: Voyennaya Literatura, 2004). Online version militera.lib.ru/science/kvachkov _vv/indexhtml, cited by Keir Giles in *Nato Handbook of Russian Information Warfare*, p. 9, which he accessed 4 July 2016. Available via Amazon from Knigamarket. It is unlikely that this book could have been published much later, and it therefore remains a crucial example of the brief window of opportunity that followed the end of the Soviet Union and the clamp-down since 2000.

across to the West's 'cyber-warfare'. Computer and internet-based activities may also be used for information-psychological purposes.[168]

Understandably, Western analysts have devoted much effort to analysing and chronicling Russian use of cyberspace. The extension of battle, and deception, into the electronic spectrum is as old as mankind's use of it. In 1914, the French set up a jamming station on top of the Eiffel Tower. In the Second World War, radio was used to spread propaganda — 'fake news' — by both sides and for the BBC to communicate with Resistance operators in occupied France. The most dramatic example of 'reflexive control' — making the enemy do what you want him to do, as well as think what you want him to think — was the creation of a 'virtual' army group, First US Army Group, in Essex and Kent using physical and electronic deception. This helped persuade the Germans to believe what they already wanted to believe, that the main Allied attack was to come across the Pas-de-Calais, and that the Normandy landings were a feint. For that reason, they held back their armoured reserves, permitting the Allies to gain a foothold in Normandy.

What makes cyber-war different now is our total dependence on the internet and our use of it not only for communications but to carry out every kind of operational and even physical task. If information is manipulated in cyberspace, the false news becomes, effectively, real. In the defence and security context, the Global Positioning Systems (GPS) used not only for navigation of manned vehicles, ships and aircraft but even in precision-guided weapons are particularly vulnerable.

The first large-scale cyber-attack from 2003 has not been attributed to Russia but to China. In 2003, an attack took place on the US, codenamed 'Titan Rain' by the US Government. Hackers gained access to many US defence contractor networks including Lockheed Martin and NASA. However, it had long been known that many Chinese computers and websites were very insecure. It looked as if a Chinese system was attacking the target, not the

---

[168] Giles, *Handbook of Russian Information Warfare*, pp. 9–10.

hacker.[169] Chinese government complicity was never proved.

The next major cyber-attack was widely attributed to Russia. It took place in 2007 against the small and highly developed Baltic country of Estonia. Being a small state and a centre of IT excellence, Estonia was a good target. In April 2007, Estonia angered Moscow by planning to move a Russian Second World War memorial, the 'Bronze Soldier of Tallinn', and Russian soldiers' graves. A series of cyber-attacks began on 27 April 2007 targeting the websites of Estonian organisations, including Estonia's parliament, banks, ministries, newspapers and broadcasters. Many believed Russia retaliated by temporarily disabling Estonia's internet, an especially harsh blow in the world's most internet-dependent economy. Most of the attacks were of the distributed denial of service (DDoS) type, in which computer networks are overwhelmed by a flood of internet messages focused on government offices and financial institutions, disrupting communications.[170] Estonian websites and the Bronze Soldier's Wikipedia page were also defaced.

The Estonian government blamed the Kremlin, which certainly had the motive, accusing it of being directly involved in the attacks. However, Estonia's defence minister, Jaak Aaviksoo, later admitted that he had no evidence linking the cyber-attacks to the Kremlin or other Russian government agencies. Russia denied accusations of its involvement, and neither NATO nor European Commission experts were able to find any proof of official Russian government participation.[171] The assessment resulted in a report issued to NATO Allied Defence Ministers in October 2007. It further developed into the creation of a cyber-defence policy and the creation of the NATO Cooperative Cyber Defence Centre of Excellence in

---

[169] Nathan Homburgh, 'The Invasion of the Chinese Cyberspies (And the Man Who Tried to Stop Them)', *Time*, 5 September 2005.

[170] Patrick Howell O'Neill, 'Web War I: The Cyberattack That Changed the World', Daily Dot, 20 May 2016, https://www.dailydot.com/layer8/web-war-cyberattack-russia-estonia (accessed 12 September 2022).

[171] 'Kremlin-Backed Group behind Estonia Cyber Blitz', *Financial Times*, 11 March 2009.

Tallinn in May 2008.[172]

In June 2008, in a similar attack, Russia punished another former republic in the Baltic. When the Lithuanian government outlawed the display of Soviet symbols, hackers, assumed to be Russian-based or sponsored, defaced government webpages with hammer-and-sickle emblems and five-pointed stars.[173]

So far, cyber-attacks had been conducted separately from more conventional operations, and that made them even more difficult to attribute. The first clear coordination of kinetic and cyber-warfare occurred in the war between Russia and Georgia starting in August 2008.

As in Ukraine in 2014, the conflict owed much to Georgian overtures to the West, and vice-versa, and to the aspirations of pro-Russian separatists in South Ossetia and Abkhazia, No part of Georgia. Another key factor is the pipeline from Baku in Azerbaijan, via Tbilisi in Georgia to Ceyhan on Turkey's Mediterranean Coast. It therefore avoids Russian territory. By April 2008, the diplomatic situation had deteriorated, and in July the United States held counter-insurgency exercises with Georgian forces, while, simultaneously, the Russians held an exercise, 'Caucasus 2008', on their side of the border in Chechnya, North Ossetia, Ingushetia, Kabardino-Balkaria and Karachayevo-Circassia. That included training to aid peacekeeping forces stationed in Abkhazia and South Ossetia. When the exercises finished at the end of July, the Russian forces did not disperse. Then, on 1 August 2008, South Ossetian separatists set off a bomb, injuring five Georgian policemen. On 7 August, the separatists began shelling Georgian villages. To put an end to these attacks and restore order, the Georgian Army was sent to the South Ossetian conflict zone on 7 August.

---

[172] NATO 'Centres of Excellence' are set up and hosted by individual NATO members, with partners from other NATO countries. The author addressed a seminar at the Centre for Defence Against Terrorism (CDAT) in Ankara, Turkey, in November 2017.

[173] 'Timeline: Ten Years of Russian Cyber Attacks on Other Nations', NBC News, 18 December 2016, http://www.nbcnews.com/storyline/hacking-in-america/timeline-ten-years-russian-cyber-attacks-other-nations-n697111 (accessed 16 February 2019).

The brief Georgian war thus included all the elements of Russian non-linear warfare. There was the use of troops for 'peace support operations' to conceal their deployment, the 'protest potential of the [pro-Russian] population' and the covert insertion of Russian forces before open hostilities began. Even the Russian media acknowledged that Russian troops had illicitly crossed the Russo-Georgian state border, through the Roki tunnel, and advanced into the South Ossetian conflict zone by 7 August before the Georgian military response.[174]

Russia launched a large-scale land, air and sea invasion of Georgia on 8 August under the pretext of a 'Peace Enforcement Operation'. Russian naval forces blockaded part of the Georgian coast. The Russian air force attacked targets beyond the conflict zone in undisputed parts of Georgia.

However, this was probably the first time that cyber-attacks preceded conventional operations, by a matter of weeks, and were conducted in concert with them. The cyber-attacks began three weeks before the 'proper war' — the kinetic war.[175] Alleged Russian hackers attacked Georgia's websites. They started by targeting Georgia's own hacking community in an attempt to disable any potential counterattack. They then gained access to over fifty Georgian military and government networks, which were highly vulnerable.

The hackers shut down official sites in Gori, including some news sites, with DDoS attacks that overwhelm the targets with massive cyber-traffic, forcing them to close down. These began just prior to launching air combat operations. Hackers hindered the

---

[174] SMI, 'Rossiyskiye voyska voshli v Yuzhnuyu Osetiyu yeshchë do nachala boyevykh deystviy' (Russian forces entered South Ossetia even before the outbreak of military action), *NEWSru.com*, 11 September 2008. See also Jon Swaine, 'Georgia: Russia "Conducting Cyber War"; Russia Has Been Accused of Attacking Georgian Government Websites in a Cyber War to Accompany Their Military Bombardment', *Daily Telegraph*, 11 August 2008, https://www.telegraph.co.uk/n ews/worldnews/europe/georgia/2539157/Georgia-Russia-conducting-cyber -war.html (accessed 16 February 2019).

[175] Daniel Hoffman, 'History's Lesson Regarding Russian Cyber Warfare', *The Cipher Brief*, 9 August 2018, https://www.thecipherbrief.com/column_article /historys-lesson-regarding-russian-cyber-warfare (accessed 19 February 2019).

Georgian government's ability to communicate, which, coupled with Russia's air, land and sea operations, degraded Georgia's defences considerably. DDoS attacks against the Georgian government, including the president's website, were well orchestrated. On the day conventional combat began, a website called 'stopgeorgia.ru' went online with a list of sites to attack, instructions on how to do so and post-attack damage assessments. Georgia's internal communications were effectively shut down.

The attackers also wanted to degrade Georgia's ability to rally international support. The Georgian Foreign Ministry released a statement on a replacement built on Google's blog-hosting service, saying that a cyber-warfare campaign by Russia was 'seriously disrupting many Georgian websites, including that of the Ministry of Foreign Affairs'.[176] Attacks targeted Georgian media, communications companies and transport. The National Bank of Georgia website was replaced with pictures of twentieth-century dictators.[177] The BBC noted that the cyber-attacks were 'a virtual echo of battles being fought on the ground by troops and tanks'. Conversely, hackers from Georgia were blamed for targeting the websites of Russian news outlets and the pro-Russian separatist government of South Ossetia.[178]

It was the first time Russia had coordinated more conventional military and cyber-action. Henceforward, cyber-action could be coordinated with physical military action. However, cyber-action alone was more common. In January 2009, as part of an effort to persuade the president of Kyrgyzstan to evict an American military base, Russian hackers shut down two of the country's four internet service providers with a DDoS attack. It worked. Kyrgyzstan removed the military base. Subsequently, Kyrgyzstan received $2 billion in aid and loans from the Kremlin.

Then, in April 2009, when a media outlet in Kazakhstan

---

[176] Swaine, *'Georgia: Russia "Conducting Cyber War"'*.

[177] Hoffman, 'History's Lesson Regarding Russian Cyber Warfare'. Also Neil Arun, 'Caucasus Foes Fight Cyber War', BBC News, 14 August, 2008, http://new s.bbc.co.uk/1/hi/world/europe/7559850.stm (accessed 16 February 2019).

[178] Arun, 'Caucasus Foes Fight Cyber War'.

published a statement by Kazakhstan's president that criticised Russia, a DDoS attack attributed to Russian elements shut down the organisation's website. In August 2009, Russian hackers shut down the social media sites Twitter and Facebook in Georgia to commemorate the first anniversary of the Russian move into South Ossetia.[179] Russian hacking attacks on target states appear to have continued ever since. In May 2014, after the re-annexation of Crimea, Russian hackers attacked the Ukrainian electoral system three days before the presidential election. Even a back-up system was taken down, but Ukrainian computer experts were able to restore the system before election day. Russia's preferred candidate lost.[180]

It was perhaps inevitable that a conflict fired by separatism in the Caucasus should spill into cyberspace. The nexus between state warfare and organised crime, as a characteristic of 'hybrid' or 'non-linear warfare', has already been noted earlier in the essay. By 2007, the time of the Estonian cyber-attack, the former republics of the Soviet Union (along with China and Brazil) were major centres of cyber-crime. Russian cyber-criminals dominated the market in online tools tailored for amateur hackers. Russia's association with cyber-crime dates back to the demise of the Soviet Union, an event that roughly coincided with the dawn of the internet in the early 1990s.

The confluence of Russian cyber-crime and non-linear warfare appears to have been serendipitous. According to the BBC News website's technology correspondent Mark Ward, cited at the time, as communism collapsed in the 1990s, computers had come to symbolise a new spirit of enterprise among young people. Russian society was suddenly, albeit temporarily, freed from close supervision and surveillance. In this uncontrolled space, they picked up expertise, in part, from a brilliant earlier generation of Soviet-era developers. These older programmers, many of whom now found themselves redundant, had devised clever software to get round

---

[179] 'Timeline: Ten Years of Russian Cyber Attacks on Other Nations'.

[180] Ibid. The website includes further details of Russian attacks on Ukraine, Germany, the Netherlands and the United States in 2015–16. Perhaps most notable was the attack on Ukraine in December 2015, just before Christmas, which took down a power station, leaving 235,000 homes without power.

the shortcomings of the cumbersome communist computers they had to use because there were no others. Although Russia's new software and computer hardware engineers had skills and intellects equal to the best in the West, they did not earn nearly as much. So, bored and underpaid, many turned their talents to hacking. Gradually, they attracted new employers from the thriving post-Soviet underworld. As the mobsters harnessed the hackers' skills, the profits from cyber-crime grew. And the hackers had been through a hard school, influenced by backward Soviet-era computing.[181]

Cyber-warfare is therefore a subset of information warfare, and, like many elements of 'non-linear warfare', its sources can be found in other fields. An example is Unit 26165, known in the United States as GRU-85 Main Special Service Center, which is believed to have run the hacking campaign to influence the 2016 US elections. It is also believed to have run the operation broken up by the Dutch security services in April 2018. Unit 26165 is believed to date back to the 1970s and to have originally dealt with cryptography.[182]

Conclusion

Throughout the development of Soviet and Russian strategic thought, numerous tributaries have fed into a widening river, as shown in Figure 5. In the most recent case, thriving cyber-crime and the need for an asymmetric state strategy to counter what is perceived as Western encirclement have merged to give Russian non-linear warfare its modern form.

---

[181] Arun, 'Caucasus Foes Fight Cyber War'. See note 100.
[182] Roland Oliphant, 'What Is Unit 26165, Russia's Elite Military Hacking Centre?', *Daily Telegraph*, 4 October 2018, https://www.telegraph.co.uk/news/2018/10/04/unit26165-russias-elite-military-hacking-centre (accessed 1 March 2019).

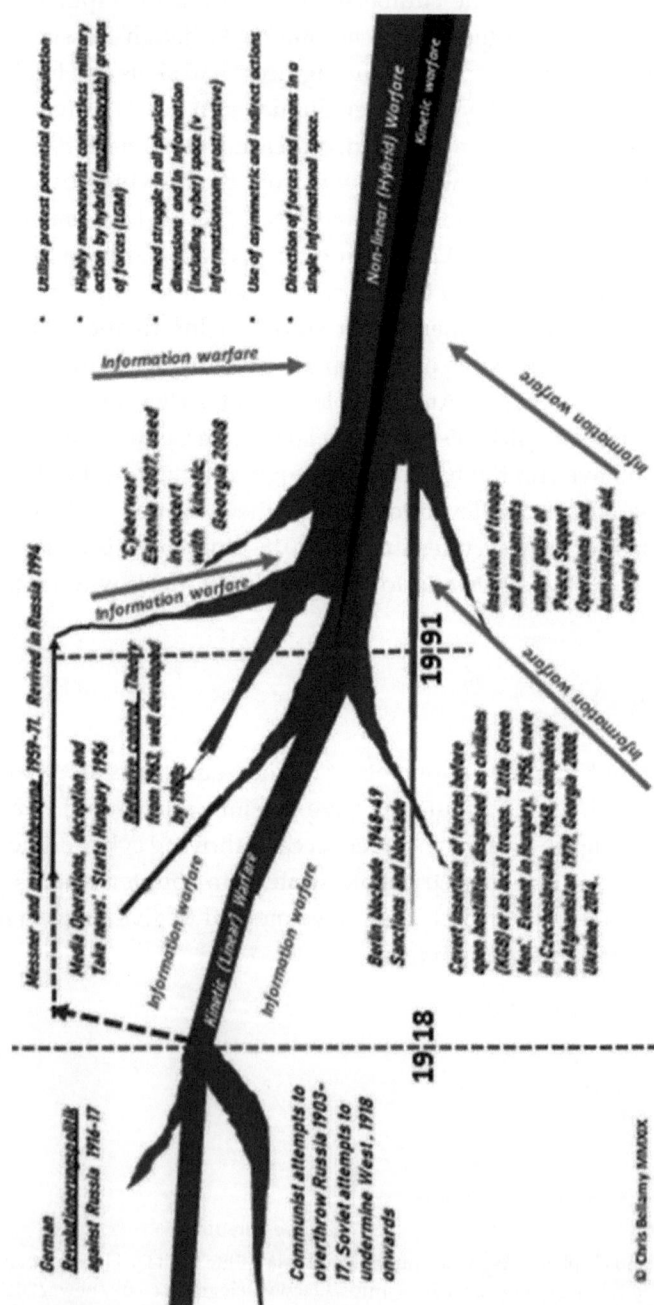

Figure 5 - Evolution of Russian and Soviet non-linear warfare, diagram by author.

The diagram shows the use of Revolutionierungspolitik by the Germans to assist the Bolsheviks in undermining first the tsarist regime and then the Provisional Government, Messner's development of myatezhevoyna in exile in South America and its adoption in Russia from 1994, the Berlin blockade of 1948–9 feeding into the stream, the covert insertion of Soviet troops — Trojan horses, from Hungary through Czechoslovakia and Afghanistan to Georgia and Ukraine — and the first use of 'cyber-war' techniques, alone in Estonia and then in concert with conventional operations the following year. 'Cyber', as noted, is not a separate category in Russia but an element of the wider field of information warfare. It affects every aspect of war and always has. Therefore, it is portrayed as the river basin from which all the tributaries that flow into the modern Russian concept of non-linear war drain. The final and most destructive element of new-type warfare, kinetic military operations, flows as a deep current, the ultimate resort, below a much wider surface.

Returning to recent times, Surkov's strategy of spreading uncertainty and 'fake news' — the oldest part of strategy — deception — clearly works. Undermining a population's confidence in its own government, and even its own political system, is very effective, as we have seen from the previous Russian attacks on Afghanistan and Czechoslovakia. But it takes a lot of work and a long time. However, that may be the strategy behind the latest component of 'hybrid' or 'non-linear' war. Without wishing to strike at anyone's confidence, it seems we may be undermined by a conspiracy, to which our dependence on the internet makes us more vulnerable. Our access to the truth is compromised. The conventional battlefield, while still relevant, and maybe still the ultimate test of nations' resolution, is less relevant and certainly less dominant than it was.

In this author's view, there is nothing new or revolutionary about the thinking and the strategy of any of the above. The means have changed, and they have certainly widened in their scope. Perhaps the only recent addition to the 'hybrid war' spectrum is that of the criminal element. But, then again, is that new? We have witnessed state armed forces fighting criminals in South America,

Africa and, perhaps most notably, against pirates at sea, for centuries. Indeed, the United States used the Italian-based Sicilian mafia in its campaign to invade Sicily and Italy in 1943.[183]

'Hybrid' or 'non-linear' warfare is not new and melds with the long-established pattern of what Kipling memorably and vividly described in 1899 as the 'savage wars of peace'.[184] Non-linear warfare, as Surkov calls it, was the very opposite of the 'black and white, two-dimensional world' his brain-damaged victim inhabits.[185] That would be a clear-cut world of 'war' and 'peace'. Instead, it is a multi-dimensional world full of shades of grey. To update Kipling: The shadow wars of peace.

It is clear from this study, and particularly from Figure 6, that what was hailed as 'Russia's new art of war'*[186] in 2014 was nothing of the sort. It was neither 'new' — this research has traced numerous precedents — nor was it peculiarly Russian.

There is an important lesson here. In 1953, Cyril Falls, the just-retired Chichele Professor of the History of War at Oxford University, warned that 'the student should not believe everything moves only when he sees the process at a glance, and stands still when he does not see it moving. It is his eyes which are at fault.'[187] He continued: 'It is a fallacy, due to ignorance of technical and tactical military history, to suppose that methods of warfare have not made

---

[183] See Tim Newark, *Mafia Allies: The True Story of America's Secret Alliance with the Mob in World War II* (Saint Paul, MN: Zenith Press, 2007); and Selwyn Raab, *Five Families: The Rise, Decline, and Resurgence of America's Most Powerful Mafia Empires* (New York: Thomas Dunne, 2005).

[184] Rudyard Kipling, 'The White Man's Burden', *McClure's Magazine* 12, no. 4 (February 1899), verse 3. 'Take up the White Man's Burden — The Savage Wars of Peace. Fill full the mouth of Famine, And bid the sickness cease ...' Alastair Horne, *A Savage War of Peace: Algeria 1954–1962* (New York: New York Review of Books, 2006 [1977]); Max Boot, *The Savage Wars of Peace: Small Wars and the Rise of American Power* (New York: Basic Books, 2014 [2002]).

[185] Surkov (Dubovitsky), *Without Sky*, p. 4.

[186] Sam Jones, 'Ukraine: Russia's New Art of War; Nato Has Struggled to Counter Moscow's Tactics in Conflict Where Traditional Might Is Only a Part', *Financial Times*, 28 August 2014,http://www.ft.com/cms/s/2/ea5e82fa-2e0c-11e4-b760-00144feabdc0.html#axzz3ID2mwpHQ (accessed 12 September 2022).

[187] Cyril Falls, *A Hundred Years of War, 1850–1950* (London: Gerald Duckworth, 1953), pp. 12–13.

continuous and, on the whole, fairly even progress.'[188] This study has shown Falls' warning to be valid. Russian understanding and implementation of non-linear warfare have evolved continuously since the First World War, and some elements—the Trojan horse of 'little green men'—go back to antiquity. What we have seen recently is an erosion of the once-clear distinction between 'war' and 'peace'. Russia sees itself as surrounded and under threat and is using every means available short of a shooting war with the West to counter that. As Robert Johnson observed: '[T]he antidotes to "hybridity" lie not in the operational or tactical sphere but in the strategic and political domains.'[189]

---

[188] Ibid., p. 13.

[189] Robert Johnson, 'Hybrid War and Its Countermeasures: A Critique of the Literature', *Small Wars and Insurgencies* 29, no. 1 (2018), pp. 141–63, http://tandfonline.com/doi/abs/10.1080/09592318.2018.1404770 (accessed 12 September 2022). The quotation is in the abstract.

4. 'NO PLAN SURVIVES CONTACT WITH THE ENEMY'

Chris Bellamy

This essay is about the military conduct of Russia's 'special military operation' from 24 February 2022 to 24 February 2023, and how it relates to the doctrine set out in the previous essay. Given the enormous intellectual capital invested by the Soviet Union and the new Russia in the study of warfare, and especially non-linear warfare, Russia's failure to achieve its objectives in the first year since 24 February 2022 is, at best, embarrassing and represents an extraordinary failure.[1] No-one can predict how this terrible and unnecessary war will end. For all the high-level education of Russian commanders and for all the advanced technology at their disposal, Russian forces have performed appallingly, not only committing atrocities but making basic military mistakes. To correct those mistakes, generals have gone far forward, and the Russians have lost many. As of 11 July 2022, the Russians had confirmed four generals dead, with Ukraine claiming another four. Three other alleged deaths among starred officers had been refuted.[2]

The essay title is a summary of the 1871 statement by Helmuth von Moltke the Elder (1800-1891), that

> [n]o plan of operations extends with any certainty beyond the first

---

[1] The chapter title quotation has been widely attributed and was obviously used in various forms by later generals, but Moltke (1800–91) was the originator. *Moltkes Militärische Werke: II. Die Thätigkeit als Chef des Generalstabes der Armee im Frieden* (Moltke's military works: II. Activity as chief of the army general staff in peacetime) *Zweiter Theil* (Second part), *Aufsatz vom Jahre 1871 Ueber Strategie* (Article from 1871 on strategy) (Berlin: Ernst Siegfried Mittler und Sohn, 1900), 287, quote at 291.

[2] See James Beardsworth, 'High Death Toll of Russian Generals in Ukraine a Blow to Military Capability', Moscow Times, 6 May 2022; Julian E. Barnes, Helene Cooper and Eric Schmitt, 'U.S. Intelligence Is Helping Ukraine Kill Russian Generals, Officials Say', *The New York Times*, 4 May 2022.

> encounter with the main enemy forces. Only the layman believes that in the course of a campaign he sees the consistent implementation of an original thought that has been considered in advance in every detail and retained to the end.³ [Author bold]

As paraphrased by Mike Tyson in 1987, then world champion boxer, "Everybody has plans until they get hit for the first time."⁴

In the last essay, we saw that the Russian playbook was set out by Chief of the General Staff Valeriy Gerasimov in two articles in 2013, the year before the successful invasion and annexation of Crimea and Russian reinforcement of breakaway separatists, mainly in the eastern oblasti (provinces) of Donetsk and Luhansk—the so-called Donbas (see Figure 1). In the overall scheme of things, the latter are quite small. With 2022 hindsight, Vladimir Putin's strategy of destroying Ukraine or ensuring that it was compliant makes complete sense. While many have suggested that President Putin - 'mad Vlad'- is insane, given his eccentric appraisal of world history, however, his actions are, to some extent, understandable given his Weltanschauung. Indeed, for all his faults, he may represent the 'rational actor' side of international relations theory.⁵

---

3 *Kein Operationsplan reicht mit einiger Sicherheit über das erste Zusammentreffen mit der feindlichen Hauptmacht hinaus. Nur der Laie glaubt in dem Verlauf eines Feldzuges die konsequente Durchführung eines im voraus gefaßten in allen Einzelheiten überlegten und bis ans Ende festgehaltenen, ursprünglichen Gedankens zu erblicken.* See note 1. The quotation has been widely attributed and was obviously used in various forms by later generals, but Moltke (1800–91) was the originator. *Moltkes Militärische Werke: II. Die Thätigkeit als Chef des Generalstabes der Armee im Frieden* (Moltke's military works: II. Activity as chief of the army general staff in peacetime) *Zweiter Theil* (Second part), *Aufsatz vom Jahre 1871 Ueber Strategie* (Article from 1871 on strategy) (Berlin: Ernst Siegfried Mittler und Sohn, 1900), 287, quote at 291.

4 "1987 August 19, Oroville Mercury-Register, Biggs has plans for Tyson (Associated Press), Quote Page 1B, Column 2, Oroville, California. (Newspapers_com)", via 'Everybody Has Plans Until They Get Hit for the First Time—Quote Investigator®', 25 August 2021, https://quoteinvestigator.com/2021/08/25/plans-hit/.

5 Alex Mintz and Karl DeRouen Jr, '4: The Rational Actor Model', in Alex Mintz and Karl DeRouen Jr, *Understanding Foreign Policy Decision Making* (Cambridge: Cambridge University Press, 2012).

The build-up to war: First encircle

The 2014 occupation and annexation of Crimea were the first stage of an incremental build- up to achieve regime change in Ukraine and to turn it back towards Russia. Putin had a useful ally in President Alexander Lukashenko of Belarus. Following the dissolution of the Soviet Union, Belarus declared independence on 25 August 1991. After a new constitution was adopted in 1994, Lukashenko was elected president, a position he has held ever since and is now in his sixth term. Only this first election is judged to have been free and fair. Lukashenko heads an authoritarian government with a poor human rights record. In 2000, the year Putin became president of Russia, Belarus and Russia formed the Union State, which still has only two members. Although there is no common currency, Belarus is effectively part of Russia in all but name. On 10 February 2009, Russia and Belarus implemented the first stage of joint military officer training programmes designed to integrate the military structures of the countries. This military collective is called the Regional Forces Group of Belarus and Russia. The goal of these operations is to ensure cohesive training, practice and implementation of military interests for the nations and were aimed at strategic and battle training taking place in February and March 2009. Furthermore, the military doctrine of the Russian Federation provides that an armed attack on the state-participant in the Union State, as well as all other actions involving the use of military force against it, should be deemed an act of aggression against the Union State, authorising Moscow to take measures in response. A two-state mirror image of NATO's Article 5.

Exercise Zapad (West) 2021 is of particular interest as it focused more than ever on integrating Belarusian forces into the Russian chain of command and also because of the exercise scenario. It has been the subject of an excellent report by the American Institute for the Study of War (ISW).[6] The Russian and Belarusian Armed

---

[6] Mason Clark and George Barros, 'Russia's Zapad-2021 Exercise', Institute for the Study of War, 17 September 2021, https://www.understandingwar.org/backgrounder/russia's-zapad-2021-exercise (accessed 13 September 2022).

Forces conducted the active phase of the Zapad 2021 large-scale annual military exercise from 10 to 16 September. The Russian Armed Forces conduct strategic exercises each year in one of Russia's four military districts (Western, Southern, Central and Eastern) on a rotating basis. The Western Military District hosted that year's exercises, dubbed Zapad 2021. The Russian Armed Forces conduct these rotating annual exercises to test the capabilities of each military district, experiment with force structure and operational concepts, and refine campaign planning. Each of these annual exercises features an active phase, a week-long scenario simulating major combat operations. The active phase is preceded by months of deployments and exercises preparing each participating unit for its role.[7]

The Zapad 2021 exercise involved ground, air, naval, air defence, engineering, logistics and chemical, biological, radiological and nuclear defence units in the Western Military District, Baltic Sea and Arctic Sea. These 'capstone' exercises are in many respects highly formalised and pre-planned actions rather than snap readiness checks or stress tests. Zapad 2021 was additionally a multinational undertaking. Many of the exercises occurred in Belarus, and forces from India, Pakistan, Mongolia, Kazakhstan, Kyrgyzstan, Armenia and Sri Lanka participated in exercises at the Mulino training ground near Moscow.

The Kremlin clearly focused Zapad 2021 on advancing efforts to integrate the Belarusian military into Russian-led structures and framed the exercise as a joint effort, unlike previous Russian capstone exercises. The Russian military formally designated Zapad 2021 a joint strategic exercise with Belarus, rather than the typical unilateral strategic command-staff exercise. Russia's annual exercises usually include several international participants supporting Russian forces but have never been designated fully joint exercises. The Kremlin made use of Zapad 2021 to further integrate Belarusian forces into Russian-led structures and deploy Russian forces into Belarus on a likely permanent basis, as ISW had previously forecasted. Russia deployed S-300 air defence systems and Su-30

---

[7] Ibid.

fighters to bases in Western Belarus in early September to support permanent joint training centres. ISW reported that additional Russian forces, including ground forces, might remain in Belarus following Zapad 2021, a forecast that proved horribly correct.[8]

The active phase of Zapad 2021 from 10 to 16 September simulated a Russian and Belarusian response to a hypothetical NATO invasion of Belarus. The Belarusian Ministry of Defence published the fictional scenario on 5 August. In the scenario, a Western coalition elects to use force to destabilise Belarus after failing to do so through non-military means—referencing repeated Belarusian and Russian claims that protests against Lukashenko since August 2020 were backed by NATO. The first phase of the exercise from 10 to 12 September simulated an offensive by the fictional states Nyaris, Pomoria and the Polar Republic (likely representing the Baltic States, Poland and a Scandinavian state, respectively) seizing territory in Western Belarus and attacking Russian naval assets. This first phase tested Russia's ability to mobilise and deploy reserves to the frontlines, counter the strategic NATO air attack that Russia expected to occur at the beginning of a European war, and begin localised counterattacks. The second phase, from 13 to 16 September, simulated a counterattack to retake Western Belarus, testing the Russian Armed Forces' ability to coordinate and conduct large-scale conventional operations. Russian, Belarusian and other international forces conducted dozens of component exercises at training grounds in Russia and Belarus as part of this active phase. Zapad 2021 was obviously the first dress rehearsal for the invasion of Ukraine five months later.

A further unambiguous indication of Russian intent came in January, when the Russians announced exercise 'Soyuznaya reshimost'' (Allied Resolve) to take place from 10 to 20 February 2022.[9] Roger McDermott of the Jamestown Foundation in Washington, DC correctly said that the unprecedented build-up to Ukraine's

---

[8] Ibid.

[9] Roger McDermott, 'Russia's Military Exercise in Belarus Prepares for War', Jamestown Foundation, Washington, DC, Euromaidan Press, 27 January 2022, https://euromaidanpress.com/2022/01/27/russias-military-exercise-in-belarus-prepares-for-war (accessed 13 September 2022).

borders effectively developed into the encirclement of Ukraine and sent a strategic message to NATO to stay out of the coming conflict. He noted, ominously, that the forces deployed were bigger than in Zapad 2021 and that the exercise areas were closer to the borders with Poland and Ukraine than those used in Zapad 2021.[10] The second dress rehearsal merged imperceptibly into the first performance.

Since 2000, Putin has stealthily courted his Belarusian ally — the two countries were effectively united. The right flank of the assault on Ukraine was secured. But the left flank was less developed and needed more investment. The seizure of Crimea by the beginning of March 2014 had, it must be said, been a masterpiece for what this author will call the Gerasimov doctrine — regardless of the ink that has been spilled on its 'doctrine' credentials.

The Russian seizure of Crimea must be a feather in Gerasimov's very large peaked cap. The compliance of the predominantly Russian-speaking population, the invisible or, at least, unattributable insertion of the 'little green people', the speed with which it was accomplished and the relative quiescence of the Ukrainian and Western governments and commentators — including me, at the time, I confess — all made it look like an irreversible fait accompli. However, the Russian involvement in the separatist movements in Donetsk and Luhansk was more complex. That included the incompetent shooting down of Malaysian Airlines Flight 17 over a pro-Russian rebel-held area on 17 July 2014 by a missile of Russian origin. Had whoever fired it used a smartphone, he or she would have been able to see that it was a civilian aircraft with flight number MH17/MAS17 en route from Amsterdam to Kuala Lumpur. At the time, I thought that if the Russians had just stuck to Crimea, they might have got away with it.

As noted in the previous essay, Crimea was an icon for Russia, but it was awkwardly dependent on Ukraine. The first issue was water. Following Russia's annexation of Crimea in 2014, Ukraine's first step was to cut off the water supply. This had profound

---

10   Ibid.

consequences for people and agriculture.[11] Some 85 per cent of Crimea's fresh water came from mainland Ukraine. Besides water, Ukraine also cut vital transportation links as Russia had no overland access to or from Crimea. There was only the ferry across the Kerch Strait (see Figure 1), which had limited capacity and was often halted by bad weather. Practical need and symbolism combined to resuscitate a project that had been on the cards since 1903: a great bridge linking mainland Russia with the re-annexed Crimean Peninsula. The longest bridge ever built in or by Russia and the longest bridge in Europe.

As a measure of the bridge's enormous importance, as an achievement and logistically, and also its symbolic significance as the first overland link between mainland Russia and the Crimean Peninsula, its security was assigned to the Kerch' Brigade of the Russian Guard (Rosgvardiya), Putin's personal Presidential bodyguard.[12] On Saturday 8 October 2022, as we shall see below, it became clear that they had not done their job.

---

[11] https://www.eurasiareview.com/author/geopolitical-monitor, 'The Water Crisis in Crimea – Analysis', Eurasia Review, 16 April 2020, https://www.eurasiareview.com/16042020-the-water-crisis-in-crimea-analysis/.

[12] 'Question of the Day: How Reliably Is the Crimean Bridge Protected from Possible Attacks by Ukraine? – We Are Covering the Agenda for You | Novye Izvestia', accessed 10 October 2022, https://en.newizv.ru/news/2021-09-13/q uestion-of-the-day-how-reliably-is-the-crimean-bridge-protected-from-possibl e-attacks-by-ukraine-389401.

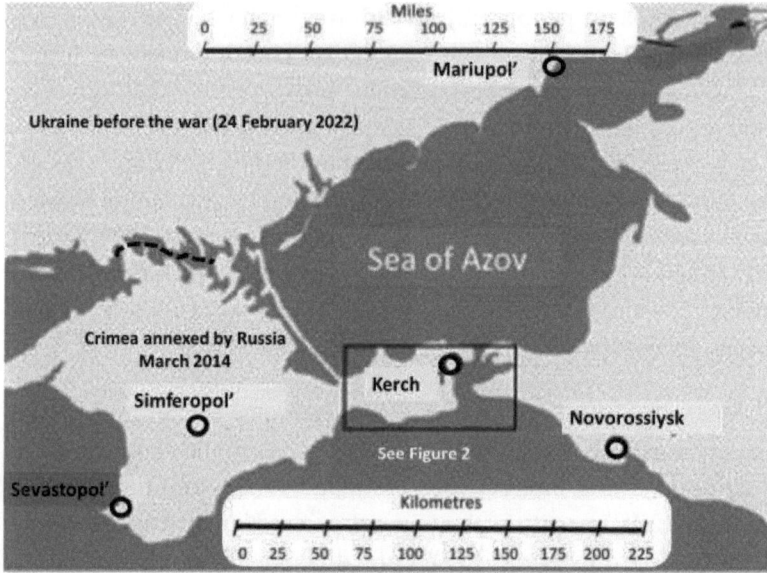

Figure 1. - Encircling Ukraine to the south. The Kerch' Strait and bridge - location. Modified by author from d-maps.com.[13]

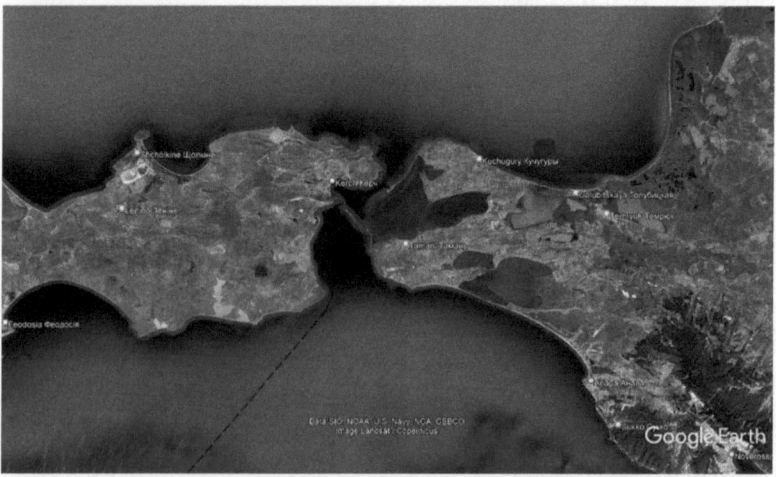

Figure 2. - Focus on the Kerch Strait. Source Google Earth redrawn by author. Low resolution image used.

---

[13] Unless stated otherwise, author maps are modified from maps of Ukraine available at https://d-maps.com/pays.php?num_pay=227&lang=en&num_pag=1, copyright of original maps is https://d-maps.com, see 'Terms and Conditions of Use', accessed 10 August 2023, https://d-maps.com/conditions.php?lang=en.

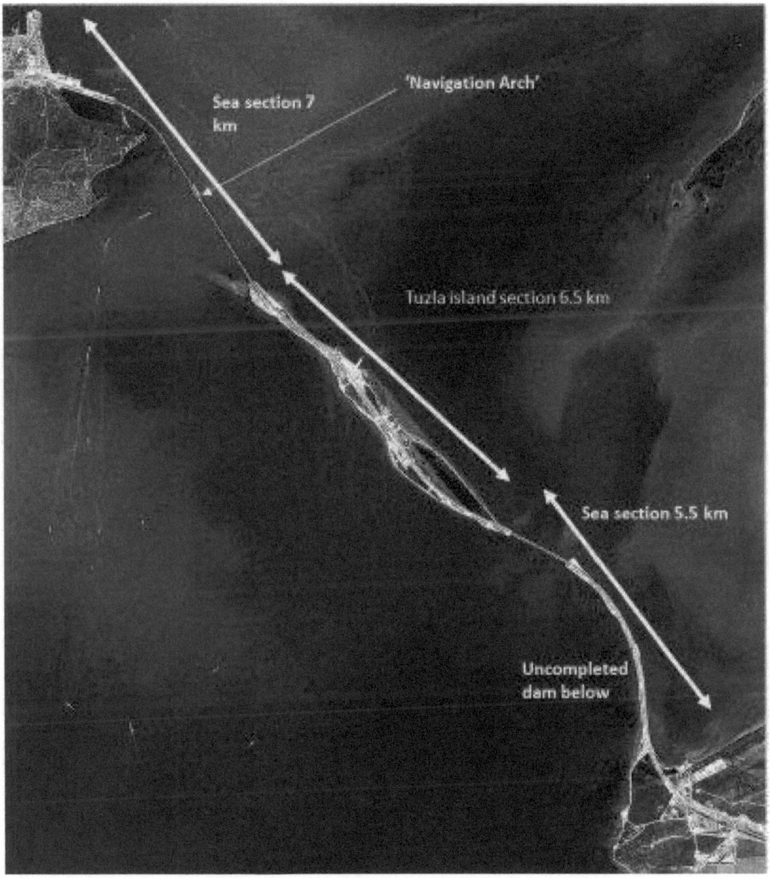

Figure 3. - Focus on the Kerch Strait. Source Google Earth amended by author. Originally 'Opening of the Crimean Bridge', Russian Geographical Society, 15 May 2018, https://www.rgo.ru/en/article/opening-crimean-bridge. Image has been previously deleted and reinstated by RGS so link is unstable. Cached on Google - http://webcache.googleusercontent.com/search?q=cache:https://www.rgo.ru/en/article/opening-crimean-bridge.

Figure 4. - The Crimean (Kerch') bridge. Central section to allow ships to pass, known as the 'navigation arch', 2018. During the November 2018 Kerch Strait incident, the Russians blocked it with a large merchant ship, to show how easily they could stop them passing. Росавтодор, *Русский: Крымский мостEnglish: Crimean Bridge*, 13 September 2019, http://rosavtodor.ru/about/upravlenie-fda/upravlenie-stroitelstva-i-ekspluatatsii-avtomobilnykh-dorog/transportnyy-perekhod-cherez-kerchenskiy-proliv/novosti/301381. Creative Commons License 4.0. Rosavtodor.ru

The opening of this bridge had been awaited for more than a century. The first plan to connect the Crimea and the Kuban was approved as far back as 1903 by the last Romanov tsar, Nicholas II. By 1910, all project documentation was ready and estimates had been drawn up, but the First World War prevented the ambitious project from going ahead[14] (rgo.ru 2018). After the German invasion of the Soviet Union in 1941, the German construction group Organisation Todt built a ropeway over the strait. Finished in June 1943, it had daily capacity of 1,000 tons. Construction of a combined road and railway bridge started in April 1943, but before it was finished, the Germans were in retreat, so they blew up the already completed parts of the bridge and destroyed the ropeway.

In 1944, the advancing Red Army constructed a 4.5-kilometre

---

[14] Ibid.

(2.8-mile, 2.43-nautical mile) bridge across the strait. This bridge, not designed to be permanent, was destroyed by floating ice in February 1945. The idea of repairing it was quickly dismissed, and the remains of the destroyed bridge were dismantled, with permanent bridge designs envisaged instead, the first of which surfaced in 1949.

In 2010, President Viktor Yanukovych of Ukraine and President Dmitry Medvedev of Russia signed an agreement to build a bridge across the Kerch Strait. Russia and Ukraine signed a memorandum of mutual understanding on the construction of the bridge on 26 November 2010. An agreement between Ukraine and the EU was shelved in November 2013, which led to greater cooperation between Ukraine and Russia and resulted in an agreement on the construction of that bridge forming part of the 17 December 2013 Ukrainian–Russian action plan. A joint Ukrainian–Russian company would handle the construction of the bridge.

The Russian annexation of Crimea and the collapse of relations between the two countries abruptly ended the bilateral Kerch Bridge agreement. President Putin announced that Russia would build a road–rail bridge over the strait on 19 March 2014, just one day after Russia officially claimed Crimea. In January 2015, the contract for the bridge's construction was awarded to the SGM (Stroygazmontazh) Group, whose owner, Arkady Rotenberg, reported to be a close friend of Putin, was internationally sanctioned in response to the Russian military's involvement in Ukraine. SGM, as its name implied, typically constructed pipelines, and had no experience building bridges, according to BBC News.[15]

Since April 2014, the Ukrainian government had actively condemned Russian construction of the bridge as illegal because it stood by its ownership of the Crimean Peninsula and has called on Russia to demolish 'those parts of that structure located within temporarily occupied Ukrainian territory'.[16] The United States and the

---

[15] 'Ukraine Conflict: Putin Ally to Build Bridge to Crimea', BBC News, 30 January 2015, https://www.bbc.co.uk/news/world-europe-31067977 (accessed 13 September 2022).

[16] 'Киев считает противоправным введение РФ запрета на судоходство через Керченский пролив' (Kyiv deems Russian restrictions on shipping in the

European Union introduced sanctions against companies involved in the construction, and from December 2018 the United Nations General Assembly repeatedly condemned the construction and opening of the bridge as 'facilitating the further militarization of Crimea'[17] and 'restricting the size of ships that can reach the Ukrainian ports on the Azov coast'.[18] Russia, inevitably, said it would not ask for anybody's permission to build transport infrastructure 'for the sake of the population of Russian regions'.[19]

Construction of the bridge began in February 2016. The bridge was christened the Crimean Bridge after an online vote in December 2017, while Kerch Bridge and Reunification Bridge were the second and third most popular choices, respectively. Putin inaugurated the road bridge on 15 May 2018; it opened for cars on 16 May and for trucks on 1 October. The rail bridge was inaugurated on 23 December 2019, and the first scheduled passenger train crossed on 25 December 2019. The bridge was opened for freight trains on 30 June 2020. A record amount of traffic was recorded on 15 August 2020, totalling 36,393 cars (avtomobiley). This appears to refer solely to motor cars, in which case we need to add a daily average of 200 buses and 2,000 trucks.[20]

Kerch Strait illegal), Interfax-Ukraine [in Russian], 11 August 2017, https://interfax.com.ua/news/general/441850.html (accessed 28 November 2019).

[17] UNGS 73/194 2019, 'United Nations General Assembly Resolution 73/194 "Problem of the Militarization of the Autonomous Republic of Crimea and the City of Sevastopol, Ukraine, as well as Parts of the Black Sea and the Sea of Azov"', United Nations Documents, 23 January 2019, https://documents-dds-ny.un.org/doc/UNDOC/GEN/N18/451/02/PDF/N1845102.pdf?OpenElement (accessed 13 September 2022).

[18] UNGS 74/17 2019, 'United Nations General Assembly Resolution 74/17 "Problem of the Militarization of the Autonomous Republic of Crimea and the City of Sevastopol, Ukraine, as well as Parts of the Black Sea and the Sea of Azov"', United Nations Documents, 13 December 2019, https://documents-dds-ny.un.org/doc/UNDOC/GEN/N19/400/94/PDF/N1940094.pdf?OpenElement (accessed 13 September 2022).

[19] 'Russia Defends Opening of Crimea Bridge against U.S. Criticism', The Moscow Times, 16 May 2018, https://www.themoscowtimes.com/2018/05/16/russia-defends-opening-crimea-bridge-against-us-criticism-a61465 (accessed 14 July 2022).

[20] 'On the Crimean Bridge a New Road Traffic Daily Record Has Been Established: Nearly 35,400 Cars Passed across the Bridge', TASS, 6 August 2020, https://tass.ru/obschestvo/9212191?utm_source=en.wikipedia.org&utm_me

Following the Russian invasion of more of Ukraine on 24 February 2022, Ukrainian plans and calls for the bridge's destruction spiralled. It was a key strategic target, and the Russians knew it. As soon as the bridge had opened for road traffic in 2018 and before the rail bridge opened at the end of 2019. The Russian commentator Viktor Zolotov, speaking to the Moscow newspaper Novye Izvestiya on 13 September 2021, underlined its importance and obvious potential vulnerability as a key target.[21]

On Saturday 8 October 2022, that very lucrative and high priority target status was demonstrated. Spectacularly. At 06:07 hours local time (three hours ahead of GMT), the day after Putin's 70th birthday, a massive explosion and fire hit the bridge's north-western section almost exactly half way between the north-west end of the Tuzla Island section and the elevated 'navigation arch' section (see figures 4, 5 and 6). The Russians almost immediately blamed a terrorist truck bomb attack, which had somehow also ignited some fuel tankers on a train standing on the parallel rail link, lying to the south of the motorway (see the two graphics in Figures 5 and 6).[22]

---

dium=referral&utm_campaign=en.wikipedia.org&utm_referrer=en.wikipedia.org (accessed 13 September 2022).

[21] Sergey Kron, 'Question of the Day: How Reliably Is the Crimean Bridge Protected from Possible Attacks by Ukraine?', *Novye Izvestiya*, 13 September 2021, http s://en.newizv.ru/news/army/13-09-2021/question-of-the-day-how-reliably-is-the-crimean-bridge-protected-from-possible-attacks-by-ukraine (accessed 13 September 2022).

[22] 'Video Shows Mystery "wave" under Crimea Bridge Just before Explosion That Threatens Putin's Plans | Daily Mail Online', accessed 7 August 2023, https://www.dailymail.co.uk/news/breaking_news/article-11293851/Massive-explosion-destroys-key-bridge-linking-Crimea-Putins-Russia.html.

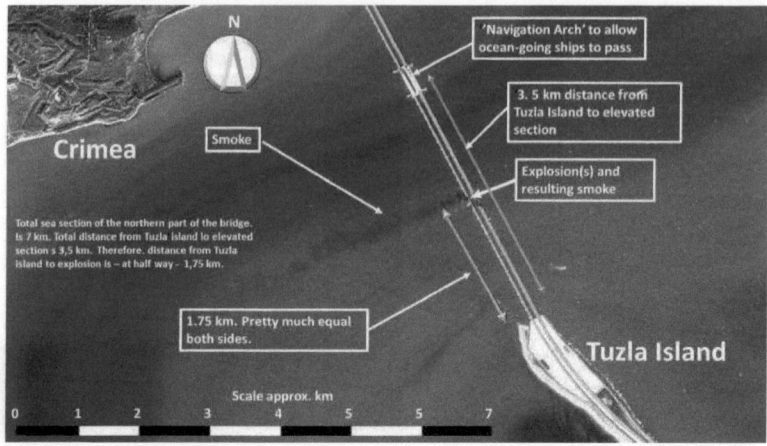

Figure 5. - The attack on the Crimean Bridge 8 October 2022. Image viaPlanet [@planet], Tweet, *Twitter*, 8 October 2022, https://twitter.com/planet/status/1578783614221058048. Accessed 15 October 2022. Low resolution image used. No rights assumed. Author annotation.

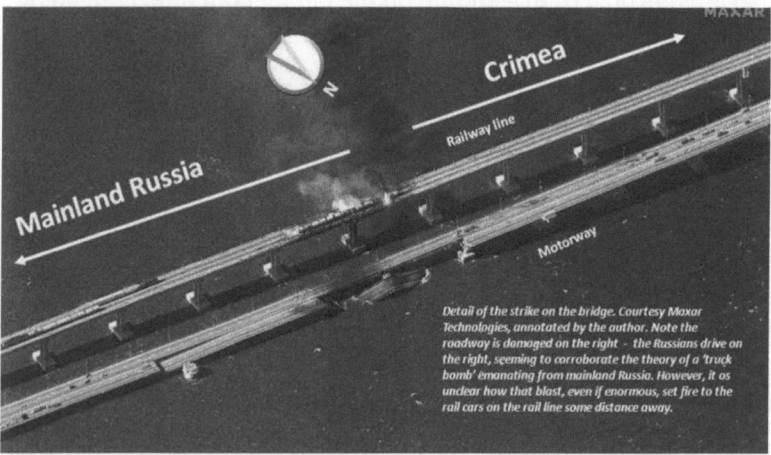

Figure 6 - Detail of the 8 October 2022 attack on the bridge, Image via Maxar Technologies, Maxar Technologies, Tweet, *Twitter*, 8 October 2022, accessed 20 October 2022, https://twitter.com/Maxar/status/1578853400195629056. Low resolution image used. No rights assumed. Author annotation.

Russia was quick to suggest this was a truck bomb, but did not say who orchestrated it. Putin accused Ukraine of attacking the bridge in an 'act of terrorism'. According to the BBC, security camera footage released on social media showed a truck - allegedly from the Russian city of Krasnodar, an hour's drive from the crossing - moving west across the bridge at the time of the explosion. Russian officials named a 25-year old Krasnodar man, Samir Yusubov, as the owner of the truck, and said an older relative, Makhir Yusubov, was the driver.

However, according to the BBC, close examination of the footage seems to show that the truck had nothing to do with the explosion. The footage shows a huge fireball erupting just behind - and to one side - of the truck as it begins to climb an elevated section of the bridge.[23]

The BBC correspondent in Kyiv thought the speed with which the truck bomb theory started to spread in Russian circles was suspicious. It suggested the Kremlin preferred an act of terrorism to a more alarming possibility: that this was an audacious act of sabotage carried out by Ukraine. In my view, blaming some dissident movement emanating from southern Russia (Krasnodar) and thereby undermining potential dissidents could well be preferable to admitting a very successful special forces strike on a Russian prestige target. At the time this book goes to press we cannot anticipate the verdict.

The BBC interviewed a former British Army explosives expert. Speaking on condition of anonymity, he said 'I've seen plenty of large vehicle-borne IEDs [improvised explosive devices] in my time. This does not look like one.' A more plausible explanation, he said, is a massive explosion below the bridge - probably delivered using some kind of clandestine maritime drone. 'Bridges are generally designed to resist downwards loads on the deck and a certain amount of side loading from the wind. They are not generally engineered to resist upward loads. I think this fact was exploited in the Ukrainian attack.'[24]

The BBC report showed a twenty second clip from a security camera. Four to five seconds in a large white truck passes over as something that looks like the bow wave of a small boat appears next

---

[23]   Adams, Ibid.
[24]   Ibid

to one of the bridge supports. At six seconds the screen goes blank, and then the picture shows a huge orange and yellow explosion.

Evidence of the existence of Uncrewed Underwater and Surface Vehicles (UUVs and USVs), known as 'drone boats', had emerged in September. On 21 September images on Russian social media showed a black uncrewed USV the size of a large kayak that had washed up near Sevastopol. The Russians examined it and then towed it out to sea and blew it up. The British explosives expert told the BBC that the Ukrainians had been developing the concept for using such remotely controlled or maybe autonomous vessels for years. If that was how Ukraine managed to attack the Kerch Bridge, hundreds of miles from Ukrainian-controlled territory, then it was one of Kyiv's most ambitious operations so far. However, the BBC report added that 'apart from a few whispers in the capital, no-one is confirming the theory. [25]

However, the Ukrainians supported the Russian explanation that that the explosion was started by a truck bomb and said that the explanation should be sought in Russia. In spite of that, and the initial report tracing the truck's origins to Krasnodar, Putin blamed the Ukrainians for 'terrorism', and the following day launched a series of missile and drone attacks in revenge for the cutting of the great Crimean bridge.[26] The attack on the bridge and Russian revenge could well be the beginning of a further bloody escalation.

The naval build-up

We now need to return to 2014 and developments in the Black Sea. While the Russians were exercising in Belarus, deployments that were expected to remain, and were building up on their own border with Ukraine, they were also reinforcing another key theatre: the Black Sea. In 2014, the Black Sea Fleet was ageing and weak, but by 2021 it could fire cruise missiles at Kyiv.[27] After the 2014 annexation

---

[25] Ibid
[26] Ibid
[27] David Axe, 'In 2014, Russia's Black Sea Fleet Was Aging and Weak: Today, It Can Fire Cruise Missiles at Kiev', Forbes, 21 December 2021, https://www.forb

of Crimea, the composition of the fleet shifted to focus on the improved Kilo-class submarines (Naval Technology 2020), and especially the improved SSK Kilo class (Type 636. 3).[28] The Russian Navy had also moved forward in the late 2010s with the construction of Project 636.3, an improved version of the Kilo class. By November 2019, six units had been built for the Black Sea Fleet and further boats were planned for the Pacific and Baltic Fleets. The improved 636,3 Kilo, nicknamed 'Varshavnika' – 'Warsaw Lady' – make of that what you will – has many qualities that make it ideal for operating in relatively shallow and littoral waters. The Type 636 submarine is considered to be one of the quietest diesel–electric submarines in the world. It is capable of detecting an enemy submarine at a range three to four times greater than that at which it can be detected itself. With a displacement of 2,325 tons surfaced and 3,075 tons submerged or 3,100 tons for the improved Kilo, it can dive to 300 metres. It can travel at 17 knots surfaced and 20 knots underwater. It has six 533mm (21-inch) torpedo tubes, and its standard armament is eighteen torpedoes and four Kalibr land-attack cruise missiles, plus twenty-four mines. However, as the Kalibr missiles are fired from the torpedo tubes, it might presumably be possible to dispense with the torpedoes and carry more missiles.

The replacement of the Black Sea Fleet's Soviet-era missile boats and corvettes with vessels of more modern design has also been a priority since 2010. A similar modernisation also took place in the Baltic Fleet and the Caspian Sea Flotilla. Utilising Russia's internal waterways provides the Russian Navy with the capacity to transfer both corvettes and other light units, such as landing craft, among its three western fleets and the Caspian Flotilla as may be required. It might even be feasible for the Russian Navy to move its Kilo-class submarines between the Black Sea and the Baltic via the internal waterways.

    es.com/sites/davidaxe/2021/12/21/in-2014-russias-black-sea-fleet-was-agin g-and-weak-today-it-can-fire-cruise-missiles-at-kiev/?sh=1a0e5d01766c (accessed 13 September 2022).

28 'SSK Kilo Class (Type 636) - Naval Technology', accessed 7 August 2023, https://www.naval-technology.com/projects/kilo/.

After the annexation of Crimea, the first major maritime incidents between Russia and Ukraine were in 2018. On 21 September 2018, a Russian Su-27 fighter, from Russian-occupied Crimea, created an air emergency, coming dangerously close to a Ukrainian Navy An-26 military transport aircraft, which was executing a scheduled task above the Black Sea. On 25 September 2018 during the Volia 2018 Ukrainian strategic command and staff exercises, Russian Su-27 fighter jets flew dangerously close to Ukrainian warships.

The big incident—the 'Kerch Strait incident'—occurred in November. On 25 November 2018, three Ukrainian Navy vessels that were attempting to redeploy from the Black Sea port of Odesa to Berdyansk on the Sea of Azov were damaged and captured by the Russian FSB security service.

On the morning of 25 November, three Ukrainian naval vessels, two lightly armoured gunboats and a tug, approached the Kerch Strait (see above). The Russians accused the Ukrainian ships of illegally entering Russian territorial waters and ordered them to leave. The Ukrainians refused, citing the 2003 Russia–Ukraine treaty on freedom of navigation in the area. The Russians attempted to intercept them and rammed the tugboat Yany Kapu several times. When they tried to ram the more agile gunboats, two Russian ships collided, and a Russian Coast Guard patrol boat Izumrud was damaged. The Ukrainian naval vessels then continued their journey, stopping near the anchorage 471 waiting zone, about 14 kilometres (7.5 nautical miles) from the Crimean Bridge (see Figures 1–4), and remained there for the next eight hours. During this time, the Russians placed 'a large cargo ship under the bridge, blocking the route into the Sea of Azov' (see Figure 4). Concurrently, Russia scrambled two fighter jets and two helicopters to patrol the strait. In the evening, the Ukrainian ships turned back to return to port in Odesa. As they were leaving the area, the Russian Coast Guard pursued them, later firing on and capturing the Ukrainian vessels about 23 kilometres (12.3 nautical miles) off the coast of Crimea, this time in international waters, even allowing for the Russian claim to waters around Crimea. The Ukrainian Navy later reported that six servicemen had been injured by the Russian actions. Berdyansk was damaged in its bridge, either by an Su-27 fighter or by 30mm naval gunfire from the Russian Coast Guard patrol ship Izumrud. Russia detained and held the twenty-four sailors.

Moscow said the gunboats and the tug had illegally entered Russia's territorial waters. Kyiv said its vessels did nothing wrong and has accused Russia of military aggression. Russia did not immediately or directly respond to the allegation, but Russian news agencies cited the FSB as saying it had incontrovertible proof that Ukraine had orchestrated what it called a 'provocation' and would publicise its evidence soon. A Crimean court ordered the twenty-four sailors, who were not accorded the status of Prisoners of War (POWs) (because, of course, there was no 'war' at this stage), to be detained for two months. However, they were later transferred to Moscow and thence to other prisons. Despite numerous protests, they were still there nine months later. Once full-scale conflict broke out on 24 February 2022, their prospects looked even grimmer. At the time of writing in August 2022, they are still in jail in Russia. The maltreatment of POWs, and the refusal to recognise them as such, is related to the overall question of genocide that this book addresses.

The situation escalated again in 2021. With hindsight, these incidents mark logical signposts on the road to war.

On 29 January 2021, three US naval vessels entered the Black Sea for the first time in three years. On 1 February, Ukrainian President Volodymyr Zelensky called for NATO membership for Ukraine. On 19 and 20 March, another significant US naval deployment to the Black Sea took place, as cruiser USS Monterey and destroyer USS Thomas Hudner entered the sea.

The Russian cruiser and Black Sea Fleet flagship Moskva made an exit to sea from Sevastopol, and on 19 March all six submarines of the Black Sea Fleet went to sea, which was an unprecedented event. Russian ground forces also started a build-up on the border with Ukraine. In April, President Zelensky began pressuring NATO to speed up Ukraine's path to membership. On 8 April, Russia started moving ten of its Caspian Flotilla warships to the Black Sea via internal waterways and conducting exercises usually associated with amphibious landings.

The last major incident before the start of full-scale war on 24 February 2022 came in late September 2021, when the Ukrainian Navy launched an operation to move the search-and-rescue ship Donbas and the tugboat Korets from Odesa to Mariupol (see Figure 1). The operation was the first deployment of Ukrainian Navy ships through the Kerch Strait area since the Russian annexation of Crimea, although the three ships in the 2018 Kerch Strait incident had been trying to. The vessels proceeded from Odesa with the forty-eight-year-old Donbas towing the forty-five-year-old Korets. Commanded by Dmytro Kovalenko, Ukrainian naval forces deputy chief of staff, the ships radioed their intention to enter the Azov Sea via the Kerch Strait as they approached it on 23 September. According to Kovalenko, this was an intentional form of 'naval diplomacy', carried out with the aim of asserting the Ukrainian claim to the surrounding waters. While the ships received pilot services from the Kerch port authority free of charge, they were also tailed by at least thirteen Russian vessels and overflown by Russian aircraft. The Ukrainian vessels complied with transit procedures, which did not require a request for permission to transit. Russia did not hinder the ships' passage under the Crimean Bridge, and they successfully reached Mariupol. In an interview with the Kyiv Post, Ukrainian naval expert Taras Chmut opined that the Russians had not expected the Ukrainian operation and so decided to take the least risky option by allowing them through. For the first time, the Ukrainians were not being merely reactive but setting their own game rules. On 14 April, a planned deployment of the two US destroyers was cancelled. On 17 April, the amphibious ships Aleksandr Otrakovsky and Kondoponga of the Russian Northern Fleet and Kaliningrad and Korolëv of the Baltic Fleet strengthened the amphibious warfare capabilities of the Black Sea Fleet.[29]

In November, further tensions started amid the build-up of Russian ground forces on the Ukraine border. On 2 November, the destroyer USS Porter entered the Black Sea, followed on 25

---

[29] Devrim Yaylali (@devrimyaylali), tweet, 17 April 2021, https://twitter.com/devrimyaylali/status/1383460240725737473 (accessed 13 September 2022).

November by the destroyer USS Arleigh Burke. In late October, the Russian Black Sea Fleet held a large exercise with a cruiser, a frigate and three corvettes.

As 2022 dawned, the indications that a conflict was imminent should have been obvious, but despite intelligence warnings that this was indeed the case, the political leadership in Ukraine and the West played them down. A 30 January report published in Naval News concluded that Russia would dominate the Black Sea in the event of all-out conflict, a conclusion that proved largely but not entirely correct. The analysis noted that '[w]hile much attention has been focused on the regional conflict and expanding militarization along the borders, the situation at sea is rarely highlighted'. The analysis correctly surmised that 'comparing the two forces is a futile effort'.[30]

Russia had been reinforcing the Black Sea Fleet with ships and submarines from the Baltic and Northern Fleets. In February, the Russian build-up around Ukraine moved into a new phase when six amphibious landing ships and a Kilo-class submarine sailed into the Black Sea. On 8 February, it was reported that the first part of a Russian Navy amphibious landing ship force had entered the Dardanelles. Due to traffic regulation, ships do not turn around. Six amphibious warfare ships and a submarine were expected to pass north into the Black Sea over the next few days. These ships had come from the Baltic and Northern Fleets. They were clearly part of President Putin's Ukraine build-up. Due to their amphibious warfare role, these ships were suitable for offensive troop landings or vital logistics support to land operations along the coast.[31] But, with hindsight, this was, at least to some extent, part of a Russian deception plan. Deliberate ambiguity, maskirovka. The ships had only

---

[30] Tayfun Ozberk, 'Analysis: Russia to Dominate the Black Sea in Case of Ukraine Conflict', Naval News, 30 January 2022, https://www.navalnews.com/naval-news/2022/01/analysis-russia-to-dominate-the-black-sea-in-case-of-ukraine-conflict (accessed 13 September 2022)

[31] H. I. Sutton, '6 Russian Warships and Submarine Now Entering Black Sea towards Ukraine', Naval News, 8 February 2022, https://www.navalnews.com/naval-news/2022/02/6-russian-warships-and-submarine-now-entering-black-sea-towards-ukraine (accessed 13 September 2022).

recently arrived at Tartus, Syria, which is Russia's forward naval base in the Mediterranean. Their stop there was fleeting, and they were soon on their way towards the Black Sea.

Western observers had been tracking the ships' progress since they left the Baltic. The ships passed north over several days. Because no official 'war' was underway, Turkey did not prevent the ships' transit under the rules of the 1936 Montreux Convention. However, the convention does limit the tonnage that can pass the straits at any one time. The first package comprised the three Ropucha-class landing ships: Minsk (127), Korolëv (130) and Kaliningrad (102). The second package followed on 9 February. This comprised the Ivan Gren-class Pyotr Morgunov (117) and two Ropucha-class ships Georgy Pobedonosets (016) and Olenegorsky Gornyak (012). The Kilo-class submarine Rostov-na-Donu (B-237) followed on 11 February.

The 6,600-ton Ivan Gren class can carry up to thirteen main battle tanks, or forty armoured vehicles, and 300 troops. It can also carry two helicopters for airborne assault and logistics. The smaller 4,080-ton Ropucha-class ships can each carry up to ten main battle tanks and 340 troops.

This gave the ships a combined capacity of up to sixty-three main battle tanks and about 2,000 troops. The exact load of the vessels was, naturally, unknown. However, the massive cargo capacity will greatly add to Russian capabilities off Ukraine.[32] The submarine, Rostov-na-Donu (B-237), was a separate variable, and it sailed independently through the Bosphorus on 11 February. But the timing of its return to the Black Sea after operations in the Mediterranean was inevitably, and correctly, seen as part of the Ukraine situation.

The submarine had been sent for repairs in the Baltic, using the long sea route through the Straits of Gibraltar. This involved spending a lot of time in the Mediterranean along the way. This is controversial because the Montreux Convention limits the reasons

---

[32] Ibid.

submarines can transit the Bosphorus.³³ It returned to the Mediterranean in March 2021 and now, eleven months later, was heading back to the Black Sea.³⁴ Its return to the Black Sea brought the Russian submarine force there up to three operational boats, all improved Kilo class. Two more remained in the Mediterranean and two were undergoing maintenance.³⁵

There was a widespread belief that Russia would carry out amphibious operations, but even before the full-scale conflict broke out, observers were sceptical, not least because such landings would probably entail huge casualties.

The 197th Assault Ship Brigade provides the Black Sea Fleet's amphibious lift, with three Alligator- and four Ropucha-class landing ships. With reinforcement from Russia's Baltic Fleet's Ropucha-class landing ships Korolëv and Minsk, this gave an amphibious lift capacity of about two naval infantry battalion tactical groups, each typically 1,000 strong.

The deployment of so many amphibious warfare ships was designed to keep the Ukrainians on edge and to make them divert attention from the war on land to guard against the ever-present possibility of an amphibious assault. The reinforced Russian naval presence in the Black Sea had a wider, strategic objective. By effectively blockading Ukraine, it would enable the Russians to strangle the country that was the breadbasket of the world (see below) and thus create pressure for a settlement favourable to Russia. Blockaded from the sea, Ukraine's economy would crumble.

The Russian exercises in Belarus, the development and integration of the Russian and Belarusian armed forces, the build-up on the Russia–Ukraine border and the reinforcement of the Black Sea

---

[33] 'H I Sutton - Covert Shores', accessed 7 August 2023, http://www.hisutton.com/Russian-Submarines-Montreux-Problem.html.

[34] Frederik Van Lokeren [@KaptainLOMA], '#BMФ #Russia's Naval Deployment in the #Mediterranean on the Morning of March 14, as Reported by #OSINT. A Significant Reinforcement of the Russian Task Force and a Possible Malfunction on Board of the Recue Tug SB-739. Https://Russianfleetanalysis.Blogspot.Com /2021/03/Russian-Forces-in-Mediterranean-Wk102021.Html Https://T.Co/n MIuCs32Tt', Tweet, *Twitter*, 14 March 2021, https://twitter.com/KaptainLOMA/status/1371044167137300480.

[35] Ibid

Fleet all looked like an attack on Ukraine, now effectively encircled, was imminent. US intelligence constantly told the president that war was coming. In addition to the evident deployments, they probably had human intelligence of Putin's intentions. But exercises, manoeuvres and movements on land and sea could all have just been means to apply pressure. And, no doubt, to persuade President Zelensky to give in to Russian demands, including to undertake never to join NATO. Perhaps the overriding opinion was that this was all sabre-ratting, and that the Russians would never be stupid enough to actually do it. It was not sabre-rattling. The sabres were already drawn.

Having encircled, then strike the head ...

The invasion began at dawn on 24 February, with infantry divisions and armoured and air support in Eastern Ukraine, and dozens of missile attacks across both Eastern and Western Ukraine. The first engagement between regular Russian troops and Ukraine's armed forces took place at about 05.00 hrs Kyiv time at Milove on the Russian–Ukrainian border (see Figure 7). The main infantry and tank attacks were launched in four spearheads, creating a northern front launched towards Kyiv, a southern front originating in Crimea, a south-eastern front launched at the cities of Luhansk and Donbas, Donetsk and an eastern front (See Figures 7 and 8).

Dozens of missiles strikes across Ukraine reached as far west as L'viv. Although the information war made it difficult to verify contradictory reports, it looks as if mercenaries from the so-called Wagner Group, including Chechens, were deployed to Kyiv to assassinate President Zelensky. The Wagner mercenaries had served in Syria and various countries in Africa. Their widespread use would lessen casualties among Russian regular troops and could, perhaps plausibly, be denied.[36] They are sometimes described as a

---

[36] Tom Ball, 'Spies Accused of Betraying Putin's Chechen Units', *The Times*, 10 March 2022, https://www.thetimes.co.uk/article/spies-accused-of-betraying-putins-chechen-units-537fj6lnr (accessed 13 March 2022). Chechen fighters loyal to the Kremlin are being betrayed by Russian spies who are leaking their whereabouts to Ukrainian forces, an aide to President Zelensky has claimed.

Private Military Company (PMC). The Ukrainian government said these efforts were thwarted by anti-war officials in Russia's FSB, who shared intelligence of the plans with the Ukrainian authorities.

Figure 7. - Situation before 05.00 hrs EEST (East European Standard Time)(Three hours ahead of GMT) 24 February 2022, showing Russian-annexed Crimea and separatist controlled parts of Donetsk and Luhansk (Lugansk), and site of first Russian attack at 03.40 EEST. Map via Homoatrox, *Russian Invasion of Ukraine — Ongoing Military Conflict in Eastern Europe since 2022 [Edit]*, 24 February 2022, 24 February 2022, https://commons.wikimedia.org/wiki/File:War_in_Ukraine_(2022)_en.png.

There were two Russian plans. The first — let us call it 'Plan A' — was to move swiftly towards Kyiv, decapitate the Ukrainian state by seizing the capital and capturing or killing the government, and install a pro-Russian puppet. That failed in the face of gallant Ukrainian resistance, and for the Russians, surprising logistical and morale problems, as well as an unexpected degree of unanimity among EU and NATO countries in opposing the Russian action. When it failed, the Russians withdrew from Kyiv and began what I shall call 'Plan B'. The seizure of the two eastern oblasti of Donetsk

---

Aleksei Arestovich said that the FSB was 'quietly passing on' information about the movements of Chechen units.

and Luhansk/Lugansk, and also an advance north, east and west out of Crimea. That was plausibly explicable, as Putin and Foreign Minister Sergey Lavrov had long said the 'liberation' of those two largely Russian-speaking and pro-Russian provinces had always been their objective.

The initial Russian land attack is shown in Figure 8. The first stage of the invasion was conducted on four fronts including one towards western Kyiv from Belarus, conducted by the Russian Eastern Military District[37] comprising the 29th, 35th and 36th Combined Arms Armies. That is of great interest as these Russian forces attacking from Belarus were originally from the Far East. So they had come a very long way. I saw Pacific Fleet marines in Chechnya, so the Independent headlined the story 'The Empire Strikes Back'. A second axis deployed towards eastern Kyiv from Russia by the Central Military District (north-eastern front) comprised the 41st Combined Arms Army and 2nd Guards Combined Arms Army. A third axis deployed towards Kharkiv by the Western Military District (eastern front), with the 1st Guards Tank Army and 20th Combined Arms Army. A fourth, southern, front originating in occupied Crimea and Russia's Rostov oblast' with an eastern axis towards Odesa and a western area of operations towards Mariupol by the Southern Military District, including the 58th, 49th and 8th Combined Arms Armies. The Southern Military District also commanded the I and II Army Corps of the pro-Russian separatist forces in Donbas.

As Figure 8 suggests, the Russians concentrated the bulk of their forces — five out of ten armies — on a rapid seizure of Kyiv. The real organisation and disposition of Russian forces, however, was far more complex. In practice, forces from these ten armies were deployed in a far more dispersed and confused way. Rather than being labelled as armies, they were described as 'groups' and 'sub-groups'. According to a map produced by the Royal United Services Institute, there were five main groups: Polessiya (equating to

---

[37] In the Great Patriotic War, Soviet Military Districts morphed into Fronts (Army Groups) on the outbreak of war. However, since the conflict in Ukraine is not a 'war', the designation Military District is retained.

the Far Eastern Military District), Northern (equating to the Central Military District's area), Belgorod, (equating to the Western Military District's area) and Donbas (equating to the two pro-Russian breakaway Army Corps).[38] Numerous sub-groups are also shown. Moving clockwise from Belarus to Crimea, they are Kilmogo, L'gov, Belgorod, Boguchar, Rostov on Don, Taganrog, Tavriya and Crimea.

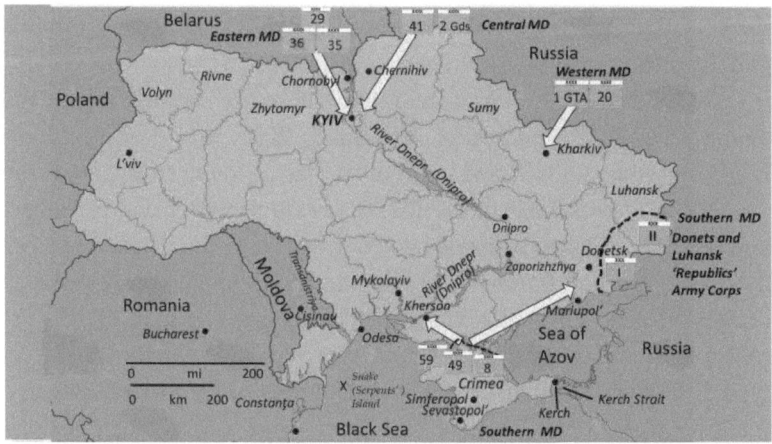

Figure 8. - Initial Russian deployments. The symbols for Armies are the standard Nato XXXX. The breakaway 'republics'' 'Army Corps' are shown with the standard Nato XXX as a Corps. As 'Corps', in accordance with common, but by no means universal, practice, they are indicated by Roman numerals.[39]

At the start of the operation, the basic fighting unit was the battalion tactical group (BTG).[40] BTGs were introduced in 2012 when the Russian Army started trying to move away from the Soviet model.

---

[38] Map produced just before 24 February 2022.
[39] Adopted from d-maps.com, maps of Ukraine available at https://d-maps.com/pays.php?num_pay=227&lang=en&num_pag=1, copyright of original maps is https://d-maps.com, see 'Terms and Conditions of Use', accessed 10 August 2023, https://d-maps.com/conditions.php?lang=en.
[40] Kyle Mikozami, 'How Russia's Battalion Tactical Groups Will Tackle War with Ukraine', Popular Mechanics, 24 February 2022, 'How Russia's Battalion Tactical Groups Work | Russo-Ukrainian War', accessed 2 October 2022, https://www.popularmechanics.com/military/weapons/a39193732/russian-battalion-tactical-groups-explained/.

There are two probable reasons. The first was that, as the Russian Army got much smaller compared to what it was under the Soviet Union, it did not need the larger structures like division headquarters as much and did not have the experienced officers to staff them. The smaller brigade structures were more flexible. A brigade could control two BTGs. The second reason is that the BTG structure allows the brigade to deploy a subsidiary unit. About one-third of Russian troops are still conscripts who, by Russian law, cannot serve outside of Russia. Therefore, the BTG is manned by the brigade's volunteers.

In August 2021, Russia had 168 BTGs, spread out across the country's eleven time zones. In January 2022, it had eighty-three BTGs massed near Ukraine, with more streaming in from across the country. The two BTGs of the 155th Naval Infantry Brigade, for example, travelled by rail nearly 4,000 miles from their barracks near the North Korean border to a position along the Ukraine–Belarus border. On 24 February 2022, Russia had more than 120 BTGs arrayed against Ukraine, more than three-quarters of the total.[41] A typical BTG might include three companies of motorised infantry totalling thirty BMP-2 or BMP-3 infantry fighting vehicles.[42] Each BMP carries seven soldiers for dismounted operations. Each includes one or two tank companies of ten T-72B3, T-80 or T-90 main battle tanks. They also include up to a half-dozen mortars, self-propelled howitzers, flamethrowers, multiple rocket launchers and Pantsir S-1 truck-mounted air defence systems.[43] In addition, there are ambulances, recovery vehicles, supply trucks, medical units and headquarters units. The result is a unit that, unlike a

---

[41] Ibid. See also Lester W. Grau and Charles K. Bartles, 'Getting to Know the Russian Battalion Tactical Group', RUSI, 14 April 2022, https://rusi.org/explore-our-research/publications/commentary/getting-know-russian-battalion-tactical-group (accessed 13 September 2022).

[42] 'BMP-2 IFV Tracked Armored Infantry Fighting Vehicle Data', accessed 7 August 2023, https://www.armyrecognition.com/russia_russian_army_light_armoured_vehicle_uk/bmp-2_ifv_tracked_armored_infantry_fighting_vehicle_data_fact_sheet.html. 'BMP-3 Infantry Combat Vehicle - Army Technology', accessed 7 August 2023, https://www.army-technology.com/projects/bmp-3/.

[43] 'Pantsir S-1', Missile Threat, accessed 7 August 2023, https://missilethreat.csis.org/defsys/pantsir-s-1/.

Russian tank regiment, could enter all types of terrain and take on the enemy and could make a 240-kilometre self-sustained bound - that is, without needing resupply - in combat. All told, a BTG is about 1,000 troops.[44] The BTGs were intended to give the Russian Army more tactical flexibility, but when the fighting started it soon became apparent that these independent, self-contained fighting units were failing. That may be why so many Russian generals were killed. A BTG is normally commanded by the commander of the battalion on which it is based. A battalion commander in the Russian Army has usually been a major, rather than a lieutenant-colonel as in, for example, the British Army. If a major-general goes forward to take over command of a BTG that has got into trouble, he becomes a lucrative target.

By the end of November it was reported that the Russians had largely replaced BTGs with a new unit called the "Assault Unit" or "Assault Detachment'. BTGs comprised perhaps 600-800 officers and other ranks but were short on infantry. They suffered 'several intrinsic weaknesses', according to the UK MoD on 29 November.*[45] The new Assault Detachments comprise two or three assault infantry companies with relatively little artillery and anti-aircraft support. The assault detachments appear designed primarily to assault urban areas or fortified positions on the edges of woods.[46]

Returning to the strategic level, the key to 'Plan A' — a swift military operation to decapitate the Ukrainian state — was to capture Kyiv. As can be seen from Figure 9, Kyiv is very close to the border with Belarus and appears very vulnerable. The Russian attack southwards bore all the hallmarks of Russian military planning. Russia apparently intended to rapidly seize Kyiv, with

---

[44] Ibid.

[45] Verity Bowman Russia largely abandons battalion tactical groups in Ukraine as weaknesses revealedThe units have played a major part in Moscow's military doctrine for the last ten years but 'has proven unsuccessful' in Ukraine. Verity Bowman, 'Russia Largely Abandons Battalion Tactical Groups in Ukraine as Weaknesses Revealed', *The Telegraph*, 29 November 2022, https://www.telegraph.co.uk/world-news/2022/11/29/russia-largely-abandons-battalion-tactical-groups-ukraine-weaknesses/.

[46] 'Thread by @Tatarigami_UA on Thread Reader App', accessed 9 October 2022, https://threadreaderapp.com/thread/1629722073487613953.html.

Spetsnaz (Special Forces) infiltrating the city, supported by airborne operations and a rapid mechanised advance from the north. Russian airborne forces attempted to seize two key airfields near Kyiv, launching an airborne assault on Antonov Airport followed by a similar landing at Vasylkiv, near Vasylkiv Air Base south of Kyiv, on 26 February. Initially, Russian forces captured key areas to the north and west of Kyiv, leading to international speculation about the city's imminent fall. However, stiff Ukrainian resistance sapped the momentum. Poor Russian logistics and tactical decisions helped the defenders thwart efforts at encirclement. The battle lasted from 25 February 2022 to 2 April 2022 and ended with the withdrawal of Russian forces. After a month of protracted fighting, Ukrainian forces mounted successful counterattacks. Russians began to withdraw on 29 March. On 2 April, the Ukrainian authorities declared that Kyiv and its surrounding province were again under Ukrainian control. The battle therefore lasted from 25 February 2022 to 2 April 2022 and ended with the withdrawal of Russian forces.

Russian forces trying to capture Kyiv sent a probing spearhead on 24 February south from Belarus along the west bank of the Dnipro River, apparently to encircle the city from the west, but it pulled back by 7 April to resupply and redeploy to the south-eastern front. It was supported by two separate axes of attack from Russia along the east bank of the Dnipro: the western at Chernihiv, and the eastern at Sumy. These were likely intended to encircle Kyiv from the north-east and east. The attack force reached the Chernobyl Exclusion Zone, established after the 1986 Chernobyl nuclear disaster, and the now ghostly city of Pripyat. Following their breakthrough at Chernobyl, Russian forces were held at Ivankiv, a northern suburb of Kyiv.

The attacks were unsuccessful due to several factors, including the disparity in morale and performance between Ukrainian and Russian forces, the Ukrainian use of sophisticated man-portable weapons provided by Western allies, poor Russian logistics and equipment performance, the failure of the Russian Air Force to achieve air superiority, and Russian military attrition during their siege of major cities. As Russian forces advanced towards Kyiv,

President Zelensky warned that 'subversive groups' were approaching the city. As noted earlier, Wagner Group mercenaries and Chechen forces were reported to have made several attempts to assassinate Zelensky. The Ukrainian government said these efforts were thwarted by anti-war officials in Russia's FSB, who gave them away.

The Russian advance was greatly hindered by logistical difficulties, partly caused by the Belarusian opposition, as dissident railway workers, hackers and security forces disrupted railway lines in Belarus. This operation, known as the 2022 rail war in Belarus, was mainly organised by individuals and three larger networks known as 'Bypol', the 'Community of Railway Workers', and the 'Cyber Partisans'. The term 'rail war' had first been used in 1943 when pro-Soviet partisans, directed from Moscow, severely disrupted German communications before and during the Kursk offensive.

A British intelligence report on 25 March 2022 said that Ukraine had retaken towns as far as 35 kilometres (22 miles) from the city as Russian forces began to run out of supplies. Following the successful Ukrainian counterattacks in late March, Russia announced it was withdrawing its forces from the Kyiv area on 29 March. Taking Kyiv was deemed to be a key objective, and their failure to take it was viewed as a setback for the campaign in general. On 25 March, the Russian Defence Ministry said the 'first stage' of the military operation in Ukraine was generally complete, that the Ukrainian military forces had suffered serious losses and the Russian military would now concentrate on the 'liberation of Donbas'.

By 7 April, Russian troops deployed to the northern front by the Russian Eastern Military District pulled back from the Kyiv offensive, apparently to resupply and then redeploy to the Donbas region to reinforce the renewed invasion of south-eastern Ukraine. As the Ukrainians recovered the territory north of Kyiv, horrors were revealed. The single most appalling incident was what is known as the Bucha massacre (Бучанська різанина- Buchanska rizanyna) in Ukrainian). Photographic and video evidence of the massacre emerged on 1 April 2022 after Russian forces withdrew from the city. According to the mayor and other local authorities, around 1,300 bodies have been recovered from the town and surrounding areas, including thirty-one children. Photos showed corpses of civilians, lined up with their hands bound behind their backs, shot at point-blank range, which suggested that summary executions had taken place. An inquiry by Radio Free Europe reported the use of a basement beneath a campsite for torture. Many bodies were found mutilated and burnt, and girls as young as fourteen reported being raped by Russian soldiers. Ukraine has asked the International Criminal Court to investigate what happened in Bucha as part of its ongoing investigation of the invasion in order to determine whether a series of Russian war crimes or crimes against humanity were committed.

Russian authorities have denied responsibility and instead claimed that Ukraine faked footage of the event or staged the killings itself as a false flag operation and that the footage and photographs of dead bodies were 'fake news'. These assertions by Russian authorities have been debunked as false by various groups and media organisations around the world. Eyewitness accounts from residents of Bucha said that the Russian Armed Forces carried out the killings.

Following the expulsion of Russian forces from the north of Kyiv, Russian attention switched to 'Plan B': their original stated intent to 'liberate' Donbas. Following the failure to decapitate the country, the fighting on land switched to a grinding war of attrition. The situation on 27 July is shown in Figure 9. The progress of the war can be followed on excellent maps produced by ISW and also by the BBC, who use ISW material and UK MoD briefings.[47]

During this period, the war at sea had not gone at all well for the Russians. On 24 February 2022, the first day of the war, the Russians had seized the tiny but strategically important Snake (Zmiinyi) Island off Ukraine's southerly coastline and very close to Romania. Snake Island became critical to the Russians after the sinking of their Black Sea flagship, the guided-missile cruiser Moskva on 14

---

[47] 'Ukraine War in Maps: Tracking the Russian Invasion', BBC, https://www.bbc.co.uk/news/world-europe-60506682 (accessed 13 September 2022).

April. Moskva had provided air defence over the western Black Sea.

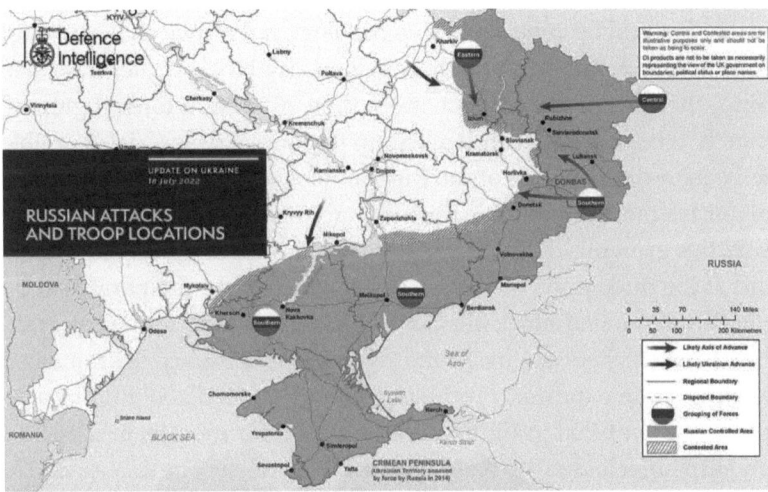

Figure 9. - Situation on 27 July 2022. Ministry of Defence GB [@DefenceHQ], Tweet, *Twitter*, 18 July 2022, accessed 22 July 2022, https://twitter.com/DefenceHQ/status/1548977862920884227. United Kingdom Open Government Licence v3.0.

That loss had to be replaced by putting air defence systems on Snake Island. The Ukrainians recaptured the island at the end of June, after bombarding it with long-range French César guns from the mainland. The vulnerability of surface warships close to the coast—Moskva had sunk after it was hit by two Ukrainian-made Neptune missiles—meant that the Russians switched to launching their very effective Kalibr cruise missiles from the Kilo-class submarines (see above). On 30 June 2022, Russia announced that it had withdrawn troops from the island in a 'gesture of goodwill' after military objectives were complete. According to Ukraine, a hasty withdrawal of Russian forces followed what Ukraine's armed forces claimed to be a series of devastating attacks on the strategically important island and any vessel bringing in troops and weapons. On 30 June 2022, Reuters reported that '[n]ew weapons sent by the West made the Russian garrison even more vulnerable, especially HIMARS, a rocket system supplied by the United States which Ukraine began fielding last week'.⁴⁸

The recapture of Snake Island was perhaps a key to help unlock what had become a massive problem, not only for Ukraine but for the world. The best way to transport dry bulk cargoes is by sea. Since the start of the conflict, more than 20 million tons of grain — mostly wheat — had been stacked up in grain silos in Odesa, unable to be exported because of the Russian blockade. One of the reasons given by the Russians for this very atypical 'gesture of goodwill' was the growing demand for the resumption of grain shipments out of the three ports of wider Odesa, which had been paralysed by the Russian naval blockade. Some 20 to 25 million tonnes of grain had been stacked in silos in the ports since February. Ukraine is a leading grain exporter, producing enough to feed 400 million people a year, but that grain had been trapped for months in silos and on ships blockaded by Russia in the Black Sea. The UN says 276 million people were severely food insecure before Russia's 24 February invasion. At the time of writing, officials projected the number to be 345 million. It is expected that the deal will bring relief to millions who have been struggling with rising food prices because of the war.⁴⁹

The war in the Black Sea had also prevented Russia from exporting its own grain, whether grown by Russians or stolen from Ukraine. But Russia is also the world's biggest producer of fertiliser and had also been hit by Western sanctions, so it had something to gain from what the UN secretary-general called a 'package deal'. Since the war, the price of fertiliser on the global market has doubled, in turn driving up the cost of crops.⁵⁰

---

[48] Max Hunders and Tom Balmforth, 'Russia Abandons Black Sea Outpost of Snake Island in Victory for Ukraine', Reuters, 30 June 2022, https://www.reuters.com/world/europe/russia-steps-up-attacks-ukraine-after-landmark-nato-summit-2022-06-30 (accessed 1 July 2022).

[49] Kaamil Ahmed, 'UN Warns Russian Blockade of Ukraine's Grain Exports May Trigger Global Famine', *The Guardian*, 18 March 2022, https://www.theguardian.com/global-development/2022/mar/18/un-warns-russian-blockade-of-ukraines-grain-exports-may-trigger-global-famine (accessed 13 September 2022).

[50] Margaret Besheer, 'Deal Signed to Get Ukrainian Grain to Global Markets', Global Security, 22 July 2022, https://www.globalsecurity.org/wmd/library/new

On 22 July, Russia, Ukraine, Turkey and the secretary-general of the United Nations signed the deal on 22 July 2022 in Istanbul. The aim was to resume Ukraine's Black Sea grain exports and facilitate Russian grain and fertiliser shipments. Russia's defence minister, Sergei Shoigu, and Ukraine's infrastructure minister, Oleksandr Kubrakov, took turns at the table signing the deal, known as the Black Sea Initiative. It was also signed by Turkey's defence minister and the UN secretary-general, António Guterres, as Turkish President Recep Tayyip Erdoğan looked on.[51] Just before the public signing of the grain deal, the UN chief and the Russian defence minister privately signed a memorandum of understanding to address the disruptions to the trade of Russian food and fertiliser.

The Black Sea Initiative did not represent an armistice or ceasefire. Within twenty-four hours of its signature, Russian missiles crashed into Odesa, supposedly aimed at 'military targets.'[52] As I write, it remains to be seen whether the initiative can be made to work. The first grain ship, the Sierra Leone-flagged Razoni, left Odesa on 1 August 2022 but was detained at Istanbul when the Lebanese purchaser of the 26,000-tonne cargo refused to accept it. He said that with the five months' delay he was unhappy about the quality of the cargo and, therefore, refused to take it for the agreed price.[53] It then headed to Syria — an ally of Putin.[54] The first grain-

---

s/ukraine/2022/07/ukraine-220722-voa02.htm?_m=3n%2e002a%2e3386%2es h0ao44kuj%2e3546 (accessed 13 September 2022).

51 Margaret Besheer, 'Deal Signed to Get Ukrainian Grain to Global Markets', VOA, 22 July 2022, https://www.voanews.com/a/deal-signed-to-get-ukrainian-grain-to-global-markets/6669862.html.. 'Turkey's Erdogan: Deal to Resume Ukraine's Grain Exports Set for Signing Friday', accessed 2 August 2023, https://www.voanews.com/a/turkey-erdogan-deal-to-resume-ukraine-grain-exports-set-for-signing-friday/6668587.html.
52 'The grain deal', The Week Staff 30 July 2022, pp. 4-5.
53 'First Ship Carrying Ukrainian Grain Leaves the Port of Odesa', New York Post, 1 August 2022, https://nypost.com/2022/08/01/first-ship-carrying-ukrainian-grain-leaves-the-port-of-odesa (accessed 13 September 2022).
54 Emiko Terazono, 'First Grain Ship to Depart Ukraine since War Appears to Dock in Syria', Financial Times, 16 August 2022, https://www.ft.com/content/85a80cfc-79c4-4ec9-9a79-23014f1f30ca?sharetype=gift (accessed 13 September 2022). 'It seems in the end the first corn from Ukraine went to Syria, a strong

carrying ship to depart from Ukraine since the Russian invasion docked in the Syrian port of Tartus—Russia's Mediterranean naval base—after it stopped transmitting its location signal early on Friday 13 August; the second big ship, the Lebanese-registered bulk carrier Brave Commander, chartered by the UN, set sail in mid-August, heading for Djibouti, in order to transfer its 23,000 tonnes of grain to Ethiopia.[55] No doubt via the railway constructed under the Chinese Belt and Road Initiative. The Initiative was due to expire on 19 November 2022 but on 17th its renewal was announced, by which time more than 11.1 million tonnes of essential foodstuffs have been shipped under its protection.[56]

Ukraine's Stalingrad: Mariupol

In assessing the Russian treatment of Ukrainians, civilians and POWs, the actions at Mariupol, a port city on the Sea of Azov (see Figures 5 and 6), deserve particular attention. Mariupol lies just within the oblast' of Donetsk.[57] Although declared a very polluted city, its city centre was, until its almost total destruction, a rather lovely multi-ethnic community on the Sea of Azov, with mosques as well as Orthodox churches. It had one of the largest Russian-speaking populations in Ukraine.

Russia recognised the breakaway so-called 'Donetsk People's Republic' (DPR) on 21 February 2022. Mariupol therefore lay (just) within the Russian-backed separatist DPR, although the part of it

---

ally of Russia', said Yörük Işık, a geopolitical and maritime analyst based in Istanbul.

[55] Carly Olson and Farnaz Fassihi, 'The First U.N. Ship Transporting Ukrainian Grain to Africa Has Set Sail', *The New York Times*, 16 August 2022, https://www.nytimes.com/2022/08/16/world/europe/the-first-un-ship-transporting-ukrainian-grain-to-africa-has-set-sail.html (accessed 14 September 2022).

[56] 'UN Chief Welcomes Renewal of Black Sea Grain Initiative | UN News', 17 November 2022, https://news.un.org/en/story/2022/11/1130727.

[57] Chapter title via Grzegorz Kuczyński, 'Russian Invasion of Ukraine: The Battle of Mariupol, or a Ukrainian Stalingrad', Warsaw Institute, 15 March 2022, https://warsawinstitute.org/russian-invasion-ukraine-battle-mariupol-ukrainian-stalingrad (accessed 14 September 2022).

where Mariupol lay was still controlled by Ukrainian forces. It was the largest city on the Sea of Azov and very important strategically. Its eventual capture gave Russia complete control of the Sea of Azov and created a land corridor from Russia through to Crimea to reinforce the link created by the Crimean Bridge (see previous essay). It was also home to the massive Ilyich and Azovstal' steelworks (see below).

After the Euromaidan Revolution in 2014, Mariupol had been swept by pro-Russian protests. By early May 2014, the war in Donbas was underway, and pro-Russian separatist forces, with considerable Russian backing, took control of the city in the First Battle of Mariupol. However, the Ukrainians recaptured it the following month. In August, the Russian-backed DPR forces captured Novoazovsk, close to the Russian border (See Figure 8). In September, they attempted to take Mariupol, leading to the second battle, but were repulsed. In February 2015, the Ukrainians launched a surprise offensive into Shyrokyne, 11 kilometres east of Mariupol, to create a firebreak separating DPR forces from the city (See Figure 10). The conflict in this area was then frozen by the 2015 Minsk II ceasefire.

One of the most important forces for the recapture of Mariupol in 2014 and its subsequent defence was the Azov Battalion, later the Azov Regiment.[58] The unit was founded in May 2014 as a volunteer paramilitary militia under the command of Andriy Biletsky to fight pro-Russian insurgents in the fighting in the breakaway Donetsk and Luhansk provinces. It was formally incorporated into the Ukrainian National Guard on 11 November 2014.[59] By 2017, its strength was estimated at between 900 and 2,500 soldiers, making

---

[58] Bojan Pancevski, 'Kiev Lets Loose Men in Black', *The Sunday Times*, 11 May 2014.

[59] Originally Special Operations Detachment 'Azov' (in Ukrainian: Окремий загін спеціального призначення 'Азов': Okremyi zahin spetsialnoho pryznachennia 'Azov'), also known as the Azov Regiment (Полк 'Азов'; Polk 'Azov) and formerly the Azov Battalion (батальйон 'Азов').

it a 'regiment' (polk) in the continental sense.[60] That is ironic because most of its soldiers are, or were, actually Russian-speaking Ukrainians.

The group has attracted controversy because, when founded, it had associations with neo-Nazi ideology. Many of its insignia were redolent of Nazi symbols. There were also allegations that members of the unit had taken part in torture and war crimes.[61] Others have argued that that the regiment has evolved beyond its origins as street militia, tempering its neo-Nazi underpinnings as it became part of the National Guard.

---

[60] In Russian and Ukrainian, a *polk* is a regiment, usually comprising three battalions. The word has an old Indo-European root, a large number of (armed) people. The same word as the English world folk.

[61] Gordon M. Hahn, *Ukraine over the Edge: Russia, the West and the 'New Cold War'* (Jefferson, NC: McFarland, 2018), p. 277. 'Inside Azov, the Far-Right Brigade Killing Russian Generals and Playing a PR Game in the Ukraine War', *Daily Telegraph*, 18 March 2022, https://www.telegraph.co.uk/world-news/2022/03/18/inside-azov-neo-nazi-brigade-killing-russian-generals-playing (accessed 14 September 2022).

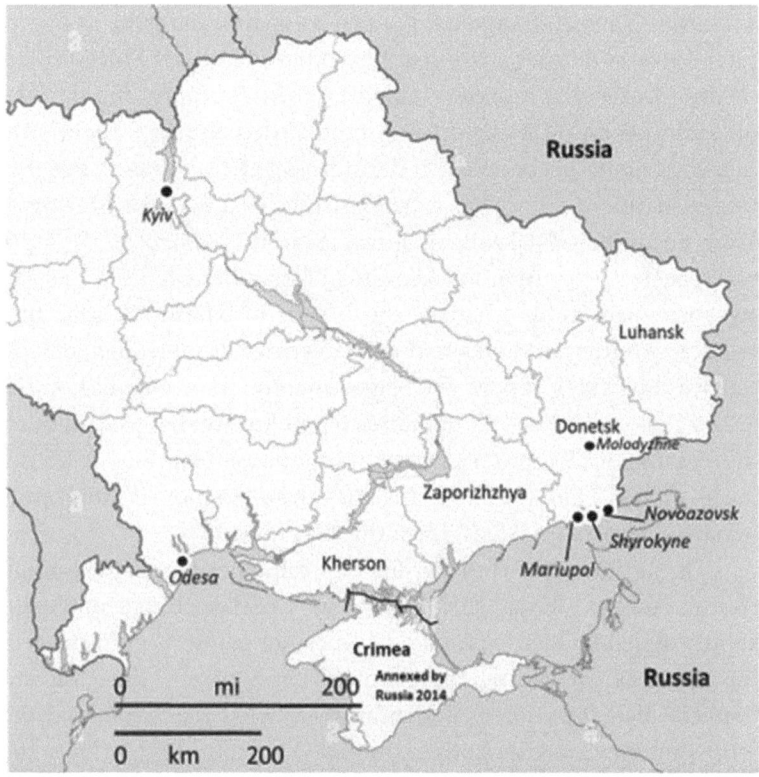

Figure 10. - Location of early fighting around Mariupol and also location of Molodyzhne (see below). Adapted by author from CIA Factbook.

Since 2014, criticism of the Azov Battalion, later Regiment, has continued. By November 2014, Azov was integrated into the National Guard of Ukraine and set Mariupol as their headquarters. As one of Putin's stated goals for the invasion was the 'denazification' of Ukraine, Mariupol was therefore an important ideological and symbolic target for the Russian forces. Like Stalingrad, it was not only a strategically important city but also a symbol. However deluded Putin may be, and whether the Azov Regiment had changed its spots, it was an important element on which Putin could play.

During the fighting in the Donbas before February 2022, Mariupol was repeatedly shelled, and the Russians mounted a major information campaign accusing the Azov Regiment, in particular, of committing atrocities against the pro-Russian separatists in the region. Prior to the siege, around 100,000 residents left Mariupol according to the city's deputy mayor. On 24 February, the day the invasion began, Russian artillery bombarded the city, reportedly injuring twenty-six people. On the morning of 25 February, Russian forces advanced from DPR territory in the east towards Mariupol. They encountered Ukrainian forces near the village of Pavlopil, north-east of Mariupol, but Ukrainian forces defeated the Russian advance. Vadym Boychenko, the mayor of Mariupol, said that twenty-two Russian tanks had been destroyed in the engagement. The Russian Navy reportedly began an amphibious assault on the Sea of Azov coastline 70 kilometres (43 miles) west of Mariupol on the evening of 25 February. It was an unopposed landing. A US defence official said the Russians may have deployed thousands of naval infantry (marines) from this beachhead.

Throughout 28 February, the city remained under Ukrainian control, despite being surrounded by Russian troops and constantly shelled. Electricity, gas and internet connection to most of the city was cut during the evening. On 1 March, the DPR announced that their forces had nearly encircled Mariupol, and the following day Russian troops completed surrounding it. Now the siege intensified. On 2 March, Boychenko announced the city was suffering from a water outage and had experienced massive casualties. He also said Russian forces were preventing civilians from leaving. A satellite view of the city is shown in Figure 11. Later, on 2 March, Russian artillery targeted a densely populated neighbourhood of Mariupol, shelling it for nearly fifteen hours. The neighbourhood was massively damaged as a result, with Deputy Mayor Sergiy Orlov reporting that 'at least hundreds of people are dead'.[62]

---

[62] 'Ukrainian City of Mariupol "near to Humanitarian Catastrophe" after Bombardment', *BBC News*, 2 March 2022, sec. Europe, https://www.bbc.com/news/world-europe-60585603.

'NO PLAN SURVIVES CONTACT WITH THE ENEMY' 209

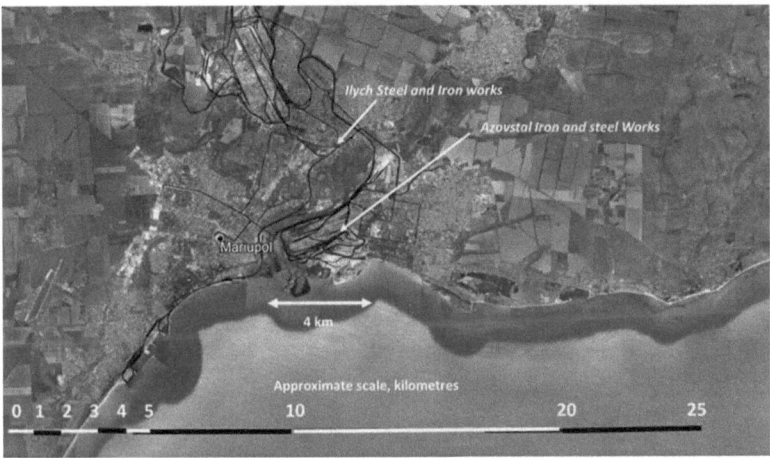

Figure 11. - Mariupol. Source: Google Earth/Terrametrics/Maxar Technologies, adapted by the author. Low resolution.

On the morning of 3 March, the city was again shelled by Russian troops. Eduard Basurin, the spokesman for the DPR forces, formally called on the besieged Ukrainian forces in Mariupol to surrender or face 'targeted strikes' and reported that DPR forces had tightened the siege and that three nearby settlements had been captured. On 4 March, Boychenko stated that the city's supplies were running out and called for a humanitarian evacuation corridor and Ukrainian military reinforcements. He also said Russian BM-21 Grad ('Hail') multiple rocket launchers were shelling the city's hospital. The Russians appear to have agreed to establish humanitarian corridors a number of times but then promptly shelled them. For example, on 7 March 2022, the US ambassador to the Organization for Security and Co-operation in Europe (OSCE), Michael Carpenter, described two incidents that occurred in Mariupol on 5 and 6 March as war crimes. He said that on both dates, Russian forces bombed agreed-upon evacuation corridors while civilians were trying to use them.

On 15 April, a Ukrainian military commander issued a plea for military reinforcements to come and break the siege of Mariupol. He also said that 'the situation is critical and the fighting is fierce' but that sending reinforcements and breaking the siege 'can be done and it must be done as soon as possible'.[63] The Azovstal iron and steel plant, the heart of one of the remaining pockets of resistance, was well defended—a 'fortress within a city'—as it was an enormous complex that made locating the Ukrainian forces difficult and had workshops that were difficult to destroy from the air. Work on it had begun in 1929, and on the first steel furnace in 1935 as part of the industrialisation of Ukraine for which Khrushchev deserves much credit. Additionally, the complex contained a system of underground tunnels, later designed to withstand a nuclear attack,[64] which would make clearing the entire complex very costly and difficult.

There were in fact two massive iron and steel plants in the city. The other one was the Ilyich steel and iron works, directly to the north of Azovstal (see Figure 11). Originally named after Vladimir Ilyich Lenin, it was renamed in 2016 after scientist Zot Illich Nekrasov due to Ukrainian de-communisation law. People in Mariupol humorously refer to it as the 'plant named after not-that-Ilyich'. It produced a wide assortment of hot-rolled and cold-rolled steel, including for shipbuilding, oil pipelines, boring gas pipelines and water pipes. In 1941, it produced armour plate for the first T-34 tanks. The company was the sole enterprise of Ukraine that produced galvanised steel and tanks for liquid gases. The products of the company are certified by international classification societies, including Lloyd's Register. It was severely damaged during the siege of Mariupol, and Russian forces stormed it on 13 April. There have been rumours that an underground tunnel connects the two steel plants, a distance of about 5 kilometres (See Figure 11), but this is not confirmed.[65]

---

[63] Peter Graff, William Maclean and Cynthia Osterman, 'Russia Says Over 1,000 Ukrainian Marines Surrender in Mariupol', Reuters, 13 April 2022, https://www.reuters.com/world/europe/russia-says-1026-ukrainian-marines-surrendered-mariupol-2022-04-13 (accessed 14 September 2022)

[64] 'Ukraine War: Mariupol Defenders Will Fight to the End Says PM', BBC News, 18 April 2022, https://www.bbc.co.uk/news/world-europe-61135901 (accessed 14 September 2022).

[65] 'All about Bomb Shelters at the Azovstal Steel Plant', Frontier India, 4 May 2022, https://frontierindia.com/all-about-bomb-shelters-at-the-azovstal-steel-plant/ (accessed 14 September 2022). Citing Irina Butorina, a professor at the St

According to Enver Tskitishvili, the Azovstal plant's general director, in an interview with the BBC, the management of the enterprise had thought about bomb shelters back in 2014, when the city was hit by heavy artillery. The general director of PJSC Azovstal Metallurgical Combine said they began to restore bomb shelters left over from the Soviet era. That was no secret or surprise. During the later Soviet period, all major public buildings and plants had been built with nuclear shelters under them.[66]

Tskitishvili said:

> We opened the archives ... in 1977 when we were reconstructing the converter shop, part of the blast furnace shop, coke production—we saw that the bomb shelter was opened and reconstructed at the plant ... five very powerful bomb shelters could withstand at least one direct nuclear strike in accordance with Soviet law—at the time, architecturally. They could withstand and save people.[67]

Then, Tskitishvili said, in 1977, there were thirty-one other bomb shelters, able to accommodate 12,006 people, adding that 10,847 people worked there at that time. He added that the thickness between the ceiling of the underground tunnels and the surface was at least 8 metres. However, there were also communication tunnels and trenches between bunkers, while the bomb shelters themselves were even deeper. These went down to maybe 50 metres.[68] All in all, 11 square kilometres of a factory complex and five nuclear bunkers and 24 kilometres of tunnels beneath it was a formidable complex to attack. Tskitishvili said that on the eve of Russia's invasion of Ukraine, plant employees had created substantial reserves of drinking water and food in bunkers, which allowed for long-term survival.

On 16 April, DPR troops seized a police station near Mariupol's

---

Petersburg Polytechnic University, a specialist in ferrous metallurgy and environmental problems of metallurgical production, who spoke to Russia Today, and Enver Tskitishvili, the plant's general director, in an interview with the BBC. This article is the best analysis of the subterranean city below the Azovstal' works that the author has found.

66 Ibid.
67 Ibid.
68 Ibid.

beach, and Russian forces were confirmed to have seized the Vessel Traffic Control Centre at the port. Several days after the port was captured, on 20 April, a Ukrainian marine officer claimed marine and Azov forces from the Azovstal plant had conducted an evacuation operation of around 500 members of the Ukrainian border guards and national police from the port, as they were running out of ammunition. According to the officer, the Ukrainian forces from the Azovstal pocket made an armoured breakthrough to the port and provided covering fire, as the 500 besieged soldiers retreated to the Azovstal plant. Subsequently, Russia announced all urban areas of the city had been cleared, claiming that Ukrainian forces only remained at the Azovstal steel plant.

On 18 April, it was estimated that 95 per cent of the city had been destroyed in the fighting. Ukrainian soldiers ignored a Russian ultimatum to surrender, deciding to fight to the end. Russia threatened to destroy those who continued to fight on. A military expert estimated that there could still be 500 to 800 Ukrainian soldiers holding out within the city, while Russian officials estimated that 2,500 Ukrainian soldiers and 400 foreign volunteers were holding out within the Azovstal plant. The plant can be seen in Figure 12.

Figure 12. - Azovstal iron and steel works. Source Google Earth/Terrametrics/Maxar technologies. The plant covers eleven square kilometres. Right (east) side indicated by dotted line. A good idea of the scale can be gained from the relative size of the athletic stadium. Low resolution image.

On 20 April, Russian and DPR forces made small advances on the outskirts of the Azovstal plant. On 21 April, President Putin ordered Russian troops not to storm the Azovstal steel plant but to blockade it instead until the Ukrainian forces there ran out of supplies. He also reported that 'the completion of combat work to liberate Mariupol is a success', while a Ukrainian official rebutted Putin's comments, saying that Russia's decision to implement a blockade rather than storming the steel plant meant that Russia had admitted its inability to physically capture Mariupol. To be fair, the battle for the plant was more symbolic than strategically important, as Ukrainian forces there could no longer impede the Russian land corridor to Crimea and its total domination of the Azov coast. Despite the ordered blockade, Russian forces advanced within 20 metres of some of the Ukrainian positions.

On 2 April, Russian forces captured the Ukrainian Security Service building in central Mariupol, after which there was no more reported fighting in the area. On 4 April, one Ukrainian battalion surrendered, with Russian officials saying two days later that they had captured 267 Ukrainian marines from the 503rd Battalion of the Ukrainian Navy. Due to the surrender, the lines between the Ukrainian 36th Independent Marine Brigade and the Azov Regiment were broken. On 7 April, the DPR announced central Mariupol had been cleared of Ukrainian forces.

Meanwhile, Russian troops had started an advance from the south-west on 1 April, leaving the Ukrainian military in partial control of the area around the south-west of Mariupol by 7 April.

On 10 April, Russian forces captured the fishing port, separating Ukrainian troops in the port from those in the Azovstal steel plant into two pockets, while a possible third pocket was centred on the Ilyich steel and iron plant to the north, which fell three days later. The next day, DPR forces claimed to have captured 80 per cent of Mariupol. Local Ukrainian forces expected the city to fall soon, since they were running out of ammunition, and analysts at the ISW believed that Mariupol would fall within a week.[69]

---

[69] Mason Clark, George Barros and Kateryna Stepanenko, 'Russian Offensive Campaign Assessment, March 29', Institute for the Study of War, 30 March

It did not. By 16 April, it became the last pocket of organised resistance in the siege. Russian forces gave the defenders until 06.00 Moscow Time (05.00 EEST) on 17 April to surrender, claiming that if they left behind their weapons they would guarantee their lives. Ukrainian forces refused to surrender, and portions of the plant remained under their control.

On 4 May, Russian troops claimed to have entered the steel plant after launching an all-out attack. However, this was refuted by Ukrainian sources, claiming they had repelled some of them. On 7 May, Deputy Prime Minister Irina Vereshchuk said: 'The president's order has been carried out: all women, children, and the elderly have been evacuated from Azovstal.'[70] 'This part of the Mariupol humanitarian operation has been completed.' The New York Times reported that the Azov 'Battalion' (Regiment) was ordered to surrender by the Ukrainian general staff on 16 May, saying: 'The supreme military command ordered the commanders of the units stationed at Azovstal to save the lives of the personnel ... Defenders of Mariupol are the heroes of our time.' Efforts were underway to evacuate the surviving troops from the bunkers.[71]

On 17 May 2022, fifty-three seriously injured people surrendered and were evacuated from Azovstal to a medical facility in Novoazovsk, and 211 people were taken to Olenivka, further north in Donetsk through the humanitarian corridor, marking the end of the combat mission in Mariupol and the defence of the Azovstal

---

2022, https://www.understandingwar.org/sites/default/files/Russian%20Operations%20Assessments%20March%2030.pdf (accessed 14 September 2022); Mason Clark, George Barros and Karolina Hird, 'Russian Offensive Campaign Assessment, April 2', Institute for the Study of War, 2 April 2022, https://www.understandingwar.org/sites/default/files/Russian%20Operations%20Assessments%20April%202.pdf (accessed 14 September 2022).

[70] 'Ukraine War: Civilians Now Out of Azovstal Plant in Mariupol', BBC News, 5 July 2007, https://www.bbc.co.uk/news/world-europe-61362557 (accessed 14 September 2022); John Dunne, 'Mariupol: All Women, Children and Elderly Evacuated from Azovstal Steel Plant', *Evening Standard*, 7 May 2022, https://www.standard.co.uk/news/world/mariupol-azovstal-steelworks-evacation-women-children-russia-b998633.html (accessed 14 September 2022).

[71] Valerie Hopkins, Ivan Nechepurenko and Marc Santora, 'The Ukrainian Authorities Declare an End to the Combat Mission in Mariupol after Weeks of Russian Siege', *The New York Times*, 16 May 2022, https://www.nytimes.com/2022/05/16/world/europe/azovstal-mariupol.html (accessed 14 September 2022).

plant after eighty-two days of fighting.

Following the capture of Mariupol by the DPR and Russian forces and the surrender of remaining Ukrainian servicemen in Azovstal, Denis Pushilin, ruler of the self-styled DPR, announced that the plant would be demolished and that 'other projects are planned in place of Azovstal'.[72]

The Red Cross had described the situation in Mariupol as 'apocalyptic', and Ukrainian authorities accused Russia of engineering a major humanitarian crisis in the city, with city officials reporting that about 22,000 civilians had been killed. Ukrainian officials also reported that at least 95 per cent of the city had been destroyed during the fighting, largely by Russian bombardments. The United Nations said it had confirmed the deaths of 1,348 civilians but said the true death toll was likely thousands higher, adding that 90 per cent of the city's residential buildings had been damaged or destroyed.

The siege ended on 16 May 2022, after what media outlets called the 'evacuation' or 'surrender' of the remaining Azov Regiment personnel from the Azovstal iron and steel works; the Russian Ministry of Defence said the Ukrainians had 'surrendered', a word Ukraine avoided using. They had not surrendered of their own volition: they had been ordered to.

The battle was a pyrrhic or symbolic victory for Russia, and the siege's humanitarian impact did disastrous damage to Russia's reputation. The siege had held down thousands of Russian troops for eighty-two days. However, the eventual loss of the city was also a significant strategic defeat for Ukraine.

That was not the end of the story, however. Some 265 defenders of Azovstal were taken prisoner, plus another fifty-one were badly wounded.[73] In all, about 1,000 prisoners were transferred to Molodizhna prison, near Olenivka, further north in Donetsk.

---

[72] 'Глава ДНР Пушилин рассказал о планах по сносу завода "Азовсталь" в Мариуполе', gazeta.ru (in Russian), 18 May 2022, https://www.gazeta.ru/social/news/2022/05/18/17761628.shtml (accessed 14 September 2022).

[73] 'Fate of Hundreds of Ukrainian Fighters Uncertain after Surrender', Al Jazeera, 17 May 2022, https://www.aljazeera.com/news/2022/5/17/russia-says-mariupol-plant-fighters-surrendered-fate-uncertain (accessed 14 September 2022).

Initially, they were kept in acceptable conditions, the Guardian newspaper reported on 24 May 2022, after they had been transferred the previous week.[74] Denys Prokopenko, commander of the Azov battalion, was able to briefly call his wife, Kateryna, who said she had also been told that the prisoners had not been subjected to violence. It was not immediately clear if Prokopenko had been able to speak freely during the conversation. 'He said he was "OK" and asked how I was,' Kateryna Prokopenko told the Guardian. 'I've heard from other sources that the conditions are more or less satisfactory.'[75]

However, things seem to have got worse. On 29 July 2022, the Russian-operated prison in Molodizhna was destroyed. Some fifty-three Ukrainian POWs were killed and seventy-five wounded. The prisoners were mainly soldiers from the Azovstal plant.

Both Ukrainian and Russian authorities accused each other of the attack on the prison. The Ukrainian general staff said that the Russians shelled the prison in order to cover up the torture and murder of Ukrainian POWs that had been taking place there, and Ukrainian authorities provided what they said were intercepted communications indicating that the Russians did it. The Russians said the Ukrainians hit the prison with a Western-supplied HIMARS rocket fired from Ukrainian-held territory.

According to experts, the Russian version of events is very likely a fabrication, as there is virtually no chance that the damage was caused by a HIMARS rocket. The most likely cause of the explosion was an incendiary device detonated from inside the prison warehouse.

Russian and DPR accounts suggest fifty-three Ukrainian POWs died and another seventy-five were wounded. A Russian communiqué initially suggested forty dead and seventy-five wounded, in addition to eight guards. The Ukrainian side suggested that about forty people were dead and 130 were wounded.

---

[74] Isobel Kosiew, 'Ukrainian Soldiers Captured at Azovstal Plant in "Satisfactory" Conditions', *The Guardian*, 24 May 2022, https://www.aljazeera.com/news/2022/5/17/russia-says-mariupol-plant-fighters-surrendered-fate-uncertain (accessed 14 September 2022).

[75] Ibid.

Both sides agree that there were captive Azov Regiment in the destroyed barracks, brought there a few days before the event. It is possible that those transferred there immediately after the fall of Azovstal had by that time been taken to prisons in Russia. Pushilin, the leader of the DPR, suggested that among the 193 inmates at the detention facility, there were no foreigners, but he did not specify the number of Ukrainians held captive. Russian officials released a list of deceased POWs. As of 30 July 2022, Ukrainian officials stated that they were unable to verify the list.

On the same day the prisoners were killed, the Russian embassy in London published a tweet containing a statement from a pro-Russian citizen of Mariupol saying that Azov Regiment fighters deserved to be hanged rather than being shot by firing squad.

The fate of the captured Azov Regiment soldiers remained an issue at the time of publication.[76] A total of 2,500 Azov Regiment officers and men are believed to have been captured in Mariupol. Many have presumably been taken to prisons in Russia, or elsewhere in the DPR. But the DPR, with Russian backing, planned to hold show trials with the prisoners displayed in cages around the time of Ukrainian Independence Day, 24 August. The show trials would be held in the Mariupol Philharmonic. 'All prisoners of war, and in particular the "Azovstal" defenders, are combatants who legally defended their country', Mykhailo Podolyak, a senior aide to the Ukrainian president, said.

He added that the 'Mariupol cages' were an 'official war crime of Russia', calling on international humanitarian organisations to intervene. Boychenko, the mayor of Mariupol, said:

> They want to hold this pantomime at the Philharmonic Hall in Mariupol somewhere around Independence Day. Russia has no success in the battlefield, so it wants to show the 'victory' over the prisoners of war. This is what is called a war crime. We had an arrangement that the soldiers who surrendered would return back to Ukraine.

---

[76] Joe Barnes, 'Russia Building Prison "Cages" to Parade Captured Ukrainian Soldiers in Mariupol Show Trial', *Daily Telegraph*, 15 August 2022, https://www.msn.com/en-gb/news/world/russia-building-prison-cages-to-parade-captured-ukrainian-soldiers-in-mariupol-show-trial/ar-AA10FTOw (accessed 14 September 2022).

Pushilin, leader of the DPR, said the trials in Mariupol would be open to the media and international representatives. 'The task is to hold the most open trial possible, so that no-one says any doubts', he added.

The report, which includes photographs of the 'Mariupol cages', adds that some 10,000 captured Ukrainians, including military personnel and civilians, were being held captive in Russian prisons, according to Ukrainian estimates.[77]

This author's conclusion is that many and multiple war crimes do not amount to 'genocide' under the terms of the UN Genocide Convention. That is a deliberate policy to destroy a race, people, nation or ethnic group. Putin has stated that Ukraine has no right to exist as a country, and the Russians have deported thousands of Ukrainians into Russia and separated Ukrainian children from their parents. So do the well documented attacks on cultural targets such as the Ukrainian Ortodox cathedral in Odesa. These constitute 'genocide' as per the UN Genocide Convention.[78] War crimes have no doubt been committed on both sides, predominantly by the Russians

Conclusion: from non-linear to linear

Having given an outline of what happened up to the time of writing in August 2022, we need to return to the scheme for non-linear warfare set out in 2013. Figure 13 is the same as Figure 3 in the previous essay. The first point in the 'New Forms and Means' column was clearly put into practice. 'Military action by groups of forces begins in peacetime' took place from 2014, with the occupation of Crimea by forces who could not be identified — the 'little green people'. Although it was not exactly military action, the build-up of forces in the Crimea and of the Black Sea Fleet were all directed towards preparation for war. The construction of the Crimean Bridge was,

---

[77] Ibid.
[78] George Wright, 'Ukraine War: Is Russia Committing Genocide?', BBC, 13 April 2022, https://www.bbc.co.uk/news/world-europe-61017352 (accessed 14 September 2022).

in this author's view, highly significant as it effectively sealed off the Sea of Azov and permitted much more efficient access to Crimea from mainland Russia. In 2018, the same year the bridge opened, the first major stand-off with the Ukrainian Navy took place, with the Kerch Strait incident. Ukrainian sailors were taken prisoner by the Russian FSB but were not POWs because this was still 'peacetime'. The exercises in Belarus, under the umbrella of the Union State, enabled the Russians to install large numbers of troops — three armies — there, and then leave them there.

The next point is clearly a reference to the BTGs. 'Highly manoeuvrist military action by hybrid [mezhvidovye] groups of forces.' Some analysts believe that in many cases this simply means 'combined arms', and they are probably right. This is obviously meant to contrast with the point at the bottom of the first column, 'Direction of military forces through a strictly hierarchical command structure.' The problem, as it emerged during the campaign, was that these BTGs could not perform as expected, in part due to officers without the necessary training and experience. Hence the need for generals to go forward.

Traditional forms and means	New forms and means
• Military action starts after strategic deployment • Frontal collision of powerful force groupings with ground forces as the basis • Destruction of personnel and weapons with the successive seizure of phase lines and areas with the aim of seizing territory • Defeat of the enemy, destruction of his economic potential and conquest of his territory • Conduct of military operations on land, in the air and at sea • Direction of military forces through a strictly hierarchical command structure.	• Military action by groups of forces begins in peacetime • Highly manoeuvrist military action by hybrid (*mezhvidovye*) groups of forces (see explanation in text) • Reduction of the military-economic potential of the [target] state by the neutralisation of critical national infrastructure in a short time • Massed use of high precision ('smart') weapons (*Vysoko Tochnye Orushtya (VTO)*), widespread use of special forces (*spetsial'nye voyska*) and weapons based on new physical principles and participation of civil-military component in military action. • Simultaneous action against enemy forces and targets throughout the entire depth of his territory • Simultaneous action in all physical dimensions and in cyberspace (*informatsionnoye prostranstvo*) • Use of asymmetric and indirect action • Direction of forces and means in a single informational space.

Figure 13. - 'Changes in the Character of Armed Struggle: attaining political targets.' Translated by the author. Original source: *Military-Industrial Courier*, 27 February 2013. p. 3 of 7.

The next point is 'Reduction of the military-economic potential of the [target] state by the neutralisation of critical national infrastructure in a short time.' The most critical part of the national infrastructure is the government, and the Russians sent in assassination squads to try to remove the president. They failed. After that, the Russians have clearly targeted national infrastructure including railways and power. They have also seized two nuclear power stations — Chernobyl and Zaporizhyya.

The naval blockade has probably been the most important attack on Ukraine's military and economic potential. Preventing the export of grain hits Ukraine hardest. But Russia cannot afford to alienate countries in the developing world whom it now needs as allies more than ever. Hence the Black Sea Initiative. Immediately after that was signed, Foreign Minister Lavrov embarked on a tour of Africa to reassure Egypt, the Republic of Congo, Uganda and Ethiopia that the shortage of grain and high prices for fertiliser were all the fault of Western sanctions.

The next point is 'Massed use of high precision ("smart") weapons [Vysoko Tochnye Orushiya (VTO)], widespread use of special forces [spetsial'nye voyska] and weapons based on new physical principles and participation of civil-military components in military action.' The Russians have been using certain high-precision weapons, especially missiles. The problem is that they are very expensive and not that numerous. It is the Ukrainians who have made more effective use of high-precision weapons, especially drones. Weapons based on new physical principles have not really been used, although the hypersonic missiles with which the Russian Navy is now to be equipped probably come into that category. However, the problem with these very high-tech weapons is that they are very expensive and in relatively short supply. Special Forces have been used, notably in the initial attempts to take out the Ukrainian government, but more novel and alarming is the 'participation of the civil-military component in military action'. That appears to mean private military companies, a definition given to the notorious Wagner Group.

'Simultaneous action against enemy forces and targets throughout the entire depth of his territory' is an old Soviet maxim, but the Russians have certainly done that. On the very first day of the hot war, missiles struck right across the country. These included missiles fired from the Black and Caspian Seas.

The next point, 'Simultaneous action in all physical dimensions and in cyberspace [informatsionnoye prostranstvo]', has also been evident. As noted in the previous essay, the Russians first used cyber-attacks simultaneously with kinetic operations against Georgia in 2008. They have kept up cyber-attacks against Ukraine throughout the war. The first major cyber-attack took place on 14 January 2022 and took down more than a dozen Ukrainian government websites. Most of the sites were restored within hours of the attack. On 15 February, another cyber-attack took down multiple government and banking services. However, 'information warfare' also refers to the propaganda and media war. In the run-up to 24 February and throughout the conflict, Russian officials have consistently distorted the truth. This is probably aimed more at the Russian population, who are banned from accessing foreign media.

Western intelligence officials believed that the physical attack on 24 February 2022 would be accompanied by a major cyber-attack against Ukrainian infrastructure, but this threat did not materialise. Cyber-attacks on Ukraine have continued during the invasion but with limited success. Independent hacker groups have launched cyber-attacks on Russia in retaliation for the invasion.

The next point, 'use of asymmetric and indirect action', has not been very evident since 24 February. 'Asymmetric action' usually refers to terrorist or insurgency tactics, whereas in Ukraine the Russians have been using fairly 'symmetric' means, including combined arms tactics and artillery and missile bombardment. More 'asymmetric' might better refer to the August killing of Darya Dugina, daughter of Putin's ally Aleksandr Dugin, in August 2022. Russia alleged that the attack, probably meant for her father, was mounted by Ukrainian security forces.[79]

That brings us to the last point: 'Direction of forces and means in a single informational space.' As the war progressed, observers noted that the four main forces shown in Figure 6 seemed to be operating largely independently. Having been stalled at Kyiv, the Russians obeyed one of their cardinal principles, which is 'reinforce success', not failure, and they switched their main effort to the east and south.

Two other key points emerge from Gerasimov's 2013 articles. He mentions private military companies. In Ukraine, the Russian use of mercenaries, like the Wagner Group, has important ramifications. They are expendable—they are not conscripts or young Russians forced to sign contracts. And their involvement is deniable. Secondly, he also noted the need to 'mobilise the protest potential of the population'. This happened in Crimea and the Russian

---

[79] 'Russia Blames Ukraine for Murder of Putin Ally's Daughter', Politico, 22 August 2022, https://www.politico.eu/article/fsb-russia-blame-ukraine-murder-vladimir-putin-darya-dugina (accessed 23 August 2022).

speaking areas of Donbas. But the Russians seem not to have taken account of the 'protest potential' of the rest of Ukraine's population. They fought back. That has cost them very dear.

5. STRATEGY IN THE AGE OF GLOBAL WAR

Philip W. Blood

The global war is on. The world finds itself embroiled in a global conflict, presenting the free world with a profound dilemma - how to navigate this global war and emerge unscathed. Western security, comprising the USA, NATO, and the EU sphere of influence, is grappling with the lingering aftermath of the unsuccessful War on Terror, the enduring socio-economic repercussions of the COVID-19 pandemic, and the uncertainties stemming from domestic political instability.

Signs that the West's cultural resilience has wavered was evident in its hesitance to become entangled in Putin's war, coupled with alarming reductions in military force and depleted weapon stocks. Putin, for his part, attributes the war to NATO expansion, yet underlying factors are at play. Firstly, NATO expansion has been a consistent topic in Russia-West political discourse since the 1990s. Secondly, Putin's war reveals a deep-seated fear of Russia's dwindling population and the subsequent decline in Russian cultural influence. Thirdly, Russia's cultural identity has been galvanized by the prospect of a resurgence, manifested in patriotic displays on national television and unwavering loyalty to Putin at community events, effectively transforming Russia into a rogue state.

If the West has poked the 'Russian bear' once too often, Putin's invasion in February 2022 has exposed the glaring lack of preparedness among Western powers. Timing was crucial to Putin's strategy and laid bare the West's vulnerability, catching them off guard. One year on, Western politicians, initially caught by surprise, have attempted to deflect blame for their complacency. Some prominent politicians claimed prior knowledge of Russia's intentions to attack

Ukraine, but their defence policies and subsequent actions reveal otherwise. Misinformed by flawed strategic analyses, their decision-making and leadership have come under serious scrutiny for their ineptitude.

Certain politicians and their advisors have consistently promised Russia's defeat, Putin's downfall, and Ukraine's victory. However, one year later, Russia maintains the strategic initiative, Putin remains in power, and the definition of Ukrainian victory remains ambiguous. The realities of the war are undeniable, and Western security has witnessed a shift in military power. Europeans are awakening to the realization that collective defence under American leadership is less assured than it once appeared.

In the backdrop of escalating tensions in East-West global relations, the far-reaching consequences of the COVID-19 pandemic, mounting concerns about climate change, and the humanitarian crisis driven by mass refugee movements, it is evident that strategic thinking has, to a significant extent, become estranged from public discourse. Drawing from my experience in international risk finance before I became an academic, subsequent involvement in Anglo-American military education during the War on Terror, and my current status as an independent author and without political affiliation, I present an alternative perspective on the unfolding landscape of strategic issues for the general reader normally excluded from debates on defence. This essay delves into the realm of the politics of strategy and the commercialisation of strategic thinking. The central query this essay endeavours to answer is why Western strategic thought has struggled to effectively grapple with the challenges of 21st-century conflicts.

This essay does not advocate a return to traditional militaristic approaches but rather aims to dissect why operational-level military analyses persist as the dominant narrative in public discourse, overshadowing alternative viewpoints about warfare. The politics of strategy has profoundly shaped NATO's political identity, and in the aftermath of Putin's aggressive actions, it prompts reflection on NATO's perceived ineffectiveness as a counterforce against Russian war objectives. This predicament should serve as a cautionary signal to Western societies. However, politicians have been reluctant to broach this topic openly, given the substantial financial and ideological investments in NATO's credibility as a defensive alliance. The prevailing question concerning NATO no longer revolves around its very existence, as propagated by Russian disinformation campaigns. Instead, it revolves around whether NATO's raison d'être has evolved into primarily a political mission, rather than a defensive one. Subsequently, this essay also contemplates whether Europe should explore alternative mechanisms for security and defence. It raises the prospect of revisiting the concept of strategic humanitarianism as a centralising doctrine to build a European army. Strategic humanitarianism, it should be recalled, played a prominent role during the Yugoslav crisis in the 1990s.

Strategy and the path to global war

The meaning and conceptualisation of strategy and strategic thinking have been in a constant flux since antiquity. Every generation of scholars and practitioners has taken ownership of strategy, repackaged it into their philosophy, be it a creed, dogma, or doctrine, to explain war, politics, corporate business, or some form of sociocultural purpose. From my extensive engagement with strategy there are two general forms: corporate strategy for business, and grand strategy for national security and defence. Both involve shuffling common attributes such as politics, ideology, resilience, scarce resources, time, mass, and information into coherent plans or doctrines. However, grand strategy is also about foreseeing problems or avoiding inappropriate paths that can have dire national consequences.[1] 'Strategy', we are informed by Earle, 'deals with war, preparation for war and the waging of war... Strategy, ... is not merely a concept of wartime but is an inherent element of statecraft at all times.'[2] Scholars of war, strategy, and military history all share a common interest in how strategy functions. Strategic thinking, in

---

[1] Lawrence Freedman, *Strategy: A History*, (Oxford: Oxford University Press), 2013.
[2] Edward Mead Earle (ed.), *Makers of Modern Strategy: Military Thought from Machiavelli to Hitler* (Princeton: Princeton University Press, 1973), p.viii.

my *Weltanschauung*, is deep in politics but shallow in military matters and framed by culture. Since pursuing research into the culture of strategy and war, my perspective has shifted beyond the conduct of war and military forces, focusing upon national security and defence resilience. Without a profound strategic vision, governments cannot conceive of a coherent national security or defence policy. According to Murray, Knox, and Bernstein: 'Strategic thinking does not occur in a vacuum, or deal in perfect solutions; politics, ideology, and geography shape peculiar national strategic cultures. Murray et al argue that 'size and location of nation', historical experience and geography, religion, ideology, and culture are the primary forces underpinning strategic thinking.[3] Thus the general theory of strategy is driven by the logic of a grand national plan in the event of war or a public statement for why the national culture must be defended.

Since 1945, western strategic thinking has been generally tied to governments rather than the militaries. After the end of the Cold War, with the end of mass standing armies and the geopolitics of power blocks, a politics of strategy became prominent. The politics of strategy, in western security thinking, has pivoted between the dogma of classical liberalism and the traditions of Just War. Liberalism has championed human progress and the freedoms of speech, religion, economics, and politics. The dogma of liberalism emerged from Britain, USA, and France, through a cocktail of philosophical ideas, the lasting precedents from great historical events (wars, revolutions, and treaties), and long-term cultural change often couched in notions of 'progress'. The concept of Just War has been a powerful thread in strategic thinking and underpins the west's moral reasons for war. However, compared with societies that embrace a different culture of war, the Just War ethos is often regarded as subjective and morally suspect. Liberalism and Just War, within English-speaking cultures, evolved in parallel with Whig history. This historical narrative embellished the onset of western socio-

---

[3] Williamson Murray, MacGregor Knox, & Alvin Bernstein, *The Making of Strategy: Rulers, States and War*, (Cambridge, Cambridge University Press, 1996), pp.3-7.

economic advances and modernity. Whig history is unfashionable in academic scholarship today, but it has not entirely disappeared from the conceptualisation of strategy especially where the 'great' thinkers are concerned. The west's 'victories' since the age of total war and Cold War have been framed in Whig history, which projects the symbolism of the champion of democracy, freedom, liberty, self-determination, and global free trade. Under modern American leadership, the western powers adapted this dogma to wage the War on Terror—and lost. The slapdash retreats from Iraq and Afghanistan have left behind chaos, catastrophe and caused a calamity within the western way of war. This same dogma was aimed at Putin—from the Maidan crisis in Ukraine, the special military operation in the Crimea in 2014, to the period leading up to the war in Ukraine in 2022—and always without success. The west's ideology can no longer openly risk war and relies upon the power of economic sanctions to force Russia to change direction or excluding Putin from prestigious global events, like the G7 conference, to isolate him. However, Putin skirted all these attempts by the west to limit his goals or blockade Russia's economy. As the west's routine of sanctions and exclusion failed, an American president resorted to insulting Russia by claiming it was only a 'regional power'. Reluctance for an escalation toward military intervention, has led the west to always back down, but in February 2022 Russia finally called the West's bluff. Avoiding nuclear Armageddon is the default excuse of western leaders, but their respective publics will not condone aggressive war. This has exposed the constraints and limitations buried within western strategy. The west played fast, and loose, and now Ukraine is the victim.

The elasticity of neo-liberalism, the compromised principles of Just War, and the fantasies of neo-Whig history were stretched beyond military failure, and western resilience is grounded with illusions. The fundamental failure of strategic thinking came from an unfounded assumption that conventional war in Europe was gone forever following the break-up of the former Yugoslavia, when the last small nations gained independence from collective nationalism. The politics of strategy turned lackadaisical as conflict resolution managed old Twentieth Century tensions and counterinsurgency (COIN) became the strategic paradigm for all future conflict. A new and reckless popular politics emerged, which subsumed defence to national security in the corridors of power. Putin exploited the growing reluctance for war in the west by exposing the hypocrisy of the western democracy's armed interventionism during the first quarter of the Twenty-First Century. He formed loose alliances that pushed a counter-agenda at the west and received backing from China and other member nations of the UN. For Putin and Russia, strategy is concerned with great power status and the legacy of a culture of military excellence. Contemporary Russian grand strategy is directed at delivering national reunification, restoration of the empire and to supercharge Russia's imperial mission.[4] There are deep cultural reasons for why Russian leaders criticised Tsarist or Soviet imperialism, but then followed the same path of Russia's manifest destiny and empire (re)building – the motherland complex. By 2022, Putin had circumvented attempts by the west to isolate him as a rogue national leader. In cahoots with China and to a lesser extent with India, Russia began to push old tropes and new challenges at the west. The three powers advocated an older form of nationalism, perhaps romanticized in the bastardisation of Marxist and socialist dogma and moulded into an aggressive form of capitalism. These powers have both rejected and pandered to the west's strategic dogma of free trade and democracy, as the situation suited them. For example, despite being America's 'most favoured nation status', China used financial loans and one-way trade to erect a counter economic revolution against free trade and continued to refuse the introduction of any western style freedoms. China's counter-capitalist challenge to western capitalism seriously undermined the western economic order, in particular the twin pillars of social democracy and welfare. To respond to an increasingly competitive global marketplace, western corporations felt compelled by the shift in trade to abandon their homelands. The corporations chose to relocate their businesses to Russia,

---

[4] Darius Staliūnas & Yoko Aoshima, *The Tsar, The Empire, and the Nation: Dilemmas of Nationalization in Russia's Western Borderlands, 1905-1915*, (Budapest: CEU Press, 2021).

China, and India, for the sole purpose of driving down operating costs, make extraordinary tax-free profits, and compete with Chinese business. There are no free lunches in business and the decision to relocate to China was tantamount to giving away the company secrets and patents. This economic shift caused a fundamental weakening in western resilience, destabilising domestic geo-economies and politics, and generating cultural tensions in the social and class order. Ironically, this process was approved, endorsed, and hailed as the future of globalism by the leading figures of western liberalism. Some corporations have gradually returned to their traditional markets; however, this has failed to restore the long-term loss to many countries or repaired the damage caused to socio-economic infrastructures. This is the Catch-22 of western dogma – the choice between unfettered capitalism or the security of national cultural resilience. For Russia, China, and India, they had successfully fended off the west's strategic aims had weakened their rivals economically and made great strides in technologically without incurring the costs of massive capitalisation while at the same time building large reserves of capital.

Inherent to the progress within western strategic theory is its commodification. The commodity of war and strategy, within English language literature, has become a powerful brand with political benefits. Strategy is a brand and sold to governments and the public alike through social media and global news. An example emerged from the Soviet-Afghanistan War, when America supplied missiles to the Taliban. Decades later a popular biopic film recreated the story and by 2014 the film persuaded American analysts to follow a similar plot against Russia over the Crimea.[5] Commercialism and strategy, doesn't always generate sound critical thinking. The American defence analysts 'hoped' that like in Afghanistan, they could cause a stream of dead Russian soldiers to be sent back to Moscow to stir domestic protest against Putin. Was it beyond their strategic vision to anticipate Putin had seen the film, or had learned the lesson of American military aid and was fully prepared in

---

[5] Universal Pictures, *Charlie Wilson's War*, 2007 based on the book George Crile, *Charlie Wilson's War* (London: Atlantic, 2003).

February 2022? Putin's war became a commodity within hours of the invasion of Ukraine as global social media and television was swamped with expert content. Experts postulated theories and outcomes ranging from the quality of Russian tyres to Russia's logistical failings, to the poor quality of Russian soldiers, and even poorer field command system. Within weeks of the war's start, the scale of extreme violence also challenged the school of genocide studies to pronounce whether the killings and destruction were genocidal. Many scholars elected to step back and wait, while others published. Virtually all military experts claimed the killings were not genocide. They argued that certain prerequisites such as extermination camps and victims, usually more than a million but always fixated on the symbolic 'six million', were not present from the evidence and therefore it wasn't genocide. Putin retained the strategic initiative, which did not deter the Clausewitzian ideologues from claiming the war was already over. By May 2022 competing publishers were on the search for authors who could explain Putin's war, but Putin defied all the experts. The Russians refused to play ball and displayed not the slightest interest in western opinions, which hasn't altered a year on. This dubious style of punditry had happened before during the War on Terror, when experts claimed the allies were winning — but lost. A year into Putin's War, we can only ponder why poor analyses and farfetched predictions have returned to the screens?

The ritual commodification of Putin's war represents a 'cultural turn' in strategic thinking, as a continuation from the War on Terror. In parallel, the presence of nostalgia biased popular history has stirred a neo-Whig history revival via social media, which has propagated notions of a national exceptionalism in war, empire, and globalism especially in Britain. Consequently, jingoistic nostalgia has radicalised how the public engage with literature about war and strategy. In academia, strategic studies, war studies and military history students were once taught the universality of strategy — across nations and time. The exponents of Sun Tzu, Clausewitz and Frunze once stood beside the historians of war and the social scientists of strategic studies, forming a school of excellence in strategy. For example, the breadth of influence upon my engagement with strategic thinking came from several scholars, courses and reading. The late Martin Edmonds advocated the combination of strategic thinking and civil-military relations.[6] In war studies, John Gooch conveyed the twin influences of Clausewitz and Michael Howard's ideas about war in history. In political theory, the influence of Machiavelli's The Prince was routinely presented as a practical handbook for politicians and strategists. The 'cultural turn' in the commodification of strategy in the present war derives from the amplification of uncritical narratives from the war on terror, and the grab for profit publications regardless of scholarship or accuracy. During the war on terror, mass publication exploited strategic theory to endorse fantasies of war. The theories of Clausewitz, Sun Tzu, and Michael Howard's constructs of war and European history were brazenly deployed like commodities in validation of popular publications. Reading Hew Strachan revealed how far this outpouring of fictitious content neither reflected the theorists' ideas nor the actualities of modern war.[7] In Putin's war, social media is carrying the fantasies of war into everyone's timelines (or at least the owners of smart phones). There is a dialectic to war which was not always precise but was central to the students of war and strategy. Commodification, however, has its own dialectic: first there is the academic research and writing. Then follows academic publication aimed at the public. Eventually the attraction of popular writing culminates in simplified books of pictures about war and strategy.[8] Before Putin's War these publications had limited value, after Putin's War they bring nothing to explain the complexities of this war or the great threat facing European civilisation.

Questions over the west's decline in strategic power have circulated since the 1990s. The west has depended upon the USA's continuing role as a global police force and the guarantor of security. America has been conflicted - often unprepared to embrace the role in full but then reluctant to let it go. David Callahan examined

---

[6] Martin Edmonds, *Armed Services and Society*, (Leicester: Leicester University Press, 1988).

[7] Hew Strachan, *Clausewitz's On War: A Biography*, (2008).

[8] Sir Lawrence Freedman, *Nuclear Deterrence*, (London: Penguin Books, 2018).

American policy during ethnic conflicts and identified the challenge of *unwinnable wars*. Already by 1998 he could identify a growing trend for misreading conflicts, and the increasing probability of false predictions from poor analyses. He recognised in the post-Cold War age that internationalism was not popular in the USA. To build positive results from policy and intervention takes time and is often hampered by setbacks. The American public have little patience for long lead times in policymaking and are not prepared to accept setbacks. The public demand immediate decisions and success from their leaders. This short termism has proven unsuccessful in countering Russia and China.[9]

Western strategic thinking has hit the buffers. The process of gradual escalation, through economic sanctions to war, has routinely failed since the end of the Cold War — in former Yugoslavia, in the War on Terror and in fending off Putin. The west did not help bring about Russia's transition to democracy and market capitalism after 1989. This was the most profound failure of western security policy in the years immediately following the dissolution of the Soviet Union. This failure was exacerbated by the west's continuing diversification of national interests away from collective security during times of peace — America's eternal strife between manifest destiny and mom n' pop isolationism, Europe's path toward communal security, British exceptionalism, and the Commonwealth's flirtations for independence — each explain why Russia was no longer a priority after the end of the Cold War and left in the mire of a post-Soviet dystopia. Consequently, the global order in the post-Cold War age was not a settled peace but heightened chaos and complexity - not envisaged or predicted in the End of History neo-liberalism.

Today, the fundamental threat to western dogma is the technological revolution, which is rendering the old economic order and national establishments obsolete. The west once ruled the globe and propagandised its democratic values, with promises of a welfare society, and the pretence to meritocracy that held societies

---

[9] David Callahan, *Unwinnable Wars: American Power and Ethnic Conflict*, (New York: Hill and Wang, 1997).

together under a rigid social order. This entire edifice is being eroded. Mathematics and computer science played a decisive part in the Second World War but code-breaking, operational research, and scientific modelling have barely featured prominently in the neo-Whig 'great man' interpretation of history. There are limits to progress within liberal culture. Artificial Intelligence has been blamed for the contemporary technological revolution, but advances in robotics and other sciences have been rapidly evolving since Reagan's Star Wars initiative. In the 1980s, computer software like *Prolog*, a logic programming language created in 1972, was once the leading edge of digital predictive analysis, but today algorithms have taken prominence. This commercialisation of science for weapons and social media devices, has been underpinned by scientific theorems such as the digital application of chaos theory, algorithms, game theory and robotics—all working toward de-skilling and removing the human interface from strategizing and generating a science dogma. The western world has continually failed to come to terms with Alan Turing's immortal question: can machines think?[10] Having failed to socialise technological advances, the west has undermined its own primary strategic ethos of progress.

The fallout from this technological revolution has already flattened socio-economic structures as industrial communities have been rendered obsolete. Capital flight has left governments to confront the socio-political fallout with the decline in financial reserves and capital. Russia and China have been able to exploit weaknesses in western capital: partly by empowering the moguls of unrestricted capitalism, and partly by the rigid compartmentalisation of their proletariat in work-to-live schemes and locked-in poverty. The freedoms of western society have forced governments into implementing intensified security measures to secure and control everyday lifestyles. Emergency security forces are assigned to protect the privileged elites and the political class, while crime escalates in UK and Europe. The inability of western leaders to confront Russia reflects the sheer scale of the domestic security challenges facing

---

[10] Robert Cooper, *The Breaking of Nations: Order and Chaos in the Twenty-First Century*, (Atlantic Monthly Press, 2004).

western societies. Putin has exploited this situation for his own ends. But liberalism is flawed having financed its own self-destruction, and the consequences are increasingly apparent to an enlightened and untrusting public. The west's strategic dilemma is not Putin but the decline in the western ethos of balanced civil-military relations and the failure to properly address the technical revolution.

The shifting sands of global strategies

The strategic situation: Russia unleashed a surprise invasion of Ukraine, designated a 'special military operation'. The initial phase in the Russian operations involved multiple assaults aimed at establishing lodgements. Russia's grand maskirovka began spewing stories, mostly depicting incompetence in a bizarre game of misinformation. The assault forces were driving forward in a rough horseshoe shaped spearhead, across an extremely long frontline, and with naval blockade indicating an Anaconda Plan was in progress. This was a short sharp flashback of classical Russian military thinking, to over-stretch the opponent across a long front. In the second phase there was 'nibbling' attrition but no identifiable *Schwerpunkt* — linking up the lodgements to form a larger battle area remained their primary aim. The emergence of supporting fire illustrated the importance of the lodgements to the Russian plan. As the lodgements joined, the shelling increased to protect them. A third phase emerged with the 'annihilation bombardments' forcing the Ukrainian Army to engage in multiple local battles to protect civilians. This prevented the Ukrainians from establishing a strategic counter and forced them to react to every Russian move. The fourth phase saw the gradual rippling of offensive activity along the entire horseshoe front, all prodding for weaknesses and attracting Ukraine's reserves. A fifth phase was mounting confusion sown between alleged humanitarian efforts to rescue Ukrainians from the 'neo-Nazis' and the deliberate massacres and rapes of civilians. Refugee corridors came under direct Russian bombardments, while the increasing devastation forced refugee numbers to swell beyond

10 million.

In reflecting on Putin's strategy, my interpretation of the war in Ukraine has been at odds with general opinion. The identification of Putin's Anaconda Plan came partly from studying security warfare during the American Civil War and partly from lessons learned about the War on Terror. Together they represented learning from the failure of western security and the declining capability to harness strategy and military power. The primary cause has been the indoctrination of Clausewitz, as the catchall theoretical solution to all things strategic and military. The first decade of the twenty-first century was awash with debates about strategy and the military, but every solution was framed by Clausewitzian orthodoxy. The decade was shaped by terror and terrorism, where the concepts of regime change, or wars for democracy, and corporate war were prominent in discourse, but the default conclusions always returned Clausewitz. When operations failed, the common excuse was the incorrect interpretation of Clausewitz. During this period, soldiers, statesmen and scholars alike notoriously predicted easy victories, which was sometimes militarily correct, but soon afterwards powerful mechanised forces became stalled in guerrilla warfare. The experts were wholly unprepared for the insurgencies in Iraq and Afghanistan — regardless of similar insurgencies in those same countries during the 1980s. Time and again, the practitioners of the *War of the Flea* (1965) outwitted the exponents of *Vom Kriege* (1832). The predictions, including strategies for victory and claims to an 'intellectual insurgency', exposed the mounting uncritical approach to strategic thinking.[11] Typical was US Army General David Petraeus and his operational plans for The Surge and sustainable security as defined in President Bush's policy document The New Way Forward, published in 2007. There was a foreboding among retired US generals, many with continuing advisory roles in national security. There was a real sense that the USA was losing its strategic grip and indications that the military were divided, and in fundamental disagreement with Bush's policymakers. However,

---

[11] The collected essays under 'Intellectual Insurgency', *The Royal United Services Institute Journal* 154, no. 3 (June 2009).

the continuing military failures did not prevent the armies in the field from trying to contain the uncontainable within the scope of The Surge.

A decade later, the authors of the winnable war theories (from Iraq/Afghan wars) began publishing counter-narratives, claiming the wars on terror were never winnable. They also began pushing their analyses of Putin's war—old analyses for a new war.[12] In 2021 a book confronted the old 'winning' narratives with an examination of British army failure in Iraq and Afghanistan.[13] This was a remarkable moment in British military history publishing—not because the book was particularly insightful but that it was virtually ignored by academia and military educators. The reality of failure was still not palatable to military educators and lessons were not learned. The book also represented a threat to the commercial interests of the strategy brand. Thus, the failed strategy from the wars on terror was repackaged for Putin's war but this time washed through social media, where memory is remarkably short. Typically, at the beginning of Putin's war, British military experts invited to radio, television, and social media, all agreed it was going to be a counterinsurgency conflict. Similar claims were made about the British deployment in Afghanistan—both were wrong—the continuity of strategic failure continues.

Looking back to past wars, we can see how strategic reality was set aside for operational dogma. It is insightful to remember what happened then, to comprehend how Putin's war is now being rationalised. There was a memorable case from early into the war in Afghanistan. In the aftermath of the US military's success in Operation Anaconda, 2-18 March 2002, Brigadier Roger Lane, Commander British Forces, Bagram Air Base, informed the British media that the 'war against Afghanistan was not over—the hunt for the Taliban goes on'. Lane explained that his challenge was to confront the Taliban to learn how they would react after their defeat at the hands of the US during Operation Anaconda. BBC Panorama filmed marines who drew on their experiences in Northern Ireland

---

[12] Theo Farrell, *Unwinnable: Britain's War in Afghanistan* (London: Penguin, 2017).
[13] Simon Akam, *The Changing of the Guard* (London: Scribe, 2021).

to rationalise why they understood the Taliban's 'guerrilla tactics'. The soldiers used their Northern Ireland experience to quantify and qualify their professionalism. Five weeks later the Royal Marines had not had contact with the Taliban and Lane was forced to accept his mission had failed. He became convinced, however, that the absence of the insurgents was evidence that British counterinsurgency strategy was actually succeeding by default. The excuses for failing mounted, while questions were raised as to whether the Taliban had successfully re-deployed out of the region or whether the local villagers the marines were interviewing for intelligence purposes were the Taliban fighters in mufti.[14] Decades later, Arthur Snell has explained that the marines were caught in a drug war between the Taliban and Afghan police.[15] Operational expertise and successes failed because there was no possibility to bring them to a strategic conclusion. And there was no overarching strategic plan because such ideas had been jettisoned for western military advances that were expected to overwhelm the warring tribes with their antiquated arms.

A year later in 2003, BBC Panorama visited Kabul to film British paratroopers serving under International Security Assistance Force (ISAF). The British soldiers confronted the scale of destruction from decades of war and were expected to work alongside the Mujahideen that boasted of victory over the Red Army—the professional soldier culture and the warrior culture visualised war differently. Major General

McColl, the commander of ISAF, recognised his forces were threatened by the invisible presence of the Taliban running through the heavily armed private armies, but was forced to mount aggressive operations with them. There was little lasting success, but it taught the Mujahideen and Taliban how to defeat western power. Time, as a strategic weapon, was on the side of the Taliban and running against the west. In 2008, retired General Sir Mike Jackson (former Head of the British Army 2003-6) was interviewed in a BBC programme about the condition of the British Army during the War

---

14 BBC, Panorama, The Hunt for Bin Laden, 2002.
15 Arthur Snell, *How Britain Broke the World* (London: Canbury Press, 2022).

on Terror and he was asked questions about Afghanistan. Jackson argued that allied manoeuvre war was stunningly successful but claimed Afghanistan was more dangerous, because of serious terrorist methods and would take longer to solve. He subtly made the contra-distinction that the decision to go to war was 'politics' but the dossier with the evidence about WMD's (the British government's reason to go to war) was 'intelligence'.[16] Those acute nuances of war, strategy, and intelligence, expressed by professionals on television were intended to lure the public into believing the war was being won. The question was whether the army believed them?

The late Richard Holmes interpretation of strategy was highly pragmatic—soldierly but realistic in how strategy should function in practice. In 2004, Holmes returned from Iraq much changed by his brief experience of the war and his observations of British Army operations. In conversation before the visit, he was focused upon using his role as Colonel of the Regiment, The Princess of Wales's Royal Regiment, to elevate discussions about how the operational war was being conducted. In public opinion there was mounting concerns, over the waste of the nation's service personnel in an unwinnable war both strategically and militarily. In his book Dusty Warriors (2006), Holmes decided to categorise the war as 'a postmodern war' but from his first briefing in Iraq, he faced uncertainty: 'a complex insurgent environment with many disparate elements working on parallel tracks without being truly united at the top. It is a polyglot mix of bad actors...'[17] He drew on the old tropes about British soldiering to deflect impressions he was particularly critical of the army or government. However, he was a cogent observer of the 'dark side' that was looming from within the British Army. His book referred to the bullying scandal in Deepcut training facility and the crescendo of 'war crimes' allegations. He partly agreed with Joanna Bourke and her article 'From Surrey to Basra, abuse is a fact of British life' in The Guardian in 2005. However, in discussions upon his return there was a noticeable and cogent change, in particular his impression that British strategy and military

---

[16] BBC, Hardtalk, General Sir Mike Jackson, 2008.
[17] Richard Holmes, *Dusty Warriors* (London: Harper Press, 2006), p.9.

operations were no longer in tandem. He elected not to write about it at that time.

In the 2008, BBC programme referred above, Jackson had been asked what did the British soldiers in Iraq die for? He replied, 'look if we take this sort of view, we will never do anything.' The question was repeated, and he replied, 'they died to bring Iraq out of the most miserable regime. Three and a half decades they had to go through, the regime of fear as it was described by some.' Jackson argued the principles remained the same: stable government, at peace with itself, peace with its neighbours, with a representative government. He was in the firing line and appeared flustered about the emotions of casualties, but this deeply inquisitive questioning turned on British strategy and its growing failure. British civil-military relations were out of sync with strategy – the question was why? In 2009 after one of his former students was killed in Afghanistan, Holmes published an article that finally questioned British strategy. He argued, 'We need a real strategy, not a sequence of tactical ploys; winning battles will not necessarily win the war.' Holmes sagely observed, 'Although the Army had considerable experience of counterinsurgency (and went on at unwise length about the fact), there is little sign that it applied its own doctrine in Iraq.'[18] Holmes and Jackson both reflected British military orthodoxy, but also revealed the dichotomies underlying western security dogma and strategy. The nature of modern war had changed, and national strategy had not kept in step; the increase in political extremism and populism undermined civil-military relations and strategy had become the plaything for politicians who foolishly believed in western supremacy. In addition, the wasting over-dependency on America had degraded the European capability to conduct sound strategic thinking.

In 2011 the Libyan Crisis led Prime Minister Cameron to take the unilateral decision to deploy military force, but it failed. Two years' later, in the UN, Putin criticised the west for adopting unilateral force, and for worsening the problem of terrorism globally.

---

[18] Richard Holmes, 'Rupert Should Not Have Died For This', *The Times*, 7 July 2009.

Putin's subsequent successful use of military intervention in Syria caught the west by surprise. This revealed an intelligent grasp of strategy, probably more advanced than most of Putin's western rivals. In deconstructing Putin's strategy, certain traits are constant. Decisiveness has been the key to his strategy, which is the golden thread that runs throughout all his wars since 1999. Putin's War does not in any form parallel the Iraq/Afghanistan wars but does reveal an underlying discipline and determination in his strategic stance, regardless of operational results. Putin retains the strategic initiative, which shows he strictly separates strategy from military operations, which Daniel Moran has explained as critical in war:

The capture of a town, the successful defence of a hill, the destruction of the enemy army in front of you — these are all undeniably victories, to be admired as such. Yet nothing is more common in war than strategically barren victory — meaning military achievements that, however impressive in their own terms, nevertheless fail to alter the political context in which they occur. Such disconnection can be demoralizing to those who fight and is a common source of civil-military discord, if not indeed of defeat.[19]

These observations about the strategic outweighing the tactical/operational are further endorsed in Murray et al: 'Mistakes in operations and tactics can be corrected but political and strategic mistakes last forever.' If we included Peter Paret's observation that statesmen and military leaders, 'live in a world of incomplete information', 'makers of strategy must cheerfully face the uncertainties of decision and the dangers of action',[20] then Putin's strategy is more than coherent. Putin, for all his wickedness, has maintained a constant posture throughout the first year of the war. Whether by chance of design, Putin has shackled together the notions of 'time is power' and the looming Russian land mass as the foundations for his strategy. After a year, he has shown that his strategy is framed

---

[19] Daniel Moron, 'Strategy', in Richard Holmes, *The Oxford Companion to Military History*, (Oxford, Oxford University Press, 2001), p.880.

[20] Peter Paret (ed), Makers of Modern Strategy: from Machiavelli to the Nuclear Age, (Oxford: Clarendon Press, 1986).

by 'persistence and the long view'.²¹ Putin has traded tactics, technology, and the minutiae of battle to retain control of strategy and the war. This was learned from history and the recent western experiences of strategic failure. The focus of the first two sections of this essay was to reflect on the western way of war in the light of Putin's war. We can now see how Putin's war has exposed serious flaws within western security and NATO in particular.

Putin and NATO - an intractable confrontation

In Moscow in August 1991 there was a failed Communist Party coup to take back control of Russia. During the coup, BBC Radio 4's Martin Sixsmith broadcast his belief that Russia was shedding autocracy for democracy. Twenty years later, Sixsmith confessed he was wrong and argued that America was also wrong. He blamed the Harvard economists sent to assist in the transition of Russia toward a market economy but revelled in the end of communism - they failed.²² In 2021 Vladimir Kara-Murza observed that following the dissolution of the Soviet Union in December 1991 Boris Yeltsin, the first democratically elected leader in Russian history, raised the question of Russia's membership of NATO.²³ Between Sixsmith and Kara-Murza there is a short history that began with hope for Russia and Europe, but has ended in Ukraine's tragedy. Sixsmith was the victim of history, whereas Kara-Murza, an opposition activist, is another victim of Putin's authoritarianism having been found guilty of treason by a Russian court and has received a twenty-five-year prison sentence.²⁴ Whereas Sixsmith dwelled on the continuity of Russian history to explain Russia's anti-democratic path, Kara-

---

21 Holmes, *Oxford Companion*, p.880.
22 Martin Sixsmith, *Russia: A Thousand Year Chronicle of the Wild East*, (London: BBC Books, 2011)
23 Vladimir V. Kara-Murza, 'A Europe "Whole and Free" Will Not Be Possible Without Russia', in Oxana Schmies (ed.), *NATO's Enlargement and Russia: A Strategic Challenge in the Past and Future*, (Stuttgart: Ibidem, 2021), p.7.
24 'Vladimir Kara-Murza: Russian Opposition Figure Jailed for 25 Years', *BBC News*, 17 April 2023, sec. Europe, https://www.bbc.com/news/world-europe-65297003. (Accessed 2 February 2023)

Murza contrasted that while NATO enlargement was a 'resounding success', it was also a 'dismal failure' for leading to 'a new dynamic of confrontation between the Western alliance and Russia...' He argued that the fundamental problem lay with recognition of Russia's place in Europe, he reflected on how integration could have been achieved and why it was mismanaged by the West in the 1990s. Kara-Murza explained it was not Yeltsin's question of NATO membership that caused difficulty, but rather NATO leadership's incoherent response to his proposal. Whereas there had been incentives for integration such as free trade, open markets, and free travel offered to some former Warsaw Pact countries, nothing was offered to Russia least of all fast-track integration, which was a central tenet of the 1992 Maastricht Treaty.[25] Kara-Murza blamed the absence of preparation and planning for the change in circumstances that led to NATO's failure to formulate a workable post-Cold War strategy for Russia.

NATO, since 1989, has pursued the politics of bureaucratic expansion through increasing membership, but has not raised the quality of its decision-making. This can be identified in the continuing claims of membership but poor regulation of budgets and the increasing failure to deter Putin since Crimea in 2014. This raises that old question that once governed bureaucratic institutions — efficiency or effectiveness? NATO is stuck in a complex paradigm beset between bureaucratic efficiency and operational effectiveness but caught in the political noose of following an anti-democratic path (expansion without wider collective agreement) and operating with underpowered forces. There is considerable scholarship that has always endorsed and approved NATO's existence.[26] As Jens Karlsbergs has observed: 'NATO faces the most complex and unpredictable security situation since the end of the Cold War.' In arguing the case for NATO, he has claimed Putin has three strategic priorities: to restore Russia's superpower status in global affairs, to disrupt European security and transform imperial Russia into a

---

[25] Kara-Murza, *NATO Enlargement and Russia*, p.8
[26] Michael O. Slobodchikoff et al, *The Challenge to NATO: Global Security and the Atlantic Alliance*, (UNP, 2021).

bastion of empire. Karlsbergs has argued that NATO's challenge is that Russia is insecure in its civil-military relations, an unstable society, and an enormous military capability.

Timothy Andrews Sayle has written an history of NATO that argues that western leaders have always feared the threat from Moscow, rather than the actuality of war. America and Britain feared Europeans would press their leaders to concede before the Red Army had crossed the front line. In effect, NATO was a means to holding member states together rather than serving as a defence community. From his research he discovered evidence that contrary to the assumption that NATO protected democracy, the alliance was held together as an 'insurance against the dangers of democracy.' NATO came to represent the *Pax Atlantica*, a means to enforcing peace through military power.[27] NATO cannot disguise the political instability within the membership ranks and entirely relies upon military ingenuity as its strategic advantage, which is also an unstable strategy. The membership is far from democratic, as some observers have often argued about Turkey resembling contemporary Russia rather than any western democracy. Britain, once a leading member of NATO, has struggled since the financial crisis of 2008 to establish a sound R&D policy for defence. These kinds of issues have always been used to question NATO's continuing existence.

Anti-NATO criticism and arguments against its existence have been in general circulation since long before the end of the Cold War. However, there has been a more critical examination by Ted Galen Carpenter, who has likened NATO to a dangerous dinosaur. He opened with President Trump's 2016 speech about the financial contributions of America's allies to collective security, NATO, and the European concerns about the future. Americans had always been animated about the balance of burden sharing, but in times of peace that balance has become a hot subject in domestic politics. Carpenter noted that American frustration increased after the 9-11 tragedy because the US military almost doubled in size while

---

[27] Timothy Andrews Sayle, Enduring Alliance: A History of NATO and the Postwar Global Order', (Cornell: Cornell University, 2019), p.2.

European powers continued to reduce their overall military budgets. The European allies, he claimed want a 'tripwire' of US military forces to ensure America's commitment to collective security. Carpenter pre-empted recent events when he wrote, 'The European desire for a renewed and enhanced U.S. tripwire has soared as worries mount about the intentions of Russian president Vladimir Putin's regime.' Carpenter was less insightful in his opinions of Russophobia and the onset of the 'new Cold War'. He was sceptical about Putin's ambitions, arguing that they were exaggerated by NATO allies and blamed the Europeans for not working harder to deter Putin from aggression. Carpenter concluded, 'Washington ought to adopt a strategy based on an orderly but prompt transfer of responsibility for Europe's security to the nations of democratic Europe.'[28] As a critic of NATO, Carpenter had valid opinions, but Putin's aggression represents a problem for all critics in being accused of backing Putin.

NATO is not transparent in its everyday work. However, NATO's actions reveal a war averse and a reluctant fighting organisation—an extraordinary position for a defence organisation. This palpable reluctance for war has been highlighted in previous military interventions and the no-fly zones implemented since the 1990s. Arguably, all NATO intervention or war-making has failed since the no-fly zones and air war over former Yugoslavia in the 1990s. However, NATO had already lost the strategic initiative to Putin by 2014 and has been on the back foot ever since. The failure to act in February 2022 was softened by President Biden's unilateral decision to stand back and watch. Jens Karlsbergs had previously claimed, alongside many analysts, that 'Russia is a declining global power while China is a rising global power.' By 2023 such claims ring hollow as the world watches powerless to prevent Russia from perpetrating genocide in Ukraine. President Donald Trump represented the ultimate threat from within regarding NATO and western security. Arthur Snell, among many former government officials and scholars, has argued that Trump 'undermined NATO'.

---

[28] Ted Galen Carpenter, *NATO: The Dangerous Dinosaur*, (Washington DC: Cato Institute, 2019), p.8 and p.52.

Trump agreed a deal with the Taliban in February 2020 signifying NATO's retreat from Afghanistan, but it was President Biden who implemented the deal in the Summer of 2021. The American failure was NATO's failure, and this is a tough lesson for the allied governments, which failed to fully appreciate the wider implications even before Russia invaded Ukraine. United Kingdom government representatives used the moment to claim it would carry on alone in Afghanistan, but it was an unrealistic claim that suited the hardline Brexit narrative of a populist regime. Putin read both Trump and Biden, out played them, and then ignored Biden prior to unleashing war on Ukraine.

The present east-west crisis dates back to the end of the Cold War but has been ramped-up by Putin's sabre rattling since 2007. His *cause célebrè* is NATO expansion. The west justifies this expansion as an expression of free will and democratic self-determination, while Russia argues that it's a direct threat to its national security — both sides have provoked the other. This has been ongoing since 1992, an intractable strategic confrontation that was always liable to escalate. In February 2007, Putin unleashed his first serious criticism of NATO expansion during a Munich Security Conference. He criticised US foreign policy, warned of 'global strategic and military consequences', cautioned against the rising tensions in world affairs, and 'openly declared the Russian categorical refusal of any NATO expansion into the post-Soviet space.'[29] In 2008, both Ukraine and Georgia became potential members in the next wave of NATO expansion. Georgia had suffered under Soviet rule and was eager to align itself to the west and join NATO. Russia responded by declaring this expansion a grave security threat and reacted violently. In August, a military manoeuvre codenamed Caucasus 2008 became the jump-off for Russian military forces to rapidly take control of Georgia in a five-day operation that resembled the suppression of Czechoslovakia in 1968.

Despite Putin's success in Georgia, the lessons learned led to doctrinal changes in Russian political and military policies. Henry

---

[29] Jan Eichler, *NATO's Expansion After the Cold War: Geopolitics and Impacts for International Security*, (Switzerland: Springer, 2021), p.79.

Kissinger and Richard Holbrooke, in Germany in 2008, initiated a general discussion regarding the incoming Obama presidency and US foreign policy. Kissinger argued that Russia was no longer a superpower but had to be treated like a superpower because of its nuclear weapons arsenal. Discussions among leading German and American officials reflected the general opinion that Russia's small wars did not alter the general trend toward further decline. The global financial crisis and the enduring failures in the War on Terror, however, caused a decline in western security influence. There was a failure to revise western doctrines and a sharp reduction in conventional military forces forced by financial constraints. The west began to falter. In 2014, at the height of the Maidan Crisis in Ukraine and the seizure of the Crimea, both Putin and Gorbachev (last Soviet leader) jointly criticised the USA for its triumphalism and unilateralism in foreign affairs since 1989. America and NATO were powerless to deter Putin. The rising tensions since 2020, Putin's sabre rattling and the general warlike rhetoric has placed Russia and the west in a head-on collision. Today the west remains unprepared for a general war.

Putin and NATO can never compromise and are bound in a permanent state of confrontation. Putin is a paternalistic authoritarian dictator and NATO is a creaking bureaucratic institution. Putin pretends to represent the interests of the Russian empire and NATO pretends to be committed to Europe's security and defence. Putin uses diplomacy, economics, espionage, and sabotage to wage cold war and is quite prepared to order Russia's military forces into invasions, interventions, and occupation. NATO's anti-democratic activities include the application of subterfuge, private forces, private contractors, espionage, and intimidation to provoke Russia and China. No side is innocent, as this has always been how great powers and power-blocks behave. At some point the bluff and bluster turns into conflict, and today an east-west global confrontation is unravelling. Putin has attacked NATO relentlessly because he knows there are political points to be gained from it in Russia. The 1990s dystopia after the end of the Soviet Union has not been forgotten and a large sector of Russian society is hostile to the west. Putin can draw on that hostility and NATO is the symbolic culprit partly because the promises of non-expansion were not observed, and western governments have been quick to side with any opponents to Putin.

It's axiomatic that political bureaucracies rarely solve the problem they were raised to resolve. NATO's existence was defined by hostility toward Russia but it's in NATO's bureaucratic self-interest to maintain Putin's war. It's self-evident that NATO have worsened Ukraine's predicament and promises of future membership have driven Russia to further intensifying military operations and genocide. NATO has justified its existence by provoking Russia, but the bluff has been called and Putin has exposed the west's military incompetence. If the west wants to formulate a common understanding with Russia, NATO must be removed from the equation. NATO and the Russia empire share similar pretences about the solidity of their regimes and their respective military power, this makes a future violent confrontation or final showdown inevitable. The sooner Europe moves away from NATO the sooner Putin's regime can be removed from office. In 2014, a New York newspaper published an article that claimed Putin had ambitions to restore the former Soviet Union but under a different management regime.[30] Does he wish to restore a failed regime or does Putin imagine the resurgence of a greater Russia, when Cossacks watered their horses in the river Seine?

The long-term failure of the west to counter or even deter Putin, and Russia, has hogtied Europe to America's unpredictable indecision and confusion in foreign affairs. American hegemony has been instrumental in intimidating Russia politically, but why did NATO strategy fail, and why did the defence systems falter? NATO leaders knew that expansion would eventually lead to confrontation. This was political intimidation without a contingency plan to counter Russian aggression — reckless war-making or bureaucratic incompetence, or both? NATO has gained nothing from failing to intervene but has preserved its political existence. That is no longer practical, and Europe should consider breaking from

---

[30] Ralph Peters, "Putin's Plan to Reclaim the Old Soviet Empire," *New York Post*, 3 May 2014.

America's domination of NATO to save Ukraine and preserve European culture.

Putin and the Russian population

Social Darwinism is alive and well and threatening a global apocalypse. Populations are central to Putin's strategic planning and the problem for western states. Once roundly rejected in Western political discourse, Social Darwinism is once again working its ways and means back into both the British Conservative Party and Putin's Russia. In the case of the Conservative Party, Boris Johnson, the outgoing prime minister, announced in his resignation speech on 7 July 2022: 'And my friends in politics, no one is remotely indispensable and our brilliant and Darwinian system will produce another leader equally committed to taking this country forward through tough times, not just helping families to get through it, but changing and improving the way we do things.[31]' Demographic pressures have been destabilising the British establishment. Today, the British government is rapidly incorporating Social Darwinist measures to shift political discourse away from the failure of Brexit and to refocus public gaze from the alarming consequences of strategic isolation. Institutional racism threatened withdrawal from the European Court of Human Rights, and the emerging impact of a social order that pushes a struggle for survival in welfare, energy and food banks exposes a country rapidly disengaging from neo-classical liberalism and embracing authoritarian national conservatism.

A few weeks before Johnson's statement, Putin hosted the Twenty-Fifth International Economic Forum, in St Petersburg, with guests including Xi Jinping, president of the People's Republic of China. In his opening speech, Putin announced: 'Russia was forced to go ahead with the special military operation. It was a difficult but

---

[31] 'Boris Johnson's Resignation Speech in Full: "Darwinian" Politics, a Westminster "Herd Instinct" and a Warning to Colleagues | UK News | Sky News', https ://news.sky.com/story/boris-johnsons-resignation-speech-in-full-darwinian-politics-a-westminster-herd-instinct-and-a-warning-to-colleagues-12647551. (Accessed 2 February 2023)

necessary decision, and we were forced to make it,' adding that 'the decision was aimed at protecting our people and the residents of the people's republics of Donbas who for eight long years were subjected to genocide by the Kievsic regime and the neo-Nazis who enjoyed the full protection of the west.' He then went on to say: 'Real, stable success and a sense of dignity and self-respect only come when you link your future of your children with your Fatherland.' With the references to social justice and population measures underpinned by economic development, his words come from another age. Reducing poverty, inequality, increasing the minimum wage and providing child support from birth to seventeen are the main performance indicators of Putin's 'new society'. The same claims have been echoed through history, but now it's official: 'Russia's future is ensured by families with two, three and more children.'[32] Weeks after official pronouncements that 'Russia was fighting for its historical future', these words now have a sinister meaning.[33] The question of Russia's declining population permeates Putin's diplomacy. In a BBC documentary, John Casson, David Cameron's foreign policy adviser claimed Putin had said in 2013: 'there is a demographic crisis in Russia, we have got an ageing population. We need more births we need more babies, if I give gay rights and marriage to the Russian people, we will have fewer babies.'[34]

The question of populations is old history regularly repackaged. Population statistics have long been the measure of great power status since industrialisation. In this over-populated and hi-tech world, it has remained the basic socio-economic measure of national success. Imperialistic nations once took pride in their population growth, which was seen as proof of industrial advancement and military power. The history of Germany, from the Kaiserreich to the Third Reich, is also a story about territorial ambitions and

---

[32] 'St Petersburg International Economic Forum Plenary Session', President of Russia, 17 June 2022, http://en.kremlin.ru/events/president/news/68669 (accessed 14 September 2022).

[33] Dr. Ian Garner (@irgarner), tweet, 5 July 2022, https://twitter.com/irgarner/status/1544273331217731591. (accessed 2 October 2022)

[34] BBC, 'Putin vs the West', Brook Lapping Productions, 2023.

declining populations. In the German scientific mindset, Lebensraum grew from an idea to improve urban squalor and population during massive growth spikes in the nineteenth century, what later underpinned a Nazi genocidal doctrine. Germany, in the period from 1919 to 1933, experienced a series of destabilising events that were not greatly dissimilar to Russia after the end of the Cold War. The Versailles treaty mandated the annexation of populations and territory on the fringes of German borders by foreign countries. This led to outbreaks of violence between local protection forces, occupiers, and foreign armies. The Allied occupation enforced reparations. For many Germans, this was revenge and plundering by the Allies. Many industrialists smuggled their business secrets out of the occupation zone.

When the Belgian occupier closed local German industries, the surge in unemployment caused outcries in the local press. Violence against the occupiers sparked periods of bitter commercial rivalries. Business learned a harsh lesson about competition especially in the rationing of investment finance.[35] Nazi Germany was a kleptocracy, not unlike Putin's Russia, but it was radicalised towards racial genocide for industrial greed. German cartels played an instrumental role in the Holocaust as both perpetrators and profiteers. They began their economic recovery from the great depression of the 1920s by acquiring small businesses and family concerns. Nazi control of the chambers of commerce smoothed the way for 'Aryanisation', the forced takeover of Jewish businesses. The chief of the SS, Heinrich Himmler, organised an inner circle of industrialists that combined security and cartel-capitalism that brought about mass slave labour and plundering of occupied nations.[36] While the degree of social violence was not as prolific as in Putin's Russia, Weimar Germany brings insights into how socioeconomic dystopia can bleed into geopolitical violence and war.

There was always a fascination and a fear of Russia within

---

[35] Philip W Blood, *Aachen in Total War*: A Study of Military History, unpublished MS.

[36] Richard Overy, *Blood and Ruins: The Great Imperial War, 1931-1945*, (London: Allen Lane, 2021).

certain British political circles. In September–October 1960, the Communist Party of Great Britain sent a delegation of British trade unionists to the Soviet Union on a political education tour. One delegate kept a collection of notes and reports that provide a remarkable snapshot of Soviet society. The party arrived in Leningrad on 24 September and were entertained in the Palace of Culture on the first evening, with 2,238 fellow trade unionists. They were shown a film of the Gary Powers' trial, who had been shot down during his U-2 intruder flight over the USSR on 1 May 1960. There were music recitals and group discussions about trade union politics in Britain and the Soviet Union. Their trip included a visit to a collective farm, a textile factory, and a new university in Moldavia, as well as an extended period in Moscow. A factory they visited advised that of 8,000 workers, 30 per cent were twenty-six years of age. There was a sporting society for everyone. In parts of the foundry, the conditions were harsh, and the managers applied piecework rules to jobs, but all workers received the full wage. Technical schools had up to 5,000 pupils. There were targets to build 1,000 new homes to increase the capacity of the industrial zone. Within the zone, they visited a children's hospital that cared for children from birth to fourteen years of age. Hospital staffing numbers were 130 doctors and 500 nurses. The tour group returned to Leningrad on 9 October for ten days of events, conferences, luncheons, suppers, museums, and the ballet.

Reading the delegation reports involves navigating through British trade union interests of wages, jobs, and politics against the Soviet attempts to project proletarian harmony, social conditioning, and the regimentation of socio-economic life.[37] In July 1961, three months after completing the first manned-space flight, Yuri Gagarin visited the union headquarters of the Rowland Casasola's in Metropolitican-Vickers, an event not included in the news broadcast. Today, social media would describe this official tour party as 'tankies'—supporters of the Stalinist and Soviet systems. In the 1960s, however, there were different viewpoints, between East or

---

[37] 'Private papers of Rowland Casasola (1893–1971), president of the Amalgamated Union of Foundry Workers. Papers held by the author.

West, bridged by a shared paternalism that underpinned socio-economic goals that have all but disappeared from modern economic thinking.

By the 1980s, the Soviet economy was stagnating, just as British historian Paul Kennedy published his study of great power history. In one section, he reflected on the Marxist notion of contradictions inherent to the capitalist system that would inevitably bring about its demise. He contrasted this to the Soviet Union's projected contradictions between its national aims and the means to achieve them. Kennedy noticed how the Soviets' adherence to the 'overriding importance of world peace' was set against their support for a massive military build-up and encouraging the spread of internal revolution across the globe. These contradictions extended to security, where Kennedy noted that Soviet concerns for absolute security compromised foreign relations with allies and opponents alike. The Soviets were committed to avoiding military inferiority and prepared to raise national production, but they were following 'the Russian tradition of devoting too high a share of national resources to the armed forces', which was negatively affecting commerce and economics.

The growing difficulties of over-militarisation at the cost of commercial development were a major cause in breaking the remaining elasticity in the Soviet economy. However, Kennedy was reluctant to predict the imminent collapse of the Soviet Union. He also advised against assuming the USSR had overwhelming power. He argued that the Brezhnev era of a balance between the military and the economy was over, and the Soviet Union was confronting serious pressures, possibly leading to an 'economic crunch'. The Soviet faith in military power largely defined its global status, and it was thereby inconceivable that Moscow would reduce or undermine its armed forces regardless of the internal and external problems the militaristic imbalance caused. Kennedy concluded this was a dilemma for both East and West, adding: '[T]here is nothing in the character or tradition of the Russian state to suggest that it could ever accept imperial decline gracefully.'[38]

Four years after Kennedy's seminal work, Francis Fukuyama, an American political scientist, declared 'the End of History'. He reviewed the recent past and itemised what he thought signalled the end of the USSR: in 1986, the Soviet press had criticised Stalin's crimes, which later spilled over to criticism of members of the last regime; in 1989, the communists tried to rig elections to the Supreme Soviet; also in 1989, the Red Army withdrew from Afghanistan; the Berlin Wall collapsed, sparking the end of the Warsaw Pact sphere of influence; and in 1990 Article 6 of the Soviet constitution no long guaranteed Communist Party leadership. Fukuyama expected the break-up to lead to 'successor states that successfully make the transition to liberal democracy'. He predicted that there would be tensions and violence as peoples transferred from historical to post-historical worlds, especially in the former Soviet Union and Eastern Europe. Fukuyama argued that 'no one ... would advocate a policy of military challenges to non-democratic states armed with powerful weapons, especially nuclear ones'.[39] With the benefit of hindsight, Fukuyama, the leading neoconservative and contributor to the Reagan doctrine, had framed the dogma that shaped the American future into the twenty-first century. The problem lay in the triumphalism of his narrative, a barely concealed arrogance over the collapse and break-up of the Soviet Union. Though little remarked at the time, Fukuyama completely ignored the 1990 Paris Charter (19–21 November) from which the new Europe was technically born. Kennedy and Fukuyama were examples of their national cultures at critical points in European history. The great powers' thesis reflected a period when Europe was at the centre of global politics and the ideological conflict between capitalism and socialism.

There is another history. Russia today is still the world's largest landmass. In 1960, during the British trade unionist visit, the

---

[38] Paul Kennedy, *The Rise and Fall of the Great Powers: Economic Change and Military Conflict from 1500 to 2000* (London: Fontana Press, 1988), pp. 488–514.

[39] Francis Fukuyama, *The End of History and the Last Man* (London: Penguin, 1992), pp. 26–8, 277–8, 280.

Russian population was 119,735,095 and growing at an annual rate of 1.4 per cent. There had been fluctuations in the population growth rate, but it then spiralled into a continuous decline from 1.24 per cent in 1962 to 0.12 per cent in 1993. From 1994 until 2008, there was significant negative population growth annually, which then stalled but returned to negative growth in 2020, which continued into 2022. In 2010, Timothy Taylor claimed the Russian population was estimated to fall to 109 million by 2050, a return to the 1954 population figure. Taylor's opinion, while not correct, illustrates the kind of American view of Russian economic performance that prevailed prior to the 2008 global financial crash. His entire discussion focused on the economic decline from post-Cold War Soviet Russia to the Russian Federation, and how Russia's political leadership had failed. Taylor referred to different perceptions of decline — in America in 2001, a 2 per cent fall might represent economic depression and difficulties, but a 50 per cent collapse of the Russian economy in 1989-95 represented a superpower catastrophe.[40] While there are fiscal and performative truths from economic decline, the deeper impact upon society, culture and politics was much harder to discern. After 1989, the sharp negative fall in population growth was reflected in the declining birth rate and the increasing rate of death. In 1989, Russia had a population of 147,341,508, a figure that had fallen to 143,086,549 by 2008 and was 144,713,314 in 2022. The seriousness of this population crisis was mentioned in a TV documentary on Alexander Navalny. In one segment, Navalny tells his followers: 'In our country people are dying before they reach 60-65 years of age. European countries are horrified by our life expectancy.'[41]

In social terms, Russia has experienced a huge surge in crime and criminality since the end of the Soviet Union. This was reflected in the institutionalisation of criminal activity at the root of Putin's mafia politics of violence. Putin's terror has a utility like that of tsarist and later Stalinist terrors. The power of arrest and political trials

---

[40] Timothy Taylor, *America and the New Global Economy*, audio lecture 8, (Wolverhampton, The Teaching Company 2008).

[41] *Navalny*, HBO, Warner Brothers, April 2022.

are aligned with assassination and state-sponsored murder. In a society framed in the maxims of security—suspicion, intimidation, and terror—cities have become places of control rather than for socio-economic development. Russia is the greatest landmass with two large cities over 5 million in population, many cities with a population of 1.6 million to 1.0 million, and then suddenly drops many smaller towns, villages, and hamlets. The break-up of the Soviet Union led to the removal of a significant segment of the population. What remains reflects the continuing problems of Russia's social change, and the continuing decline in population.

The rise of organised crime came in parallel with Russia's turn towards a market economy. Vouchers representing shares in former Soviet state industries were issued to the masses. Their real value was not realised by the public. A few entrepreneurs saw an opportunity for the cheap acquisition of wealth and acquired the vouchers through sharp practices and began to take control of state industries. The cash for vouchers, usually a few dollars, took advantage of masses scrambling to find the means to stave off starvation. This marked the rise of 'gangster capitalism', which would lead to one the largest transfers of national resources from state to private ownership. The new owners took away enormous margins from a small initial return on investment. This ill-gotten wealth attracted violent criminals that preyed off the new rich and, as the BBC's Martin Sixsmith observed, turned Moscow into the murder capital of Europe. This became, in Sixsmith's words, a 'wild west capitalism'. Violence was rife in the cities, like Moscow, as private security groups and organised gangs began to rule everyday life. Those who emerged as top dogs, the seven oligarchs, had established a mafia-capitalism.[42] They had taken control of media, public utilities, raw materials, and industries. By the 1990s, Russian society was brittle and began to fracture as pensions were not paid, there was a massive increase in unemployment and politics lost all credibility. Confidence in the market system fell to an all-time low after the euphoria at the end of the Cold War.

During a speech at the International Economic Forum, in 2022,

---

[42] *Citizen K*, Passion Pictures, 2018.

Putin charged: 'After declaring victory in the Cold War, the United States proclaimed itself to be God's messenger on Earth, without any obligations and only interests which were declared sacred.' He continued by referring to 'other' countries (meaning the US and NATO interventions in Iraq and elsewhere): 'They still treat them like colonies, and the people living there, like second-class people, because they consider themselves exceptional. If they are exceptional, that means everyone else is second rate.' His more insidious comment went unnoticed: 'In April, less than a hundred thousand children were born in Russia, almost 13 percent less than in April 2020 ... the magnitude of the extraordinary demographic challenge we are facing.' In June 2022, a tweet by Kevin Rothrock, reposted from a Russian tweet about babies born in Russian-occupied Kherson (Ukraine) since February 2022, and noted they had been given Russian citizenship.[43] The thread acquired other notable content including an article in a London-based newspaper that claimed Kirill Stremousov, one of Putin's 'puppet governors', had been filmed swinging a baby around his head in 2017.[44] The more important issue is whether Putin's claims of the denazification of Ukraine was a cloak for the more insidious campaign to counter Russia's declining population and put an end to the negative birth rate through mass kidnapping. Putin's invasion of Ukraine will continue to raise challenges of interpretation, but the searched for children and the presence of citizenship experts have all the hallmarks of racial profiling and engineering. This is Russianisation and it is driven by deep socio-economic problems and terminal superpower decline. Putin's maskirovka disguises, and Putin's genocide shields, the more sinister project of mass kidnapping and enforced demographic change.

Why does Russia strategize population? Part of the reason is historic; mass has been the logic of Russian power. Traditionally,

---

[43] Kevin Rothrock (@kevinrothrock), Tweet, 16 June 2022, https://twitter.com/KevinRothrock/status/1537315381924216832. (Accessed 2 October 2022)

[44] 'Man Who Swung Baby around His Head Now One of Putin's "Puppet Governors"', *Metro*, 13 May 2022, https://metro.co.uk/2022/05/13/man-who-swung-baby-around-now-one-of-putins-puppet-governors-16636048 (accessed 14 September 2022).

the horde had been deployed to overwhelm Russia's enemies. This suited an empire built on agriculture and land mass. industrialisation barely changed the demographics of Russia and even Soviet collectivisation could not remove the dependency on agriculture. In the age of total war, Soviet sophistication was largely limited to certain groups of weapons that were developed, like artillery and tanks, against more advanced weapons which developed much more slowly. In the age of advanced technology, Russia can manipulate cyberwar and break western internet trade, but the economy has not replaced the shortfall of skilled labour with advanced technology. The masses, the old workers, and peasants, do not have a powerful middle class hovering over their existence. This makes Russia a bipolar society and explains why there is a resort to strategizing the masses. In regard to Ukraine, Russia is prepared to throw masses at the problem until the Ukraine is absorbed. Ukraine represents a quick fix for Putin, a massive increase population and the acquisition of an educated social group. Once absorbed, Russia's losses will be made good by a pacified society incorporated into the Russian system. Refugees will scattered to never to return to Ukraine, further reducing internal opposition Russia. For the west, with its prominent middle class or bourgeois social orders, is incapable of comprehending Russia, preferring to dub it a backward society rather than recognise the cultural dystopia of Putin's regime.

Strategic humanitarianism and the case for an European army

NATO has failed European security and the European member states have failed NATO. Europeans have failed to secure their continent. Populist politics has replaced strategic thinking. This is not in the same meaning as the Clausewitzian maxim for war and politics, but an alternative vision of war. Despite all the military education, the West is bereft of rational and pragmatic thinking about war. Universities have dabbled in teaching military history, mostly for commercial opportunities, but the primary function has been the commoditisation of war studies and intelligence. The experts of war studies have become the influencers of governments, and since the kudos of government adviser outweighs the dull routines of academia, selling military expertise and intelligence during a conflict has proven highly lucrative for all involved. There are always consequences, and perhaps the gravest concern for democracies are how this non-democratic influence, by unelected advisers, can cause distortions and disruptions in security and defence policy. For example, the overt over-promotion of counterinsurgency doctrine in UK over conventional forces, has deformed the armed forces into an incoherent budget disaster. Prime Minister Johnson's annual defence review was rendered shambolic by the ramifications of Putin's war in Ukraine. Added to such woes is America's continual failure to deter Russia from successive invasions of Chechnya, Georgia, Crimea and now Ukraine. America will abandon Europe, according to Ian Kearns (@IanKearns_), who posted a Twitter thread on this subject in June 2022.[45] Putin's invasion has restored war to the centrepiece of European history and Europeans have shuddered. In the continuing hostilities, the world has experienced a roller-coaster of change. Initially, the war rejuvenated the old-world order, but since May 2022 the war has shuffled nations into a new world order. The rise in anti-NATO sentiment represents strong politics in Europe, and if galvanised to act in concert would form a significant protest movement. One Irish MEP has been continually vocal against NATO and its involvement in Ukraine and its ramifications.[46] Regardless of the deep anti-war sentiments, Europe needs to examine the practicalities of forming a European army if only to restore the territorial integrity of its security.

NATO has failed as a force for humanitarian intervention. In the case of bombing Serbian forces in Kosovo, Arthur Snell observed that it was the first sustained use of force in NATO's history.

---

[45] Ian Kearns (@IanKearns_), tweet, 24 June 2022, https://twitter.com/iankearns_/status/1540438166632599552 (accessed 16 September 2022).

[46] Mick Wallace (@wallacemick), tweet, 29 August 2022, https://twitter.com/wallacemick/status/1564263909196009472 (accessed 16 September 2022).

Eventually the air war was extended to ground operations alongside Russian forces. British intervention in Kosovo, according to Snell, defined British foreign policy in the first quarter of the twenty-first century.[47] However, humanitarian intervention looks very different to those people bombed and the ramifications from that war still resonate within Russo-Serbian alliance building. Russia felt threatened by NATO's use of force. The neo-liberal economics of 'shock doctrine' has failed Western security.[48] America's 'shock doctrine' capitalism in the former Soviet Union, almost buried Russia in a third world-style dystopia. Whether by accident or by design, Western societies have widely transitioned toward Shock Doctrine styled government, which has greatly undermined the old establishment structures and the social welfare safety nets. This is a civil–military relations dilemma since societal resilience to war has been significantly reduced. This is most apparent in the privatisation of public utilities, the cost of energy and the decline in the supply of essential commodities. Long-term privatisation of the public utilities is a serious strategic failure. In the Summer of 2022 Germany's modern railway network, failed to cope with a sudden surge of customers during peacetime, how would that network perform under the pressures of war?[49] This is the reality of western strategic resilience, societies that once were once configured for communal civil–military relations are no longer in sync with national strategic doctrines. Interestingly, Michael Howard's warning that Bobbitt's 'market-states' could only 'reduce their vulnerability' and victory would mean avoiding defeat is pertinent to this strategic problem. Instead of constructing a new strategic architecture for confronting Russia, NATO dismantled the old strategic architecture in the misguided delusion that the West won the Cold War. The outcome was the strategic failure in February 2022. This is the strategic reality of European societies trying to confront Putin's aggression.

---

[47] Snell, *How Britain Broke the World*, p.18-19.
[48] Naomi Klein, *The Shock Doctrine* (London: Penguin, 2007).
[49] Dr Philip W Blood (@historianblood), Tweet, 29 August 2022, https://twitter.com/HistorianBlood/status/1564170938119344128. (Accessed 2 October 2023)

In February 2022, US President Biden unilaterally announced that NATO would not become involved or initiate a no-fly zone over Ukraine. This decision confirmed the United States' ownership and control of NATO. Europeans, in NATO, acquiesced since they had no other option. Several NATO countries have promised to supply weapons and money to Ukraine. Politicians who had once accepted Putin's financial benevolence with little democratic oversight began to introduce economic sanctions against Russia. There was an avalanche of political and military content uploaded across social media has largely deceived the public. Thousands of news platforms delivered multiple layers of information to the global public, but it caused information overload. The surge of refugees from Ukraine fleeing to the West rapidly reached 10 million and continued to rise, with many more rendered homeless in-country. From the UK, Prime Minister Johnson immediately engaged with Ukraine unilaterally. This was his Bismarckian moment to deflect public gaze away from the mounting troubles in domestic politics and the continual failure to deliver the promises of Brexit. Johnson's eagerness to deflect his political problems exposed the inadequacy of British defence policy, the catastrophe of inadequate weapons procurement and the depleted condition of the armed forces. As criticism of the western response increased, attention began to turn on nations regarded as not doing enough. The spotlight of criticism fell on Germany, causing disturbances within the body politic since Chancellor Merkel's regime had facilitated many of Putin's excesses and had blocked Ukraine's membership of NATO. Chancellor Olaf Scholz announced a rise in defence expenditure and the supply of weapons to Ukraine, thus ending Germany's post-war policy of not interfering in a war zone. This was popular among the chattering classes in Berlin but was not well received elsewhere within Germany.

In the confused hopes that Putin's war would degenerate into an insurgency, several stalwarts from the War on Terror reappeared. Experts offered Ukraine urban warfare expertise, while the fighting was primarily in the swamplands. Former Iraq war 'experts' like Eliot Cohen waded into the arena to refight their old wars

but wholly inappropriate to the war in Ukraine.⁵⁰ They brought a thinly veiled agenda of turning the war into America's war. Putin's war, in the guise of a special military operation, is not war within the context of a NATO-style military operations, rendered American style conventional war-making dogma irrelevant. The level of televised warfare coverage was like the war related news broadcasts in the wake of the 9-11 terror attacks. The screening of replays of the terror attacks was balanced by news slots about military hardware in action, as a visual means to reassure the public that retribution was not far away, and irrespective that Osama Bin Laden continued to evade capture. In Putin's war, social media splices time between images of military action and other incidents culminating in a war narrative that more likely resemble the script from the film *Wag the Dog* (1997). In real terms, Putin has outfoxed the news broadcasts by engaging in conflicts with longer timeframes to outlast the patience of the newsmakers and the public alike. Long term, Russia has revealed a social media resilience, whereas Europe is fractured, and America is fighting a political war for Biden's re-election — high in cash but low in body-counts. Europe must build an army of common defence to defend Europe's interests and culture against future Russian aggression.

Breaking away from the relative comfort zone of the status quo of Anglo-American strategic thinking is tantamount to mutiny. However, the rising crescendo of increasingly narrow debates about battlefield minutiae had gone too far, and the logic of Anglo-American exceptionalism had reached the zenith of absurdity. British attitudes against European led defence can be traced in the writings of the late Michael Howard. His criticism of Europe began with The Continental Commitment (1972), when he set out to understand Britain's commitment to the common defence of Europe. However, almost from the first page he was distinguishing the UK from Europe:

> The British Isles still lie adjacent but not contiguous, to a European continent

---

50 *Rambo III, Counterinsurgency, & Ukraine w/ Hannah R. Gurman/New FBI Documents on 9/11 & Saudi Arabia w/ Branko Marcetic*, 2022, https://open.spotify.com/episode/557Ni0MuubPxM64TmpGbhQ.

peopled by nations whose culture has no more in common with our own than has that of countries founded by men of our own stock in such inconveniently distant parts of the world as North America, the Antipodes and even Sothern Africa.[51]

He appealed to the long traditions of those institutions that were once the bedrock of empire and liberalism — trade, the military, politics, and culture. Howard concluded in doubt for the future, pertinent to Brexit Britain: 'We are unlikely ever again to have statesmen — or, come to that, strategists — who maintain that the security of the United Kingdom can be considered in isolation from that of our Continental neighbours east as well as west of the Rhine.'[52]

In 1976, Howard set forth a war narrative for the nuclear age and European professional armies. His interpretation was set in the binary ideological confrontation of the time - liberal capitalism versus Soviet socialism. By the 1950s, according to Howard, war was regimented by two superpowers, and all the predictions about future war were based upon the general expectation that they would decide the character of any conflict. In one sense, this strategic setting granted Howard a remarkable foresight: 'A war in Europe would be a local conflict within a confrontation of global dimensions and could be considered and planned for only within that context.' In regard to conventional forces, he thought missiles would contest crewed armoured vehicles and aircraft, and that 'portable infantry' would change the face of the battlefield. The advanced technologies, he claimed, were the fruits of the military–industrial complexes of the leading nations, while the drones of Ukraine have made all nations equals in war. However, Howard also pondered the demise of soldiering in the culture of modern European societies. There was no place of pride for the nations in arms, with few exceptions: in France, for example, where Bastille Day harked back to the revolution and republicanism, or in Britain, where Trooping the Colour reinforced monarchy. In West Germany, the population had virtually outlawed war and militarism. Howard argued that European societies had raised generations of

---

51 Michael Howard, *The Continental Commitment* (London: Temple Smith, 1972), p.9.
52 Ibid., p. 149.

people 'uninterested in military affairs, sceptical of the military virtues and regarding the armed forces with a mixture of suspicion, incomprehension, and contempt'.[53] He was sceptical of the 'make love, not war' generation's 'relaxed' lifestyles. Young males in society, traditionally the rifle bearers, had traded guns for guitars. The prospect of nuclear war rendered reservists and regiments obsolete in the court of public opinion. He was sceptical about societies that had turned their back on 'traditional military values', arguing 'such confidence may prove immature'.[54] Could Howard ever have imagined twelve years of Conservative governance, since 2010, that continuously implemented incoherent and calamitous defence policies? Howard's prophecies for the future were blinkered.

The 1970s was a strange decade, a confusing time in British history. Howard's *War in European History* was an interpretation that suited the British university syllabus, which struggled to teach war as a viable academic option. Some leading scholars had participated in the CND marches or joined the anti-Vietnam protests or were activists in the anti-racism battles with popular right-wing extremists – there was deep reluctance among scholars to teach even the history of war. In reply, Howard's book was dismissed by European scholars as an overtly Anglo-American tract, which they argued oversimplified the complexity of European cultures. Certain politics departments were also critical. Scholars of Western European security argued Howard's closing chapter was overly generalising and didn't engage with the complexities of prevailing concepts such as deterrence, mutually assured destruction (MAD) in nuclear exchange theory, forward defence, or flexible response. They also observed Europe's thriving military–industrial complex, which was generally committed to hardball competition with their American rivals. This pointed to the existence of an entirely different attitude to war within Europe's commercial establishment. Latterly, the civil–military relations school criticised Howard for avoiding the political dimensions of armies and society. War,

---

[53] Michael Howard, *War in European History* (London: Oxford University Press, 1976), p. 142.
[54] Ibid.

security, and defence were administered by governments for domestic and foreign policy, and not just for confronting the Soviet Union. *War in European History* was completed just four years before the Cold War began to turn sharply confrontational. Howard's vision ignored post-colonial conflicts, and he failed to predict the imperialistic conflicts of the superpowers, as in the Soviet invasion of Afghanistan or America in Grenada or Britain and the Falklands. Regardless of the criticism, Howard reinforced his opinion in his Huizinga lecture of 1985 – '1945: End of an Era' – that European history had ended. In 1978, War and the Liberal Conscience completed Howard's ideological foundations of a Western way of war and rooted in war studies and military history education for British and American audiences.

In 2002, Philip Bobbitt's *The Shield of Achilles* was hailed as a blockbuster and essential reading for anyone interested in the West and war. In a time just before social media and in the wake of the 9-11 tragedy, it was initially regarded as a cogent explanation for the war against terrorism. The book was lionised because it claimed law and strategy had shaped the West, and it was framed around the long period of war from 1914 to 1990. Forgotten in the passing of Bobbitt's thesis was Howard's foreword, which read like a 'new' epilogue for 'The Nuclear Age' from his *War in European History*. Howard explained that Bobbitt's interpretation of war argued the case for Western liberal capitalism, which after the French Revolution had led to the rise of the modern state and then evolved into the nation state. This was portrayed as inevitable, which underscored Bobbitt's narrative of Anglo-American exceptionalism. With the benefit of hindsight, it was tedious triumphalism for a post-Cold War era and delivered just as America took a different historical direction. Howard described how westernised ideological progress had overcome Hegelian concepts of forging nation states through war - in both 1945 and 1918. After 1945, liberal democracy had successfully confronted the 'authoritarian socialism' of Soviet Russia, in a process that concluded with the Paris Charter in 1990 and that finally settled the Second World War. Howard added praise of Fukuyama's concept of 'the end of history' and a future world framed by the ideas of Kant, Bentham, Woodrow Wilson, and F. D. Roosevelt. The Paris Charter had recognised human rights, while Germany and Russia acceded to 'western-values, and the balance of power in favour of the USA'. Europe was wholly ignored in this interpretation, but it was European culture that supported the Howard-Bobbitt narrative.

Explaining the reasons behind American hegemony, Howard pointed to its economic power, superior weapons systems, and the global appeal of its popular culture. However, in the wake of 9-11, he expected an outbreak of squabbles in Europe descending into petty conflicts, the emergence of new nations, and ethnicity in an age of vague citizenships (an unfavourable acknowledgement of identity as an emerging cultural genre). He reflected upon the failure of humanitarianism and collective security structures in the former Yugoslavia, the failure of states that were unable to transform into proper nations and the continuing decline of the former great powers from the Second World War. The Soviet Union, he claimed, was defeated by American 'soft power' rather than superior weapons, but this had proven transitory and without tangible substance. This was a roundabout way of criticising the progress of the 'new' Russia without any critical observations of Russia's changing trajectory under Putin. Howard concluded that although 'instant communications' had created the global community, it was only a destructive phase, just as 'guns destroyed the feudal order, railways destroyed the dynastic order, computers destroyed the nation-state'. Howard's neo-liberalism encouraged him to oversimplify his criticism of the Marxist state, which he claimed had formulated dystopias without the primary options for war. Failures of western war-making were entirely ignored. This was an unusual interpretation of war and Howard concluded that Bobbitt's 'masterpiece' was similar in global impact to Oskar Spengler's Decline of the West (1918) — 'mankind facing a tragedy'. To a certain extent, old Cold War dogma reinforced Howard's opinion about modern war at a time when modern war was transitioning. Putin's strategy shattered any illusions of Howard's strategic confidence and delusions of western supremacy, because the Russian army is simply 'doing it' partly the old way and virtually in de-modernised form. The lessons of war are profound but thus far the west has found no strategic answer.

In 2008, Howard revised *War in European History* with an epilogue: 'The End of the European Era'. The opening paragraphs buried European history in yet more of his Anglo-American rhetoric: '1945 marked the end of an era' to 'European history ended ... in a single week in December 1941.' This epilogue continued his faith in the End of History paradigms. Howard described Europe as a collection of client states, lying in the sensitivity zone between the superpowers and conventional armies acting solely as the 'trip-wires' for confrontation. Howard informs his readers that from out of this confrontation emerged the EU and NATO. Since the EU never properly incorporated security or defence (although the French tried and failed numerous times), he thought it was largely irrelevant to any thoughts of European security. In contrast, NATO had turned this 'unwieldy group of auxiliaries' to serve the United States, and its role was more political than military. He once again argued Europeans could no longer treat war as an acceptable policy. There were numerous social changes that flourished in the Cold War – America had drifted away from a hard military posture towards a social order that embraced civil liberties, the Europeans became more united, but in Britain there was division, the mutually exclusive contradictions of the colonial past and the futuristic attraction of European unity. Howard's hardening stance towards Europe, across thirty-two years, projected his political thoughts of British military history and war studies - pro-American and anti-European. This deep cynicism of Europe was Brexit in style long before Brexit became a reality. Howard's preference for opinion over substance (critical analysis) remains the troubling polemic that reflects the culture with the British military education establishment.

Whether Howard was a Brexiter before Brexit is not the issue. Re-reading Howard is to isolate the significance of the absence of empire and genocide in historical narratives. These recurring themes from academic history can no longer be ignored by military historians of the Whig school. The Rwandan genocide stemmed from empire, genocide in former Yugoslavia originated from old ethnic hatreds and enmities from long before the Second World

War that became weaponised following Tito's death in 1980. Putin's perpetration of genocide in Ukraine is the next phase from his crimes in Chechnya and Syria, which is a serious warning to Europe. Putin's war-making is about colonisation, denazification, and genocide, his response to Russia's decline in population and other socio-economic forces. All Western dogma, the End of History thesis and even Howard's Liberal Conscience are rendered irrelevant by Putin's existential struggle for the Russian empire. The West's failure to rationalise and make good its failures in foreign affairs and military interventions has undermined strategic thinking. Globally it has granted Putin all the excuses necessary to justify war to the Russian people and the United Nations.[55] Howard's ideas from 1976 framed his dogma for 2008, by 2020 his ideas had nailed western security to US uncertainty. The dogma of isolation and manifest destiny were in freefall during the bitter debates between presidential candidates that divide the country. The long period of Western hegemony became fragile in 2022 like that experienced by the Soviet Union in 1989. This is not a story of the decline of the West, but the reality of a false euphoria of victory at the end of the Cold War. Thus, when we re-examine why the NATO and Anglo-American responses to Putin were so weak before the invasion, and so ineffectual at deterring war in February 2022, we must also reflect on the fundamental failings of western military education and seek a European solution.

Interestingly, since Putin's war started there have been calls for a European defence. This ran counter to Howard's rhetoric from 2008. For example, Christoph Nübel (@christoph_nubel) posted a Twitter thread about the European Defence Community (EDC) from 1951. He charted the emergence of the common defence of Western Europe from the Korean War. In the early days, there was deep concern over the rearming of Germany, but compromises over the formation of the EDC stemmed from a deeper culture pressure within Germany over national sovereignty.[56] One factor arising

---

[55] Refer to Snell, *How Britain Broke the World*.
[56] Christoph Nübel (@christoph_nubel), tweet, 4 July 2022, https://twitter.com/c hristoph_nubel/status/1544048091862646785 (accessed 16 September 2022).

from reading Nübel's thread was how the North Atlantic-centric experts have generally avoided the subject. However, Ulrike Franke (@RikeFranke) retweeted one of her older tweets from 2021 about European security among the different political parties in Germany. The thread very quickly descended into the habitual distrust of Germany as reflected by concerned tweets about a place on the UN Security Council. European vision, expansion and security had always run counter to US defence policy even when America advocated European independence and championed a European army. This dichotomy was rarely presented to European society because of NATO's imperialistic designs of political expansion, and the unregulated European Union bureaucratic enlargement—both without democratic oversight.

Since 1990, war has barely featured in the political discourse of the European Union's progress, but hardly a year has passed when wars or conflicts have not impacted on European culture and society. The expansion of Europe followed on from the end of the Cold War, incorporating former Warsaw Pact states, as the former Soviet Union appeared to at first retreat and then disband and divide. There was no serious offer or thoughts of granting a 'democratic' Russia EU membership, regardless of UK Eurosceptics' claims that the EU wanted to expand to the Urals. Fear of the Soviet Union was replaced by disdain for a failed state that had struggled to come to terms with Western-style economic liberalism. In February 1992, the Treaty on European Union was signed in Maastricht by the twelve member states. The treaty envisaged a single market, a social policy (the UK opted out), an increased membership and made claims for regulation and democratic oversight. The Maastricht Treaty introduced the concept of a common European citizenship, with integration and free movement. A weakness, which would come to haunt the concept, was to hinge citizenship to member nations, rather than an entirely European identity. The Maastricht Treaty of 1992 appeared to open the door for Russia's possible candidature, but membership was not forthcoming. By 2008, notions of embracing Russia within a European community were long gone as geopolitical tensions over places such as Kaliningrad (the former German city of Königsberg) were once again stirred.

The more NATO was perceived as unnecessary, the more it became entangled in conflicts to construct vague notions of necessity. Whenever new member states joined the European Union, the expansion of NATO has generally followed. Hand-in-glove, NATO and the EU symbolised the marriage between the values of social-democratic capitalism in everyday European life and the liberal capitalist face of security stretching from America to the borders of Russia, China, and the Middle East. NATO expanded beyond its original mission, transforming the strategy of 'forward defence' into an existential ideological dogma. Similarly, the EU grew from the twelve member states that signed the treaty in 1992 to the fifteen in 2002, to the twenty-one in 2016 and to the twenty-seven in 2022 after the UK ended its membership. In parallel, NATO has grown from twelve original member nations in 1949 to thirty in 2022. Regardless of the massive bureaucratic institutionalisation by the EU and NATO, European security has not been enhanced, war has not been avoided, while the future prospect of war, even nuclear war, remains a stark reality.

On the evening of 21 February 2022, many Europeans went to bed without any thought of war coming to Ukraine. The shock at Putin's invasion was palpable. Yet Russia had invaded the Crimea in 2008, and an irregular conflict then simmered just below boiling point. War over the Donbas region broke out in 2014, and years later Putin penned his vision for the glory of Russia and the demise of Ukraine. The fighting staggered on until the 2022 invasion. Throughout 2019 to 2021, the COVID pandemic distracted the West's attention as tensions mounted between Poland, Ukraine, and Russia. Just before Christmas 2021, Putin warned Ukraine and the West about the prospect of future conflict. Europeans ignored the warning, more fixated on recovering from COVID, or the natural disasters from the summer, or managing the growing economic crises. The opponents and critics of Putin push for a confrontation that could escalate to all-out global war. Some opponents fear to tread too heavily, as in the case of NATO, and rely on the 'hope' that by drip-feeding advanced weapons systems into Ukraine, they will tilt the balance. There are multiple high-risk strategies facing the West, but there is a high risk for Ukraine if Russia begins to lose.

The threat turns into the release of limited nuclear weapons.

Putin's illegal and criminal war has unfurled a humanitarian disaster of apocalyptic proportions. The world is horrified at the scenes on news broadcasts of widespread devastation, the long lines of refugees fleeing to frontiers, the stories of starvation, the bombardments, the vicious fighting, and the deaths of many civilians, especially children. Since February, when the war started, there has been a feeling that the world is on the edge of Armageddon. The information war, thus far controlled by Ukraine, has uplifted 'expert' observers who revel in armchair militarism but has caused deep apprehension and anxiety among those less warlike and more responsible corners of society. A significant proportion of societies are bemused by the absence of any efforts at peacekeeping or attempts to stop the war. Indeed, when Putin claimed to redirect the war from a 'second phase', many of these experts claimed it was the end of the war, and that they had predicted all along. Putin's war continues, and the experts have moved on with their hindsight, poor judgement, and the flip-flops. War in Europe has transformed over the last 100 years and is in the process of change. Putin has unleashed absolute war in Europe, but with the added brutality of genocidal violence firmly directed at the civilian population. The 'shock and awe' of Putin's illegal war is heightened by the calculated decision to ignore all war crimes precedents. In effect, by calling his war a special military operation he was superficially skirted the rules of war. The siege of Mariupol was over by 18 March 2022, less than a month into the campaign. The planned and deliberate positioning artillery, with pre-set grid coordinates, enabled Putin's artillery to systematically reduce the city by the hectare. Artillery has remained the 'God of War' in the Russian way of war in the drone age when conventional artillery should be almost extinct. This is a harsh lesson for western analysts. At the time of finalising this essay, October 2022, the BBC are still reporting explosions in Lviv in western Ukraine. While bombardments are unleashed, more attention should be given to the humanitarian case.

Humanitarianism is not always well served. A Twitter thread by Amnesty International has exposed the kind of self-righteous dogma that stalks certain humanitarian institutions. In August

2022, Amnesty issued a report that claimed Ukrainian combat tactics were endangering Ukrainian civilians. The report began in April, several weeks into the war, but took no account of how invading forces, especially with surprise and superior numbers, dictate the fighting. When people criticised the report, instead of replying, Agnes Callamard, the secretary general, tweeted: 'Ukrainian and Russian social media mobs and trolls: they are all at it today attacking amnesty investigators.'[57] Dogma, whether political or ideological, has weakened the defence of Ukraine. Predictions aside, the world needs a fresh attitude toward war.

In 1996, Christopher Bellamy published Knights in White Armour: The New Art of War and Peace. For a decade, it was the classic study of modern peacekeeping from the years immediately following the end of the Cold War to 9-11. The tragedy of 9-11 galvanised American opposition to peacekeeping, and within a few years, not only was the concept of peacekeeping dismissed from Western security doctrine but also the United Nations had been compromised through several attempts by the United States and the UK to present false evidence against Iraq to secure a mandate for war. Bellamy had followed the classic approach of strategic analysis by first identifying war(s), presenting historical cases of intervention, and isolating the potential causes for future wars — new actors, WMDs, the clash of civilisations, global warming — all still challenges to civilisation. He then cited forms of peacekeeping or limiting war, such as airpower, sea power and wars of intervention. Bellamy was also concerned with the new or 'future warriors' with corporate agendas, rogue mercenaries and leaders, robots, and genetic engineering.

In the final chapter of the book, 'Legion Patria Nostra', the author proposed a permanent UN peacekeeping force. The motto of the French Foreign Legion — 'The Legion Is Our Country' — was perhaps an unusual starting point to present the case for the UN.

---

[57] Agnes Callamard (@AgnesCallamard), tweet, 4 August 2022, https://twitter.com/agnescallamard/status/1555234095982149632 (accessed 16 September 2022); 'Ukraine: Ukrainian Fighting Tactics Endanger Civilians', Amnesty, 4 August 2022, https://www.amnesty.org/en/latest/news/2022/08/ukraine-ukrainian-fighting-tactics-endanger-civilians (accessed 16 September 2022).

Bellamy's experience from reporting on peacekeeping had taught him time and speed were critical. In his Evolution of Land Warfare (1992), he had explained their importance in war. This time, he advocated its importance for the not insignificant observation that the 'UN Rapid Reaction Force, in Bosnia in 1995, was not rapid.' He was aware of the very critical issues arising from religions, cultures, and racism in war—and argued that all UN interventions had to be mindful of prejudices. He then discussed the proposed size of UN forces and optimal levels of equipment. Bellamy's book has disappeared from memory and is no longer in print. As with so many 'analogue' books from before the post-2006 age of information-digitalisation, they have no links to modern scholarship. When discussed in forums, most people have expressed surprise and have searched for library copies. The reason for mentioning this book during Putin's illegal war is the absence of any calls for intervention or restraint, or the intervention by a peacekeeping third party. Regardless of Putin's obvious determination to destroy much of Ukraine, such a force could have facilitated the safe relief or escape of many civilian refugees. As this brutal war unfolds, the UN has been reduced to an echo chamber for all sides to hurl accusations. If one lesson is to be learned from this war, the world needs a third force, a peacekeeping force.

There is however hope in the groundswell of humanitarianism offered to the people of Ukraine by the peoples of Europe. Humanitarian aid, whether organised by local groups, or municipalities or charity organisations, has filled a gap in the aid programmes. While the press and social media have focused upon weapons and cash, ordinary people volunteered to organise aid and help. This aspect of European neighbourliness has bridged the east-west confrontation between Putin and NATO. This represents hope for the future for a unified and secure European continent.

6. PUTIN'S WAR, RUSSIAN GENOCIDE

Philip W. Blood

Putin is an anachronism, the twentieth-century's last political soldier still active in politics. His political identity was moulded in the guardian units raised by regimes to protect extreme political parties or movements. Once established in power, the guardian units turned into secret police institutions, an example being Nazi Germany's SS. In 1917, the Bolsheviks established the All-Russian Extraordinary Commission, which became known as the Cheka. As the Soviet Union consolidated control and power transitioned from Lenin to Stalin's rule, the security service developed from the Cheka to the GPU (1923), then the OGPU (1923–34), the NKVD (1934–43), NKGB (1943–6), MGB (1946–54) and KGB (1954–91). The simplistic name changes disguised a long process of institutionalised internal security that bound Soviet Russia together even in times of greatest crisis. Less well appreciated was the culture of security that shaped the process of socialisation within these institutions. Medals, uniforms, regalia, traditions, and customs are the trappings of a unique organisational culture, and they reinforced the dogma of guardianship of the regime and the political identity as protector of the nation. The identity changed outwardly, but the working practices within were turned into the rituals of security, transforming the security complex into a regime within the regime. This made the KGB one of the most powerful and effective security organisations in the world.

    Putin joined the KGB in 1975 and trained in a Leningrad academy. In 1985, he was posted to Dresden, then part of the DDR. During his time in Dresden, he was known to have assisted the terrorist group the Red Army Faction. In 1991, he resigned from the KGB. Later that year, Boris Yeltsin issued a decree that transferred the

KGB to the FSK (Federal Counter-Intelligence Service), which remained operable until April 1995 when it became the FSB (Federal Security Service), which is still active at present. The SVR (Foreign Intelligence Service) was formed in 1991 and has also remained in service. Putin's story, therefore, began with Soviet Russia, carried over into the Gorbachev and Yeltsin regimes, and despite his resignation from the KGB, he was appointed director of the FSB in 1998. Putin's KGB training first socialised him as a guardian of the state and later of Russia. In that mindset, security has an entirely different outlook from the traditional forms of military defence. This mindset went to war against Ukraine.

Putin's terror

The priorities of the politics of security and the politics of violence inevitably turns to the institutionalisation of security violence. This was common to all the guardian formations of the twentieth century. Observing Putin's efforts to both localise the war to Ukraine and the resort to crimes, we immediately recognise the behaviour of a guardian prosecuting security violence in the name of Russia. Compare the words of two anti-Putin activists: 'There is no reason to expect a regime that tramples on the rights of its own people and violates its own laws to respect international norms or the interests of other nations.'[1] This points to the progress of his crimes and genocide in Ukraine as an extension of domestic policy. And also:

"Putin has repeatedly mentioned that the Russian Federation's sovereign interests dictate the conditions of the world's survival. ... The Kremlin's nuclear threats are addressed both to the country itself and outside. ... The Russian population is seen as the threat that could change the regime by either refusing to obey or starting a radical uprising.[2]"

---

[1] Vladimir V. Kara-Murza, 'A Europe "Whole and Free" Will Be Possible without Russia', in Oxana Schmies (ed.), *NATO's Enlargement and Russia: A Strategic Challenge in the Past and Future* (Stuttgart: Ibidem-Verlag, 2021), p. 10.

[2] Gleb Pavlovsky, 'Strategic Decentering: Moscow's Ideological Rhetoric and Its Strategic Unconscious, 2012–2020', in Schmies, *NATO's Enlargement and Russia*, p. 215.

Putin's training and mindset is suited to the national security paradigm, which toxified western political leadership during the War on Terror. The covert actions, spying and assassinations suit a security agency but, in the presidency, they blend an unpredictable dimension to strategy and war. Regardless of Putin's past and his Caesarism tendency, the regime he has crafted is a dictatorship for the twenty-first century. Gleb Pavlovsky, an anti-Putin scholar, has been particularly descriptive about the regime, although his predictions of the war have been less accurate. He referred to the regime's 'moral unscrupulousness', 'the global gold standard of insolence' and described Putin as a tyrant from the Renaissance age.[3] Putin is also a bully. In 2007, Putin allowed his dog to intimidate Angela Merkel, knowing she had a morbid fear of dogs. She responded later: 'I understand why he has to do this—to prove he's a man. He's afraid of his own weakness. Russia has nothing, no successful politics or economy. All they have is this.'[4] But had Putin successfully intimidated Merkel?[5]

Early into Putin's first presidency, there were a series of domestic terrorist incidents that have remained a mystery. The Moscow terror bombings in September 1999 led to more than 300 people killed, while responsibility is still unknown. John Dunlop found a wealth of circumstantial evidence that the bombings were carried out by the Russian secret service. He concluded that if the secret service had carried out the acts of terror, then the chain of command reached Putin. The FSB blamed Chechen rebels, which granted Putin the excuse to prosecute genocide against Chechnya. However, as with many conspiracy theories, at its heart was the suicide

---

[3] Ibid., pp. 212, 213.
[4] 'Famous Negotiators: Angela Merkel and Vladimir Putin', Program on Negotiation, Harvard Law School, 29 August 2022, https://www.pon.harvard.edu/daily/international-negotiation-daily/merkel-and-putin-a-difference-in-negotiating-style (accessed 16 September 2022).
[5] 'Germany Agonises over Merkel's Legacy: Did She Hand Too Much Power to Putin?', *The Guardian*, 5 March 2022, https://www.theguardian.com/world/2022/mar/05/germany-angela-merkel-power-to-vladimir-putin-russia (accessed 16 September 2022).

of a leading figure adding a sense of speculation to the mystery.[6] On 23–26 October 2002, there was a hostage incident in a Moscow theatre. Forty terrorists held 850 people hostages, and in the ensuing breach by security forces using a chemical agent all the terrorists were killed together with 171 hostages. In September 2004, a terrorist incident occurred at a school in Beslan, in the northern Caucasus of Russia, involving about 1,100 hostages. After it was over, 333 people died, including 186 children and thirty-one terrorists.[7] Dunlop has examined all these incidents and found the official explanations less than forthright. Given Putin's political alchemy, he no doubt used these incidents to reinforce his power, almost like the Nazis and the Reichstag Fire. In theories of security, great political value is drawn from domestic incidents because they identify enemies or alien social groups, which are used as reasons to introduce extreme legal measures.

Putin's exploitation of Russian youth represents another pointer of his use of power. Russian society had traversed waves of social change from the stratified Soviet systems of conformity to the more 'open' society from 1992, while also heightening political, religious, and cultural pressures that pushed for conformity. Putin's Nashi movement was typical of how political motivation could target social groups. The movement began in March 2005, and during its existence there were as many 120,000 to 150,000 youth members. The manifesto was anti-fascist but also anti-democratic. One spokesperson claimed: 'Constitutional action sometimes means street fighting.' During one meeting, Putin was recorded explaining to young Nashi followers that Britain forgets it's no longer a colonial power. By 2013, Nashi was finished, but in eight years its followers had been deeply radicalised.

Putin has also exploited low-level football hooligan violence as a form of soft power in his geopolitics. During the 2016 European championships, Russian football hooligans burst into the global

---

[6] John B. Dunlop, *The Moscow Bombings of September 1999* (Stuttgart: Ibidem-Verlag, 2014).

[7] John B. Dunlop, *The 2002 Dubrovka and 2004 Beslan Hostage Crises* (Stuttgart: Ibidem-Verlag, 2006).

arena of football violence. Within hours, Putin made a comment about the hooligans, implying a few Russians could beat a thousand English fans, which one British newspaper headlined as nationalistic chauvinism.[8] At that time, TV commentators were fixated on the old tropes of troubled youths and outcasts. They saw a gang culture as nationalistic in tone but not as state-sponsored in form. These reports overlooked Putin's deliberate radicalisation of youth through the Nashi movement. Putin revealed a deviousness in the radicalisation of youth, but worse was his application of this in soft power diplomacy, once again revealing that lurking inner violence. By 2018, Nashi had ceased to exist, but the footy gangs were still prominent in Russia's culture of violence. They had transformed into hardened extremism. By 2022, many of the former Nashi members and football hooligans are middle aged but still fervent followers of Putin. Their radicalisation granted Putin a cadre of hardened followers embedded in Russia's social order. Russia's democratic future will have to confront these kinds of cultural legacies. Hooliganism in the east was radicalised and was weaponised. Gang culture was carried into 'battalion culture', which is a feature of the modern Russian armed forces.

There are also the parallels with Stalin and the removal of opponents and critics like Trotsky. Putin targets individual critics and opponents for a peculiarly vile form of retribution. The irradiated cup of tea, that oxymoron of Putin's trademark barbarism, has involved the use of radiological substances or the nerve agent Novichok to permanently silence critics. The most well-known critic is Alexander Navalny, currently residing in a Russian prison, and who became the subject of TV documentary that exposed Putin's assassins confessing to trying to assassinate him.[9] The most prominent and consistent political opponent to Putin is Vladimir Kara-Murza. He has worked strenuously to bring about US sanctions against certain members with Putin's clique that later led to the 2012 Magnitsky Act. In 2015 Kara-Murza was hospitalised

---

[8] Philip W. Blood (@HistorianBlood), tweet, 28 February 2022,
[9] HBO TV, Navalny, 2022.

following severe organ failure after being poisoned.[10] At the time of writing he is in a Russian prison awaiting a sentence after being found guilty of treason. The most notorious case of Novichok poisoning took place in Salisbury (UK) against Sergei and Yulia Skripal in March 2018.[11]

Another dimension is in foreign affairs, Putin has appealed to a shared Slavic nationalism. Serbia is a fertile ground of ideological fanaticism for Putin, a boiling pot of Slavic nationalism within Europe and a military ally. The relationship between Russia and Serbia was reawakened during the time Putin was still in the KGB and radicalised through the Yugoslav wars. Charles Clover has written that the fighting in Yugoslavia attracted many contemporary Russian nationalists, 'who saw in Serbia a fellow Orthodox Slavic civilisation under siege', and in 'microcosm' the end of the Soviet Union. The Serbs were portrayed as heroic fighters on Russian television even as the cases of genocide mounted. Two battalions of Russians volunteered to serve with the Serbians. Once again, the prominence of the 'battalion' was the core social unit for bonding volunteers and mercenaries. Clover also observed that in 2008, when the United States floated the idea of NATO membership to Georgia and Ukraine and had recognised the state of Kosovo, they created for Putin an 'object and the prize for a new Cold War …'[12]

Serbia's part in the collapse of the former Yugoslavia did have an influence on the post-Soviet Russian way of war and Putin's notions of war. The Yugoslav wars were a cocktail of conflicts—civil wars, ethnic violence, independence, insurgencies, and nationalism—and the fighting raged for ten years from 1991 to 2001, preceding Putin's methods. The grotesque manifestations of the wars included sexual violence, ethnic cleansing, war rape, crimes against humanity and genocide. The destruction of Vukovar between

---

[10] 'Who Is Vladimir Kara-Murza, The Russian Activist Jailed For Condemning The Ukraine War?', accessed 2 August 2023, https://www.rferl.org/a/russia-vladimir-kurza-profile/32367146.html.

[11] 'Salisbury & Amesbury Investigation | Counter Terrorism Policing', accessed 2 August 2023, https://www.counterterrorism.police.uk/salisbury/.

[12] Charles Clover, *Black Wind, White Snow: The Rise of Russia's New Nationalism* (New Haven: Yale University Press, 2016), pp. 211, 309.

August and November 1991 resulted from an eighty-seven-day siege after Croatia declared independence. The fighting killed 3,000 Croatians and saw 20,000 deported, and there were many Serbian-perpetrated massacres.[13] In 1992 Sarajevo, in Bosnia–Herzegovina, came under a siege that lasted almost four years and killed 5,434 civilians. The mass killing of civilians through bombardment was a key military operation during the war and has been a prominent feature of Putin's war-making. This was later labelled as 'urbicide' (violence against urban communities).[14] There were other atrocities besides the bombardments, including sniper killings, mass executions of Serbs and a short-sharp-surprise shelling (five minutes long) of a marketplace that cost seventy lives. The fighting for Srebrenica, during the Bosnian War, involved an eleven-day massacre of 8,400 Bosnian Muslims, men, and boys that has since been labelled ethnic cleansing and genocide. During the wars, Russia, the United States, NATO, the EU, and the UN all struggled to find an appropriate diplomatic stance or interventionist position. One confusion in the role of external powers was NATO's air war against Serbia during the Kosovo War (1999). Even the codenames were confused - NATO assigned Operation Allied Force and the USAF assigned Operation Noble Anvil. Both claimed victory through bombing, but it's difficult to judge what victory meant then or now. One expert later wrote: 'We may never know for sure what mix of pressures and inducements ultimately led Milosevic to admit defeat.'[15] There is an anti-Western legacy in Serbia from the bombing, which Putin stokes in his war rhetoric and psychological warfare. Putin referred to the NATO bombing in his presidential address of 24 February 2022. In January 2019, Russia held talks with Serbia, which opened with a visit to an exhibition of diplomatic documents from 1804 to 1918. Putin joined the Serbian president to pay their respects at monuments to the liberators of Belgrade and fallen

---

[13] Misha Glenny, *The Fall of Yugoslavia* (London: Penguin, 1996).
[14] 'Russia's Campaign of Urbicide in Ukraine', Newlines Institute, 7 June 2022, https://newlinesinstitute.org/power-vacuums/russias-campaign-of-urbicide-in-ukraine (accessed 16 September 2022).
[15] Benjamin S. Lambeth, 'NATOs Air War for Kosovo', Rand Corporation, 2001, p. 14. Slobodan Milošović was president of Yugoslavia.

Soviet soldiers. The two countries agreed to work on a strategic partnership with advanced military equipment and nuclear research.[16]

There is another aspect to the Serbian legacy. Partly it was the blueprint for Putin's war-making and partly it informs the West of the difficulties in prosecuting a national political leader as per the case of Slobodan Milošević, the Serbian communist who presided over the Socialist Republic of Yugoslavia after Tito's death. His rise to power came through economic and constitutional reforms. However, he began to embrace a deeply Serbian nationalistic agenda, initially to confront the Croatian independence movement and later the Bosnian Muslim communities. Understanding Milošević's use of genocide provides insight into Putin's methods, since both have similarities. Both men used the communist movement and its methods to erect nationalism in one country, just as the Stalinist dialectic had once declared 'socialism in one country'. Both exploited religious conflict, and both employed genocide to inflate their conventional military capability. Both adopted long periods of attrition conflict with deep penetrating violence. Both Milošević and Putin were Yeltsin's creatures and nurtured like mafia underlings and protégés, dispensing with the usual discourse of state politics of previous Soviet politruks.

Serbia has also proven to be a fertile recruiting ground for mercenaries. The 'great sniper' Dejan Berić, a Serbian volunteer mercenary, served in the pro-Russian Donbas of Ukraine when he was made the subject of a documentary film—The Sniper's War (2018). 'Deki', as he is portrayed in the film, recalled: 'I never forgot what NATO did to Serbia' as one of his reasons for volunteering. He explained that his reputation was born when he was wounded in 2014 during a battle at the site of a Second World War memorial (erected in 1963) at Savur-Mohyla in the Donbas. The memorial site was a key position, a height on the Donets Ridge about 3 miles from the Russian border. The fighting was intense, and the position changed hands up to eight times; eventually, the massive war memorial

---

16 'Russian–Serbian Talks', President of Russia, 17 January 2019, http://en.kremlin.ru/events/president/news/59689 (accessed 16 September 2022).

collapsed due to the intensity of the fighting. The film followed Deki to revisit the site, where he recalled: 'This is where the legend of the great sniper was born.' The camera panned across the smashed memorial and the graves of his comrades from the Vostok Battalion, reflecting the symbolic bond of the battalion in the social order of Russo-Serbian shared military culture. The film moved to an apartment block, described as the front line at Oktyabrsky, focusing upon elderly people struggling to live in the face of shelling and sniping. The scenes of extensive destruction included large apartment blocks, factories, roads, and villages. The filmmakers drove through the village of Spartak to meet villagers to hear their accounts of the shelling. The film then moved on to the parade for the seventy-first anniversary of the Second World War—the Great Patriotic War. Later, the film recorded the sight of a war-scarred Russian Orthodox church with relatives tending the graves of loved ones. The film ends with Deki being wounded by a Ukrainian sniper and retiring to Russia—outlawed from returning to Serbia. Wikipedia informs that Deki authored a book, *Kad mrtvi progovore* (*When the dead speak*), which details his life from 1974. Since writing this section, the Wikipedia page has been edited to include he received a medal 'for the return of crime'. After the war started, he was involved in recruiting Serbian volunteers and in December 2022 was recorded greeting the volunteers upon their arrival.[17]

Putin's resort to mass destruction and mass death has been a feature of the Russian way of war since his orders first to destroy Grozny in 1999. Aleppo in 2016 was a game changer. The Russian forces that supported the Assad regime in Syria used the insurgency as a testing ground for weapons of mass destruction.[18] Putin learned that just as the allied powers were able to bombard Afghanistan and Iraq with impunity, he could do the same or worse. The use of chemical weapons included dropping barrel loads of chlorine on the insurgents and civilians. The scale of bombardment

---

[17] 'Dejan Berić', Wikipedia, last edited 4 July 2022, https://en.wikipedia.org/wiki/Dejan_Berić (accessed 16 September 2022 and second access 22. March 2023, 11.25am).

[18] Mark Galeotti, *Putin's Wars*, (London: Osprey 2022), pp.202-228.

turned entire conurbations into dead zones, and very soon dead cities. These paralysing methods were harnessed to a command system that was increasingly falling into step with Putin's logic for aggressive wars underpinned by political violence. Then in 2021 Putin issued an essay in which he announced his aim to recreate the Russian Empire.[19] Putin had changed the agenda to the preservation of the Russia empire, through both population and culture, and by aggressive social engineering. Biographies of Putin, like Catherine Belton's *Putin's People* (2020), will be overlooked in the wake of war.[20] Her conclusions before the war and my observations here suggest Putin is far from being a typical war criminal or dictator. To summarise, Putin is a complex character but also a global catastrophe. He threatens Europe like an old Roman emperor with the means of modern war—Caesarism with nukes. Putin's 'will' to save Russia twists old Soviet logic of confronting the capitalist world with the old Tsarist slogans behind the creation of the Russian empire. Whether Putin is removed or not, his legacy will be difficult to eradicate without a European war.

Putin's special military operation—Russian security warfare

From a strategic standpoint, Putin was careful not to declare war on Ukraine. He dressed up his illegal war as a special military operation (SMO) for political-security purposes. He wanted to circumvent all legal restrictions and the constraints of international law. Although he intended to avoid an outright declaration of war, his invasion constitutes an aggressive act of war against an internationally recognised and independent nation state. Since Putin cannot circumvent the laws of war, the measures adopted by the Russian

---

[19] 'Putin's New Ukraine Essay Reveals Imperial Ambitions', Database of the Russia Forum, Putin's List, 19 July 2021, https://www.spisok-putina.org/en/news-about-the-persons/2021-07-19/putins-new-ukraine-essay-reveals-imperial-ambitions (accessed 16 September 2022).

[20] Catherine Belton, *Putin's People: How the KGB Took Back Russia and Then Took On the West* (London: Farrar, Straus and Giroux, 2020).

Army should not be ignored because of this illegality but scrutinised to explain the character of this war. An open-ended and ill-defined 'mission' enables Putin to keep the boundaries of success flexible and the goals purposefully vague. An SMO grants multiple options, generates tasks, and enables goals to be claimed after a success that were not set prior to the mission. In theory, Putin could claim victory and declare war afterwards. The SMO, if successful, will allow him to adopt any historical narrative that suits his political ends, and if he loses, he can adopt plausible deniability. In some respects, losing offers Putin greater options, as Pavlovsky observed: 'Even when an operation goes wrong, the Kremlin wants its failed attempt to be noticed. In the end, a successful special operation is a simple matter of luck, whereas its failure is a sensation.'[21] The SMO is political since it empowers Putin to determine victory or defeat, and it also allows him to set measurements for success or failure within the operation, but most of all it grants a wide range of options for escalation. Thus, Putin's SMO against Ukraine incorporated genocide as an operational priority.

At the operational level, the SMO can generate sub-missions within an overall plan, it has a high degree of flexibility and can allow the redirection of fighting units to different tasks; it can alter or change doctrine to accommodate fluctuating conditions; and it can blend military units into security missions. These kinds of catchall doctrines or sweeping instruments can have serious legal consequences. If an SMO strays from specific military tasks, it will fall within the governance of civil-criminal litigation. Under these conditions, waging combat in urban areas exposes soldiers to charges of murder and offers no protection from notions of collateral killing as has been the case with conventional wars. This situation is magnified when the SMO deliberately directed bombardments against civilian conurbations with large concentrations of civilians. The open-ended mission is often introduced as license for all kinds of behaviour outside the laws and customs of war. The usual political explanation for adopting these measures is that they empower the military and soldiers. The extent of empowerment

---

[21] Pavlovsky, 'Strategic Decentering', pp. 206–7.

includes the motivation for individual soldiers to use their initiative. In June 2022, Putin met with graduates from the leading military schools. He hailed them as '[t]oday's Russian officers and soldiers—the successors of the generation of victors, grandchildren and great-grandchildren of the Great Patriotic War heroes—[who] are selflessly fighting for the Fatherland'. He went on to explain the advancement of Russia depended on efficient law-enforcement systems, special services, and the internal security services. Their task was to protect Russian citizens 'in an uncompromising fight against terrorist and extremist threats ...'[22] The logic behind Putin's SMO defies Western defence analysts and their predictions because it incorporated extremism as an extension of Russian operations, which are mostly mistaken as inefficient.

Throughout history, open-ended operations have mostly been directed towards security aims. Governments turn to such instruments to address a political problem, a threat to national security or in defence of spheres of influence or colonies. The intervention of the Russian Army to preserve the Habsburg monarchy put an end to the 1848 revolution in Hungary. The imperial German government issued vague instructions to its generals during the Boxer Rebellion (1900) and in the Herero War (1904) to encourage brutality in the fighting. The imperial German Army combined doctrines for war with regulations for occupation to formulate a unique form of ideological war that I described as security warfare.[23] This kind of warfare was employed in the German colonies, in the rear areas especially in the east during the Great War, to crush left-wing revolutions in Germany, especially in the Battle of Munich in 1919, and in the contested areas mandated to foreign nations under the Treaty of Versailles (1919). Throughout the period 1871 to 1942, the Germans refined security warfare to suit different political scenarios without specific definition. When the general staff planned to employ military power for security tasks, they worked against the

---

[22] 'Meeting with Graduates of Higher Military Schools', President of Russia, 21 June 2022, http://en.kremlin.ru/events/president/transcripts/68685 (accessed 16 September 2022).

[23] Philip W. Blood, *Hitler's Bandit Hunters: The SS and the Nazi Occupation of Europe* (Washington, DC: Potomac Books, 2006).

rules of war because they routinely referred to circumventing the Lieber Code (1861) or Geneva Conventions. In August 1942, Nazi Germany adopted Hitler's *Bandenbekämpfung* Directive, setting a generic anti-bandit rhetoric to the prosecution of security warfare through genocide across occupied Europe. This might be likened to an earlier form of war on terror. Thus, the German incorporation of brutal methods, excused on the grounds of the military necessity of national security.

Long before the 2022 invasion, there was insightful criticism of Putin's strategic dogma. Pavlovsky argued Putin used escalation to build conflicts locally with the sole purpose of maximum media coverage. He claimed: 'This is not old-school geopolitics. This is the Russian way of using asymmetry between Russia and the west. ... a policy of aggressive globalism—not of a nation-wide mobilization. ... The system does not have a strategic objective' and relies on 'special operations and infiltration' to gather intelligence.[24] Pavlovsky added this strategy 'exaggerates the player's potential' while maximising confusion to the outside observer. This strategy is primarily directed against the Russian population, as a means of internal social control, because of deeply rooted fears of a coup like 1917 or 1991. This internal fear resembled the Nazi fears of the hunger winter 1916–17 and the reason behind the war against the Soviet Union in 1941. In 2021, Jakob Hauter concluded the Donbas War had caused division 'between two camps supporting diametrically opposing characterisations of the war has not only appeared among political organizations and mass media around the world but also in academic debate'.[25] Putin's war is not actually about external national goals in the traditional sense but is framed in security warfare form to reinforce his regime's authoritarian control over the Russian people.

Restoring the authoritarian state by prosecuting security warfare in Ukraine is old school politics. On 24 February 2022, Putin gave a televised address to Russia. He claimed justification for his

---

[24] Pavlovsky, 'Strategic Decentering', p. 207.
[25] Jakob Hunter (ed.), *Civil War? Interstate War? Hybrid War? Dimensions and Interpretations of the Donbas Conflict 2014–2020* (Stuttgart: Ibidem-Verlag, 2021).

actions under Article 51 of the UN Charter, any nation's right to engage in self-defence. This was intended to reinforce the legitimacy of his actions to the Russian public. Putin accused NATO of aggressive expansion and assisting the genocidal actions of neo-Nazis in Ukraine. He announced the 'noble' goal of protecting the Russian community in Ukraine. He announced a 'special military operation' in the Donbas region and called upon Ukrainian forces to lay down their arms and return to their homes. He warned that all bloodshed would be the responsibility of Ukrainians. There was no declaration of war, no territorial aims, no specific targets, and no statement of what constituted final victory. Russian operations have followed a predictable series of phases. The first phase saw multiple assaults aimed at establishing lodgements. The grand maskirovka was unleashed as the assaults formed a rough horseshoe shape, across an extremely long frontline, and set in a westerly direction. In addition, the Black Sea was closed placing Ukraine in an Anaconda vice-like grip. This was classical Russian strategy intended to over-stretch the opponent on a long front. The aim being to force Ukraine to commit forces and reserves, wasting them in attrition. Putin then donned the trappings of the righteous and persona of the rational actor.

The second phase began the 'nibbling' away of attrition. There was still no identifiable Schwerpunkt (centre of gravity on the battlefield) since building the lodgements into a larger battle area was the operation mission. The emergence of supporting fire illustrated how important the lodgements were in Russian thinking. The need to build larger or extended areas was about preparing for future aggressive and offensive operations. As the lodgements joined, the scale of shelling increased to protect them. At that point, 'experts' on social media misread the signs and focused upon the roads, the mud, and the tyres of Russian vehicles. Contrary to myth, the Russians had always used roads, long before the Soviet days. The Russians could get bogged down in war, but opponents were also bogged down and unable to take advantage. There was a discussion about failing Russian leadership and capability, and the impact of weak logistics following the withdrawal from Kyiv. Those discussions faded away as the scale of operations continued to increase. A third phase was identified with the opening of the 'annihilation bombardments' forcing the Ukrainian Army to fight multiple local battles and protect civilians. This also represented the mix of classical and modern doctrines. Forces on the ground prod and prod until they meet concerted resistance. This forces the opponent to commit more reserves into the battle. The logic of attrition kicks-in as reserves melt, leaving overwhelming superiority in places designated for offensive operations. The attrition, however, is also being directed at Ukrainian cities and civilians. This was apparent when Putin declared all disregard for war crimes and indirectly announced his plans to destroy Ukraine.

The fourth phase has seen the gradual rolling of offensive activity across the entire horseshoe front, all prodding for weaknesses. This has been most visible in southern Ukraine. Russian war-making unleashed barrages flattening villages, towns, and cities. The 'annihilation bombardment' has included massive displays of multiple launch weapons, self-propelled howitzers and towed artillery firing from long distances at pre-planned grid-references. This crescendo of war, twinned with a mechanised genocide, was being orchestrated in complete contrast to the west's war-making — or so it appeared. The people of Iraq have a different opinion. The fifth phase was the deliberate confusion regarding humanitarian efforts. Corridors for refugees perpetually come under fire, while increasing devastation has pushed refugee numbers towards 10 million and rising. This conforms to Putin's terror — driving refugees towards the West to spread fear and trepidation.

The regular progress assessments of this SMO have followed patterns of typical security warfare. In April, Putin met with Sergei Shoigu, the Russian defence minister, for a monthly military situation conference. Shoigu informed Putin that Mariupol had been 'liberated'. He claimed the city had been turned into 'a powerful stronghold and the base of far-right Ukrainian nationalists ... the capital of the Azov Battalion'. A body count identified 8,100 Ukrainian troops known to have been in the city in March. Since then, 4,000 were 'neutralised', 1,478 were POWs and the rest (2,000) were still resisting in the Azovstal plant. The numbers didn't balance. Shoigu claimed in the retreat, the Ukrainian Army had used civilians and residential buildings as shields.[26] In May, Putin met with Russian border guards. He told them:

> "In June 1941, the fighters of the Soviet frontier posts fearlessly engaged in the first heavy combat despite being outnumbered, and then valiantly battled on the fronts of the Great Patriotic War and in the partisan detachments ... and made a huge contribution ... to the eradication of the Banderites and other henchmen of the Nazis...[27]"

During the July conference, Shoigu adopted a more military format of command and forces, which indicated the SMO might be about to change again. After the command summary, the report noted twenty-five localities had been taken under control, including Severodonetsk and Zolotoye, and operations had ended the previous day with the 'liberation of Lisichansk'. This covered 670 square kilometres that had fallen under Russian control. Regarding Ukrainian casualties, there was a large 'body-count' of 5,470 of which 2,218 had been killed and 3,252 wounded—in other words, no unwounded POWs. The captured booty included thirty-nine tanks, forty-eight Javelin and NLAW systems, eighteen Stinger systems and other material. Russian forces were 'de-mining' the city of Lisichansk, and humanitarian supplies were being driven in. The report signed off with: 'The Russian Armed Forces are continuing the special military operation.'[28] At the time I wrote: 'We should regard this as an indication of an impending change to the SMO and heightened military operations.'—which we now know happened.

Western experts and scholars have entirely misunderstood the symbiotic relationship between security warfare and genocide. Putin's politics of violence display similarities to imperialistic power, like the colonial wars of the nineteenth century and

---

[26] 'Meeting with Defence Minister Sergei Shoigu', President of Russia, 21 April 2022, http://en.kremlin.ru/events/president/transcripts/68254 (accessed 16 September 2022).

[27] 'Greetings on Border Guards Day', President of Russia, 28 May 2022, http://en.kremlin.ru/events/president/transcripts/68500 (accessed 16 September 2022).

[28] 'Meeting with Defence Minister Sergei Shoigu', President of Russia, 4 July 2022, http://en.kremlin.ru/events/president/transcripts/68815 (accessed 16 September 2022).

including the wars against terror of the twenty-first century.[29] Typically, security warfare campaigns adopt a vague mission statement, low numbers of conventional forces, a grindingly slow war of maximum attrition and acts of extreme violence (bombardments, shootings, rape and beatings). The methodology applies violence against indigenous populations, forcing them to become refugees, causing chaos, destabilising communities, and sowing fears nationwide. Putin's security warfare began to succeed very early on by forcing a humanitarian calamity on the West—initially, 5 million refugees fled westwards, a figure that doubled in less than two weeks as progressive destruction was pounded into Ukraine. Putin's security warfare has imposed genocide through the mass bombardments of civilian communities, placing Mariupol under siege and destroying hundreds of towns and settlements along all fronts. On the local level, there were several atrocities and wilful mass killings of civilians. The politics of security warfare has shapeshifted into a vast area of occupation as the lodgements were extended while those more exposed infiltrations were rapidly shut down in the Kyiv area. Even as the Russians began a withdrawal from several lodgements, it was obvious the Russian general staff could still manage complex operational plans and shift troops with agility through the railway network. Thus, from this emerging horror, Putin's deliberate employment of conventional military forces for strategic goals reached beyond 'normal' political ends because of his genocidal agenda. Putin's goal is now known: the eradication of Ukraine, as we know it, and the grinding socio-cultural attrition against the West.

Observing the horror of security warfare being unleashed, where humanitarian catastrophe and war crimes are manifestly central to Russian operations, Western military experts have struggled to come to terms with Putin's war-making. The problem lies with judging Russian methods against NATO's standards of rehearsed manoeuvres and battle school wargames. Similarly, genocide scholars were bizarrely slow to recognise how genocide was being conducted so wilfully before social media. Far too many

---

[29] Blood, *Hitler's Bandit Hunters*.

genocide experts relied on inappropriate ideological structures or the historical precedent of victims in big numbers, or the generalisation of 'millions' before coming to a decision. Slow to comprehend Putin's genocidal agenda, it was weeks into the war before many began to realise their error. The prediction of genocide, since the Rwandan genocide, relied too heavily on historical processes rather than comprehending the actions of an aggressor. Elements within this conflict's development explain how this war was genocidal from the start. The ongoing war, since the invasion of Crimea, had become a stalemate of attrition that some observers believed suited Putin's methods of 'freezing conflicts in the hot spots' without developing 'a long-term strategy'.[30] Throughout history, the deliberate bombardment of civilians was rarely judged a war crime if there was no direct military connection. In most military narratives, civilians killed by an artillery salvo during war were usually blamed on collateral damage. At 154 days into the war, experts were still struggling to come to terms with the Russian way of war, or the deliberate bombardment of civilians.[31]

Putin's genocide: holocaust by bombardment

There is an impression that this is an artillery war. Russian artillery has pounded with impunity. The absence of Ukrainian air cover, or a NATO no-fly zone, has encouraged the artillery to take control of the fighting. If the artillery could be countered, this would spell a major defeat for Russia. Security warfare is about conventional military and police forces employed to non-specific missions. It can be conducted within conventional war but rarely has the strength of forces to engage in a protracted or attrition war. Putin's operations are framed in terms of security warfare of the hammer and anvil — the artillery bombardment is the hammer, and the ground forces

---

[30] Pavlovsky, 'Strategic Decentering', p. 215.
[31] 'The Russo-Ukrainian War of 2022: Day 154 (Ground Actions)', Mystics and Statistics blog, 27 July 2022, http://www.dupuyinstitute.org/blog/2022/07/27/the-russo-ukrainian-war-of-2022-day-154-ground-actions (accessed 16 September 2022).

are the anvil—applied to break Ukraine's will to fight. In 2004, Benjamin Valentino published a study of genocide that received much criticism. Dan Stone, in his Historiography of Genocide, argued Valentino had 'overemphasize(d) the role of political and military leaders in genocide' (p.52).[32] However, it was Valentino's chapter, 'The Strategic Logic of Mass Killing', that has some relevance to Putin's illegal war. In this interpretation, the adoption of genocide for strategic purposes pointed to a deeper insidiousness in the application of Russia's politics of violence. While some of this language seems dated, he did note that genocides had been adopted to transform societies according to a doctrine. In another opinion, Valentino noted that 'sometimes mass killing is simply war by other means'.[33] However, regardless of the thin Clausewitzian tone, it was his next observation that spoke directly to the present conflict: 'Coercive mass killings occur in major conflicts when combatants lack the capabilities to defeat their opponents' military forces with conventional military techniques.'[34] Has Putin resorted to genocide because he recognised Russia could not easily defeat Ukraine, or was genocide Putin's answer to the waning power of Russia's war machine?

After 1917, a unique tradition of artillery developed in the military culture of the Russian way of war. This was not always a successful or efficient tradition, as Alexander Hill has explained.[35] The study of Soviet doctrines such as 'deep battle' or 'deep operations' are many; however, Russian artillery doctrine has not been at the forefront of research since the Cold War. If we imagined three examples of the key artillery pieces during the Second World War, we immediately turn to the Katusha multiple rocket launcher, the self-propelled 152mm howitzers and the masses of towed artillery. According to The Military Balance (2022), the multiple missile

---

[32] Dan Stone ed, *The Historiography of Genocide*, (Basingstoke: Palgrave MacMillan, 2008), p.52.

[33] Benjamin A. Valentino, *Final Solutions: Mass Killing and Genocide in the 20th Century* (Ithaca, NY: Cornell University Press, 2004), p. 81

[34] Ibid.

[35] Alexander Hill, *The Red Army and the Second World War* (Cambridge: Cambridge University Press, 2017), pp. 32–8, 50–1.

launcher, the self-propelled howitzers and towed artillery are still the largest segment of conventional army hardware. The Russian order of battle identifies at least 4,894 artillery pieces as opposed to 2,927 main battle tanks and 1,700 armoured vehicles.[36] Artillery, the 'God of War', reigns supreme. Between 1945 and 1995, the artillery was in the background. In securing the Warsaw Pact and Soviet spheres of influence, the Red Army conducted two large-scale intervention operations — Hungary 1956 and Czechoslovakia 1968 — without artillery. In in the stealth of nigh time, Russian forces invaded Czechoslovakia in 1968, and Red Army armoured forces entered Prague. The Russian pretext was that counter-revolution had to be prevented to save the Warsaw Pact. The Red Army deployed tanks, light armour, and infantry for their mobility for power-projection, rather than destruction, and they used roads. Noticeable in all these internal operations was the relative youth of the troops and the use of surprise. There were skirmishes and casualties, but the full force of bombardment was avoided. A story emerged that young Red Army soldiers had not been told they were being sent to suppress the Czech people. This would seem to echo the remarks of young recruits captured in Ukraine at the start of Putin's war.[37] In 1979, in Afghanistan, the Red Army adopted the coup de main, the fast mobile forces but ran into trouble. Helicopter gunships were deployed for heavy support, but they were countered by supplies of US anti-aircraft missiles supplied to the Mujahideen. An account of this US support was published in 2003, which was popularised in the film Charlie Wilson's War (2007), starring Tom Hanks, Julia Roberts, and Philip Hoffman.

The Soviet War in Afghanistan, led to an 'Afghansty syndrome' the Russian version of the Vietnam syndrome. Afghansty defined the stark social difference between those who served and those who hadn't. Russian soldiers dubbed it Afghansty but the veterans likened themselves to 'soldier-interventionists' from the

---

[36] IISS, *The Military Balance* (London: IISS, 2022), pp. 413–15.
[37] Background reading from the Russian perspective included: David Marples, *Motherland: Russia in the Twentieth Century* (London: Routledge, 2002), and Ronald Grigor Suny, *The Cambridge History of Russia*, vol. 3, *The Twentieth Century* (Cambridge: Cambridge University Press, 2006).

wars of national liberation wars supported by the Soviet Union during the Cold War.[38] The Red Army's defeat ended forty years of invincibility, while the supply of arms was reinterpreted as the triumph of capitalism. The same dogma explains USA and NATO's efforts to defeat Putin. An alternative scenario has emerged. The drip-drip-drip of weapons to Ukraine has undermined Ukrainian strategy and caused attrition against its manpower reserves. We should be cautious that Putin and the Russian Army learned from that experience and have calculated to neutralise the threat.

In December 1991, the Soviet Union was officially disbanded. However, the constitutional crisis of October 1993 brought open conflict to the streets of Moscow for the first time since 1917. Under Yeltsin's orders, Russian Army tanks fired on the White House and saved Yeltsin's regime. In December 1994, the Russian Army launched three offensive operations towards Grozny, in the opening of the First Chechen War. The conflict lasted until August 1996. It was a calamity for Russia, with casualties reaching somewhere between 4,000 and 14,000 and defeat by Chechnya. Yeltsin was entirely responsible for escalating the conflict, but within specific operations there were serious flaws in the performance and capability of the Russian armed forces. The Battle of Grozny was the change point in operations. Russian heavy bombardment returned to Europe for the first time since 1945. Air raids and bombardment flattened the city. The Russians sustained significant losses of armoured fighting vehicles and casualties in less than two months. However, they had inflicted more than 25,000 civilians killed. There were indications that rogue elements within the Russian high command system were working against the army's cohesion. Human rights bodies began to investigate mounting evidence of war crimes and extreme cases such as the Samashki massacre—categorised as a cleansing action by the United Nations Commission on Human Rights.[39] On 16 April 1996, a battalion of the 245th Motor Rifle

---

[38] Rodric Braithwaite, *Afgantsy: The Russians in Afghanistan 1979–1989* (Oxford: Oxford University Press, 2011).

[39] UN Commission on Human Rights, 'The Situation of Human Rights in the Republic of Chechnya of the Russian Federation', Report of the Secretary-General,

Regiment was ambushed in Shatoy. The column was savaged, and an official report (alternatives in brackets) claimed fifty-three (seventy) killed and fifty-two (100) wounding.[40] The fighting turned into a vicious insurgency. Captain Vladimir Vermolin recalled convoys and columns were ambushed and everyone killed. Chechen videos were used to attract foreign volunteers and finance. A Chechen counter-offensive caught the Russians in a moment of operational complacency and destroyed the column. When Putin became President, according to his aids he became fixated on succeeding in Chechnya. He adopted an aggressive and rough tone about the Chechens: 'If we catch them in the toilet that's where they'll die.' Eventually, under heavy bombardment the war turned in Russia's favour and Shatoy was 'avenged' in 2000. Andrei Illarionov, a Putin adviser, has told how an assistant came into the room and handed Putin a communique. Illarionov said, 'Putin read it. His face lit up. He was jubilant.' He recalled Putin said, 'Well, we have rolled over Shatoy.' The victory raised Putin's popularity.[41]

In 2008, the Russian Army embarked on a modernisation schedule of its older equipment while introducing new weapons. Self-propelled artillery was a particular weapon system being upgraded with the 2S35 Koalitsiya-SV being introduced to replace the 2S19 Msta-S, which had begun service in the 1990s. A similar programme was applied to tanks, with T-90M main battle tanks being introduced, while the T-80BVM and T-72B3M were modernised versions of tanks already in service. Many of the new weapon systems were placed on show in 2015 with expectations of their coming into service in 2022.[42] While Russia's armed forces were passing through another phase of hardware modernisation, cultural transformations—from the Soviet Red Army to the present-day—are less well understood. The Russian way of war has managed decline

---

26 March 1996, http://hrlibrary.umn.edu/commission/country52/1996_13.htm (accessed 16 September 2022).

[40] Since most sources referring to the ambush have been removed or lost on the web, please refer to https://en.wikipedia.org/wiki/Shatoy_ambush

[41] BBC, Putin, Russia and the West: Taking Control (part one), Brook Lapping Productions, 2011

[42] IISS, *The Military Balance 2021* (London: IISS, 2021), pp. 166–78.

while retaining its great power status. Putin's programme for military reform was planned for completion by 2020. There were overruns and delays, and the plan was not achieved. This of course raises questions over whether those reforms that did happen were properly wedded into the military system, and the Russian troops properly trained or worked up to meet the new equipment doctrines.[43]

The artillery remains the power within the Russian Army's order of battle and the central force of Putin's anaconda plan in Ukraine. According to Lester Grau and Charles Bartles: 'The Soviet Army was an artillery army with many tanks. The Soviets structured their army around artillery. The Russian Army is also artillery-centric.' They have written about 'manoeuvre by fire', whereby artillery remains in positions firing on one or shifting to several targets without moving positions. The artillery is used to smash targets over a short or extended period. Manoeuvre by fire can also shift fire to support several offensive operations from different directions. The artillery mission is to gain superiority over an opponent, and this is known as the 'massed artillery gambit'. Thus, Russian artillery doctrine still affirms the benefits of massed artillery. The artillery missions are normally arranged by type of target. The main mission is 'annihilation', the purpose being to render the opponent virtually powerless. Indirect fire is planned mathematically to achieve 70 to 90 per cent probability of destroying an individual target, or in the range of 50 to 60 per cent for an area target. Within the framework of this mission, the rubblising of urban centres or 'flattening' became a self-fulfilling logic for bombardment. Artillery commands plan for the high expenditure of ammunition. When destruction is planned and plotted by the hectare, it was assumed drones would be used for reconnaissance. In the past, questions were raised about the efficiency of fire control communications. Given these concerns, it's possible the artillery is operating with different levels of communications. The positioning of artillery and its

---

[43] IISS, *The Military Balance 2010* (London: IISS, 2010), pp. 211–14.

specific operations are beyond the remit of this essay.[44] However, it should be noted that with railways providing a constant flow of supplies, the artillery could continually pummel targets from 20 kilometres without the front troops having to do much more than hold the line. Thus, we can begin to recognise that Putin's anaconda plan has wider benefits if the artillery is the primary offensive arm, and the anti-cultural genocide was served as punitive bombardment.

The classifications and numbers of artillery in the Russian Army are bewildering. The multiple rocket launchers, the self-propelled howitzers and the towed artillery reflect the Second World War heritage. Examining these weapons in the context of Putin's war in Ukraine is to confront the realistic potential for mechanised genocide. Given the large populations in Kyiv or Kharkiv, the bombardment by heavy ordinance from grid coordinates is not only a very real prospect but the potential casualties to the civilians could match the numbers in Grozny — per Ukrainian city. The Msta-S, to take one self-propelled howitzer as an example, has a 152mm howitzer, with a range of 15 kilometres, can be set up to fire in thirty minutes, fire four or five 15 kilo shells per minute and then move off. A battery of these guns could rubblise vast areas in a short time.[45] The Russian specialist forces deploy flamethrower forces as part of the NBC Defence Regiments in a military system that internally plans to survive and thrive if ever there was a tactical nuclear confrontation. The TOS1 Buratino is a multiple rocket launcher, flamethrower system that fires thirty 220mm missiles in 7.5 seconds, within the short range of 4 kilometres. They are a thermobaric weapon that causes deep shockwaves and were used in Afghanistan because the weapon has advantages in mountainous terrain. They have the potential to utterly devastate municipalities because they dominate the urban battle space, clearing enemy forces and smashing bunkers.[46] Aviation raises a further dimension but is

---

[44] Lester W. Grau and Charles K. Bartles, *The Russian Way of War: Force Structure, Tactics and Modernization of the Russian Ground Forces* (Fort Leavenworth, KS: Foreign Military Studies Office, 2016), pp. 233-4.
[45] Ibid., p. 232.
[46] Ibid., pp. 320-1.

outside of this essay's remit.

Thirty years ago, Vukovar was destroyed at the start of a decade of bitter conflict. Many pundits at the time claimed this was the first-time total war had been experienced in Europe since 1945. Afterwards, Sarajevo was placed under 1,400 days of siege, and in Srebrenica, where UN assigned French General Morillon was appalled by the scale of the humanitarian tragedy. Later, there was a massacre of 8,000 Bosnians that revealed how rapid escalation functions in genocidal conflicts. Mariupol, in the last month, has surpassed Vukovar in the scale of destruction seen since 1945. In less than four weeks, a vibrant municipality has been reduced to a dead city. The appearance of genocide in Ukraine has 'shocked' social media. In the change world of social media, past conflicts like those in the former Yugoslavia and Chechnya were no longer prominent in the digital age. The images of the genocide and ethnic cleansing in Yugoslavia largely disappeared from public memory. In Yugoslavia, the United States, NATO, and the UN had claimed the determination to confront genocide. In the 1990s, air power was effective in forcing the aggressors to withdraw but they didn't end the killing. These lessons are conveniently forgotten in Ukraine, where the West has recoiled before Putin's threat to use nuclear weapons. The West faces imploding as Putin's economic warfare bites deeper, undermining the rigid structures that are unable to counter food shortages and exorbitant fuel prices.

By June 2022, Putin's armed forces had committed outrages that were classifiable under the five criminal activities that the UN recognises as genocide.[47] The Russian way of war has tightly woven genocidal acts to military operations. The destruction of Mariupol took less than four weeks. Volnovakha and many towns around Kyiv and Kharkiv have also been obliterated. This was achieved in record time through the deliberate positioning of artillery in pre-constructed positions. Massive excavations, the size of quarries, were cut into large areas far behind the national frontiers. Then targets were pre-set as grid coordinates, which enabled the artillery to

---

[47] Dan Stone (ed.), *The Historiography of Genocide*, (Basingstoke: Palgrave MacMillan: 2008), p.14.

flatten targets systematically by the hectare. The annihilation bombardment is the signature mission of Russian artillery doctrine, and the flattening of Ukraine's towns and cities has also been extended to destroying crops. In addition to the destruction of archives and other cultural buildings, there is evidence that the Russians are avoiding the destruction of Orthodox churches. Forcing the break-up of Ukraine also has parallels with the break-up of Yugoslavia. Thus, bombardment to annihilate was more than coincidental to both conflicts, with sieges lasting for extended periods and in one case up to more than 1,400 days. This imposition of extreme conditions to cause mass suffering was a deliberate act of genocide. French General Morillon was profoundly shocked at the condition's the masses were forced to survive under — he elected to stay in the city to expose the horrors to the world. Milošević's resort to crimes against civilians followed several patterns: the killing of large numbers of men, mass rapes and the employment of paramilitary forces to 'cleanse' communities. Milošević incorporated war crimes and crimes against humanity from the beginning of the conflict in 1989. In response to the terror, the Croatians and Bosnians turned to mass killings and atrocities. This is the logic of genocidal conflict, locking both sides into the spiralling violence of survival. Deliberately directing missiles and aiming guns at a city was treated as collateral damage in military circles. However, modern European cities are densely concentrated with civilians. Pointing guns at densely populated communities is not collateral damage - it's a deliberate act of genocide. Russian annihilation bombardments are a deliberate act of genocide when directed at Mariupol or any other Ukrainian city.

The precedents to these operations were the Serbian bombardments of Vukovar in 1991 and the Russian bombardments of Grozny in 1996 indicate a Serbo-Russian operational methodology. Few realise today that there was an older historiography of humanity in war and crimes against civilians, where bombardment was noted as controversial but treated as a peculiar aspect of British naval methods during the nineteenth century and was imitated by other European powers. Bombardments were largely improvised, not specifically aimed at civilians, but conducted in parallel with a more deliberate policy of using starvation in siege warfare. Gradually, indiscriminate bombardment became a feature of modern warfare. From the latter half of the twentieth century up to the present day, aerial bombardment developed into the most destructive force against civilians, and doctrines were drafted for the sole purpose of delivering cost-efficient mass death.[48] Since Grozny (1996), and during the civil wars in the former Yugoslavia, there has been an increased trend for all belligerents to target civilians with modern and highly lethal weapons. In the first decade of the twenty-first century, the nature of modern war was once again the subject of debate in the wake of 9-11. During a conference in 2001, Steve Crawshaw from Human Rights Watch said: 'Military acts like those against Dresden, which were already controversial at the time, have since been codified into international law.'[49] Crawshaw thought there was little to be gained from bombing Iraq. Two years later, a journalist from The New Yorker reported as cruise missiles began exploding in Baghdad. Jon Lee Anderson wrote: 'That night, the "shock and awe" bombardment began. The first bombs hit at precisely nine o'clock, and we had a front-row view of the conflagration.'[50] Perhaps memories fade and history lost, but the bombardment of civilians has been central to the way of war of most industrialised nations. The problem lies in how to prosecute the perpetrators of war crimes and national political leaders that resort to genocide, when all nations are guilty of extremism.

The case of the individual perpetrator

In Russia, the 'battalion' can be a variety of identities from the military equivalent to a community, a hooligan gang, or a private army. Battalions normally peak around 500–700 officers and

---

[48] Geoffrey Best, *Humanity in Warfare* (London: Methuen, 1980), pp. 108–12,

[49] Steve Crawshaw, 'Military Activities and Human Rights', in Patrick Mileham, 'War and Morality', Whitehall Paper 61, Royal United Services Institute, London, 2004, p. 129.

[50] 'The Bombing of Baghdad', *The New Yorker*, 31 March 2003, https://www.newyorker.com/magazine/2003/03/31/the-bombing-of-baghdad (accessed 16 September 2022).

ordinary ranks, but their fighting power usually fluctuates between 250-400 soldiers. They operate in a variety of configurations, from squads and patrols of five to fifteen soldiers to platoons of forty to fifty soldiers to companies of 120 to 150 soldiers and are managed by a command staff of officers, specialists, clerks, and cooks. The usual desirable outcomes of raising a battalion are their socio-culture order and its fighting prowess. This culture is often described in terms like 'élan', 'elite', or corps d'elite. Roger Beaumont identified several categories of elite units: the ceremonial, the combat-proven, the Praetorians, the ethnic forces, the ideological, the romanticised, the tech-proto-cybernetic and the functional.[51] There is another group of battalions bonded in blood: trigger-pullers, killers, war criminals and perpetrators of genocide. They can build a darker form of elitism. Regimes have raised battalions to commit state-sponsored crimes or conduct genocide, but some detachments within battalions have broken out of the bonds of military discipline to build an inner culture based on bloodlust.

The research literature on fighting formations that have descended into criminal acts or conducted bloodlust actions are not as numerous as the popular books of heroic fighting forces. The great gap that once existed between the extreme methods of the Waffen-SS units, often in conventional fighting, and the more heroic accounts of 'Tommies' and 'Yanks' at war, are gradually being bridged. The individual war crimes' perpetrator in the guise of the ordinary soldier, the regular police officer, the militia volunteer or the recruit have appeared in every modern army. In colonial wars, the British, German, French, American, Italian, Japanese, Russian and Spanish all shared unflattering histories of war crimes or crimes against humanity. Police forces no longer stand alone as history's trigger pullers in the politics of violence. Set against the backdrop of the wars in the former Yugoslavia, Christopher Browning conceptualised the 'ordinary men' as Hitler's perpetrators, but it was Daniel Goldhagen that coined the phrase 'Willing Executioners' about the deep-seated hatred for Jews in Germany that led to

---

[51] Roger Beaumont, *Military Elites* (London: R. Hale, 1974), p. 3.

the Holocaust.⁵² A decade later, two researchers investigated the dark recesses of unit culture that was rooted in the memory of war crimes. The jacket cover of the book advertised 'the story of a group of elite soldiers in Vietnam who spin dangerously out of control and went on a seven-month rampage'.⁵³ My research on the Holocaust in Poland focused upon a Luftwaffe battalion that incorporated game hunting methods to hunt Jews and Soviet partisans during operational training.⁵⁴ Training soldiers for war by killing civilians blooded and brutalised recruits early in their service. While the narratives of these books categorised the participants in genocide as victims, bystanders, perpetrators, the infinite varieties of war crimes and genocide undermined simplistic conclusions about genocide. In other words, the general conclusion that perpetrators were willing killers became less convincing when ordinary soldiers were scrutinised in similar detail.

Soldiers are trained to kill, which, as many military historians will explain, is about overcoming the natural human trait of a reluctance to kill. Few have imagined the ramifications of professional armies embracing killing as a norm. Theories about killing in war have raged over the decades since 1945 in Anglo-American literature. One of the first to observe the reluctance to kill, or even fire weapons, was S. L. A. Marshall's study of US Army soldiers in war.⁵⁵ In 1976, a psychologist examined the organisational behaviour of military cultures to explain their inherent incompetence. He was less insightful in explaining cultures of killing.⁵⁶ In 1995, Dave Grossman reiterated the opinion that soldiers were generally reluctant to kill, but he also examined themes such as desensitisation training, the 'dark power of atrocity', and identifying the 'black

---

52   Christopher Browning, *Ordinary Men* (New York: HarperCollins, 1993), Daniel J. Goldhagen, *Hitler's Willing Executioners* (New York: Alfred A. Knopf, 1996).
53   Michael Sallah and Mitch Weiss, *Tiger Force: A True Story of Men and War* (New York: Little, Brown, 2006).
54   Blood, Birds of Prey.
55   S. L. A. Marshall, *Men Against Fire* (Alexandria: Byrrd Enterprises, 1947).
56   Norman Dixon, *On the Psychology of Military Incompetence* (London: Jonathan Cape, 1976).

areas' of executions.⁵⁷ The recognition that group killing can lead to unit cohesion, even toward a dark elitism (an elite crafted in atrocity), undermines decades of theories about humanitarianism in war. The conundrum facing Western armies has been to train men to kill, and after they had killed, hoping they do not turn into killers. The one exception to that theory of men at arms was the German army, which trained soldiers to become aggressive warriors as the cultural norm through discipline and expertise.

Since the 1980s, Western armies have claimed the fantasy known as Auftragstaktik, a postwar fantasy of the German soldier's fighting power granted an advantage during the Second World War. Few military analysts acknowledged key salient points: the Germans lost both world wars, they rarely succeeded without a pre-emptive strike, and only when they held the advantage of armoured concentration enhanced with air power. These fantasies of German fighting power were constructed from books that were published after the war and had no empirical value. Nonetheless attempts to institutionalise the word have informed western military education. Noticeably the leading German military historians have strenuously dodged the word.⁵⁸ Military analysts face a conundrum, even if Auftragstaktik had existed, it would have been instrumental to Hitler's annihilation warfare and form a serious conclusion about the German army's resort to genocide. Anglo-American armies and NATO forces have tried to anglicise Auftragstaktik into 'mission command'. The dilution of military control handed to junior officers is to place considerable responsibility on the moral integrity of the soldiers. If a junior officer was ordered to complete a mission successfully, regardless of costs or consequences as was assumed with Auftragstaktik, then the potential for

---

57   Dave Grossman, *On Killing: The Psychological Cost of Learning to Kill in War and Society* (New York: Little, Brown and Co., 1995).
58   Stephan Leistenschneider, *Auftragstaktik im preussisch-deutschen Heer 1871 bis 1914* (Berlin: Mittler & Sohn, 2002), Werner Widder, 'Auftragstaktik and Innere Führung: Trademarks of German Leadership', *Military Review* 82, no. 5 (September–October 2002), pp. 3–9. In silent reply avoiding the word or its existence, Gerhard P. Gross, *The Myth and Reality of German Warfare* (Kentucky: University Press of Kentucky, 2016).

crimes is considerable. Promoting 'mission command' raises questions. If 'mission command' was normal dogma for operations in Iraq and Afghanistan, does this explain the random cases of war crimes? If war crimes did occur due to 'mission command', must ultimate responsibility lie with the senior commanders? If this was the common practice in Western forces, then there are consequences for judging the behaviour of the Russian Army.

Members of the Russian forces have committed serious crimes against Ukraine's civilians on almost every front and in every city where there has been fighting. This has included mass killing, rape, physical harm, deportation and killing of children. To disguise the evidence, bodies were buried in mass graves. There has also been looting and plunder. Pavlovsky observed, 'when a nation believes it has embarked on a just war. The rationale fades as the carnage mounts, and the soldiers no longer fight for a cause, but to survive and to help their comrades do the same.'[59] He also cautioned: 'Although operationally ineffective, formations such as the Wagner Group serve as an important device that produces newsworthy events.'[60] According to Ken Silverstein observed: 'Private Warriors have a financial and career interest in war and conflict as the power and connections to promote continual hard line policies.'[61] Regardless of the social media claims and counterclaims, the number of civilians killed in brutal acts by Russian soldiers has been constantly mounting. We should consider two questions: Is Putin's resort to genocide enhancing the fighting power of the Russian forces, and how quickly are Russians being initiated into war crimes? Looking at several cases in history and recent judgements may help address these questions.

On 23 May 2022, Russian Army Sergeant Vadim Shishimarin was found guilty of war crimes by a Ukrainian court. He is a twenty-one-year-old Siberian, born in Ust-Ilimsk in the Irkutsk oblast. During the opening phase of Putin's invasion, he was designated as a squad leader in the 4th Guards Kantemirovskaya Tank

---

[59] Pavlovsky, 'Strategic Decentering', p. 319.
[60] Ibid., p. 207.
[61] Ken Silverstein, *Private Warriors* (New York: Verso, 2000), p. ix.

Division. On 28 February, Shishimarin was driving through the village of Chupakhivka when he was ordered by Makeev Nikolai Olegivich to kill Oleksandr Shelipov. He refused. A senior lieutenant intervened and ordered him to shoot the sixty-two-year-old Ukrainian civilian. He justified the killing on the grounds that the civilian was using his mobile phone, and he didn't want him to warn Ukrainian forces of their positions. Shishimarin shot and killed Olegivich with his AK-47 automatic rifle. Shelipov's wife heard the shots and rushed out of the house to see Shishimarin and his comrades drive off in a vehicle. The next day (29 February) Shishimarin surrendered to Ukrainian forces. After cooperating with Ukrainian interrogators and prosecutors, he confessed to the war crime, and the court in Kyiv sentenced him to life imprisonment.[62]

Historically, the most lethal exponents of war crimes within military operations were the German armed forces. On 29 May 1943, Corporal Nonnig, a Luftwaffe Oberjäger (Luftwaffe corporal of rifles), led a three-man patrol through Białowieża Forest in the Białystok region of Poland. It was 8.30am and they were on raised ground approaching Okulniki when several persons broke cover from a tree line. They began moving through a field towards more forest and were possibly walking through the firebreaks used to prevent forest fire. In an after-action report, Nonnig unslung his rifle and without warning fired several shots. He killed two people described as 'Jews' from up to 500 metres. After examining the two dead bodies, he continued the patrol on to Okulniki, where he reported that three remaining 'Jews' had fled into the forest, possibly wounded, and leaving a blood trail. With the delay in searching for the bodies and then completing the patrol, the area began to fall into darkness and under the battalion standing orders, the troops waited in their strongpoint. At around 3.00am, they received orders from the battalion commander, a Luftwaffe-Major to return to the scene and track the area for the other 'fugitives'. The major believed there was a bunker in the area where the 'Jews' were hiding, and

---

[62] Sergey Vasiliev, 'The Reckoning for War Crimes in Ukraine Has Begun', *Foreign Policy*, 17 June 2022, https://foreignpolicy.com/2022/06/17/war-crimes-trials-ukraine-russian-soldiers-shishimarin (accessed 20 September 2022).

he wanted it found and the fugitives killed. Under the leadership of Luftwaffe-Lieutenant Spies, a patrol including Nonnig located a camouflaged bunker where Jews were hiding from the Holocaust. After a grenade was thrown in the bunker, a young male survivor was apprehended and tortured for information. After he told the Germans of other Jews cohabiting the bunker, a trap was set, and they were killed. The report was sent to Luftwaffe headquarters in Königsberg, and Nonnig was mentioned in dispatches for skills as a marksman.[63] If this was Auftragstaktik, then it graphically illustrates the inherent dangers of 'loose' command dogma. The ordinary German soldiers were formed into squad and nearly always led by junior NCOs. Prior to combat, senior officers would pass orders to the squad leader, with a recommendation to act in any suitable way to complete the mission. From patrols to combat, the ordinary soldier looked to the NCOs for leadership in the field, as well as guidance and motivation.

Those who follow the gang or crowd have often been the most prolific perpetrators of genocide. In March 1993, Borislav Herak, a Bosnian Serb soldier, was found guilty of genocide by a Sarajevo military court.[64] During the civil wars in the former Yugoslavia in the 1990s, the violence erupted into ethnic cleansing, religious extremism, and genocide. Herak confessed to thirty-two murders and sixteen rapes and remains in prison serving a life sentence. He was the only soldier found guilty of genocide during a decade of violent conflicts. During the trial process, Herak confessed before cameras about his crimes and represents an important record of how an individual was turned into a mass murderer. He had an unremarkable upbringing. Then he was conscripted and trained by a police officer in how to kill pigs with a large knife. His first killing followed soon afterwards. His unit was attacked by Bosnians. They fled but captured six men from Visoko, in uniform, and they were disarmed. He was ordered to kill them with a knife, like killing pigs.

---

[63] Blood, *Birds of Prey*, pp. 350–1.
[64] 'A Public Show in the Sniper Season', *The Guardian*, 13 March 1993, https://www.theguardian.com/world/1993/mar/13/warcrimes (accessed 20 September 2022).

One was knocked to the floor and struck with a gun. Herak was told to kill him, and he confessed—he took the man by the hair, forced his head to the floor and then 'slit his throat once'. Then the rest were killed in the same way. He later confessed to observing the Serbian Army conduct mass killings, and afterwards, the grave pits were filled up by bulldozers. While on guard duty of Bosnian prisoners, he shot one who tried to escape. During these confessions, he described in detail the rape of young women and afterwards killing them. He was told to participate in the rapes because it would improve his morale. To kill the women afterwards was excused because there were too many women and not enough rations. In their warped rationale as Serbian soldiers, they shot the women in the forehead, to spare them from further suffering.[65]

Another war crime example falls within the parameters of 'mission command'. On 15 September 2011, while on patrol in Afghanistan, Sergeant Alexander Wayne Blackman, a Royal Marine serving with 42 Commando, shot and killed a Taliban insurgent. Simon Akam gave a full account of the crime in his examination of British accountability in Iraq and Afghanistan.[66] However, there is a recording of Blackman and his comrades killing the insurgent that was still accessible on YouTube at the time of writing.[67] The recording is evidence - the voices of the soldiers, their dialogue about an enemy, and the sound of the killing pistol shot informs us of the killing. The behaviour of the marines constituted a war crime: from their assessment of the insurgent's medical condition - 'I hate to say it we'll have to administer first aid to this individual'; to the pistol shot, and then the after-kill elegy—'Shuffle off this mortal coil, you cunt', and then the acknowledgement of criminal behaviour—'I've just broken the Geneva convention'. A moment when modernity, advanced technology and war etched in the politics of violence - the soldier's headcam had recorded the crime. The more profound

---

[65] John F. Burns, 'A Killer's Tale: A Special Report; A Serbian Fighter's Path of Brutality', *The New York Times*, 27 November 1992.

[66] Simon Akam, *The Changing of the Guard: The British Army since 911* (London: Scribe, 2021), p. 374.

[67] 'LISTEN: Sickening Audio of British Marine Shooting Afghan', YouTube, 8 November 2013, https://youtu.be/KjtzgWzh9fk (accessed 20 September 2022).

problems concerned why a British soldier wilfully ignored military discipline, mocked the laws of war after the insurgent was killed and why the headcam recording survived.

The four cases bring into sharp focus the difficulties of predicting or identifying war crimes or acts of genocide. They also reveal forensic analysis is key to establishing the train of events of the perpetrator and the victim. From the four cases, the genocidal crimes of Herak represent the most threatening to the war in Ukraine. He was initiated into murder while serving in a militia. His confession was depressingly timeless, random killing. His confessions had similarities with the massacres of Jews in Vilnius in 1941. The large force of militias serving with the Russian Army represent a serious threat to civilians in Ukraine. Alexander's case exposes the hypocrisy of Western criticism of Russia. On 20 December 2016, Nick Ferrari, the LBC radio presenter, claimed a miscarriage of justice when Alexander was denied bail. Ferrari fumed over the decision and compared the case to the treatment of Rolf Harris[68]: 'We have a system where bail is afforded to rapists and to paedophiles, but not to a soldier.'[69] Once the moment had passed, Alexander disappeared from the headlines. On 16 March 2017, Ferrari announced: '[C]elebrations will echo across the land when Marine A[lexander] is released.' He added: '[I]f we cannot look after the men and women who defend this country, well frankly what the bloody hell is this country about?'[70] Shishimarin was the first soldier to be prosecuted for a war crime during Putin's illegal war. An alternative interpretation of Shishimarin's actions could easily have treated his crime as the collateral consequence of military necessity if place before a more 'generous' court. A civilian caught up in a conflict killed while

---

[68] Rolf Harris was found guilty of indecent assault of female victims and imprisoned for 5 years.
[69] 'Nick Ferrari Fumes at "Shocking Miscarriage of Justice" over Marine A', LBC, 22 December 2016, https://www.lbc.co.uk/radio/presenters/nick-ferrari/nick-ferrari-fumes-at-marine-a-bail-refusal (accessed 20 September 2022).
[70] 'Celebrations Will Echo across the Land When Marine A Is Released: Nick Ferrari', LBC, 16 March 2017, https://www.lbc.co.uk/radio/presenters/nick-ferrari/celebrations-echo-across-land-marinea-nick-ferrari (accessed 20 September 2022).

holding a mobile phone could be regarded as a threat to military security. The absence of his officers, who avoided responsibility and justice, is a constant problem in war crimes jurisdiction. Nonnig's case exposes the dangers of military efficiency within a totalitarian regime. Nazi racism was subsumed into German military practice, and this was weaponised in Nonnig's automatic response to training. His actions came under the civilian codex, but he followed battalion standing orders. His defence might have been 'orders are orders', but if the report was presented as written he would have been found guilty under 'normal' military law largely because he fired before giving a warning. The only difference between Shishimarin and Nonnig was the verbal confession and the after-action report. We assume both were processed through the prevailing military system without criminal investigation.

The myths about Russian armies have been constant since the Napoleonic Wars. 'The myth of Ivan began in the midst of war', wrote Catherine Merridale. The army was the backbone of regimes from tsarist times to the present day, but the modern version is a shadow of the reputation gained by the Red Army. However, Merridale also tried to research Red Army crimes and sexual violence where she could but constantly faced the blank refusal of access to the archives. She wrote: 'Whole areas of wartime life, including desertion, crime, cowardice, and rape were banned from public scrutiny and several specific crimes, such as the Katyn massacre were buried in denial.'[71] In 1979, the Red Army marched into Afghanistan. The coup de main succeeded in neutralising the political leadership, but military operations were less successful and eventually the acknowledgement of failure led to withdrawal. Over 620,000 Soviet soldiers served in Afghanistan, of which 15,051 were killed, 50,000 wounded and 10,000 left disabled, including suffering from PTSD. 'The blows that then struck the Soviet army came close to destroying it as an effective military force.' The fallout from the disintegration of the Soviet Union also fell on the army.

---

[71] Catherine Merridale, *Ivan's War: Inside the Red Army 1939–45* (New York: Metropolitan Books, 2006), pp. 462–5.

Post-mortems of social media and genocide

On 9 August 2022, The Telegraph, a leading British newspaper, ran the headline: 'I Was Raped in Ukraine by a Russian Soldier: He Was the Same Age as My Son'. The article told Viktoria Martsyniuk's story, a forty-two-year-old Ukrainian woman from Borodyanka (near Kyiv), who was sexually assaulted on 9 March. Three soldiers abducted her and another woman, a neighbour. They shot and killed her neighbour's husband when he tried to resist. She could not recall the rapist's features, except that his name was Dania, and he was tall. The experience caused her to suffer PTSD and she has since received therapy.[72] The Telegraph webpage reduced the story to search words, all lower case: 'raped — ukraine — russian — age — son'. We have become used to commodifying social media events and reducing their impact to keywords. In 1945, similar keywords would have been adopted, if the internet was around, but replacing 'ukraine' with 'german'. In March 2022, Wikipedia published a page: 'Sexual Violence in the 2022 Russian Invasion'.[73] Wikipedia's content dates to 2014 but also includes references to sexual violence against Ukrainian refugees in Poland and Germany and incidents caused by Ukrainian security forces. The page also refers to Lyudmyla Denisova, the ombudsman for human rights in Ukraine, who 'speculated that sexual violence was being used as a weapon of choice by Russian forces'. How far Putin and the armed forces have encouraged this behaviour is open to speculation. In my first essay, I suggested there are strong grounds for assuming Putin has conjured up the Soviet past, the 1945 rapes, to intimidate the West. This is part of Putin's power-games, as revealed in his intimidation of Merkel and the licence for Russian soldiers to behave criminally.

On 7 April, The Jerusalem Post adopted a Ukrainian military spokesperson's comment as the sub-headline: 'Russian soldiers are

---

[72] 'I Was Raped in Ukraine by a Russian Soldier: He Was the Same Age as My Son', *The Telegraph*, 9 August 2022, https://www.telegraph.co.uk/news/2022/08/09/raped-ukraine-russian-soldier-age-son (accessed 20 September 2022).

[73] 'Sexual Violence in the 2022 Russian Invasion of Ukraine', Wikipedia, last edited 20 September 2022, https://en.wikipedia.org/wiki/Sexual_violence_in_the_2022_Russian_invasion_of_Ukraine (accessed 20 September 2022).

"rapists without any moral boundaries".'[74] The stereotype is old, but has Putin invoked these old tropes for his illegal invasion? During the 1950s, Germans expelled from the east after the war began to record their experiences. These testimonies became part of a large collection of eyewitness reports known as *Die Vertreibung der deutschen Bevölkerung aus den Gebieten östlich der Oder-Neiße*. Robert Moeller referred to the case of Anna Schwartz, a seamstress from Danzig, who recorded her memories in 1952. He found that rape and sexual violence preceded her imprisonment in a Soviet labour camp where she worked as a slave labourer, was forced to live on meagre rations and suffered wasting disease before being extradited to Germany. Moeller wrote: 'Rape, the loss of loved ones, the separation of families, expropriation, humiliation, and physical, emotional, and psychological abuse — these were extraordinary experiences that became altogether too ordinary for many Germans …'[75] On 3 April 2022, Anne Applebaum wrote on Twitter: 'We know that in the territories even briefly occupied by Russian troops there was rape, looting, random killings, assaults on schools and hospitals. This is what the Red Army did in central Europe in 1944-45, and apparently nothing has changed.'[76] There is a danger in assigning exceptionalism since presumably Ukrainian soldiers serving in the Red Army also committed crimes? Some of the Soviet graffiti scrawled on the Reichstag walls came from soldiers who had come from Ukraine.

Confronting memory over fact is a major issue in war crimes investigations. Moeller shows how Germans recalled the memories to formulate a 'national political culture'. His findings undermine the myth that the West knew nothing of the rapes until Antony Beevor published a book, as discussed in my first essay. The Red

---

[74] 'Ukraine Claims over 300 cases of rape, sexual violence by Russian forces', *The Jerusalem Post*, 7 April 2022.

[75] Robert Moeller, *War Stories: The Search for a Usable Past in the Federal Republic of Germany* (Berkeley: University of California Press, 2003), pp. 51–60. Translated, the collection is: 'The expulsion of the German population from the regions of the Oder-Neisse'.

[76] https://twitter.com/anneapplebaum/status/1510427182149033991 (accessed 22 March 2023).

Army's crimes were known and documented; the problem was why it took so long for that record to reach Anglo-American media. Social media has turned the scenario upside down: today, there is too much speculation, while the common denominator between 1945 and 2022 is the importance of forensic evidence. The second conclusion concerns the case of Anna Vorosheva who was sent to Olenivka jail, a Russian detention centre, after being arrested delivering humanitarian supplies to Mariupol. She described 'screams from soldiers being tortured, overflowing cells, inhuman conditions, a regime of intimidation and murder'.[77] Olenivka is already building a reputation as a torture centre, and the Russian perpetrators are using the search for Nazis as an excuse for their crimes. In legal terms, the only real solution to exposing barbarism is by detailed documented evidence. The wars in the former Yugoslavia degenerated into genocide: ethnic cleansing, crimes against humanity, war rape and sexual violence. There was extensive media coverage of Yugoslavia, but the sectarian violence led to accusations of bias. The lesson from the conflict in Yugoslavia was the international recognition that all belligerents had committed crimes and all sides had claimed victimhood. The war in Ukraine has turned into a social media battle between pro-Putin and pro-Ukraine — an inherent danger is that both sides cancel each other out. The only solution to issues of bias or sectarianism is the long and arduous task of acquiring forensic evidence.

On 26 September 1998, twenty-one members of the same family were massacred in a forest nearby Kosovo. Within two days, Human Rights Watch had issued an official statement about the killing of eighteen adults and five children in a forest. This story from Kosovo highlights the importance of forensic science but also the necessity of diplomacy in enforcing the investigation of

---

[77] '"Absolute Evil": Inside the Russian Prison Camp Where Dozens of Ukrainians Burned to Death', *The Guardian*, 6 August 2022, https://www.theguardian.com/world/2022/aug/06/russian-prison-camp-ukrainians-deaths-donetsk?CMP=share_btn_tw (accessed 20 September 2022).

genocide.[78] Once the story was a news headline, NATO threatened to bomb Belgrade if a forensic mission was refused. The Serb government reluctantly agreed, and Professor Helena Ranta (Finland) was assigned by the EU to examine the reported massacre sites: Gornje Obrinje, where men, women and children were massacred by the Serbian armed forces, and Klečka, where Serbian civilians were killed by the Kosovo Liberation Army (Albanian separatists). In November 1998, Channel 4's Dispatches (UK TV) broadcast 'Mission Impossible', which followed Ranta's forensic investigation team in Kosovo. Ranta's endurance under harsh political pressure from both Serbian and Albanian officials was remarkable. Both sides wanted investigations of their victims but were opposed to investigations of their crimes.

The investigations had no documentation, only bone and body fragments. A Serbian judge, Danica Marinković, claimed the Albanians had constructed lime ovens. There were only 'carbonised bones' and remains. Ranta was followed as they navigated through ghost towns wrecked by conflict, and under constant military observation from both sides. Ymer Deliaj, remained in the area and had marked the graves of the bodies of his family. After the massacre, he found his dead wife covering their child, who died soon afterwards. Baskim Delijai described how the soldiers assaulted from behind tanks to occupy their town and one had thrown a grenade through the second-floor window of his home. Ranta explained before the cameras how critical exhumations and post-mortems were in building evidence for criminal investigations. There had been weeks of demanding and difficult work, negotiating with authorities, and acquiring resources and people to assist in the process. The perpetrators had used bayonets, axes, and hammers to kill. The Serbian government realised the Albanians in Kosovo would not let all their officials into the area. They demanded Danica Marinković travel with Ranta's team. Enroute, a vehicle broke down, and the team were forced to withdraw because a Serbian army unit

---

[78] 'Eighteen Civilians Massacred in Kosovo Forest', Human Rights Watch, 28 September 1998, https://www.hrw.org/news/1998/09/28/eighteen-civilians-massacred-kosovo-forest (accessed 20 September 2022).

demanded entry, claiming to be forensic scientists with armoured cars and AK-47s. Later, Commander Shkupi of the KLA revealed he had orders to shoot the investigators if they were accompanied by Serb officials.

The lasting trauma of genocide has been a humanitarian challenge for pos-1945 societies. The shock of Hitler's Holocaust and Nazi genocide has become the benchmark for scholars and media alike. The genocide committed across the territorial boundaries of former Yugoslavia is still shocking, especially the rapid descent to genocide, which represents a serious parallel to the war in Ukraine. Robert McNeil, a UN forensic technician, later recalled arriving in Bosnia and being informed about the dynamics of the conflict. His Bosnian advisor explained, McNeil's brackets:

In 1991 the Croats (who are mainly Catholics) went to war against the Serbs (who are mainly Orthodox Christian), who invaded parts of our country and killed many hundreds of Croats and Bosnian Muslims. Then later in 1992 the Croats joined the Serbs to get rid of the Bosnian Muslims in Bosnia-Herzegovina so they could claim back that part of Bosnia for themselves. Later still, the Croats and the Bosnian Muslims and together we fought and defeated the Serbs. ... There were two aggressors in the war in Bosnia: Serbs and Croats, there was one victim: the Bosnian Muslims.[79]

McNeil's account of his work in Bosnia is dark and chilling. From an opening chapter entitled 'The Body Factory', the reader faces the stark reality of genocide. From the pungent smell of death to the dozens of body bags piled high, and all oozing black liquid, any lasting illusions about genocide are very quickly erased. The forensic teams were forced to work in the primitive ruins of war and nearby Bosnian families struggling to survive — both groups co-existing in heavily damaged buildings, no electricity, no water, and irregular rations. Ratko Mladić, a Bosnian Serb, was the central perpetrator ordering his troops to carry out deportations, looting, rape, and murder of Bosnian Muslims. Pre-empting the flight of young Muslims to the forests, the Serbs carried out manhunts and

---

[79] Robert McNeil, *Grave Faces: A Forensic Technician's Story of Gathering Evidence of Genocide in Bosnia*, (Coral Springs: Behar Publishing, 2022), pp.12-13.

dragnet killing actions. However, gathering the evidence was hard enough, but prosecuting the criminals proved much harder. The media, in misunderstanding the important operational difference between the killer-perpetrators and the deskbound-perpetrators, was critical of the prosecution of low-ranking soldiers. Then in June 2001 Milošović was arrested in his home, but a heart attack and subsequent death cheated justice. However, the media was more approving. Then in 2011 Ratko Mladić, after sixteen years on the run, was arrested and in 2017 found guilty of genocide and crimes against humanity. He received a life sentence and in 2021 his appeal was denied.[80]

As to the war in Ukraine, on 7 July 2022, the BBC reported 21,000 crimes were being investigated and there are expectations for prosecutions.[81] This essay was initially drafted in June 2022, rewritten in August, restored to the original in November and then re-edited in March 2023. A reflection of how writing about a war and genocide in progress can distort perspective. Since February 2022, we can identify the traits and themes of this war. Putin's willing executioners have run amok on the battlefield, it was rapid, but it wasn't random. Genocide will be Putin's legacy, regardless of who prevails in the war, the crimes will be rooted in memory for many future generations. In trying to save the Russian empire, Putin has donned the robes of a latter-day emperor. He controls the strategic initiative from Moscow while his willing killers commit heinous crimes—will he be arrested at his home like Milošović? I have serious doubts especially since from another perspective, Russia and Putin have lost the control of the war—the treadmill of escalation is working against him. If Russia loses this war, will Putin deploy a nuclear device—this is the conundrum facing the west. Thus, his threats to go nuclear are only sustainable if he goes nuclear.

---

[80] McNeil, p.284.-285
[81] 'Ukraine War: 21,000 Alleged War Crimes Being Investigated, Prosecutor Says', BBC, 7 July 2022, https://www.bbc.co.uk/news/world-europe-62073669 (accessed 20 September 2022).

7. CRIMES, WAR, AND GENOCIDE

Dustin Du Cane

Russia's attack on Ukraine has legal repercussions which are directly connected with the military, moral, political, and historical aspects of this war discussed in other essays of this book. It is not true that war is the root of crimes committed in war, especially genocide. A war, even a war of aggression, can be waged without genocide, though crimes are a certainty in war, hence the need for law in war and justice during and after war. A war however can be waged for a previously existing criminal purpose, that is genocide, as the Nazi and Russian war started in Poland by Hitler and Stalin, in 1939 and thus the intent to commit genocide leads to war, as is the case for this war—Putin intends genocide on Ukraine, Ukrainians and Ukrainness.[1] This essay explores how genocide, as a legal concept, has deep roots, academic and personal, in the European areas stretching from Germany's western border to St Petersburg and the Ukrainian borders with Russia, with the particular importance of Ukraine. This essay details the development of international criminal, as well as what the term genocide means for its author and what it means in international law, especially in the context of Russian history.

---

[1] I like many others authors quoted in this chapter, do not conflate Russia with Soviet out of ignorance or laziness. The USSR was a rebranded Russian empire.

A genocide lawyer is born

> "Here were imprisoned Polnische Banditen
> In Sonder Abteilung" — Mirosław Łebkowski, "Auschwitz
> (In Sonder Abteilung)", 1943[2]

Danuta Dziwińska was born in then Lwów, a beautiful city now called Lviv, in Ukraine, deep in what Poles called Kresy.[3] This city lies just across the Polish border, functioning as Ukraine's secondary capital and Western supply transport hub during the Russian invasion. Danuta's mother, Olga, was ethnically Ukrainian but married a Polish officer, making their situation precarious during the Second World War.[4] Danuta eventually married Mirosław Łebkowski, the author of the quote, who built a successful post-war career writing popular songs, the Auschwitz poem not being his first and last work. Their grandson studied and practised law in Warsaw, as an attorney, living for some time at ul. Kredytowa 6 in Warsaw, where a great-grandson, Oscar, also lived for the first months of his life... and at the same address where a Russian Empire-born Polish Jewish lawyer from the renowned University of Lwów, lived and practised. That Polish Jewish lawyer, Rafael Lemkin, will receive particular attention throughout this essay because he coined the word genocide to describe a supreme type of atrocity that Nazis mastered. That word is in this book's title. Lemkin's links with Ukraine, especially Lviv, are also significant.

Lemkin practised law at the Kredytowa address, as an attorney from 1934, after stints as a prosecutor and judge, until the German

---

[2] Author is my grandfather. Translated by June Friedman in Adam A. Zych, ed., *The Auschwitz Poems: An Anthology*, 2. revised and extended ed. (Oświęcim: Auschwitz-Birkenau State Museum, 2011)., 266. Thank you Museum (Jadwiga Pinderska-Lech) for my copy of the translation.

[3] My grandmother. Ukrainian readers please forgive for using the name Lwów for the period before 1945. The reference to 'return' is an historical juxtaposition with the fate of Bialystok, where my grandmother's husband was born.

[4] Timothy Snyder, 'The Causes of Ukrainian–Polish Ethnic Cleansing 1943+', *Past & Present* 179, no. 1 (1 May 2003): 197–234, https://doi.org/10.1093/past/179.1.197.

and Soviet invasion in 1939.⁵ Lemkin was a graduate of Uniwersytet Lwowski, Lwów University. It is ironic that this was an institution the equally brilliant and Jewish Hersch Lauterpacht tried to study at but left because of anti-semitism.⁶ Lwów University's brilliant professors, some virulently anti-semitic but not genocidal, were mostly murdered by a German Einsatzkommando extermination unit in July 1941 as part of the policy of cultural and physical genocide of Slavs.⁷ Cultural genocide often takes away the need to exterminate the entire nation — that was the Nazi plan, and it is Putin's towards Ukraine with the same type of kill lists of officials and intellectuals, especially lawyers, that the Nazis and the Soviets used in 1939.⁸

Polyglot and quiet genius Lemkin avoided death in Poland and after an epic journey arrived in America in the spring of 1941 where he began work on many projects, including coining of the term genocide as part of his analysis of Axis occupation laws and crimes.⁹ Both the Nazis and Soviets would have killed him — he was known by name to Soviet show trial lawyers for criticizing the Soviet pseudo-legal nihilistic system and the Nazis had their racial, as well as kulturkampf reasons to kill a Jewish Polish lawyer.¹⁰

---

5   The photo of the plaque in Lemkin's Wikipedia article as of time of writing and subject to Wiki edit wars, is at the entrance to the building I lived and sometimes worked in. 'Rafał Lemkin', in *Wikipedia, wolna encyklopedia*, 8 February 2023, https://pl.wikipedia.org/w/index.php?title=Rafa%C5%82_Lemkin&oldid=69535320.

6   Philippe Sands, *East West Street: On the Origins of Genocide and Crimes Against Humanity* (London: W&N, Weidenfeld & Nicolson, 2016).

7   Slavs and Jews were not the only victims of genocide, see Anton Weiss-Wendt, *Eradicating Differences: The Treatment of Minorities in Nazi-Dominated Europe* (Newcastle: Cambridge Scholars, 2010).

8   Erica Kinetz, 'Russians Hunt Down Ukrainians on Lists | FRONTLINE', accessed 24 March 2023, https://www.pbs.org/wgbh/frontline/article/russians-h
unt-down-ukrainians-on-lists/.

9   Raphael Lemkin and Donna-Lee Frieze, *Totally Unofficial: The Autobiography of Raphael Lemkin* (New Haven: Yale University Press, 2013). xii-xiii.

10 For Bismarck's kulturkampf as a precursor to the Holocaust - Dustin Du Cane, 'Grandfather Genocide', *Fallout* (blog), 12 September 2022, https://fallout.substack.com/p/bismarck-was-genocidal. Further and better Stefan Ihrig,

Lemkin was a brilliant and tragic product of history, blood, the spilt and married kind, and geography of the borderlands. As a child, Lemkin linked the literature of Henryk Sienkiewicz, a major if not the national Polish Catholic patriot author, of the nineteenth century, in Quo Vadis, on the slave pits of Rome to regular and numerous antisemitic pogroms in Russian-occupied Białystok.[11] During his studies, Lemkin, according to his anecdote, questioned criminal law professor, converted Jew and anti-semite Juliusz Makarewicz, about the legal circumstances of the Soghomon Tehlirian trial. Tehlirian had assassinated, in Berlin, the former Grand Vizier of the Ottoman Empire, Mehmed Talat Pasha, for the massacre of Armenians in general in the Ottoman Empire between 1915 and 1917, and the murder of Tehlirian's mother, among eight-five relatives, in particular.[12] Lemkin, who in turn had forty-nine relatives killed by Nazis, would later describe the atrocities of the Armenian genocide as a key example to him personally and in the history of genocide and the term.[13] In a connected tragedy, Lviv's large émigré Armenian population was liquidated during the Second World War by bullet, train and Siberia, by Stalin, not Hitler.[14] Lemkin asked in particular why Tehlirian was on trial for the murder of one man while his victim, the murderer of millions, had never been put on trial.[15] Professor Makarewicz, even though he was a

---

Justifying Genocide: Germany and the Armenians from Bismarck to Hitler (Cambridge, Massachusetts: Harvard University Press, 2016).

[11] Lemkin and Frieze, *Autobiography*. 20. Also Douglas Irvin-Erickson, *Raphael Lemkin and the Concept of Genocide* (University of Pennsylvania Press, 2017), https://www.jstor.org/stable/j.ctv2t4ds5., 23-24. About pogroms, Yasha Levine's personal family account, Yasha, 'My Ukrainian Grandma and Our Lost History of Pogroms', Substack newsletter, *Yasha Levine* (blog), 14 June 2022, https://yasha.substack.com/p/my-ukrainian-grandma-and-our-lost..

[12] Irvin-Erickson, *Concept*. 36.

[13] Thomas De Waal, *Great Catastrophe: Armenians and Turks in the Shadow of Genocide* (Oxford ; New York: Oxford University Press, 2015), 132-133. Seda Kerobi Gasparyan et al., *Raphael Lemkin's Draft Convention On Genocide And The 1948 UN Convention: A Comparative Discourse Study* (Yerevan: Yerevan State University Press, 2016). is written and published by Armenians for a good reason.

[14] Irvin-Erickson, *Concept*. 35.

[15] If interested, Tehlirian was found 'not guilty' by a Berlin jury for reason of insanity caused by the extermination of his family.

comparatively progressive lawyer, author of an enlightened penal code, Kodeks Makarewicza, is anecdotally supposed to have explained the principle of state sovereignty that allowed these massacres, in these rather brutal terms: 'Let us take the case of a man who owns some chickens. He kills them. Why not? It is not our business. If you interfere, it is trespass.'[16] Lemkin however viewed sovereignty as 'conducting an independent foreign and internal policy, building schools, construction of roads, in brief, all types of activity directed toward the welfare of people.'[17]

Historians and Lemkin himself have suggested that the Armenian genocide had a particular role in initiating and shaping Lemkin's work, even before his ethnic group suffered the Holocaust and his country suffered the Nazi and Soviet Russian exercise of sovereignty in 'doing their business'.[18] This essay opens with an introduction about the people of the lands between Russia's western border and Poland's eastern border, especially Lemkin, because of their importance in shaping the twentieth and now twenty-first century definition, discussion, and prosecution of genocide.

Towards the Holocaust

Before Lemkin coined the term genocide, international law had been developing over the centuries to create a nascent framework within which Lemkin would operate while also looking to the future. Until international treaties began regulating international criminal law there were recurring common practices and "thinking" in the engagement of civilisations and states between each

---

[16] Irvin-Erickson, *Concept*. 36. Sands, *East West Street*. 152-156.
[17] Lemkin and Frieze, *Autobiography*.20. Makarewicz also taught Hersch Lauterpacht, a British QC, dynamo of international law, who advanced international law studies in general and human rights law specifically.
[18] Lemkin and Frieze.10 and John Cooper, *Raphael Lemkin and the Struggle for the Genocide Convention* (Basingstoke [England]; New York: Palgrave Macmillan, 2008). 14. Gasparyan et al., *Raphael Lemkin's Draft Convention On Genocide And The 1948 UN Convention: A Comparative Discourse Study*.52-53. Lemkin was also a historian as well as a lawyer, Dominik J. Schaller and Zimmerer Jürgen, The *Origins of Genocide: Raphael Lemkin as a Historian of Mass Violence* (London: Routledge, 2013).

other in times of the classical states, relating to diplomacy and friendship (such as embassies), the initiation of war (what lawyers still call jus ad bellum-law towards war) and finally the conduct of war (jus in bellum-law in war). Common practices and thinking bring us custom and international law in our times. The most pertinent rules of conduct from classical times are laws relating to conduct in war through Hebrew, Greek and Roman practice and rules concerning the obligatory or prohibition against, massacres of prisoners, respecting temples and the sanctity of ambassadors.[19] The key developments of jus in bellum up to the twentieth century are:

- The war crimes trial of Peter von Hagenbach-hung after a trial in 1474 for his brutal oppression and rule via mercenaries committing 'murder, rape, illegal taxation and wanton confiscation of private property'[20]
- Gustavus Adolphus. Adolphus with Sweden's 'Articles and Military Lawes to be Observed in the Warres' of 1621 which forbade rape of women and murder of clergy and teachers outright as well unauthorised pillaging and stealing.[21]
- The Peace of Westphalia ended the Thirty Years War when various disparate states first came together *en masse* to create international rules.[22] This was an 'agreement of kings' that created the historical and legal concept of 'Westphalian sovereignty'.[23]
- The horrors of the Crimean War and then the Battle of Solferino 1859 in the Italian war of liberation, during a time of

---

[19] David J. Bederman, *International Law in Antiquity*, 1st ed. (Cambridge University Press, 2001), https://doi.org/10.1017/CBO9780511494130.
[20] Edoardo Greppi, 'The Evolution of Individual Criminal Responsibility under International Law', *International Review of the Red Cross* 81, no. 835 (1999). 533-535.
[21] Leslie C Green, 'The Law of War in Historical Perspective', n.d., 49-50.
[22] Malcolm N. Shaw, *International Law* (Cambridge, United Kingdom: Cambridge University Press, 2008)., lxxxii, list of treaties starts with Westphalia. Andreas Osiander, 'Sovereignty, International Relations, and the Westphalian Myth', *International organisation* 55, no. 2 (2001): 251–87, https://doi.org/10.1162/00208180151140577.
[23]

supposed progress and enlightenment, led to the creation of the Committee of the Red Cross in 1863 as well as the adoption in 1864 of the first Geneva Convention for the Amelioration of the Condition of the Wounded of Armies in the Field" (Geneva Convention 1864) — creating a category of Geneva Law protecting civilians, the sick, prisoners of war and wounded as the victims of war. [24]

- The 1868 Declaration of St Petersburg (St Petersburg Declaration) was the first international treaty prohibiting the use of certain weapons in war, in this first case in the form of an exploding and light (below 400 grams), bullet.[25] Tsar Alexander II sought to ban the usage of this Russian invention between *civilised* states, not against savages. This led to two Hague Conventions on land warfare of 1899 and evolutionary 1907 (Hague Convention 1899, Hague Convention 1907).[26] A category of Hague Law regulating conduct in war, 'lawful' ways of warfare, would be subsequently created.[27]

---

[24] Green, 'The Law of War in Historical Perspective'.51-52. Mark Lewis, *The Birth of the New Justice: The Internationalization of Crime and Punishment, 1919-1950* (Oxford: Oxford University Press, 2016). 15-16.

[25] 'Declaration Renouncing the Use, in Time of War, of Explosive Projectiles Under 400 Grammes Weight. Saint Petersburg, 29 November / 11 December 1868.', IHL Databases, accessed 2 March 2023, https://ihl-databases.icrc.org/en/ihl-treaties/, https://ihl-databases.icrc.org/en/ihl-treaties/st-petersburg-decl-1868.. Nineteen signatories still existing and in force.

[26] 'Law of the Hague | How Does Law Protect in War? - Online Casebook', IHL Databases, accessed 2 March 2023, https://casebook.icrc.org/a_to_z/glossary/law-hague. Green, *The Law*, 55-56/.

[27] For an example of how Hague Law is completely misunderstood by a highly flawed Amnesty International report Oksana Pakalchuk, Oksana Pokalchuk, 'Opinion | Why I Quit Amnesty International in Ukraine - The Washington Post', Washington Post, 13 August 2022, https://www.washingtonpost.com/opinions/2022/08/13/amnesty-ukraine-civilians-at-risk-why-i-quit/. and Uriel Epshtein, 'Amnesty Got It Terribly Wrong', POLITICO. POLITICO, 15 August 2022, https://www.politico.eu/article/amnesty-ukraine-report-wrong/.. For a better review on urban warfare Laurent Gisel et al., 'Urban Warfare: An Age-Old Problem in Need of New Solutions', *Humanitarian Law & Policy Blog*, 18 November 2021, https://blogs.icrc.org/law-and-policy/2021/04/27/urban-warfare/.. For the utterly predictable results, refer to Meduza, Meduza, '"Into Military Targets" How Russian Propaganda utilised and Distorted Allegations by Amnesty International That Ukrainian Troops Endanger Civilians', 6

Hague and Geneva law can be referred to as international humanitarian law. Nineteenth and very early twentieth century attempts to create a permanent international tribunal or mechanisms to enforce Geneva and Hague law did not achieve much success and encountered much state push-back, especially relating to the prosecution of individuals and any form of international justice—apart from state civil reparations for breach of law.[28] Reparations however would need to be agreed upon diplomatically or executed via occupation. These reparations were introduced to the treaties in 1907 at the second Hague Conference at the initiative of the German delegation, perhaps because the German General Staff had been caught publishing a book stating that 'attempts to humanise warfare with the law had completely failed' and Kriegsraison (war necessity) justified atrocities in war.[29] The Nazis, Soviet Union and Western powers would repeat the lie that fierce (brutal) means of warfare shortened wars and were those more humane in the long run. War necessity is even written into international law, though not as a catch-all exemption and justification for war-crimes.[30]

While lawyers discussed lofty issues of responsibility and redress to the contempt of 'professional soldiers' of European empire, a quiet but massive genocide was occurring in the Belgian Congo, privately owned by King Leopold II against the areas enormous collection of tribes, and also in German colonised Africa specifically against the Herero people.[31] German military tactics in the twentieth century of which much has been written, were polluted by their

---

August 2022, https://meduza.io/en/feature/2022/08/06/into-military-targets. and my commentary.Dustin Du Cane, 'The Amnesty International War Crime Defence', *Fallout*, 18 August 2022, https://fallout.substack.com/p/the-amnest
y-international-war-crime.

[28] Lewis, *Birth*.16-17. ICRC, 'Rule 150. Reparation." Customary IHL - Rule 150. Reparation' (n.d.), 150, https://ihl-databases.icrc.org/customary-ihl/eng/docs/v1_rul_rule150.

[29] Lewis, *Birth*. 17.

[30] Larry May, *War Crimes and Just War*, 1st ed. (Cambridge University Press, 2007), https://doi.org/10.1017/CBO9780511841002.

[31] Martin Ewans, *European Atrocity, African Catastrophe: Leopold II, the Congo Free State and Its Aftermath* (London: Routledge, 2015) and Blood, Hitler's Bandit Hunters.

paranoia over francs-tireurs as well as their Herero extermination operations.³² In the First World War German soldiers applied what they had learned in Africa and during the Franco-Prussian war.³³ This time the murder of some 6.500 white Belgians and French civilians in 1914 would not evaporate into the darkness of the heart of Africa unlike the murder and maiming of millions of black people.³⁴ Brutal occupation methods, martial law imposed on occupied Western Europe and deportation of forced labour caused shockwaves throughout civilised Europe, reaching even the United States.³⁵ The severity of hostile occupation increased moving east, but even nowadays it is difficult to find English or even Slavic language sources on atrocities by both sides in Eastern Europe during that war.³⁶

A legal revolution was brewing after the First World War which would lay the ground for the Nuremberg trials and modern international criminal law-the widespread idea of personal liability for breach of customs and legal conventions as well as limiting

---

32 Ibid., 33-35, 79, 370 and 396.
33 Russia simply applies all the barbarism it learnt and utilised effectively over the centuries, especially towards other Slavic nations. Łukasz Adamski, 'Vladimir Putin's Ukraine Playbook Echoes the Traditional Tactics of Russian Imperialism', *Atlantic Council* (blog), 3 February 2022, https://www.atlanticcou ncil.org/blogs/ukrainealert/vladimir-putins-ukraine-playbook-echoes-the-tra ditional-tactics-of-russian-imperialism/. 'Battle of Praga', in *Wikipedia*, 13 March 2023, https://en.wikipedia.org/w/index.php?title=Battle_of_Praga&ol did=1144403001; Oliver Bullough, *Essay. In Let Our Fame Be Great: Journeys among the Defiant People of the Caucasus*, 7-8 (New York: Basic Books, 2012).
34 John Horne and Alan Kramer German Atrocities, *A History of Denial* (New Haven, CT: Yale University Press, 1914). 175-225 and in general. Famously the Belgian Congo regime inspired Joseph Conrad, 'Heart of Darkness', in *Story. In Youth; Heart of Darkness; Typhoon* (New York: Modern Library, 1993).
35 Mykhailo Tkach, '"It Was Hard to Watch" How Ukrainian Journalists Turned Footage from a Russian Soldier's Phone into a Short Documentary', n.d., https:// /meduza.io/en/feature/2022/05/20/it-was-hard-to-watch. Lucian Staiano-Daniels, 'The Russian Army Is an Atrocity Factory', *Foreign Policy*, 18 May 2022, https://foreignpolicy.com/2022/05/18/russia-atrocities-ukraine-soldiers/.
36 Alexander Watson, '"Unheard-of Brutality": Russian Atrocities against Civilians in East Prussia, 1914-1915', *The Journal of Modern History* 86, no. 4 (2014): 780-825, https://doi.org/10.1086/678919. Lewis, *Birth*. 65-68. Lemkin and Frieze, *Autobiography*. 19.

sovereignty.37 This would then combine with Lemkin's future work to provide the framework for discussion of genocide. The French and Belgians were, in particular, furious at the invasion, occupation of their land and German atrocities on their civilians while the UK, Canada and the United States had been angered by the mistreatment of POWs, unrestricted submarine warfare and some high-profile atrocities. Germans were widely labelled as 'Huns' in newspapers.38 A concept not dissimilar to that of the Russian 'Orc' or rashist in Ukrainian friendly social media in 2022.39

The British particularly, via Lloyd George's very public demand to 'Hang the Kaiser', had made clear they would seek to punish the Kaiser personally, but he managed to escape to Holland when he lost power in revolution. There is a simple logic to pursuing leaders, civil and military superiors, and order givers. How can a soldier be tried for breaking the laws of war when he raises the defence of following orders?40 Can we say that the soldier is guilty of breaking the law but the person giving the order is not? A soldier is subject to discipline, and can we demand that a man who can be shot if he refuses to carry out an order, refuse the order if we don't demand responsibility for the superior?41 Rejection of the 'just following orders' defence demands that we try to punish superiors and preferably hold them to greater account than the person following orders. Appropriately, articles 228 and 229 of the Versailles

---

37 Lewis, *Birth*.
38 David Welch, 'Images of the Hun: The Portrayal of the German Enemy in British Propaganda in World War I', *Propaganda, Power and Persuasion*, 2014, https://doi.org/10.5040/9780755694334.ch-002..
39 Mansur Mirovalev, '"Orcs" and "Rashists": Ukraine's New Language of War', *Russia-Ukraine War News | Al Jazeera. Al Jazeera*, 3 May 2022, https://www.aljazeera.com/news/2022/5/3/orcs-and-rashists-ukraines-new-language-of-war.
40 Geoffrey Robertson, *Crimes against Humanity: The Struggle for Global Justice* (New York: The New Press, 2013). 304.
41 A favorite defense of German war criminals and often raised by the ignorant in defense of the 'ordinary' soldier who committed atrocities is that soldiers were threatened with execution if they refused an atrocity—this was widely disproven by later research, see David H. Kitterman, 'Those Who Said "No!"': Germans Who Refused to Execute Civilians during World War II', *German Studies Review* 11, no. 2 (1988): 241–54, https://doi.org/10.2307/1429971. 100 cases of refusing to kill civilians were examined, no soldier was executed.

Treaty of 1919 foresaw the handing over of persons accused of having committed acts in violation of the laws and customs of war" to "military tribunals". The Germans flatly refused to do so after receiving a list of names but agreed to try a tiny number in Germany under German law. The results of 'loser's justice' were predictable.[42]

Of the pared down list of 900 war criminals (out of 20,000 suspects!) sought for extradition, only twelve were brought to trial in Leipzig. This was a very different result in 1921 from what had been expected in 1918.[43] Trials were carried out on charges of German law (mostly the Penal Code) being violated by Germans, not of directly violating international established customs of law.[44] So the charges were e.g. assaulting prisoners, machine-gunning lifeboats, neglectful treatment, and insulting prisoners' honour. The most significant case involved a general accused of ordering massacres of POWs and the major carrying out the orders. The general 'proved' he gave no such 'direct' orders while the major was found deranged, and not subject to punishment, under the German Penal Code for one massacre and sentenced to two years in a civilian prison for another.[45] Subordinates were sought for punishment, not those giving orders. Genocide, as such, as we would recognise it in later times, was not a significant issue in the Leipzig trials. The Germans were brutal to Belgians and French, but they were not attempting to exterminate them in whole or part. Something different was occurring in what the West regard as a 'minor' sector, the south-east of the conflict.

The Ottoman war may have been a secondary battlefront, but a proto-genocide was declared during the war by the Western Allies against the Ottoman Empire: '[Crimes] against humanity for

---

[42] Refer to Gerd Hankel and Belinda Cooper, *The Leipzig Trials: German War Crimes and Their Legal Consequences after World War I* (Dordrecht, Netherlands: Republic of Letters Publishing BV, 2014). Also Claud W. Mullins, *The Leipzig Trials* (London: Witherby, 1921)..

[43] Ibid., 21.

[44] Ibid., 51-173 for the details on crimes.

[45] Ibid., 168, suggests the general very strongly hinted that a massacre should take place.

which all members of the Turkish Government will be held responsible together with its agents implicated in the massacres.' The crimes weren't an atrocity against enemy civilians or even enemy soldiers, but of a state's actors against citizens of that state, Armenians—a circumstance not mentioned in Geneva or Hague law.[46] After significant British pressure, actual trials occurred in Constantinople after the war, with some Ottoman military leaders rounded up, but these trials collapsed amidst the violent birth of Turkey as a modern nation.[47] The most senior war criminals escaped justice, leading to the assassination of the Grand Vizier already discussed earlier in this essay. A string of similar assassinations and attempts on Central Power war criminals became embarrassing enough for an attempt to be made to create an international criminal justice tribunal under the aegis of the League of Nations—but without much support in the period before the apocalypse of the Second World War.[48]

Most accounts would jump from the post-First World War legal and extra-legal attempts to seek justice for atrocities straight to the even worse atrocities of the Second World War and the Nuremberg trials of Nazis, but it would be wrong to do so. The Russian Civil War and the Holodomor tie back to Lemkin. The Russian Civil War was fought with no civility to paraphrase Bob Dylan.[49] In this conflict no laws, customs, rules or other measures mattered.[50]

---

[46] Roger S. Clark, 'History of Efforts to Codify Crimes Against Humanity', in *Essay. In Forging a Convention for Crimes against Humanity*, ed. Leila Nadya Sadat (New York: Cambridge University Press, 2011).

[47] Vakahn N. Dadrian, 'The Turkish Military Tribunal's Prosecution of the Authors of the American Genocide: Four Major Court-Martial Series', *Holocaust and Genocide Studies* 11, no. 1 (1997): 28–59, https://doi.org/10.1093/hgs/11.1.28.

[48] Robertson, *Crimes*.305-306. Robertson raises the pertinent question, would have hanging the Kaiser dissuaded Hitler. Anya Loukianova Fink and Olga Oliker, 'Russia's Nuclear Weapons in a Multipolar World: Guarantors of Sovereignty, Great Power Status & More', *Daedalus* 149, no. 2 (2020): 37–55, https://doi.org/10.1162/daed_a_01788. Nuclear sovereignty or nuclear immunity?

[49] A more nuanced approach is contained in Matthew Rendle, *The State Versus the People: Revolutionary Justice in Russia's Civil War, 1917-1922* (Oxford: Oxford University Press, 2020)..

[50] Eugene Huskey, 'A Framework for the Analysis of Soviet Law', *Russian Review* 50, no. 1 (1991): 53, https://doi.org/10.2307/130211.

'Soviet legal nihilism' from this period, though reminiscent of earlier imperial subjugation via law, continues to inform the Russian approach to law and deserves further study, especially in its civil war roots-my other essay covers some of its consequences.⁵¹ Putin's ultra-me puppet, Medvedev, even squawked about its negative impact on the Russian state back when he was pretending to be a liberal.⁵² Jews suffered terribly at all hands during the Russian Civil with multiple pogroms occurring one after the other at one location.⁵³ After the period of the Russian Civil war came the even darker days of Stalinist dominance.⁵⁴ Lemkin writes later of Soviet genocide against Ukrainians, Ukraine and Ukrainism as nothing new:

> "Instead, it has been a long-term characteristic even of the internal policy of the Kremlin—one which the present masters have had ample precedent for in the operations of Tsarist Russia… Each is a case in the long-term policy of liquidation of non-Russian peoples by the removal of select parts.⁵⁵"

Note that Lemkin often conflates Russia and the Soviet Union—he does not do it out of ignorance or laziness. Lemkin lists Tsarist and Soviet genocides leading up to the Ukrainian genocide: Crimean

---

51 Kathryn Hendley, 'Who Are the Legal Nihilists in Russia?', *Post-Soviet Affairs* 28, no. 2 (2012): 149–86, https://doi.org/10.2747/1060-586x.28.2.149.

52 Robert J. Einhorn, *The U.S.-Russia Civil Nuclear Agreement: A Framework for Cooperation* (Washington, DC: CSIS Press, 2008). Medvedev currently threatens international courts with nuclear missiles - Al Jazeera, 'ICC Concerned by Russia's "Threats" over Putin Warrant', accessed 24 March 2023, https://www.aljazeera.com/news/2023/3/23/icc-concerned-by-russian-threats-over-putin-arrest-warrant.

53 Yasha Levine, 'My Ukrainian Grandma and Our Lost History of Pogroms." My Ukrainian Grandma and Our Lost History of Pogroms', *Yasha Levine* (blog), 14 June 2022, https://yasha.substack.com/p/my-ukrainian-grandma-and-our-lost?s=r.

54 Refer to Bernard A. Ramundo, 'Soviet Criminal Legislation in Implementation of The Hague and Geneva Conventions Relating to the Rules of Land Warfare', *American Journal of International Law* 57, no. 1 (1963): 73–84, https://doi.org/10.2307/2196177.. This contains details on Soviet interwar neglect of international law criminal law implementation requirements despite recognizing 'conventions relating to the Red Cross'.

55 Raphael Lemkin, *Raphael Lemkin. Soviet genocide in Ukraine (article in 33 languages)*, ed. Roman Serbyn and Olesiā̃ Stasiūk (Kyïv: Vydavnytśtvo Marka Mel'nyka, 2020). 31.

Tatars, the mass murders of Ivan the Terrible's 'SS', the Oprichnina, the extermination of Polish nationalist leaders, the murder of Ukrainian Catholics by Nicholas I, the Jewish pogroms, the Soviet annihilation of the Ingerian nation and the Don and Kuban Cossacks as well as the crushing of the Baltic nations of Lithuania, Estonia, and Latvia-as one genocidal thread of Russian (Soviet) history.[56]

The Ukrainian nation is too numerous to be liquidated en masse, but Lemkin notes, 'However, its leadership, religious, intellectual, political, select and determining parts, are quite small and therefore easily eliminated.'[57] This is a key example of what genocide meant for Lemkin when writing his speech in 1953, as compared to what it means in the Genocide Convention (not the same). Lemkin estimated that 75 per cent of Ukrainian intellectuals, i.e., teachers, writers, artists, thinkers, and political leaders, were liquidated, imprisoned, or deported in Western Ukraine—which included areas annexed by the Soviets after 1939.[58] This completely disproves the 'incompetence' and 'kulak' narrative of collectivisation as primary or only cause of the Holodomor. Murder of a Ukrainian 'kulak' was cake and eat it for the Soviet Russian state - as the murder of an political enemy to both the Soviet state and an ethnic enemy of the Russian empire. Collectivisation in other parts of the empire brought similar multiple genocidal benefits. The rhetoric of the 1920-1921 Soviet war against the newly independent Polish state was similar, showing good honest Soviet (Russian)

---

[56] For an extended history, see Serhii Plokhy, *Lost Kingdom: A History of Russian Nationalism from Ivan the Great to Vladimir Putin* (Penguin Books, 2018).. This is a truncated list of genocides throughout Russian history. Also Amos Fox, 'Russo-Ukrainian Patterns of Genocide in the Twentieth Century', *Journal of Strategic Security* 14, no. 4 (January 2021): 56–71, https://doi.org/10.5038/1944-0472.14.4.1913.

[57] Lemkin, *Soviet genocide*. 31-32. Tjorben Studt, 'The Necessity of a Structural Investigation into the Cultural Genocide in Ukraine', *Völkerrechtsblog*, 15 February 2023, https://doi.org/10.17176/20230215-113003-0.

[58] There are more exact and better estimates available in the works already cited.

bayonets skewering fat capitalists (Poles).⁵⁹

Lemkin writes plainly:

> "And yet, if the Soviet program succeeds completely, if the intelligentsia, the priests and the peasants can be eliminated, Ukraine will be as dead as if every Ukrainian were killed, for it will have lost that part of it which has kept and developed its culture, its beliefs, its common ideas, which have guided it and given it a soul, which, in short, made it a nation rather than a mass of people.⁶⁰"

Lemkin made a key point-genocide does not necessarily involve shooting or gassing every member of a group. It can involve targeted annihilation of the group via destruction of culture, language and society.⁶¹ Lemkin notes that the Ukrainian Orthodox Church, separate from the Muscovy patriarchate, was deliberately destroyed. Another important element of genocide mentioned by Lemkin was seeding Ukraine with non-Ukrainian minorities—including Russians. When Russians in 2023 state that the majority of the inhabitants of Crimea are Russian, this is a truth borne of centuries of, and recent, ethnic cleansing of Crimean Tatars and Ukrainians and Russian colonisation.⁶² The most important aspect of Soviet, Stalin's, genocide, was the destruction, mostly via hunger of Ukrainian farmers, some Jewish, of which Lemkin estimates 5 million died. Nazis and their collaborators almost wiped out the

---

⁵⁹ '20 Posters from the War That Saved the World from Communism - Russia Beyond', Russia Beyond, accessed 14 October 2022, https://www.rbth.com/history/329877-20-posters-from-polish-war.

⁶⁰ Lemkin, *Soviet genocide*. 35. Also Yuriy Gorodnichenko, Marianna Kudlyak, and Ayşegül Şahin, 'The Effect of the War on Human Capital in Ukraine and the Path for Rebuilding', *IZA Policy Paper*, Policy Paper Series, no. 185 (2022), https://docs.iza.org/pp185.pdf.

⁶¹ Naseer Ganai, 'Ukraine War: How Russian Invasion Targeted Ukraine's Cultural Heritage And Books Became Instruments Of War', https://www.outlookindia.com/, 22 February 2023, https://www.outlookindia.com/international/ukraine-war-how-russian-invasion-targeted-ukraine-cultural-heritage-and-books-became-instruments-of-war-news-264443. In detail Lionel Gernholtz, 'Ukrainian Culture Under Attack | PEN America Report', accessed 24 March 2023, https://pen.org/report/ukrainian-culture-under-attack/.

⁶² Austin Charron, 'Russia's Recolonization of Crimea', *Current History* 119, no. 819 (21 September 2020): 275–81, https://doi.org/10.1525/curh.2020.119.819.275.

rest of the Jewish population, and now Putin's rabidly anti-semitic Russia is renewing ethnic cleansing.[63] The harvest in 1932 was taken as taxed, unharvested, or exported. Mass executions played a smaller role than hunger in destroying Ukrainians, but nevertheless occurred.

Soviet Genocide in Ukraine was written in the 1950s but at the time of Holodomor Lemkin was aware of what was happening across the Polish border, as was the Polish government and society then and today.[64] As the Holodomor was winding down in 1933, Lemkin, was by now a much-respected lawyer in Poland and internationally. Lemkin even published critical commentary work on the Soviet legal code, which he identified as an instrument of oppression, not justice. Simultaneously Lemkin played a key part in drafting the diametrically different and advanced Polish criminal code of 1932… nicknamed after his lecturer at Lwów, with whom he now worked.[65] Lemkin later claimed that Article 113, for which he took credit, was the first in the world to outlaw public encouragement of a war of aggression.[66]

Lemkin was not working in a vacuum. Lemkin's other mentor, Emil Stanisław Rappaport, luminary of law, and Hersch Lauterpacht (famously a leading British barrister, QC, and architect of the European Human Rights Conventions) as well as international

---

[63] Nora Berman, 'I Worried Antisemitism Would Engulf Ukraine after Russia Invaded. I Was Wrong', The Forward, 16 February 2023, https://forward.com/opinion/536547/antisemitism-ukraine-russia-invasion-unified/.

[64] Roman Wysocki and Philip Redko, 'Reactions to the Famine in Poland', *Harvard Ukrainian Studies* 30, no. 1/4 (2008): 49–67, https://www.jstor.org/stable/2361 1466.

[65] Ludwik Dworzak et al., *Kodeks Karny Republik Sowieckich* (Warszawa: F. Hoesick, 1926). and Rafał Lemkin and Wacław Makowski, *Kodeks Karny Rosji Sowieckiej* (Warszawa: F. Hoesick, 1928).

[66] President of the Polish Republic, 'Polish Criminal Code 1932. - Rozporządzenie Prezydenta Rzeczypospolitej z dnia 11 lipca 1932 r. - Kodeks karny' (n.d.), https://isap.sejm.gov.pl/isap.nsf/DocDetails.xsp?id=WDU19320600571. Irvin-Erickson, *Concept*.40-41. Lemkin knew that propaganda was the first step to atrocity, as we can see in Ukraine. Tom Porter, 'Kremlin Propaganda Is Directly Responsible for Russia's Genocide in Ukraine, War-Crime Investigators Say', *Business Insider. Business Insider*, 20 May 2022, https://www.businessinsider.co m/russia-shifted-propaganda-amid-ukraine-setbacks-fuel-genocide-investigat ors-2022-5?IR=T.

lawyers Vespasian V. Pella and Henri Donnedieu de Vabres were better known at the time and afterwards.⁶⁷ However, since this book is about genocide, a term that Lemkin coined and that concerns Ukraine, a nation close to his heart, he will be written about it in more detail. In 1933 Lemkin was denied the opportunity to promote his already developed ideas to 'outlaw the destruction of national, racial, and religious groups' at one of the most important inter-war international law conferences in Madrid. After being attacked in a nationalist tabloid attack, Lemkin was denied travel documents and the opportunity to personally present his paper suggesting clearly expressing in treaty five crimes from the 'laws of nations': barbarity, disrupting international communication and spreading human, animal, or vegetable contagion and vandalism provoking catastrophes in international communication. ⁶⁸ All of these crimes are being deliberately committed in Ukraine in 2022 or earlier — see even the MH17 attack by Russia.⁶⁹ The Polish witch hunt was particularly appalling because Lemkin had also been denounced for his work by the Soviet prosecutor general. Igor Krasnov, Putin's head prosecutor, perhaps should have a look at the current Russian Federation Criminal Code article 354, wouldn't want any Polish Jew contaminating rodina's Criminal Code in 2022.⁷⁰ Stalin's favourite murder lawyer, Andrey Vyshinsky took

---

67 Cherif M. Bassiouni, 'A Glimpse at the Association's History and Some of the Contributions of its Members', *Revue internationale de droit pénal* 86, no. 3-4 (2015): 817–28, https://doi.org/10.3917/ridp.863.0817.

68 Douglas Irvin-Erickson, 'Raphaël Lemkin, Genocide, Colonialism, Famine, and Ukraine', *East/West: Journal of Ukrainian Studies* 8, no. 1 (2021): 193–215, https://doi.org/10.21226/ewjus645. Barbarism was the destruction of the destruction of collectivities — social, ethnic, or religious. This included via rape and murder. Vandalism was cultural destruction. The tabloid attack seemed fuelled by the fear that an international treaty would grant the same rights to the Jews as ethnic Germans were granted in Poland. Lawyers of international law like to stick to the sometimes true, sometimes myth, that this type of law is mostly an expression of already existing customs, rather than being created in a positivist, man created, manner - see the already mentioned Martens Clause.

69 As documented exhaustively by Bellingcat, yes it was Russia.

70 Promoting war of aggression, see later notes on this area of Russian law. *Rodina* is one of the Russian terms for mother-land, and a name for a nationalist political party forming part of Putin's fake loyal opposition. It is an evocative term. 'Rodina (Political Party)', in *Wikipedia*, 30 September 2022, https://en.wikipedi

particular offence at Lemkin's 'limiting state sovereignty'...[71] To add injury to insult, Lemkin lost his government jobs within a few weeks of his trip being cancelled.

The Holodomor and Lemkin's later response to it is covered in this essay because the Holodomor often disappears from discussions of the development of international criminal law in the shadow of Nuremberg. However, as is apparent in Ukraine, this should not be the case. The Holodomor negatively affected the text of the Genocide Convention with the Soviet Union manoeuvring to remove 'political groups', 'kulaks', from the text—even if their genocide was an ethnic one against Ukraine - see later in this essay. Efforts to create transnational courts stuttered during the interwar period, especially where the issue of sovereignty as the right to slaughter citizens, within or across borders, like a farmer does chickens was concerned.[72] Interwar failure to create international courts to hold the powerful and evil to account just before the Holocaust was unleashed, despite the centuries of previous experience and the example of the Armenian Genocide and Holodomor shows how short-sightedness dooms millions to death.[73] The Germans and their allies, unfortunately including Baltic and Ukrainian collaborators, then carried out the Holocaust and other genocides in Europe. An introductory bibliography on these subjects would be

---

a.org/w/index.php?title=Rodina_(political_party)&oldid=1113184416. 'The Many Ways to Say "Motherland" in Russian - Russia Beyond', Russia Beyond, accessed 13 October 2022, https://www.rbth.com/education/333909-rodina-motherland-russia. The phrase "Motherland calls-Rodina-zovet-Родина зовет" appears on the iconic Soviet war poster with a personification of Mother Russia with bayonets behind her, 'Exhibition Themes | The Art Institute of Chicago', accessed 13 October 2022, https://archive.artic.edu/tass/motherland-calls/.. Also the equally iconic poster "For motherland, for Stalin-Za rodinu za Stalina-За Родину. За Сталина" poster by the same artist, Irakli Toidze.. Rodina appears through this and the next essay as an expression of military mystical messianism and fascism. Dustin Du Cane, 'Genocide, Atrocity and War Propaganda Pt 1', Substack newsletter, *Fallout* (blog), 12 October 2022, https://fallout.substack.com/p/genocide-and-war-propaganda-pt-1.

[71] Irvin-Erickson, *Concept*. 49.

[72] Robertson, *Crimes*. 79.

[73] Lewis, *Birth*. This book extensively covers the subject of the developments and more importantly the failures of international criminal law in the period between the world wars in chapters 3-5.

longer than this book.⁷⁴

The Holocaust and the law

In his chapter in From Nuremberg to The Hague: The Future of International Criminal Justice, Richart starts his story of the revolutionary Nuremberg trials with leading Nazi Richard Ley, in his cell in Nuremberg, writing a long letter refuting the victor's right to try him.⁷⁵ This was a position Ley shared and continues to share with many lawyers of his time and even now.⁷⁶ What was the basis of the trials? Ley said he broke no codified law (Lemkin proved this untrue re: Hague and Geneva law in his key work, discussed later). As Nazi atrocities became apparent during the Second World War, to a degree shocking even to the Soviets, the Allies realised that some sort of justice would be needed, without repeating the farce of the Leipzig trials, and quickly found a way to apply justice and a legal basis to do so. The legal issue of the basis for trials was initially so vexing that the British intended throughout the war just to quick shoot any high-ranking Nazis they caught.⁷⁷ On their hand, American lawyers feared legal mischief from the Fuhrer if he was ever brought to a fair trial. The Munich, 'Beer Hall', Putsch trial which Hitler had turned around into a trial of Versailles, the Weimar Republic and other enemies of Germany (Communists and/or Jews) had already had terrible consequences for the fate of

---

74 Omer Bartov, *Germany's War and the Holocaust: Disputed Histories* (Ithaca, NY: Cornell University Press, 2003)., Alexander B. Rossino, *Hitler Strikes Poland: Blitzkrieg, Ideology, and Atrocity* (University Press of Kansas, 2018). Léon Poliakov, *Harvest of Hate: The Nazi Program for the Destruction of the Jews of Europe* (New York: Schocken Books, 1979). or Olaf Jensen and Claus-Christian W. Szejnmann, *Ordinary People as Mass Murderers: Perpetrators in Comparative Perspectives* (Basingstoke: Palgrave Macmillan, 2014)..

75 Richard Overy, 'The Nuremberg Trials: International Law in the Making', in *Essay. In From Nuremberg to The Hague: The Future of International Criminal Justice*, ed. Philippe Sands (Cambridge: Cambridge University Press, 2003)..

76 European Court of Human Rights (ECHR Court), former third division, Kononov v. Latvia, No. 36376/04 (ECtHR 24 July 2008)..

77 Kevin Jon Heller, *The Nuremberg Military Tribunals and the Origins of International Criminal Law* (Oxford: Oxford University Press, 2012).

Germany, Germans, Europe's Jews, Slavs and the world in general.[78] But even before Nuremberg, there were other trials of captured Nazis.[79] The most significant and with a contrasting legal basis to the Nuremberg trials are those carried out in Krasnodar in July 1943 (Soviet traitors) and Kharkiv, now in Ukraine and a frontline city, in December 1943. Carefully stage-managed trials, accessible to Western journalists, found Germans and Soviet traitors guilty of the murder of Soviet citizens, in breach of Soviet law, without reference to Jews.[80] The mass murder of Jews was classified as 'massacres of Soviet citizens'. [81] Ghettoisation was correspondingly a form of 'kidnapping of Soviet citizens'. The Soviets had already been promising justice in their Great Patriotic War—'from the lance-corporal in the army to the lance-corporal on the throne'.[82] Something that is of critical importance to understanding the Soviet and now Russian mindset and key to understanding Nuremberg is that for the Russians the great crime committed by the Germans was not the mass murder of Jews, not the Holocaust.[83] Instead the crime of all crimes was the crime of war of aggression, and in its worst possible form-an attack on Russia, the rodina, the heart and soul of the whole world, imperial or communist. This would later be the central element of Nuremberg: 'The central crime in this

---

[78] David King, *The Trial of Adolf Hitler: The Beer Hall Putsch and the Rise of Nazi Germany* (New York: Norton & Company, 2018).. The title says it all.

[79] Greg Dawson, *Judgment before Nuremberg: The Holocaust in the Ukraine and the First Nazi War Crimes Trial* (New York: Pegasus Books, 2012).

[80] Dustin Du Cane, 'How Many Times Do the Russians Mention Jews at Nazi Trials?', Substack newsletter, *Fallout* (blog), 1 October 2022, https://fallout.substack.com/p/how-many-times-do-the-russians-mention.

[81] Ibid.

[82] Daniel Rothbart et al., 'Genocide Studies and Prevention: An International Journal. Issue 13.1. Special Issue: Revisiting the Live and Work of Raphaël Lemkin', *Genocide Studies and Prevention*, 1 January 2019, https://www.academia.edu/39000729/Genocide_Studies_and_Prevention_An_International_Journal_Issue_13_1_Special_Issue_Revisiting_the_Live_and_Work_of_Rapha%C3%ABl_Lemkin.

[83] Nathalie Moine and John Angell, 'Defining "War Crimes against Humanity" in the Soviet Union: Nazi Arson of Soviet Villages and the Soviet Narrative on Jewish and Non-Jewish Soviet War Victims, 1941-1947', *Cahiers Du Monde Russe* 52, no. 2–3 (15 November 2011): 441–73, https://doi.org/10.4000/monderusse.9346..

pattern of crimes, the kingpin which holds them all together, is the plot for aggressive wars' — Justice Robert H. Jackson (Chief of Counsel for the United States), July 26, 1946.[84] An attack on rodina, is the great crime Jews, Slavs and others will of course disagree, violently. Any discussion of Nuremberg needs to start with this Russian obsession with crimes against the great country rodina and we can look at that through the legal framework of the Kharkiv trials. Around the time that the Kharkiv trials were being held, Lemkin had been feverishly working on a key new concept. The 674 pages of his magnus opus, Axis Rule In Occupied Europe are mostly a collation and discussion of occupation laws.[85]

Lemkin labels the laws he describes as instruments of genocide and writes: 'Obviously, such regulations amount to a violation of the laws of humanity as invoked in the preamble to The Hague Convention.' Lemkin was referring to the Martens Clause of Hague Law that allowed (acknowledged) customary international law to be in force between parties apart from what they had codified.[86] More importantly, in Chapter IX of Axis Rule, aptly named 'Genocide', Lemkin defines the term genocide:

> "New conceptions require new terms. By "genocide" we mean the destruction of a nation or an ethnic group. This new word, coined by the author to denote an old practice in its modern development, is made from the ancient Greek word genos (race, tribe) and the Latin cide (killing), thus corresponding in its formation to such words as tyrannicide, homicide, infanticide, etc.".[87]

Lemkin tells us that genocide is a new word for an old practice. The

---

[84] Office of Chief of Counsel for the Prosecution of Axis Criminality, *Nazi Conspiracy and Aggression* (Washington: United States Government Print. Off, 1948)..

[85] Raphael Lemkin, *Axis Rule In Occupied Europe: Laws of Occupation, Analysis of Government, Proposals for Redress* (Washington D.C: Carnegie Endowment for International Peace, 1944).

[86] Rupert Ticehurst, 'The Martens Clause and the Laws of Armed Conflict', *International Review of the Red Cross* 37, no. 317 (April 1997): 125-34, https://doi.org/10.1017/S002086040008503X.. The Martens Clause, named after the Russian representative, prof Martens, Russia has always bought good foreign lawyers, arose from arguments about shooting *franc-tireurs* out of hand, which the major powers very much wanted to do.

[87] Lemkin, *Axis Rule*.79.

next sentences are key to understanding why we call this book 'Russian Genocidal Warfare':

> "Generally speaking, genocide does not necessarily mean the immediate destruction of a nation, except when accomplished by mass killings of all members of a nation."

Lemkin qualifies genocide as coordinated plans of different actions destroying the foundation of the life of national groups. You can go straight to genocide through the bullet, artillery shell, bomb, and gas chamber but you can also destroy a group's political and social institutions. Annihilate the 'culture, language, national feelings, religion, and economic existence' and the group is destroyed.[88] A group without 'personal security, liberty, health or dignity' also ceases to exist. A Ukrainian made to live as a Russian, speaking Russian, with a Russian passport, in a Russian state, is a living victim of genocide.[89] Shooting artillery at a Ukrainian museum to destroy Ukrainian culture past and future is also how Lemkin understood genocide.[90] In this context, the Holodomor was already an attempt at genocide against the Ukrainians. Nowadays, when Russia kidnaps Ukrainian children to make them into little Russians in both senses of the term, it is committing genocide, less brutally but

---

[88] Marianna Tzabiras, 'Report Exposes Putin's War on Ukrainian Culture', IFEX, 5 December 2022, https://ifex.org/report-exposes-putins-war-on-ukrainian-culture/. Ukraine has also been destroying old Russian textbooks, regrettable. However Ukrainian literature will collapse if Russia occupies Ukraine while Russian literature will easily survive losing Russia's war of genocide. The same act can be genocidal depending on the circumstances and intent.

[89] Kyiv Independent Staff, 'Russia Forces Russian Passports on State Workers in Occupied Territories', accessed 24 March 2023, https://kyivindependent.com/news-feed/russia-forces-russian-passports-on-state-workers-in-occupied-territories.

[90] Tomasz Kamusella, 'Premonition: The Kremlin's Quest to Destroy Ukrainian Language and Culture', in *New Eastern Europe - A Bimonthly News Magazine Dedicated to Central and Eastern European Affairs*, 2022, https://neweasterneurope.eu/2022/07/22/premonition-the-kremlins-quest-to-destroy-ukrainian-language-and-culture/..

as effectively as shooting, or bombing them.[91] Which it also does.[92]

In *Axis Rule*, the key aspect of genocide is that a criminal action against an individual occurs because of their membership of a (national) group.[93] For Lemkin, genocide was not limited to the massacre of Jews at Nazi hands. Lemkin being a Polish Jew born and raised in the Kresy among Jews, Ukrainians, Lithuanians, Poles, Russians, and Armenians, pogroms and massacres made him sensitive to genocide being a type of atrocity repeating throughout history.[94] Chapter IX of *Axis Rule* is essential and short reading. In part III of that chapter, Lemkin states that the 'Hague Regulations' contain 'technical rules' dealing with 'some rights of the individual' about 'state sovereignty' but finds those protections lacking in a war of unheard-of atrocity and for the future. Lemkin lists many violations of existing Hague law by Nazi occupation forces. The Nazis, including Ley, were breaking existing codified international law in the Second World War as well as the law of occupied countries. Most of the Nuremberg defendants could have received the death sentence under Polish law for crimes committed against Poles or in Poland. Lemkin however writes: "It will be advisable in the light of these observations to consider the place of genocide in the present and future international law."[95] Lemkin makes an important point that genocide is an atrocity of both war and peace, as

---

[91] Laurie R. Blank, 'Forcible Transfer of Children in Ukraine: An Element of Genocide?', 21 April 2022, https://www.jurist.org/commentary/2022/04/laurie-blank-russia-invasion-ukraine-genocide/. This was written long before the International Criminal Court warrants which do not mention genocide. 'Little Russia', in *Wikipedia*, 4 October 2022, https://en.wikipedia.org/w/index.php?title=Little_Russia&oldid=1114031752.

[92] Azeem Ibrahim, 'Russia's War in Ukraine Could Become Genocide', *Foreign Policy*, 27 May 2022, https://foreignpolicy.com/2022/05/27/russia-war-ukraine-genocide/.. It is not *could*, it *is* genocide.

[93] The Jewish Holocaust and the Armenian Genocide though given as specimens of genocide in *Axis Rule*, were not 'prototypes,' Gasparyan et al., *Raphael Lemkin's Draft Convention On Genocide And The 1948 UN Convention: A Comparative Discourse Study*. 51-52. Lemkin in later work would expand genocide to cover political groups.

[94] Cooper, *Struggle*. 58. Lemkin is therein criticized for using the term genocide 'too freely' while 'exaggerating the physical danger to Poles'… something my grandfather and a couple of million dead might contest.

[95] Lemkin, *Axis Rule*. 92.

future genocides, civil wars notwithstanding, prove. Lemkin was always looking forward, always thinking about how to protect while cataloguing the evil of the past and present, as we should be. Lemkin's writing about genocide shows how ridiculous the Soviet assertation, repeated by of aggression does not necessarily lead to genocide. Genocidal intent however always requires a war of aggression if genocide is aimed at a neighbour. A war of genocide has as its reason genocide. Mein Kampf came before the invasion of Poland. Any assertion that a war, which can mostly avoid the civilian population en large, such as that waged by NATO against Serbia is a greater crime than a domestic or foreign genocide is an insult to the victims of genocide, such as those of Serbia in its local wars.[96]

This essay will now go into the Nuremberg trials and to some extent Lemkin's role in them. The major thing to remember going in is that the trials were not built around genocide or the Holocaust as such, at least for the first major trial, the case of twenty-three Germans. That case we call the Nuremberg Trial colloquially (properly "the International Military Tribunal"). The major allies, the UK, the United States and the USSR made their Moscow Declaration (Conference) on 30th October 1943 which foresaw that: 'Fascist chiefs and army generals known or suspected to be war criminals shall be arrested and handed over to justice.' [97] German officers, men and Nazi party members were to be arrested and sent to the countries they had committed crimes in and to be tried under local law. Since war crimes were still occurring, Germans were notified both practically and formally of their consequences. The clumsy adjective 'Hitlerite' betrays Russian etymology.[98] Compare with the modern

---

[96] Dustin Du Cane, 'Calling Crime of Aggression the "supreme Crime" Is an Insult to the Victims of Genocide', Substack newsletter, *Fallout* (blog), 11 January 2023, https://fallout.substack.com/p/calling-crime-of-aggression-the-supreme.

[97] 'Avalon Project - Documents in Law, History and Diplomacy', *"The Moscow Conference*, October 1943, https://avalon.law.yale.edu/wwii/moscow.asp.

[98] Refer to Francine Hirsch, *Soviet Judgment at Nuremberg: A New History of the International Military Tribunal after World War II* (New York, NY: Oxford University Press, 2020). and Francine Hirsch, 'The Soviets at Nuremberg: International Law, Propaganda, and the Making of the Postwar Order', *The American Historical Review* 113, no. 3 (2008): 701–30, https://doi.org/10.1086/ahr.113.3.701. for many examples, including the book "The Criminal Responsibility of the

Russian indiscriminate and flawed use of Nazi to label Ukrainian defenders, including the famously Jewish Nazi, president Zelensky, who they also compared to that other Nazi of 'Jewish descent', Adolf Hitler.[99] We haven't yet had a Kyiv Declaration on bringing Russian war criminals to justice — but Putin's incredibly brazen stupidity has already secured him international warrants, which will be discussed later in this essay.[100]

After VE Day, the summer and autumn of 1945 saw feverish work in London, under the eye of Justice Robert H. Jackson, delegated from the United States Supreme Court, in preparing the subsequent "Agreement for the Prosecution and Punishment of Major War Criminals of the European Axis [London Charter]" of 8 August 1945.[101] The London Charter was a framework of crimes to be tried

---

Hitlerites," published after the Kharkiv trials. The author, Aron Trainin, built a concept of complicity and a global conspiracy against peace. He saw comparisons with gangs and criminal organisations, which was quite apt for the Nazi mafia like structure and is particularly apt for David Levene, Luke Harding, and Laurence Topham, 'Putin's Russia: Dictator Syndrome and the Rise of a "Mafia State" — Video', *The Guardian. Guardian News and Media*, 20 June 2022, https://www.theguardian.com/world/video/2022/jun/20/putins-russia-dictator-syndrome-and-the-rise-of-a-mafia-state-video.. Complicity had been widely used as a charge in the Moscow show trials during the great purges. For genesis of the term war of aggression, see Francine Hirsch, 'How the Soviet Union Helped Establish the Crime of Aggressive War', *Just Security*, 25 March 2022, https://www.justsecurity.org/80599/how-the-soviet-union-helped-establish-the-crime-of-aggressive-war/.

[99] 'Israel Outrage at Sergei Lavrov's Claim That Hitler Was Part Jewish', *BBC News. BBC*, 2 May 2022, https://www.bbc.com/news/world-middle-east-61296682.. Hans Frank, lawyer to Hitler, war criminal, here appears as the author of Hitler Jewishness claim.

[100] Guardian Staff, '"It's Justified": Joe Biden Welcomes ICC Arrest Warrant for Vladimir Putin | Joe Biden | The Guardian', *The Guardian. Guardian News and Media*, 18 March 2023, https://www.theguardian.com/us-news/2023/mar/18/joe-biden-welcomes-icc-arrest-warrant-vladimir-putin. See the nonsense qualifier that the US doesn't 'recognise' the International Criminal Court. It does, including in law, however it does not submit to its jurisdiction. You don't recognise a country or institution if you don't admit it legitimacy.

[101] 'Agreement for the Prosecution and Punishment of Major War Criminals of the European Axis [London Charter', *International Terrorism: Multilateral Conventions (1937-2001* 472 (n.d.): 82 279, https://doi.org/10.1163/9789004478428_056 .. Refer to Quincy Wright, "The Law of the Nuremberg Trial," *American Journal of International Law* 41, no. 1 (1947): pp. 38-72. https://doi.org/10.2307/2193853.

and trial procedures. Lawyers had been considering the legal issues connected with dealing with Axis criminals throughout the war but their viewpoints had been rapidly changing with developments, including that of the publication of Axis Rule.[102] Lauterpacht played an important role in framing the legal response to Nazi rule in the terms of 'Crimes against Humanity'[103] Lemkin also worked on the legal documents, as did many eminent or in the Soviet case, notorious, lawyers. Some famous lawyers would be Robert H. Jackson, a Roosevelt New Deal judicial ally–chief United States prosecutor at Nuremberg trials and Iona Nikitchenko, Soviet military lawyer, notorious show trial 'judge', Soviet Supreme Court who was also a Nuremberg judge. There were impartiality issues. Nikitchenko declared before the trials:

We are dealing here with the chief war criminals who have already been convicted and whose conviction has been already announced by both the Moscow and Crimea declarations by the heads of the governments... The whole idea is to secure quick and just punishment for the crime.[104]

Note the Crimea reference here, this is in connection to the (in)famous February 1945 'Yalta' conference between Roosevelt (dying), Churchill and Stalin in Ukraine. [105] Jackson was appalled at Nikitchenko's approach to justice but himself served as a prosecutor based on a charter he had prepared as a framer. An 'International Military Tribunal' (IMT) was foreseen with arrest and extradition authority–but countries who had their hands on criminals

---

[102] Refer to Lewis, *Birth*. 158-183. Also Cooper, *Struggle*.66-67 and Chapter 4 in its entirety.

[103] Cooper, *Struggle*. 66. Lauterpacht also spent a busy war, one of his important works was H. Lauterpacht, 'The Law of Nations and the Punishment of War Crimes', *British Year Book of International Law* 21 (1944): 58, https://heinonline.org/HOL/Page?handle=hein.journals/byrint21&id=64&div=&collection=.- dealing with war crimes, the law of nations and their sources and superior orders.

[104] Telford Taylor, 'The Nuremberg Trials', *Columbia Law Review* 55, no. 4 (1955): 488-525, https://doi.org/10.2307/1119814. Which references George A. Finch, 'International Conference on Military Trials', *American Journal of International Law* 43, no. 4 (1945): 835-36, https://doi.org/10.2307/2193307.

[105] Yalta as a word evokes anger amongst many Slavs and Balts, see Serhii Plokhy, *Yalta: The Price of Peace* (London: Viking, 2011)..

could try them locally if they could and chose to. This is the also case with the modern International Criminal Court ("ICC") which does not replace properly functioning, able and willing national courts for most accused. The key elements of law are in Article 6 of the London Charter, which covers crimes against peace, war crimes (violations of Hague and Geneva law), crimes against humanity and culpability for conspirators in these crimes. Genocide is not named. Article 6 (c) on crimes against humanity is an unhappy word jumble where the Holocaust and genocide disappears among other atrocities. Two very important additional rules were that heads of state and officials alike were not immune to punishment if fulfilling their duties (Article 7) and that superior orders could only mitigate punishment but not eliminate responsibility (Article 8).

After proceedings which would now seem lightning quick, from November 1945 to October 1946, the IMT reached verdicts on the first and major set of defendants: nineteen convictions and three complete acquittals. The acquittals infuriated the Soviets.[106] In Soviet Russia and nowadays in Putin's Russia, important (or any) trials do not end in acquittals.[107] All defendants were indicted of conspiracy for a crime against peace, but only Göring, Hess, Jodl, Keitel, Neurath, Raeder, and Ribbentrop were found guilty. That verdict was a major failure for the Soviet attempt to label the entire Nazi government as a criminal conspiracy against peace. There is a serious issue here that is not addressed by those calling for an international tribunal to try Russians for the crime of aggression. That crime is difficult, not easy to prove as Nuremberg proves — plus there exists the easy whataboutism of the invasion of Iraq 2003.[108]

---

[106] Hirsch, 'The Soviets at Nuremberg: International Law, Propaganda, and the Making of the Postwar Order'. Note role of Aron Trainin, Soviet jurist in formulating the charge of 'aggressive war.'

[107] 0,4 per cent in 2015, Jan Strzelecki, 'Russia behind Bars: The Peculiarities of the Russian Prison System', *OSW Centre for Eastern Studies*, 25 February 2019, https://www.osw.waw.pl/en/publikacje/osw-commentary/2019-02-07/russia-behind-bars-peculiarities-russian-prison-system..

[108] Andreas Paulus, 'Second Thoughts on the Crime of Aggression', *European Journal of International Law* 20, no. 4 (1 November 2009): 1117–28, https://doi.org/10.1093/ejil/chp080. George Monbiot, 'How Many of Those Calling for Putin's Arrest Were Complicit in the Illegal Invasion of Iraq?', *The Guardian. Guardian*

Gordon Brown in particular should not be talking about an international trial. The ICC does not have jurisdiction for the crime of aggression in the case of Russia against Ukraine for reasons discussed later in this essay.

On the subject of responsibility of propaganda for crimes, which will be further discussed in the Russian case in my other essay, Judge Nikitchenko dissented against the acquittal of Hans Fritzsche, a Nazi radio flunky.[109] I agree with Nikitchenko's assertion that propaganda is a factor in preparing and conducting acts of aggression, as it was and is in the Ukraine war.[110] It is worth mentioning that Fritsche was subsequently convicted by a de-Nazification court and sentenced to nine years imprisonment.

News and Media, 20 March 2023, sec. Opinion, https://www.theguardian.com/commentisfree/2023/mar/20/putin-arrest-illegal-invasion-iraq-gordon-brown-condoleezza-rice-alastair-campbell-russia. I do not share all Monbiot's points and I do pronounce judgment on the Iraq invasion as illegal, though it looks like it but I certainly object to key figures ignoring their role. This whatabout is being already used by Russia, "[T]he international community has not yet recovered from the catastrophic consequences of American adventurist interventions in Iraq…" - Martin Belam et al., 'Russia-Ukraine War Live: Russians Urged Not to Adopt "Stolen" Ukrainian Children; Bakhmut Battle Has "Badly Damaged" Wagner Forces', *The Guardian*. Guardian News and Media, 29 March 2023, sec. World news, https://www.theguardian.com/world/live/2023/mar/29/russia-ukraine-war-live-zelenskiy-fears-war-could-be-hampered-by-washington-divisions-moscow-starts-drills-with-new-icbm.

[109] On the importance of radio for the Nazi regime, Keith Somerville, *Radio Propaganda and the Broadcasting of Hatred: Historical Development and Definitions* (Basingstoke: Palgrave Macmillan, 2012). Fritszche was subsequently convicted by a de-Nazification court and knew about the atrocities, refer to Gregory S. Gordon, "The Forgotten Nuremberg Hate Speech Case: Otto Dietrich and the Future of Persecution Law", Ohio State Law Journal, p. 579. https://papers.ssrn.com/abstract=2457641.

[110] Carsten Stahn, 'Putting Criminal Accountability into Perspective: Russia, Ukraine and the ICC', *Universiteit Leiden*, 18 March 2022, https://www.leidenlawblog.nl/articles/putting-criminal-accountability-into-perspective-russia-ukraine-and-the-icc. Also Randall L. Bytwerk, 'The Argument for Genocide in Nazi Propaganda', *Quarterly Journal of Speech* 91, no. 1 (2005): 37–62, https://doi.org/10.1080/00335630500157516..

Figure 1 - Accompanied by the Reich Minister of Propaganda, Hitler visits the state of the art media giant UFA production facility in 1936 - via Bundesarchiv, Bild 183-1990-1002-500 / CC-BY-SA 3.0. Nazi propaganda never stated genocidal intent as openly as Russian media does, the closest was Goebbels' deliberate mistake during his infamous *Sportpalast* speech where he started to say Jews would be exterminated before 'correcting' this to 'evacuated'.[111]

---

[111] 'Goebbels' 1943 Speech on Total War', accessed 1 August 2023, https://research.calvin.edu/german-propaganda-archive/goeb36.htm.

Figure 2 - Accompanied by Russia Today television editor, Russian Federation president Vladimir Putin visits media giant Russia Today state of the art television facilities. Margarita Simonyan: 'Ukrainian people have turned out to be engulfed in the madness of Nazism', one of her regular wolf-whistles to genocide.[112] Others go much further.[113] Goebbels framed the war as existential to Germans, as does Russian state media to Russians, excusing genocide as kill or be killed in his *Sportspalast* speech. Picture via Kremlin.ru. Creative Commons Attribution 4.0 International - image converted by author to grayscale.

This was the first of a set of a dozen trials, the later trials were before purely United States military courts called the 'Nuremberg Military Tribunals' (not the IMT), as Allied cooperation with the Soviet broke down, though in the same rooms with a similar procedure.[114] As a final note, the neologism genocide was already being used in materials at the Nuremberg trials though not as a legal definition to

---

[112] Andrew Roth, 'Fears Genocidal Language in Russian Media May Prompt More War Crimes', *The Guardian. Guardian News and Media*, 7 April 2022, https://www.theguardian.com/world/2022/apr/07/russian-media-coverage-ukraine-genocidal-streak..

[113] Alexey Kovalev, 'Russia's Ukraine Propaganda Has Turned Fully Genocidal', *Foreign Policy*, 9 April 2022, https://foreignpolicy.com/2022/04/09/russia-putin-propaganda-ukraine-war-crimes-atrocities/..

[114] Refer to Heller, *The Nuremberg Military Tribunals and the Origins of International Criminal Law*.. The trials were thematically grouped as 'medical', 'legal', 'race policy', 'economic', 'military' and 'political and government'.

be used in indictments.[115]

Since the time of the trials, the 'orders are orders', 'superior orders', and 'just following orders' defence first mentioned with von Hagenbach, has been known as the Nuremberg defence. It's already raised in Ukrainian trials of Russians prosecuted for war crimes, mostly ineffectively.[116]

Genocide codified

During the war, one of Roosevelt's and Churchill's major projects had been to create a world organisation to replace the toothless League of Nations. Ironically, the League of Nations project had severely hampered the prosecution of Central Powers war criminals– their prosecution was left toothless at President's Wilson pressure, to avoid 'offending' Germany to a point it withdrew from the great project. The United Nations was then the great international project that came from the ashes of the Second World War. There are two key United Nations organs, the General Assembly and the Security Council. The United Nations Security Council is dominated by its five permanent members.[117] That list of permanent members is shaped by war — France, the United States, the United Kingdom, China (the government replaced during the civil war) and Russia.

---

[115] William A. Schabas, *Genocide in International Law the Crime of Crimes* (Cambridge: Cambridge University Press, 2009). 17 and 48-52.

[116] 'Superior Orders', in *Wikipedia*, 25 February 2023, https://en.wikipedia.org/w/index.php?title=Superior_orders&oldid=1141563011. ICRC, 'Defence of Superior Orders', accessed 29 March 2023, https://ihl-databases.icrc.org/en/customary-ihl/v2/rule155. Also raised obscenely to justify Russian soldiers posing as athletes to participate in international sport, as a human right.Sean Ingle, 'Russian Soldiers Should Be Allowed to Compete at Olympics, Says UN Expert | Paris Olympic Games 2024 | The Guardian', *The Guardian. Guardian News and Media*, 27 March 2023, https://www.theguardian.com/sport/2023/mar/27/russian-soldiers-ukraine-olympic-games-united-nations-paris. As Kitterman, 'Those Who Said "No!"' showed, soldiers can refuse orders. Perhaps the Nazis were more lenient on their soldiers than the Russian state is currently but perhaps not.

[117] For history and practise refer to Vaughan Lowe et al., eds., *The United Nations Security Council and War: The Evolution of Thought and Practice since 1945* (Milton Keynes, UK ;Oxford: Lightning Source UK Ltd; Oxford University Press, 2011).

It is legally unclear why the Russian Federation replaced the United States SR at the Security Council, but it might be difficult to remove.[118] The absurd mechanisms of the United Nations have led to Russia, whose president is an indicted war criminal, heading the Security Council.[119]

One of the many organisations created by the United Nations was the International Law Commission which got to work on establishing the precedents and laws coming out of the Nuremberg Trials. That commission established the principles of international criminal law: personal liability for breaching international law, lack of command immunity, no 'order's defence' and crimes against peace, war crimes, crimes against humanity and complicity in these crimes, are specifically punishable.[120] These are principles that more or less constitute accepted current international law–as expressed in current customary law and treaties, especially establishing the ICC.

Lemkin informally joined the nascent United Nations convention in 1946. Lemkin's previous work in Axis Rule and preparing the Nuremberg Trials had been noticed by leading lawyers and politicians and he was becoming widely known and respected.[121] The word genocide first appeared widely in a Washington Post editorial on Lemkin on 4 December 1944:

> '[A] noted Polish scholar and attorney, Prof. Raphael Lemkin, now on the faculty of Duke University had coined the word genocide to describe wanton ethnic killing.'

As a result, and considering Lemkin's work and Axis atrocities, a proposal was tabled for the United Nations to declare genocide an international crime in the future. The United Nations could not

---

[118] Riet and Joris, 'No, Russia Cannot Be Removed from the UN Security Council', *Universiteit Leiden*, 22 March 2022, https://leidenlawblog.nl/articles/no-russia-cannot-be-removed-from-the-un-security-council.

[119] 'The Danger of Russia Becoming President of the U.N.', Time, 14 March 2023, https://time.com/6262698/danger-russia-president-u-n-security-council/.

[120] United Nations, *Yearbook of the International Law Commission 1950, Vol. II*, Yearbook of the International Law Commission (UN, 1950), https://doi.org/10.18356/cc800c08-en..

[121] Cooper, *Struggle*.62-65.

legislate international law, so a convention of nations was planned.[122] Peace-time genocide was an obvious glaring future legal issue, what if the Nazis had just murdered all the Jews they could find within the Reich borders without attacking Poland with the Russians? (Again this shows the absurdity of calling crime of aggression the 'supreme crime' and a throwback to sovereignty and rodina war nonsense). A resolution was passed on 11 December 1946 defining the crime of genocide:

Genocide is a denial of the right of existence of entire human groups, as homicide is the denial of the right to live of individual human beings; such denial of the right of existence shocks the conscience of mankind, results in great losses to humanity in the form of cultural and other contributions represented by these human groups, and is contrary to moral law and to the spirit and aims of the United Nations.[123]

A special convention of the United Nations was planned to agree on international law regarding the punishment and prevention of genocide. The first United Nations Secretary-General, set up a working group to prepare the legal framework.[124] The group consisted of Lemkin, who had been lobbying informally but hard in literal back rooms for a change 'in the world' on which he could advise, de Vabres, the French Nuremberg judge and Pella, then president of the International Association of International Law.[125] Lemkin seems to have been the main author of the subsequent so-called 'secretariat draft' of a future convention. In that draft, Lemkin deliberately avoided any specific connection with the Holocaust

---

[122] Schabas, *Genocide in International Law the Crime of Crimes*. 53-54.
[123] "United Nations High Commissioner for Refugees, 'Refworld | The Crime of Genocide', Refworld, accessed 3 March 2023, https://www.refworld.org/docid/3b00f09753.html.. Schabas, *Genocide*, 52-53.
[124] The United Nations can organise a convention which then passes international law. A passing vote by the General Assembly does not bind the world. States must sign and ratify the law which follows which are treaties by another name. The same would happen with the Geneva Conventions of 1949.
[125] Cooper, Struggle. 80. Schabas, *Genocide in International Law the Crime of Crimes*. 61.

in the text to make the crime more universal and applicable.[126]

The manoeuvring in the backrooms and corridors of the United Nations around the future convention was Byzantine, reflecting the flaws of the United Nations process from the beginning of its existence. For instance, the Soviets variously privately opposed or supported the convention while the British declared support—planning to kill the convention procedurally.[127] Even the term genocide was threatened with replacement by 'extermination'. Listing 'political groups' as subject to genocide was opposed by the Soviet Union.[128] An international court to try crimes of genocide was ruled out by the super-powers and minnows alike as a threat to 'sovereignty'. The real elephant in the room for the democratic world was the United States' treatment of 'Negroes' as the term was then used, along with other genocides such as against Native Americans. The United States would sign the future convention but the United States Senate, 'worried' about citizens being sought by evil international lawyers and judges, blocked ratification until 1988(!). Lemkin personally began to be irritated with his lawyer colleagues delineating violent, 'physical', and nonviolent, 'cultural', means of genocide. That led to 'cultural genocide' being downgraded to a 'nonviolent' crime.*[129] There was a real threat that the convention would be killed in committee.

The manoeuvring and in-fighting are described because it explains the differences in contents of the secretariat draft Genocide

---

[126] Jim Fussell, 'Genocide Convention Drafts." The Genocide Convention - Secretariat (1947) and Ad Hoc Committee(1948) Drafts', *Prevent Genocide International*, n.d., http://www.preventgenocide.org/law/convention/drafts/.. Compare with suggestions in Lemkin, *Axis Rule*. Cooper, *Struggle*. 81.

[127] Irvin-Erickson, *Concept*. 155-158.

[128] The secretariat draft lists political groups as subject to genocide.

[129] "Article I: Definitions: II. 3.[Cultural genocide] Destroying the specific characteristics of the group by:(a) forcible transfer of children to another human group; or(b) forced and systematic exile of individuals representing the culture of a group; or(c) prohibition of the use of the national language even in private intercourse; or(d) systematic destruction of books printed in the national language or of religious works or prohibition of new publications; or(e) systematic destruction of historical or religious monuments or their diversion to alien uses, destruction or dispersion of documents and objects of historical, artistic, or religious value and of objects used in religious worship.", secretariat draft.

Convention and then what became international law. Political groups being protected from genocide was a very difficult concept for the right and left.[130] The idea of political group paradoxically touched on Russian ethnic nationalism: 'Soviet ideological xenophobia fanned Russian nationalism which regarded Diaspora nationalities (Koreans, Germans, Poles and Finns) living on the borders of the Soviet Union as disloyal because of conflicts over land and their resistance to the collectivisation of farms.'[131] The Soviet deportations of national groups during the Second World War could have easily qualified as genocide and at the time Vyshinsky was making serious trouble in and out of committee sniffing a capitalist plot, conspiracy again, to intervene in the Soviet Union. World conspiracies are a popular mental crutch for the Kremlin Soviets and now Russians.[132] Lemkin famously asked the President of the General Assembly, "Mr President, who is making international law for the world–Vyshinsky or the General Assembly?"[133] Unfortunately, both political groups as a target and cultural genocide were still removed from the draft. These committee contortions led to a ridiculous argument over whether the Holodomor was a genocide under the final convention.[134] If the Ukrainian peasants were exterminated as a political group, kulaks, there was no genocide in the legal definition. If they were exterminated as 'Ukrainians', it would be classed as genocide. The committee's distortions of the concept of genocide have also led to the current contortions among academics at the beginning of the Ukraine war on whether Russia's

---

[130] Irvin-Erickson, *Concept*. 167-168.
[131] Cooper, *Struggle*.102.
[132] Michael P. Ferguson, 'Putin's Jedi Mind Trick in Ukraine: How Truth Decay Shapes the Operational Environment', *The Strategy Bridge. The Strategy Bridge*, 10 June 2022, https://thestrategybridge.org/the-bridge/2022/6/9/putins-jedi-m
ind-trick-in-ukraine-how-truth-decay-shapes-the-operational-environment..
[133] Cooper, *Raphael Lemkin*, 103 citing Herbert Yahraes, 'He Gave a Name to the World's Most Horrible Crime', *Collier's Weekly*, 3 March 1951., pp. 28-29 and 56-57. That article states that forty-nine of Lemkin's relatives had been killed by the Nazis... The Soviet Union is variously referred to as Russia in the text. Yahraes knew.
[134] Irvin-Erickson, *Concept*. 188.

actions constituted genocide.[135] When a politician post invasion says genocide, we should also look at what Lemkin defined as genocide in Axis Rule or the secretariat draft. They are valid definitions of genocide in the same way as saying calling a killing murder does not require reference to the legislation of every country (and state) in the world. There are however significant consequences for Russia fulfilling the convention definition of genocide as will be discussed later in the essay.[136] Going forward we could consider reverting the Genocide Convention to the secretariat draft, with cultural genocide and political groups, including 'nonviolent' genocide, to underline the many tactics of genocide.[137] Russia is particularly bent on destroying Ukrainian culture, as an affront to its view that Ukraine is simply 'Little Russia'.[138]

On 9 December 1948, after some last-minute wrangling, the General Assembly passed the 'Convention on the Prevention and Punishment of the Crime of Genocide'.[139] 'Universal Declaration of

---

[135] Zack Beauchamp, 'Is Russia Committing Genocide in Ukraine?" Vox', *Vox* (blog), 13 April 2022, https://www.vox.com/23020696/ukraine-russia-genocide-allegations.. Professor Finkel mentioned in the article that he admitted changing his mind during the invasion. This was the professor and authority on genocide used by the GRU to attempt to infiltrate the ICC. Also, Kate Cronin-Furman, Eugene Finkel, and Peter Balakian, 'The Politics of Calling the Russia-Ukraine War a Genocide', *NPR Illinois*, 19 April 2022, https://www.nprillinois.org/2022-04-19/the-politics-of-calling-the-russia-ukraine-war-a-genocide..

[136] Elizabeth Whatcott, 'Compilation of Countries' Statements Calling Russian Actions in Ukraine "Genocide."', *Just Security*, 10 June 2022, https://www.justsecurity.org/81564/compilation-of-countries-statements-calling-russian-actions-in-ukraine-genocide/.. This list will doubtless be longer as of publication of this book.

[137] Clara Apt, 'Russia's Eliminationist Rhetoric Against Ukraine: A Collection', *Just Security* (blog), 15 June 2022, https://www.justsecurity.org/81789/russias-eliminationist-rhetoric-against-ukraine-a-collection/..

[138] Paul D. Shinkman, 'Russian Attempts to Wipe out Ukraine's Culture 'Looks Systematic', *U.S. News*,", 10 June 2022, https://www.usnews.com/news/world-report/articles/2022-06-10/russian-attempts-to-wipe-out-ukraines-culture-looks-systematic-u-s-diplomat-says.

[139] 'Convention on the Prevention and Punishment of the Crime of Genocide, 9 December 1948', in *Treaties, States Parties, and Commentaries. ICRC*, n.d., https://ihl-databases.icrc.org/ihl/INTRO/357..

Human Rights' was passed on the next day.[140]

The key provisions of the Genocide Convention are:

> "**Article 1-**The Contracting Parties confirm that genocide, whether committed in time of peace or in time of war, is a crime under international law which they undertake to prevent and to punish.
>
> **Article 2-**In the present Convention, genocide means any of the following acts committed with intent to destroy, in whole or in part, a national, ethnical, racial or religious group, as such: (a) Killing members of the group; (b) Causing serious bodily or mental harm to members of the group; (c) Deliberately inflicting on the group conditions of life calculated to bring about its physical destruction in whole or in part; (d) Imposing measures intended to prevent births within the group; (e) Forcibly transferring children of the group to another group.
>
> **Article 3-**The following acts shall be punishable: (a) Genocide; (b) Conspiracy to commit genocide; (c) Direct and public incitement to commit genocide; (d) Attempt to commit genocide; (e) Complicity in genocide.
>
> **Article 4-**Persons committing genocide or any of the other acts enumerated in article III shall be punished, whether they are constitutionally responsible rulers, public officials or private individuals.
>
> **Article 5-**The Contracting Parties undertake to enact, in accordance with their respective Constitutions, the necessary legislation to give effect to the provisions of the present Convention, and, in particular, to provide effective penalties for persons guilty of genocide or any of the other acts enumerated in article III."

Note that Article 5 covers the domestic implementation of the convention, especially with domestic penalties, a major subject of my other essay. However, the convention does not need the implementation to come into force for the citizens of a state. Specifically, if genocide was not a crime in Russian law (which it nowadays is, in theory), it would still be an international crime. Article 6 states that genocide might be tried by the courts of a country in which genocide occurred (Ukraine) or an international tribunal. Article 7 lifts protection from extradition for political crimes. Article 8 allows states to petition the United Nations organs for protection—and in the case of Russia's 2022 attack on Ukraine, a veto stopped that procedure. Article 9 covers the International Court of Justice's (ICJ)

---

[140] United Nations, 'Universal Declaration of Human Rights', United Nations (United Nations), accessed 3 March 2023, https://www.un.org/en/about-us/universal-declaration-of-human-rights..

jurisdiction in interpreting the convention between states, but this does not mean it holds criminal trials against individuals.[141] As a note here, the current case of Ukraine vs Russia at the ICJ does not concern Russian genocide, but Russia's allegation of Ukraine committing genocide as a pretext of invasion.[142] Going back to Article 2, it imposes a very significant hurdle for genocide to be called genocide under the convention—'intent to destroy'. So, there is a huge theoretical burden of proving intent. However, in the case of Ukraine, Putin's closest allies have publicly promised and demanded a genocide of Ukraine while Putin has circuitously said the same.[143] The Genocide Convention was then variously ratified and forgotten in legal practise and realpolitik about until the 1990s.

Justice for Genocide

The Second World War had shown the flaws and limitations of previous international humanitarian law. Riding the wave of legal enthusiasm and following the Genocide Convention, four new Geneva Conventions (Geneva Conventions 1949) were signed in 1949,

---

[141] The ICJ is not to be confused with the ICC. It was created along with the United Nations and handles disputes between states. It has extensively adjudicated Ukrainian claims against Russia and Russia ignores the rulings. Refer to Schabas, *Genocide*, chapter 9, "State responsibility and the role of the International Court of Justice".

[142] ICC, 'Allegations of Genocide under the Convention on the Prevention and Punishment of the Crime of Genocide (Ukraine)', accessed 24 March 2023, https://www.icj-cij.org/case/182. Anecdotally a majority of politicians, journalists and lawyers, if they have heard of the case, wrongly think its about Russian geocide.

[143] This article links further into pieces describing the evidence for genocidal intent, particularly pieces by professor Finkel and Francine Hirsch, Vox Ukraina, 'Will Russian Atrocities in Ukraine Be recognised as Genocide? Here Is What the Researchers Say about This', accessed 3 March 2023, https://voxukraine.org/en/will-russian-atrocities-in-ukraine-be-recognised-as-genocide-here-is-what-the-researchers-say-about-this.. The European Parliament has called Russian actions genocide, European Parliament, 'Motion for a Resolution the Fight against Impunity for War Crimes in Ukraine' (2022), https://www.europarl.europa.eu/doceo/document/B-9-2022-0283_EN.html. Holly Ellyatt, 'Putin's Supporters Call for the Liquidation of Ukraine as "genocidal Rhetoric" Swells', CNBC, 25 November 2022, https://www.cnbc.com/2022/11/25/putins-supporters-call-for-the-extermination-of-ukraine.html.

combining the two threads of law, Hague and Geneva, to increase the protection of civilians and victims during conflict:

- The First Geneva Convention-'for the Amelioration of the Condition of the Wounded and Sick in Armed Forces in the Field' which updated the 1864 and 1829 conventions,
- The Second Geneva Convention 'for the Amelioration of the Condition of Wounded, Sick and Shipwrecked Members of Armed Forces at Sea' replaced The Hague Convention (X) of 1907 with content like the First above,
- The Third Geneva Convention 'relative to the Treatment of Prisoners of War' which replaced the 1929 Geneva Convention relating to prisoners of war.
- The Fourth Geneva Convention 'relative to the Protection of Civilian Persons in Time of War' which gave many new protections to civilians.[144]
- As time went by it was noticed that additional and better protections would be needed which gave us:
- Protocol I (1977) 'relating to the Protection of Victims of International Armed Conflicts'
- Protocol II (1977) 'relating to the Protection of Victims of Non-International Armed Conflicts'
- Protocol III (2005) 'relating to the Adoption of an Additional Distinctive Emblem–covering emblems for medical staff aka Russian targets. The next essay will start with this subject'.

As Robertson notes in Crimes Against Humanity, 262-263, Article 35 of Protocol I (1977) sums up the development of the rules of war, with its basic principles:[145]

"**Article 35**-Basic rules

---

[144] 'The Geneva Conventions of 1949 and Their Additional Protocols' (2010), https://www.icrc.org/en/doc/war-and-law/treaties-customary-law/geneva-conventions/overview-geneva-conventions.htm. The regularly updated commentaries by Jean S. Pictet, *The Geneva Conventions of 12 August 1949: Commentary* (Geneva: International Committee of the Red Cross, 2006). provide in-depth analysis.

[145] Robertson, *Crimes*.

> 1. In any armed conflict, the right of the Parties to the conflict to choose methods or means of warfare is not unlimited.
> 2. It is prohibited to employ weapons, projectiles and material and methods of warfare of a nature to cause superfluous injury or unnecessary suffering.
> 3. It is prohibited to employ methods or means of warfare which are intended, or may be expected, to cause widespread, long-term, and severe damage to the natural environment."

Protocol I (1977) was the work of the centuries of development of international humanitarian law and perhaps requires updating but is very much applicable in the current war, for instance in:

- protecting civilian populations (Part IV — including also cultural objects),
- protecting the wounded and sick (Part II),
- covering armed conflicts which also includes so-called 'special operations' (Article 3 in connection with Geneva Conventions 1949),146
- treatment of POWs (Part III section II, includes mercenaries and protection of persons not in the military formally,147
- legal advisers on humanitarian law must be provided to commanders and troops instructed on the law (Articles 82 and 83, covered in the next essay).

The Russian Federation is on record as actively and enthusiastically abusing all of the above. 2.000 pages listing broken rules of war and giving examples hitherto uncovered could easily be written. [148] The

---

[146] 2022 is a war. And it started in 2014.

[147] See the Office of the United Nations High Commissioner for Human Rights (OHCHR) report on treatment of prisoners of war — Russia routinely mistreats prisoners of war, up to the regular execution of captured soldiers. Executions have also been reported on the Ukrainian side. Needless to say, these are grave breaches of international law. See OHCHR, 'OHCHR Report on the Treatment of Prisoners of War and Persons Hors de Combat in the Context of the Armed Attack by the Russian Federation against Ukraine: 24 February 2022-23 February 2023', accessed 24 March 2023, https://www.ohchr.org/en/documents/country-reports/ohchr-report-treatment-prisoners-war-and-persons-hors-de-combat-context.

[148] This project is gathering evidence on the ground. 'CCL." Центр Громадянських Свобод - Center for Civil Liberties', 19 September 2021, https://ccl.org.ua/en/. Refer to 'War Crimes in the 2022 Russian Invasion of Ukraine',

United Nations Human Rights Council created an Independent International Commission of Inquiry on Ukraine in March 2022. After a year, a report was published finding:

It [Commission] has concluded that Russian authorities have committed numerous violations of international humanitarian law and violations of international human rights law, in addition to a wide range of war crimes, including the war crime of excessive incidental death, injury, or damage, wilful killings, torture, inhuman treatment, unlawful confinement, rape, as well as unlawful transfers and deportations.[149]

This report did not 'find a genocide in Ukraine' but with the disclaimer 'we have noted that there are some aspects which may raise questions with respect to that crime... but we have not yet put in any conclusion here'.[150] Too much shouldn't be read into this, the United Nations has strict guidelines on using the term — therefore a finding of genocide: 'must be done by a competent international or national court of law with the jurisdiction to try such cases, after an investigation meeting appropriate due process standard.[151]

Going back to the history of international law, after the flurry of initial enthusiasm for human rights and a rule-based order of international justice, the world found itself in the Cold War. International treaties descended into products of convention junkets in

---

in *Wikipedia. Wikimedia Foundation,* 12 June 2022, https://en.wikipedia.org/wiki/War_crimes_in_the_2022_Russian_invasion_of_Ukraine.

[149] OCHR, 'War Crimes, Indiscriminate Attacks on Infrastructure, Systematic and Widespread Torture Show Disregard for Civilians, Says UN Commission of Inquiry on Ukraine', accessed 24 March 2023, https://www.ohchr.org/en/press-releases/2023/03/war-crimes-indiscriminate-attacks-infrastructure-systematic-and-widespread. Most of the report details crimes committed by the Russian military, with notes on 'limited' cases involving the Ukrainian military.

[150] Stanislav Pohorilov, 'UN Commission Fails to Find Evidence of Russia's Genocide in Ukraine | Ukrainska Pravda', accessed 29 March 2023, https://www.pravda.com.ua/eng/news/2023/03/16/7393761/.

[151] UN Office on Genocide Prevention and the Responsibility to Protect, 'Guidance Note - When to Refer to a Situation as Genocide', accessed 29 March 2023, https://www.un.org/en/genocideprevention/documents/publications-and-resources/GuidanceNote-When%20to%20refer%20to%20a%20situation%20as%20genocide.pdf.

Geneva, The Hague, Vienna, Rome, and New York.[152] The most significant international conflict for the next forty years was the Korean War where the Security Council decided to act because the Soviet Union boycotted the vote, a mistake it would not repeat.[153] While the world repeated 'never again' about the Holocaust in the 1950s, Stalin crushed the remnants of opposition to Communism and Russian occupation in Hungary, Poland, and East Germany, in imperial violence, often targeting leaders in genocide aimed at politicians. [154] A decade after Stalin's death, the Soviet regime reminded the Czechs that freedom was still not on its way. A quarter of a million Bangladeshi women were raped in the Pakistan invasion of 'East Pakistan'. [155] Mao quietly genocided, using Lemkin's definition, China with the Great Leap Forward which apart from sparking random useless violence also targeted intellectuals. Human rights and treaties were ignored in the name of the progress of communism and in combating communism. Kissinger's beloved Realpolitik and Soviet and American exceptionalism continue to poison the world, particularly via Putin's Russia, where Lavrov takes his lead from Kissinger's example.[156]

The Cold War and post-Cold War world suffered from what could be called the 'Don't call it genocide' Disease as this example shows: '"As a responsible Government, you don't just go around

---

[152] Robertson, *Crimes*.49.

[153] UN, 'Russia Vetoes Security Council Resolution Condemning Attempted Annexation of Ukraine Regions | UN News', 30 September 2022, https://news.un.org/en/story/2022/09/1129102.

[154] European Parliament, '"Never Again": EP Commemorates International Holocaust Remembrance Day: Aktualności: Parlament Europejski', *European Parlia* (blog), 27 January 2022, https://www.europarl.europa.eu/news/pl/press-room/20220120IPR21417/never-again-ep-commemorates-international-holocaust-remembrance-day. Note the date.

[155] Notice how regimes whose soldiers like to rape deny the existence of other entities… such as with 'Little Russia' or in the Yugoslav horror lands. Nayanika Mookherjee, 'Mass Rape and the Inscription of Gendered and Racial Domination during the Bangladesh War of 1971', in *Rape in Wartime*, 2012, 67–78, https://doi.org/10.1057/9781137283399_5.

[156] Ivan Witker, 'Ivan Witker: Sergei Lavrov, El Kissinger Ruso', *El Líbero*, 14 March 2022, https://ellibero.cl/opinion/ivan-witker-sergei-lavrov-el-kissinger-ruso/. Jamie Dettmer, 'No Lie Too Great', *POLITICO. POLITICO*, 29 July 2022, https://www.politico.eu/article/heart-lavrov-darkness-russia-ukraine-war/..

hollering 'genocide," David Rawson, the United States Ambassador to Rwanda, said in an interview. "You say that acts of genocide may have occurred, and they need to be investigated."'[157] See the diplomatic and academic reaction to President Biden calling the genocide in Ukraine a genocide in April 2022. [158] Perhaps the most significant genocide of the Cold War occurred in Cambodia under the Khmer Rouge, which Robertson in Crimes Against Humanity blames mostly on Kissinger and the Vietnam War.[159] As an example, this genocide does not qualify under the UN guidelines mentioned earlier as warranting the official label genocide—because there was no international court adjudicating this...[160]

During the 1980s, the Cold War ended much to the surprise of all, including Kissinger, with the collapse of communist regimes. As Yugoslavia descended into a bloody war, atrocity and genocide appeared again in Europe. The bloodshed in Yugoslavia was televised and shocking, resulting in public calls for action. An International Criminal Tribunal for the Former Yugoslavia (ICTY) was duly established by the UN Security Council via resolution in May 1993 to prosecute individuals responsible for the new atrocities.[161] A weakened Russia, desperately dependent on Western aid, did not veto this action. This tribunal did not do much publicly at first, mostly for lack of defendants to be tried, but some key behind-the-scenes legal preparatory work was occurring. Meanwhile, Serbian

---

[157] Douglas Jehl, 'Officials Told to Avoid Calling Rwanda Killings "Genocide."', *New York Times*, 10 June 1994.

[158] John Hudson, Adele Sulliman, and Jennifer Hassan, 'As Leaders Debate "Genocide," a Growing Focus on Atrocities in Ukraine' (Washington Post, 13 April 2022)..

[159] Robertson, *Crimes*.57. Kissinger has been infamously vocal about Ukraine giving up land to Russia, Nathan Gardels, 'Kissinger: The next Steps in Ukraine', *NOEMA*, 10 June 2022, https://www.noemamag.com/kissinger-the-next-steps-in-ukraine/. Please stop, Kissinger.

[160] UN Office on Genocide Prevention and the Responsibility to Protect, 'Guidance Note'.

[161] Robertson, *Crimes*.448. The Security Council in general has the power to 'decide what measures shall be taken to maintain or restore international peace and security under article 39 of the UN Charter and this has become the precedent that it can establish *ad hoc* tribunals, in the Nuremberg fashion.

nationalists called and still call their Croatian enemies 'Nazis'.[162] It's easy to genocide Nazis-and here's the Lemkin, not convention, definition of genocide which covers political categories is used. It is not even a crime, it's justice in the eyes of the perpetrator. Political prisoners in Soviet prisons were called fascists, which was a synonym for Nazi, no difference, for this psychological reason.[163]

Before the first major criminals from the Yugoslav conflict could be brought to justice or even before the major symbolic atrocity of that Balkan war, Srebrenica, a terrible atrocity was being perpetrated in Rwanda. After the suspicious death of Rwanda's moderate Hutu president in 1994, Tutsis and moderate Hutus were hunted down in scenes reminiscent of Cambodia or the Congo under Leopold's rule. The entire incident was shameful to a degree that cannot be described. It is lucky for Ukrainians that they are not black Africans on a separate continent so the West cannot say it should avoid interfering in 'black on black violence', an idea pushed by the British Foreign Office at the time.[164] Six months after the Tutsis won the civil war and stopped the genocide, the UN Security Council, again in a resolution, decided to create an international tribunal under Chapter VII of the United Nations Charter—which was active in trying major Hutu criminals who mostly escaped Rwanda to avoid summary trial and execution by firing squad.[165] The trials in The Hague by an international tribunal, the "International Criminal Tribunal for Rwanda", constitute valuable case law which will be used in the future.[166] That case law covers genocide as well as various crimes against humanity and war

---

[162] Associated Press, 'Croatia Celebrates 1995 Blitz; Serbia Calls It Nazi Policy', 5 August 2018, https://www.voanews.com/a/croatia-celebrates-1995-blitz-serbia-compares-to-nazi-policy/4514354.html..

[163] 'Many Days, Many Lives', *Gulag*, n.d., https://gulaghistory.org/exhibits/days-and-lives/prisoners/3.html..

[164] Robertson, *Crimes*. 98-101.

[165] Ibid., 101-102.

[166] Jennifer Trahan et al., eds., *Genocide, War Crimes, and Crimes against Humanity: Topical Digests of the Case Law of the International Criminal Tribunal for Rwanda and the International Criminal Tribunal for the Former Yugoslavia* (New York: Human Rights Watch, 2004). Bakhtiyar R.Tuzmukhamedov, referenced in other chapter, was nominated as the Russian appointed judge in 2009.

crimes.¹⁶⁷

We then come back to genocide, war crimes and crimes against humanity on the European continent with the Yugoslav civil wars which started before the Rwanda genocide and continued after it had finished. As Robertson points out in Crimes Against Humanity, General Mladić, contemptuous of law, looked down on Srebrenica and promised genocide on Serbian television in July 1995, long after the Rwanda tribunal and even the ICTY was set up. In 2022 and 2023 we have Russian genocidal criminals broadcasting their genocidal intent, secure in their belief in nuclear immunity.¹⁶⁸

At Srebrenica in Bosnia, men of fighting age were taken under the eyes of Dutch 'peacekeepers' to be 'screened for complicity in war crimes.¹⁶⁹ Only a minor Serbian torturer was waiting for trial in The Hague while Serbs massacred the men of Srebrenica and besieged Sarajevo. Nobody was taking the ICTY or the ICTR seriously in 1995.¹⁷⁰ However in 1998 NATO began arresting senior Serbian leaders like General Krstić, one of the butchers of Srebrenica and General Galić who had bombarded Sarajevo. In all 161 people have been indicted. The list is mostly Serbs (ninety four) but has Croats (twenty nine) and a mixture of other ethnicities.¹⁷¹ Some of the key

---

[167] Refer to ICRC, 'Statute of the International Criminal Tribunal for Rwanda, 8 November 1994', accessed 3 March 2023, https://ihl-databases.icrc.org/en/ihl-treaties/, https://ihl-databases.icrc.org/en/ihl-treaties/ictr-statute-1994..

[168] Ron Jackson, 'Russian TV Host Threatens to Nuke Any Country That Detains Putin', accessed 24 March 2023, https://www.newsweek.com/russian-tv-host-threatens-nuking-any-country-that-detains-putin-1789307.

[169] Robertson, *Crimes*, 103. Also, Oksana Rasulova and Yuliana Skibitska, 'The Russians Send Men from Mariupol to Filtration Camps. They Are Kept There and Not Allowed to Communicate with Relatives. Their Wives Try to Save Them - and This Is What They Say', Babel, n.d., https://babel.ua/en/texts/78606-the-russians-send-men-from-mariupol-to-filtration-camps-they-are-kept-there-and-not-allowed-to-communicate-with-relatives-their-wives-try-to-save-them-and-this-is-what-they-say.

[170] If the timeline is confusing, refer to the Criminal Tribunal for the former Yugoslavia, ICTY, 'Court Timeline', Criminal Tribunal for the former Yugoslavia, accessed 6 August 2022, https://www.icty.org/en/content/print..

[171] 'List of People Indicted in the International Criminal Tribunal for the Former Yugoslavia', in *Wikipedia. Wikimedia Foundation*, 10 May 2022, https://en.wikipe

figures would be Slobodan Milošević–Serbian President 1989-1997 and rump Yugoslavia president 1997-2000, Dragomir Milošević-Republika Srpska commander and besieger of Sarajevo and Ratko Mladić-Colonel General and former Commander of the Main Staff of the Bosnian Serb Army between 1992 and 1995. There are politicians, field generals, camp commanders, mid-level officers ordering massacres and some low-level scum. The ICTY likes to underline that nobody from their list of persons indicted for war crimes in 2000 has escaped trial.

An example of mid-level criminals would be Goran Jelisić, a fraudster turned 'police-man' turned concentration camp commander, who famously murdered a man while on camera.[172] Bellingcat, created to find the persons responsible for shooting down MH17, one of Russia's most serious atrocities in its earlier war, should serve as a terrifying internet Batman to future war criminals. The TikTok and Telegram posting Russian soldiers documenting their atrocities should consider Jelisić's fate: forty years in prison which at his age practically means life.[173] Identification of war criminals is getting easier, especially when grown men record and publish videos of their war crimes like teenagers record and publish Tiktok video and organisations like Bellingcat hunt the more intelligent war criminals even using bread crumbs of data found on the internet.[174]

---

dia.org/wiki/List_of_people_indicted_in_the_International_Criminal_Tribunal_for_the_former_Yugoslavia.

[172] Alona Mazurenko, 'Bellingcat Investigators Have Identified the Occupier Who Tortured and Executed a Ukrainian Soldier', *Ukrainska Pravda*. *Ukrainska Pravda*, 5 August 2022, https://www.pravda.com.ua/eng/news/2022/08/5/7362088/. Also Bellingcat, 'Tracking the Faceless Killers Who Mutilated and Executed a Ukrainian POW', 6 August 2022, https://www.bellingcat.com/news/2022/08/05/tracking-the-faceless-killers-who-mutilated-and-executed-a-ukrainian-pow/.

[173] Brendan Cole, 'Video of Russian Soldier Allegedly Castrating Ukraine POW Sparks Outrage', *Newsweek*, 29 July 2022, https://www.newsweek.com/russia-ukraine-castrate-torture-video-1728988.

[174] DATALLION, 'Ukraine War Footage Database', accessed 24 March 2023, https://dattalion.com/; Ukrayinska Pravda, 'Database of Russian Executioners of Ukrainians Created | Ukrayinska Pravda', accessed 24 March 2023, https://www.pravda.com.ua/eng/news/2022/06/18/7353259/. Joshua, '"TikTok Warriors": What Are Chechen Fighters Doing in Ukraine? | Euronews', accessed 24

The ICTY is proud of its effect on developing international criminal law which ranks in volume and significance with the work of the Rwanda tribunal.[175] The case law built by both tribunals is significant. In fact the already mentioned United Nations guidelines qualify the Tutsi genocide and Srebrenica as genocide, the only two 'official' examples in the guidance.[176] If Russian officers and leaders are prosecuted, we can expect the largest and most complex trials since the Second World War, perhaps larger than the Nuremberg or Tokyo trials as a whole. This not because Russian crimes are greater than Nazi or Japanese ones, they're not, at least for now, but because this field of law and the technology to identify and prosecute perpetrators is significantly different and expanded.[177] That said it has been pointed out that in the ICTY and ICTR jurisprudence is that 'genocide would cease to be genocide if Hutu, Tutsi, Serb, Croat, Bosnian Muslim were administrative categories, or political groups, instead of ethnicities'.[178] Maybe Putin cunningly labels Ukrainians as Nazis for his genocide because Nazis are a political group. Milošević was the most famous war criminal tried by the ICTY and his arrest was a breakthrough, comparable only to the trial of Göring at Nuremberg—the most significant warrant until Putin overplayed his hand kidnapping Ukrainian children during war-time. Milošević's hand-over was closely

---

March 2023, https://www.euronews.com/2023/01/20/mad-dogs-what-are-chechen-fighters-doing-in-ukraine.

[175] ICC, 'Achievements." Achievements | International Criminal Tribunal for the Former Yugoslavia', n.d., https://www.icty.org/en/about/tribunal/achievements..

[176] UN Office on Genocide Prevention and the Responsibility to Protect, 'Guidance Note'.

[177] Flynn Coleman, 'To Prosecute Putin for War Crimes, Safeguard the Digital Proof', *Foreign Policy*, 10 April 2022, https://foreignpolicy.com/2022/04/10/prosecute-putin-war-crimes-evidence-bucha-safeguard-digital-proof/. Al Jazeera, 'ICC Sends 42-Member Team to Probe Alleged War Crimes in Ukraine', ICC News | Al Jazeera. Al Jazeera, 17 May 2022, 42, https://www.aljazeera.com/news/2022/5/17/icc-sends-largest-ever-investigative-team-to-war-torn-ukraine. Chris Oxendine, 'Ukraine: Open-Source Data Aided Response and Documents Damages and Atrocities', *Esri*, 16 June 2022, https://www.esri.com/about/newsroom/blog/ukraine-open-source-intelligence/. 'Conflict Observatory', *Conflict Observatory*, 30 June 2022, https://conflictobservatory.org/.

[178] Irvin-Erickson, *Concept*. 238.

connected with a massive aid package for Serbia. Milošević had already been indicted back in 1999 for a 100-word list of crimes, which starts with genocide—as the crime of crimes. Putin will have an even longer charge sheet, though for now it's limited to the war crime of kidnapping children, which could easily be qualified as genocide at a later time.[179] At trial, Milošević, a lawyer by education like Putin, used the usual war criminal defence of whatabout/tu quoque,[180] raising for instance British actions in Northern Ireland. Milosevic died in 2005 during the trial. Russian propaganda is already whatabouting Iraq for the threat of an international tribunal indicting Putin for the crime of aggression. There is currently a strong intellectual movement to bring Putin to trial on this charge, led both by Ukrainians understandably and Westerners, such as Philippe Sands, admirably and very much less admirably by Gordon Brown.[181] This concept seems to be confusing the public and public figures alike—as to what a tribunal is supposed to do—some seem to think a special tribunal is necessary to deter Russian atrocities (war of aggression is not an atrocity as such), despite the existence of the ICC which very much has jurisdiction for most of Putin's and friend atrocities.[182] Crime of aggression as a concept is an alien one even for lawyers, unlike say war crimes. There are also

---

[179] 'Situation in Ukraine: ICC Judges Issue Arrest Warrants against Vladimir Vladimirovich Putin and Maria Alekseyevna Lvova-Belova', International Criminal Court, accessed 22 March 2023, https://www.icc-cpi.int/news/situation-ukraine-icc-judges-issue-arrest-warrants-against-vladimir-vladimirovich-putin-and. See later for notes on Rome Statute and crimes. The other indicted person ironically bears the name of the city of Lviv in her Russian surname.

[180] Normally called the 'Tu quoque' defence, refer to Katerina Borrelli, 'Between Show-Trials and Utopia: A Study of the *Tu Quoque* Defence', *Leiden Journal of International Law* 32, no. 2 (June 2019): 315–31, https://doi.org/10.1017/S0922156519000074.

[181] Janet H. Anderson, 'Everything You Need to Know or Argue about a Special Tribunal on Russia's Crime of Aggression', *JusticeInfo.Net* (blog), 13 December 2022, https://www.justiceinfo.net/en/110201-everything-you-need-to-know-argue-special-tribunal-russia-crime-of-aggression.html.

[182] Jennifer Rankin, 'Ukrainian Nobel Peace Laureate Calls for Special Tribunal to Try Putin', *The Guardian. Guardian News and Media*, 27 February 2023, sec. World news, https://www.theguardian.com/world/2023/feb/27/ukrainian-nobel-peace-laureate-oleksandra-matviichuk-calls-for-special-tribunal-to-try-vladimir-putin.

significant legal issues here—firstly the Security Council will not authorise a tribunal, such as ICTY or ICTR because of the Russian veto.[183] This raises the issue of who can authorise the trial, maybe the General Assembly of the Security Council which does not seem legal under international law.[184] If the trial is not truly international then there's the issue of (sovereign) immunity for a triumvirate of a country's major figures.

I need to try and quickly explain this frankly absurd concept, which has no treaty or constitutional basis. Basically international law, somehow by custom, holds that 'heads of state [presidents, monarchs], heads of government [prime ministers, chancellors] and foreign ministers enjoy "full immunity" from foreign jurisdiction and inviolability'.[185] I will not attempt to explain how the Nuremberg trials put Donitz (Reich President), Goring (successor to Hitler by law) and Ribbentrop were on trial at Nuremberg because that subject is both confusing and contradictory. The current concept is that 'international courts' can try these persons. An ICC warrant for instance binds member countries. A particularly thorny issue arises at the time of writing for South Africa, an ICC member. The government had previously ignored an ICC international arrest warrant for the President of Sudan when he visited in 2015. This led to it losing domestic and international cases.[186] At that time, the

---

[183] Olivier Corten and Vaios Koutroulis, 'Tribunal for the Crime of Aggression against Ukraine - a Legal Assessment', n.d., https://www.europarl.europa.eu/RegData/etudes/IDAN/2022/702574/EXPO_IDA(2022)702574_EN.pdf.

[184] Kevin Jon Heller, 'The Best Option: An Extraordinary Ukrainian Chamber for Aggression - Opinio Juris', accessed 29 March 2023, https://opiniojuris.org/2022/03/16/the-best-option-an-extraordinary-ukrainian-chamber-for-aggression/.

[185] Miguel Lemos, 'The Law of Immunity and the Prosecution of the Head of State of the Russian Federation for International Crimes in the War against Ukraine', *EJIL: Talk!* (blog), 16 January 2023, https://www.ejiltalk.org/the-law-of-immunity-and-the-prosecution-of-the-head-of-state-of-the-russian-federation-for-international-crimes-in-the-war-against-ukraine/.

[186] HRW, 'ICC: Ruling on Sudanese President's South Africa Visit - Sudan | ReliefWeb', 6 July 2017, https://reliefweb.int/report/sudan/icc-ruling-sudanese-president-s-south-africa-visit. 'Al-Bashir Case: ICC Pre-Trial Chamber II Decides Not to Refer South Africa's Non-Cooperation to the ASP or the UNSC', International Criminal Court, accessed 24 March 2023, https://www.icc-cpi.int/

government could have weakly argued the law was not clear on the subject, what with the (ridiculous for this author) custom despite the wording of the ICC treaty which will be discussed in the paragraph below.[187] Putin was invited to visit South Africa for a BRICS summit in 2023 before the ICC indicted him for the war crime of kidnapping Ukrainian children…[188] This poses a conundrum for the South Africans as well as Russia. To sum up this concept, the international legal concept of immunity says an Ukrainian court would not be able to try Putin or Lavrov for any crimes, if they were to fall into Ukrainian hands — something I submit would very much not be the case if this ever happened, as a new legal concept would quickly be forged to try him in Ukraine if it chose to do so - much like the crime of aggression was pulled out of a hat for the Nuremberg trials (that is not to criticise the trials or forging new law as necessary, however lawyers often desperately pretend they are not creating new law, especially in the field of international law).

Around the time Milosevic, another person shielded by personal immunity, in the time before an international tribunal was created for Yugoslavia, was indicted, an enormous change in international criminal law was made through the signing of the statute of the ICC on 17 July 1998 ("Rome Statute").[189] Russia, like the United States, signed, but did not ratify the treaty-leading to some complicated questions on status which we don't have to worry about for reasons to be discussed, their status is they have signalled they do not 'intend to ratify'. Note that Russia was already under Putin's rule while the United States president was Bill Clinton, with four democratic changes in the US, since then while Putin has remained formally or informally in power. The Genocide Convention

---

news/al-bashir-case-icc-pre-trial-chamber-ii-decides-not-refer-south-africas-non-cooperation-asp-or.

[187] Doctors without Borders, 'Doctors without Borders | The Practical Guide to Humanitarian Law', accessed 24 March 2023, https://guide-humanitarian-law.org/content/article/3/immunity/.

[188] S'thembile Cele, 'Putin Arrest Warrant Prompts South Africa to Seek Legal Advice', *Bloomberg.Com*, 24 March 2023, https://www.bloomberg.com/news/articles/2023-03-24/putin-arrest-warrant-prompts-south-africa-to-seek-legal-advice.

[189] 'Rome Statute of the International Criminal Court' (2022), https://www.icc-cpi.int/sites/default/files/RS-Eng.pdf.

in 1948 had already foreseen an international tribunal to deal with that crime but nothing had come to realise that part of Article VI for decades. After the Cold War, the Balkan and Rwandan genocides had energised the international community to some degree, especially considering the obvious feelings of impunity among Balkan and Rwandan murderers, torturers and rapists. There were various views on how a court should operate ranging from a powerful independent court (most of Western Europe) to a Security Council dependent court (United States), and a mixture was eventually agreed upon.[190] The Rome Statute still has many flaws which were mostly written into the text to keep the United States as a party to it.[191] Of particular note is that the preamble of the Rome Statute states: "Emphasising in this connection that nothing in this Statute shall be taken as authorising any State Party to intervene in an armed conflict or in the internal affairs of any State," written in the period just before the series of the interventions (invasions/occupations, choose favourite) in Afghanistan, Iraq and Libya. The United States ferociously fought to keep the crime of aggression outside the jurisdiction of the ICC, except for cases between parties or when referred by the Security Council (where the US has a veto, like Russia).[192] As note Russia was a non-ratified signatory to the ICC in those heady pre-Putin days when it paused in its legal nihilism. Even the signature was later withdrawn, in light of

---

[190] Robertson, *Crimes*. 503-504.

[191] For machinations affecting development of twentieth and 21st century law refer to Mark Lattimer, ed., *Justice for Crimes Against Humanity* (Oxford: Hart, 2006). Especially chapters 4, Timothy McCormack, *"Their* Atrocities and *Our* Misdemeanours: The Reticence of States to Try Their 'Own Nationals' for International Crimes", 9, William Aceves and Paul Hoffman, "Pursuing Crimes Against Humanity in the United States: the Need for a Comprehensive Liability Regime". Also, Robertson, *Crimes*, chapter 10, "The International Criminal Court".

[192] Astrid Reisinger Coracini, 'The Kampala Amendments on the Crime of Aggression Before Activation: Evaluating the Legal Framework of a Political Compromise (Part 1)', *Opinio Juris* (blog), 29 September 2017, http://opiniojuris.org/20 17/09/29/the-kampala-amendments-on-the-crime-of-aggression-before-activ ation-evaluating-the-legal-framework-of-a-political-compromise/; Harold Hongju Koh and Todd F. Buchwald, 'The Crime of Aggression: The United States Perspective', *The American Journal of International Law* 109, no. 2 (2015): 257–95, https://doi.org/10.5305/amerjintelaw.109.2.0257.

investigations of the annexation of Crimea.[193]

The ICC is a criminal court that deals with persons—even though it encounters states and international institutions like the United Nations and organs like the UN Security Council. We must always remember that the ICC functions within the sphere of Realpolitik, and it does not have an army or police force.[194] It relies on the soldiers and policemen of the states interested in justice and their relative power. The Rome Statute builds on the work of centuries, including Geneva and Hague Law, the Nuremberg Trials, the ICTR and ICTY tribunals, and consolidates and changes international criminal law, along with creating a court. The pertinent material elements of the Rome Statute are that:

- crimes against humanity can be committed in peace and prosecuted,
- sexual violence was codified as a form of war crime,
- command responsibility was raised to a provision of international treaty law,
- grave breaches of international humanitarian law, the laws in war, are specifically treated as criminal acts,
- genocide receives special attention and is given a real treaty prohibition supported by an enforcement mechanism.

Specifically, crimes within the jurisdiction of the court (Article 5^1 of the Rome Statute):

> "shall be limited to the most serious crimes of concern to the international community as a whole.
> The Court has jurisdiction in accordance with this Statute with respect to the following crimes:
> (a) The crime of genocide;
> (b) Crimes against humanity;
> (c) War crimes;

---

[193] ICC, 'Russia Withdraws from International Criminal Court Treaty', BBC News. BBC, 16 November 2016, https://www.bbc.com/news/world-europe-38005282.

[194] For a detailed look at the Rome Statute, Otto Triffterer and Kai Ambos, *Commentary on the Rome Statute of the International Criminal Court: Observers' Notes, Article by Article* (Oxford: Beck/Hart, 2015).) with 2300 pages.

(d) The crime of aggression."[195]

The ICC does not replace local courts. So a nineteen year-old conscript who shoots a Ukrainian civilian is not usually in the purview of the ICC because Article 1 says the court deals with: 'most serious crimes of international concern, as referred to in this Statute, and shall be complementary to national criminal jurisdictions.' and the case has 'sufficient' gravity, under Article 17 par. 1 (d).[196] Ukraine will perhaps have to deal with thousands of lesser Russian offenders who have no place at The Hague under current rules and practise. The Rome Statute takes the sovereignty of national courts seriously and doesn't act as a replacement for normal proceedings... except in cases where national courts are 'unwilling' to prosecute, under general rules in Article 17. Article 6 of the Rome Statute is identical to Article II of the Genocide Convention. Article 7 par 1 and 2 of 'Crimes Against Humanity' is a long list of the horror that humankind has thought up ranging from murder, deportation, torture, and rape to forced sterilisation. Article 8 is even longer and covers violations of Hague and Geneva Law as international humanitarian law, coming under par. 2 (a): 'Grave breaches of the Geneva Conventions of 12 August 1949, namely, any of the following acts against persons or property protected under the provisions of the relevant Geneva Convention:....' and (b): 'Other serious violations of the laws and customs applicable in international armed conflict, within the established framework of international law, namely, any of the following acts:..'[197] It should be noted here that

---

[195] (d) is as of 2010.

[196] Ukraine has its own Criminal Code, which most definitely applies. Crimes committed in Ukraine or against Ukrainians give the Ukrainian legal system jurisdiction. The Russian Criminal Code also applies to Russians committing crimes in Ukraine (as if they will be prosecuted), refer to next chapter. For unofficial translation refer to: 'Criminal Code of the Republic of Ukraine (English Version' (n.d.), https://sherloc.unodc.org/cld/uploads/res/document/ukr/2001/criminal-code-of-the-republic-of-ukraine-en_html/Ukraine_Criminal_Code_as_of_2010_EN.pdf.. Refer to "Chapter XX. Criminal Offenses Against Peace, Security Of Mankind And International Legal Order" and Article 442-Genocide.

[197] For instance, torture, wilful killing, extensive damage of property, forced conscription of prisoners, deportation, intentional attacks on civilians and civilian

Articles 6-8 are in the jurisdiction of the court where one side of a conflict is a party to the treaty or where a victim state has accepted the jurisdiction without ratifying the Rome Statute. Article 27 deals with immunities -'official capacity as a Head of State or Government' does not 'exempt a person from criminal responsibility' or 'mitigate punishment'.

For complicated internal legal and political reasons, Ukraine is not a party to the Treaty of Rome, but it has accepted the exercise of jurisdiction in this war under the above provisions.[198] The ICC has jurisdiction in this war for investigation of genocide, crimes against humanity and war crimes, regardless of Russia's current status with the ICC.[199] There's no statute of limitation for the ICC so hopefully, we will see 100-year-old Russians responsible for Bucha in court, in the future like the centenarian Nazi camp guard finally at trial in June 2022.[200] As the ICC doesn't hold trials in absentia so the court has to have its hands on the indicted to try them which will be an issue with the hyper-powerful and hyper-rich Russians at the top of the command pyramids. About wealth, Article 75 of the Rome Statute foresees reparations for 'any damage, loss and injury to, or in respect of, victims'. Let us hope we can find some oligarchs among Russian war criminals captured by Ukraine or others.

A short history of the ICC's activities might be appropriate at

---

property, attacks on hospitals, large scale looting, using poison or toxins, large scale sexual violence, starvation warfare and using child soldiers. The list would cover pages of this book.

[198] Interfax-Ukraine, 'Rada Amends Constitution of Ukraine in Part of Justice', *Interfax. Interfax-Ukraine*, 2 June 2016, https://en.interfax.com.ua/news/general/347592.html..

[199] ICC, 'Ukraine', International Criminal Court, n.d., https://www.icc-cpi.int/ukraine.. The issue of the crime of aggression is too complex to be covered here. The ICC does not have jurisdiction over Russia regardless of Ukraine status—unless the Security Council, Russian veto, refers the crime to the ICC. Dustin Du Cane, 'Charge of War of Aggression in Ukraine Invasion', *Fallout*, 16 August 2022, https://fallout.substack.com/p/charge-of-war-of-aggression-in-ukraine.

[200] The Week Staff, '100-Year-Old Former Nazi Concentration Camp Guard to Face Trial', *The Week UK. The Week*, 3 August 2021, https://www.theweek.co.uk/news/world-news/europe/953692/nazi-trial-100-year-old-former-concentration-camp-guard..

this point even though the ICC has not had many occasions to exercise its authority through a combination of circumstances both political and historical. The genocide in Sudanese Darfur in 2005 and the atrocities in Libya in 2011 were referred to the ICC via the Security Council, surprisingly without vetoes—even though those countries were not parties to the Rome Statute and did not refer their situations to the ICC.[201] Uganda, on the other hand, as a party to the Rome Statute and interested in punishing its foreign supported rebels, referred the situation regarding the Lord's Resistance Army (LRA) in Uganda to the ICC directly.[202] Various LRA leaders are sought by the ICC, one, Dominic Ongwen surrendered himself and is currently on trial. Of the other notable persons sought by the ICC, Sudan's former President Omar Al Bashir, already mentioned, has an outstanding ICC warrant from 2009. There was even an ICC arrest warrant against Libyan dictator Muammar Mohammed Abu Minyar Gaddafi—but he was beaten to death by a mob in 2011. A case against his intelligence chief and torturer, Abdullah Al-Senussi, was deemed inadmissible in 2014 because the Libyan domestic system was deemed 'willing and able to try him—currently he is awaiting his death sentence to be carried out or other developments, such as Gaddafi's son being elected president.[203] As can be seen, for complex reasons, the ICC has, concentrated on African defendants leading to accusations of it being an anti-African institution.[204] As of the time of writing in late 2022, the ICC has open investigations in Uganda, Democratic Republic of Congo, Darfur (Sudan), Central African Republic, Kenya, Libya, Côte d'Ivoire, Mali, Georgia, Burundi, Bangladesh/Myanmar (bordering states), Afghanistan, State of Palestine, Republic of the Philippines, Venezuela

---

[201] 'Darfur, Sudan', International Criminal Court, n.d., https://www.icc-cpi.int/darfur.

[202] 'Uganda', International Criminal Court, 20 April 2022, https://www.icc-cpi.int/uganda..

[203] ICC, 'Al-Senussi Case: Appeals Chamber Confirms Case Is Inadmissible before ICC', *International Criminal Court*, n.d., https://www.icc-cpi.int/news/al-senussi-case-appeals-chamber-confirms-case-inadmissible-icc..

[204] M. Cherif Bassiouni and Douglas Hansenn, 'Africa Debate - Is the ICC Targeting Africa Inappropriately?', *The International Criminal Court Forum*, n.d., https://iccforum.com/africa..

and Ukraine.[205]

Figure 3 - Internet infamous meme Joseph Koy, sought by the ICC, Via ICC arrest warrant. International Criminal Court, 'Kony Et Al', n.d. https://www.icc-cpi.int/uganda/kony.

---

[205] Refer to Robertson, *Crimes*. For instances ICC and other tribunal activities for instance in Sierra Leone, Lebanon, and Cambodia. He also covers a whole litany of atrocities and abuses by the 'West' which will form the basis of *whatabout* legal defences in any international proceedings against Russians.

CRIMES, WAR, AND GENOCIDE 373

Figure 4 - Two other war criminals—also sought by the ICC, via Kremlin.ru. 'Встреча с Уполномоченным По Правам Ребёнка Марией Львовой-Беловой', Президент России, 10 March 2022, http://kremlin.ru/events/president/news/67949. Creative Commons Attribution 4.0 International, converted image to grayscale

Two areas of ICC investigation touch on Russia and Russian nationals—Georgia and Ukraine. Russia has been causing trouble around its borders forever and after the collapse of the USSR with subsequent Georgian independence, a convenient flashpoint was found in South Ossetia, which led to armed conflict or war, in 2008. Georgia is a party to the Rome Statute and at the time of conflict/war, Russia had signed but not ratified the treaty.[206] Since 2008, the ICC has: 'gathered information on alleged crimes attributed to the three parties involved in the armed conflict—the Georgian armed forces, the South Ossetian forces, and the Russian armed forces. It seemed for a time that the ICC would not be needed but investigations in Georgia and Russia stalled despite there being 6,335 victims found at that point in investigations. The Russian invasion of Ukraine and subsequent annexation of Crimea finally led to the ICC waking up

---

[206] 'Georgia', International Criminal Court, n.d., https://www.icc-cpi.int/georgia..

to the Georgia situation.²⁰⁷ Those investigations have not yet led to arrest warrants being issued at the time of writing.

So, at this point, we have the ICC having jurisdiction over genocide, war crimes and crimes against humanity committed by Russians, or Ukrainians, on the territory of Ukraine. This also includes those persons giving orders in Russia. The legalese of the terms used by Ukrainian declarations on the subject is unnecessarily limiting, but there are also multiple and valid 'State Party' referrals. ²⁰⁸ The ICC doesn't have jurisdiction over the crime of aggression as potentially committed by Russia, the trickiest field of ICC jurisdiction, and it is improbable it would gain it as a Security Council referral would be needed.²⁰⁹ Even so, as mentioned there are some very loud and prominent voices calling for a non-ICC tribunal to tackle Russian nationals over the crime of aggression.²¹⁰ I again refrain from attempting to explain how 'a hybrid' tribunal for the crime of aggression, which somehow involves international elements with Ukrainian ones (an option favoured by Germany and France, not Ukraine), has jurisdiction to try a country's president when a domestic court somehow doesn't. It's not established law

---

[207] Nika Jeiranashvili, 'How the ICC Can Still Be Meaningful in Georgia', 28 May 2019, https://www.justiceinfo.net/en/41542-how-the-icc-can-still-be-meaningful-in-georgia.html.

[208] Declarations are linked on the ICC Ukraine page; Ukraine is trying to limit jurisdiction to Russian nationals and 'DNR and LNR terrorists'.

[209] Shane Darcy, 'Aggression by P5 Security Council Members: Time for ICC Referrals by the General Assembly', Just Security, 9 May 2022, https://www.justsec urity.org/80686/aggression-by-p5-security-council-members-time-for-icc-referrals-by-the-general-assembly/.. For my notes on the subject including discussion of ICC jurisdiction for other crimes - Du Cane, "Charge of War of Aggression in Ukraine Invasion".

[210] Gordon Brown, 'Statement Calling for the Creation of a Special Tribunal for the Punishment of the Crime of Agression Against Ukraine', March 2022, https://gordonandsarahbrown.com/wp-content/uploads/2022/03/Combined-Statement-and-Declaration.pdf.. Refer also to Tom Dannenbaum, 'Mechanisms for Criminal Prosecution of Russia's Aggression against Ukraine', Just Security, 12 March 2022, https://www.justsecurity.org/80626/mechanisms-for-criminal-prosecution-of-russias-aggression-against-ukraine/..

no matter the meagre precedents presented.[211]

That said Putin's performative kidnapping and Russification of Ukrainian children will stand in the annals of international law as an example of what not do. Putin has appeared on television discussing and congratulating the main organiser of the kidnapping of Ukrainian children – he is therefore directly implicated along with his henchwoman.[212] As I have mentioned, this war crime can also be re-qualified as genocide. Why then are intelligent, active and educated voices crying for an international tribunal for the crime of aggression, an abstract crime promoted by the Russians at Nuremberg (!) to minimize the Holocaust claim of greatest crime of the war, when Putin has been kidnapping children to Russify them?[213] The evidence for the genocidal kidnapping of children is horrific, stunning and clear.[214] It might be cynical but necessary for me to point out that the ICC issuing arrest warrants in March 2023 might be an attempt to remind the world of the ICC's existence and jurisdiction for actual serious atrocities, not the 'supreme crime' nonsense that the Russian Soviets forced on the world at Nuremberg.

As we can see, the state of international criminal law at the end of the twentieth century and the beginning of the twenty-first is completely different to that of the end of the nineteenth and beginning of the twentieth. Lemkin, Lauterpacht, De Vabres, Pella and

---

[211] An excellent article which might still be too complex for the layman - 'A New Court to Prosecute Russia's Illegal War?', 29 March 2023, https://www.crisisgroup.org/global-ukraine/new-court-prosecute-russias-illegal-war.

[212] International Criminal Court, 'ICC Arrest Warrants in the Situation of Ukraine: Statement by President Piotr Hofmański - YouTube', accessed 29 March 2023, https://www.youtube.com/watch?reload=9&v=FbKhCAaRLfc&embeds_euri=https%3A%2F%2Fwww.icc-cpi.int%2F&feature=emb_imp_woyt.

[213] Dustin Du Cane, 'Calling Crime of Aggression the "supreme Crime" Is an Insult to the Victims of Genocide', Substack newsletter, *Fallout* (blog), 11 January 2023, https://fallout.substack.com/p/calling-crime-of-aggression-the-supreme; Luke Harding, '"It's a Slam Dunk": Philippe Sands on the Case against Putin for the Crime of Aggression', *The Guardian*. Guardian News and Media, 31 March 2022, https://www.theguardian.com/law/2022/mar/30/vladimir-putin-ukraine-crime-aggression-philippe-sands.

[214] 'Russia's Systematic Program for the Re-Education & Adoption of Ukraine's Children - Ukraine', 14 February 2023, https://reliefweb.int/report/ukraine/russias-systematic-program-re-education-adoption-ukraines-children.

Makarewicz would be shocked or delighted that even the head of a continent-sized superpower armed with weapons of incomparable power, could even be threatened with criminal proceedings by a super-national Hague-based court. We have more or less defined crimes of genocide, war crimes and crimes against humanity. We have implemented complicated judicial procedure mechanisms. We have countries declaring never again... and building mechanisms in theory to stop them.

But we are wary of declaring genocide, as discussed earlier in the case of the United Nations. There is a legal reason for the fear of politicians and diplomats to use the genocide word. In 2005 the UN held one of its regular World Summits. That produced a 'World Summit Outcome Document, nr A/RES/60/1:[215]

> "138. Each individual State has the responsibility to protect its populations from genocide, war crimes, ethnic cleansing and crimes against humanity. This responsibility entails the prevention of such crimes, including their incitement, through appropriate and necessary means. We accept that responsibility and will act in accordance with it."

The contents of paragraphs 138-140 were reframed by the UN Secretary-General in 2009 to provide us with three 'Pillars' of what was labelled 'the Responsibility to Protect':

- Pillar one-The protection responsibilities of the State,
- Pillar two -International assistance and capacity-building,
- Pillar three-Timely and decisive response.216

Look at pillar three. The world powers who happily signed the declaration in 2005 seem worried at the Responsibility to Protect being leveraged to force an actual intervention against Russia.[217] Perhaps

---

[215] UN, 'United Nations Office on Genocide Prevention and the Responsibility to Protect', United Nations, n.d., https://www.un.org/en/genocideprevention/about-responsibility-to-protect.shtml..

[216] Secretary General, 'Report of the Secretary-General: Implementing the Responsibility to Protect - United Nations and the Rule of Law', United Nations, n.d., https://www.un.org/ruleoflaw/blog/document/report-of-the-secretary-general-implementing-the-responsibility-to-protect/..

[217] On diplomatic nuances, Nicolas Tenzer, *Ukraine: Let's Be Careful Not to Divide Europe - and the Alliance." Desk Russie* (Nicolas Tenzer, 2022), https://en.desk-russie.e

at the time the resolution was passed it was thought that only non-European conflicts would be covered by the responsibility to protect and drones and black-clad ninja special soldiers could be used to kill or capture, mostly kill, brown and black people. That assumption completely ignored Russian incursions at its borders and the rise of Russian fascism as well as the fact that Srebrenica had happened just a decade before. 'Responsibility to protect' in 2022 is currently a legal fiction of the type that the Genocide Convention was for decades after 1948. Russia murders, burns, and rapes and some of the world send weapons to Ukraine but mostly looks on. This is not new, since 2005, the world has not prevented atrocities in Afghanistan, Syria, Libya, Yemen, Somalia, Myanmar and elsewhere.[218] The charge of ignoring the declaration may be a tad unfair in the case of Libya because the responsibility to protect was mentioned at the time of a Security Council resolution which became the basis of NATO air strikes in 2011.[219] Gaddafi did not have nuclear weapons, which may have been his 'mistake' as they would have given NATO pause. Putin however has plenty of them. So, for now, the world shirks from 'officially', Biden missteps aside, calling the war in Ukraine genocide, presumably because:

> "A finding that genocide has occurred is widely perceived as carrying a special stigma, and as entailing an imperative to treat the conduct in question as the worst of the worst." — Todd Buchwald, U.S. Ambassador and Special Coordinator for Global Criminal Justice from 2015-2017.

Buchwald also stated there are no binding responsibilities for the

---

u/2022/05/28/ukraine-lets-be-careful.html. Aslo Todd Buchwald, 'Genocide Determinations and Ukraine: A Q&A with Fmr. Ambassador Todd Buchwald', *Just Security*, 6 July 2022, https://www.justsecurity.org/81903/genocide-determinations-and-ukraine-a-qa-with-fmr-ambassador-todd-buchwald/..

[218] Peter Lee, 'Ukraine the UN's "Responsibility to Protect" Doctrine Is a Hollow Promise for Civilians under Fire', *The Week*. The Week, 8 March 2022, https://www.theweek.in/wire-updates/international/2022/03/08/fgn24-un-doctrine-ukraine-crisis.html.. For a more balanced review, Noamane Cherkaoui, 'Policy as Implementation: Reconsidering the Responsibility to Protect Doctrine', *Policy Center*, 13 May 2022, https://www.policycenter.ma/publications/policy-implementation-reconsidering-responsibility-protect-doctrine..

[219] UN Security Council, 'Resolution S/RES/1970 (2011) | United Nations Security Council', accessed 13 October 2022, https://www.un.org/securitycouncil/s/res/1970-%282011%29.

world to prevent and counteract genocide. Buchwald even says that whether there are 'moral' responsibilities is 'complicated'. The railway to Auschwitz is open with "In this sense, the responsibility would be no greater or less in the context of genocide than in the context of these other crimes."

As I end this essay on words of the fear of calling genocide, genocide, I would discuss Lemkin's life after the (deeply limited) Genocide Convention was agreed upon. As the world divided into Cold War blocs and genocide erupted in the wake of decolonisation and Soviet and American imperial wars, Lemkin's final years were unhappy.[220] The United States refused to ratify the Genocide Convention causing much despair to Lemkin, who spent much of his time lobbying Lithuanian, Polish and Ukrainian diasporas, to convince their representatives of the need to ratify it, see Soviet Genocide in Ukraine. Lemkin fell into contradiction when he realised that the American right was fearful of the Genocide Convention being used against American segregation policies and he became a paradoxical supporter of McCarthyism and vocal critic of civil-rights protests.[221] Lemkin died in 1959, perhaps thinking that his great project had failed. Supposedly however he was at peace and enjoying life by that time.[222] Lemkin's last great final hurrah was the afore-mentioned Soviet Genocide in Ukraine, a speech which sadly was never officially published in his lifetime and disappeared for a long time into his archives like much of his unfinished work.[223] Lemkin at the end of his life could not understand why the United States could not use Soviet genocide in Ukraine against the Soviet Union for its democratic political purposes but also above all for justice and prevention.

> "For the Soviet national unity is being created, not by any union of ideas and

---

[220] For the politics of the period, see Anton Weiss-Wendt, *A Rhetorical Crime: Genocide in the Geopolitical Discourse of the Cold War* (New Brunswick: Rutgers University Press, 2018)..

[221] Anton Weiss-wendt, 'Hostage of Politics: Raphael Lemkin on "Soviet Genocide"', *Journal of Genocide Research* 7, no. 4 (December 2005): 551–59, https://doi.org/10.1080/14623520500350017..

[222] Irvin-Erickson, *Concept*. 229.

[223] Ibid., chapter 7, subchapter: "The Cold War and the Civil Rights Movement"

of cultures, but by the complete destruction of all cultures and of all ideas save one – the Soviet." – Raphael Lemkin.²²⁴

Replace Soviet with Russian.

Russian culture is weaponised in the current war.²²⁵ Russians are loudly objecting to removal or limiting of Russian cultural symbols in Ukraine and the West, viewing it as an existential threat and proof of evil outside intentions while physical genocide is taking place.²²⁶ Meanwhile hated Soviet monuments, as symbols of occupation and oppression, are toppling all over Central and Eastern Europe as populations realize that the bear of the rodina military, drunk on genocide and false history vodka, will never be happy and cannot be celebrated as it genocides across Ukraine.²²⁷

> "The ICC occupies an important place in the ecosystem of international justice, and the United States supports the investigation by the ICC Prosecutor, who received an unprecedented referral of the situation in Ukraine by 43 States Parties last year." - Beth Van Schaack, Ambassador-At-Large For Global Criminal Justice Office Of Global Criminal Justice²²⁸

As a final note we have a situation where the United States supports ICC investigation of Putin and Russian international crimes in

---

[224] Lemkin, *Soviet genocide*. 36, the last sentence in his speech.
[225] Peter Dickinson, 'Putin Has Forced Ukrainians to View Russian Culture as a Weapon of War', *Atlantic Council*, 8 August 2022, https://www.atlanticcouncil.org/blogs/ukrainealert/putin-has-forced-ukrainians-to-view-russian-culture-as-a-weapon-of-war/.
[226] UN Press, '"Russophobia" Term Used to Justify Moscow's War Crimes in Ukraine, Historian Tells Security Council | UN Press', accessed 15 March 2023, htt ps://press.un.org/en/2023/sc15226.doc.htm. Also see Ian Garner, *Z Generation: Into the Heart of Russia's Fascist Youth* (S.l.: Hurst & Co, 2023).
[227] Aaron Eglitis, 'Latvia Topples Soviet-Era World War II Monument in Swipe at Russia', *Bloomberg.Com*. *Bloomberg*, 25 August 2022, https://www.bloomberg.com/news/articles/2022-08-25/latvia-topples-soviet-world-war-ii-monument-in-swipe-at-russia. See a report on Ukrainian destruction of Russian language books in response to the invasion. Guy Davies, 'How the Russia-Ukraine Conflict Became a Cultural War', ABC News, accessed 3 March 2023, https://abcnews.go.com/International/russia-ukraine-conflict-cultural-war/story?id=97332345.
[228] 'Ambassador Van Schaack's Remarks', *United States Department of State* (blog), accessed 29 March 2023, https://www.state.gov/ambassador-van-schaacks-remarks/.

Ukraine.[229] But the United States is not a party to the Rome Statute and shows no burning intent to join. And neither is or does Ukraine, possibly because of too much consultation with American politicians and soldiers on the of hypothetical threats of international criminal justice to our brave soldiers who have never committed any war crimes and never will. A viewpoint the Russians, who undoubtedly and undeniably commit the vast majority of crimes in Ukraine also share with them — our soldiers are always saints, only yours are criminals, always. This essay started with a comment on the need for justice in war and justice after it, for all criminals and victims, though there are many more Russians in the former category and many more Ukrainians in the latter. The paradoxes of international criminal law are many. But an imperfect system is still a system. Good is better than unobtainable perfect, something the whatabout Iraq, Syria, Palestine crowd forget.[230]

---

[229] Guardian Staff, '"It's Justified": Joe Biden Welcomes ICC Arrest Warrant for Vladimir Putin | Joe Biden | The Guardian'.

[230] Amnesty International USA [@amnestyusa], 'BREAKING: Amnesty's Annual Report Paints a Disturbing Picture of the State of Human Rights in 2022. As Hypocritical States Pick and Choose Which Rules to Ignore with Impunity, Worldwide Respect for Human Rights Is Deteriorating. Read for Yourself', Tweet, *Twitter*, 28 March 2023, https://twitter.com/amnestyusa/status/1640715614934237185. Hypocritical is an apt word to use when describing Amnesty International which managed to accuse the Ukrainian military of not saving civilians from being shot at by Russians in 2022. Sergei Kutzenov, 'Zelenskyy [SIC!] Slams Amnesty International over Critical Military Report — POLITICO', accessed 30 March 2023, https://www.politico.eu/article/ukraine-rejects-amnesty-international-report-accusing-troops-of-endangering-civilians/.

8. RUSSIAN LAW OF WAR

Dustin Du Cane

"Gawd, those Ukrainian grannies would spend their burial savings to be raped by Russian soldiers... They [Ukrainian children] should have been drowned in the Tysyna River. Just drown those children, drown them" - Antoni Krasovsky, Russia Today tv (RT) director of broadcasting, journalist, March 6th 2023[1]

This essay will examine Russian law within the context of:

- domestic implementation of international humanitarian law, i.e., putting it into Russian books of laws,
- internalisation of the law, whether the Russian military and executive are aware of the law and attempt to follow it, as well as notes on the application of law in practise.

This essay attempts to give the reader a basic legal framework to assess the undeniable atrocities committed, being committed and that will be committed, in Ukraine, by Russia, in the context of the past, present and future.

Another fundamental question raised in this essay is how and if Russia attempts to follow international humanitarian law and criminal law—specifically how the law is communicated to its soldiers - considering how its soldiers, politicians and propagandists and politicians seem to hold the concepts of Geneva and Hague law in contempt. They seem to hold the law in contempt while either committing, ordering, and inciting genocide. An attempt is made to answer are they aware of the law or do they even care?

---

[1] Julia Davis, '"Morality Shouldn't Get in the Way" — Russia's Genocidal State Media', CEPA, 13 March 2023, https://cepa.org/article/morality-shouldnt-get-in-the-way-russias-genocidal-state-media/; *RT's Director of Broadcasting Anton Krasovsky Suggests Drowning or Burning Ukrainian Children*, 2022, https://www.youtube.com/watch?v=8lkshypC2Rk (accessed 30 April 2023).

Knowing the law

> "Since Western diplomats have signed these treaties, they ought to insist that the Soviet Union, having also signed them, should explain to its soldiers, officers, and generals what they contain, and should include in its official regulations special paragraphs forbidding certain acts in war. Only then would there be any sense in painting on the huge red crosses." — Bogdanovich Rezun - Victor Suvorov.[2]

Major Vladimir Bogdanovich Rezun, of Victor Suvorov pseudonym fame, finished the elite Frunze Red Banner Higher Military Command School in Kyiv and the even more elite GRU Military Diplomatic Academy in Moscow. The quote is about Rezun not knowing what red crosses on ambulances meant during some NATO exercises that he watched after defection. Exasperated by his ignorance, Western officers explained to him that the Soviet Union had signed treaties that mean appropriately marked ambulances were not legal targets. Rezun explained back that did not matter because Soviet soldiers would view red crosses as aiming points.[3] Rezun had spent the first part of his Soviet life in advanced Russian military education and the second part as a 'diplomat', a cover for his role as spy. If anybody in the Soviet system should have known what the red crosses on vehicles meant, it should have been him, but he did not. What chance did a semi-literate non-Russian speaking conscript from a Soviet Asiatic republic in the 1970s have of knowing what red crosses meant? Or in 2022?[4]

> "According to all conventions, it is forbidden to touch medical crosses at all, but for Russians, it is like a target, " says the girl."[5]

---

[2] Viktor Suvorov, *Spetsnaz: The Story behind the Soviet SAS* (London: Grafton, 1989).

[3] Shooting at Red Cross marked vehicles is not a specific crime under current Russian law unlike say Ukrainian.

[4] Amy Mackinnon, 'Russia Is Sending Its Ethnic Minorities to the Front Lines in Ukraine', accessed 15 March 2023, https://foreignpolicy.com/2022/09/23/russia-partial-military-mobilization-ethnic-minorities/.

[5] Victoria Andreeva, 'She Pulled the Dead from the Car to Help the Living. Frontline Stories of Combat Medicine', *Pravda UA*, 15 July 2022, https://life.pravda.com.ua/society/2022/07/15/249554/. Also 'Destruction and Devastation: One

The quotes from Rezun and the Ukrainian medic above set up two questions– how does Russia implement in its legal system and then teach and apply the rules of war? The two subjects are intimately connected. A law on paper means nothing if not communicated to the addressee (through information on international or implemented domestic law) and then accepted, respected and followed by that addressee (the process of application via internalisation). This was an issue recognised by the deeply practical authors of the Geneva Conventions:

> "The High Contracting Parties undertake to respect and to ensure respect for the present Convention in all circumstances". – common article 1 to all the Geneva Conventions."[6]

More importantly for this book, Article 5 of the Genocide Convention requires states to implement necessary legislation and to provide effective penalties for persons guilty of genocide. The lawyers drafting international law knew that bayonets on the ground needed to be taught right and wrong. They also wished to invalidate the 'orders are orders' excuse. That defence had appeared as far back as the von Hagenbach trial centuries earlier.

The Genocide Convention and Geneva Conventions do need to be implemented into domestic law—they are part of international criminal law and binding on all persons and states. Domestic implementation is useful for three reasons:

- Ease of communication—those affected can read the law in their own language;

Year of Russia's Assault on Ukraine's Health Care System - Ukraine | ReliefWeb', 21 February 2023, https://reliefweb.int/report/ukraine/destruction-an d-devastation-one-year-russias-assault-ukraines-health-care-system. For the murder of a Red Cross helper see Meduza, '"They Weren't Fighting Soldiers - They Were Fighting Regular People" the 17 Civilians Killed during the Russian Occupation of Andriivka', 20 August 2022, https://meduza.io/en/feature/202 2/08/20/they-weren-t-fighting-soldiers-they-were-fighting-regular-people.

[6] Refer to Luigi Conorelli and Laurence Boisson Chazournes, 'Common Article 1 of the Geneva Conventions Revisited: Protecting Collective Interests', *ICRC. 1*, 31 March 2000, https://www.icrc.org/en/doc/resources/documents/article/other/57jqcp.htm. International Committee of the Red Cross [ICRC].

- Reinforcement of acceptance and confirmation of the binding nature of international law - implementation underlines that international law is not just a political but a solemn undertaking by the state;
- Providing effective sanctions mechanisms—the Genocide Convention and Geneva Conventions are not criminal and criminal procedure codes in that they do not cover investigative, procedural and punishments frameworks (note that the Rome Statute does) and domestic law provides an interpretation, investigative, procedural and punishment framework for internal and international purposes. A local policeman or prosecutor will find it easier to operate within domestic law.

Turning to Russia specifically, a few, not all, specific breaches of the Geneva Conventions were implemented in the Soviet law books as punishable offences via the Criminal Code of the Russian Soviet Federative Socialist Republic of 1960—but without direct reference to the Conventions.[7] This shows how little value the Soviet state attached to the Geneva Conventions as such, as discussed in Rezun's quote. The Russian Federation inherited these provisions as a successor to the Russian Soviet Federative Socialist Republic.[8] The current Criminal Code of The Russian Federation of 1996 (amended 2012) ("Russian Criminal Code"), goes into more detail in Chapter 34. Crimes Against the Peace and Security Mankind with the following headings and crimes:[9]

"Art 353—Planning, Preparing, Unleashing, or Waging on Aggressive

---

[7] Refer to USSR Soviet, 'Criminal Code of the Russian Soviet Federative Socialist Republic (1960)', accessed 5 May 2022, https://en.wikisource.org/wiki/Criminal_Code_of_the_Russian_Soviet_Federative_Socialist_Republic_(1960). Article 266-269, covering battlefield pillage, violence towards inhabitants of a battle-zone, mistreatment of POWs and illegal wearing of symbols of the Red Cross and Red Crescent—note that in line with Rezun's quotes, this does not cover shooting at Red Cross or Red Crescent marked vehicles and personnel.

[8] Legal successor to RSFSR or the USSR or just a renaming (rebranding)?

[9] Russian Federation Parliament, 'Criminal Code Russia - Imolin' (n.d.), https://www.imolin.org/doc/amlid/Russian_Federation_Criminal_Code.pdf.—unofficial translation.

War[10]

Art 354 - Public Appeals to Unleash an Aggressive War[11]

Art 355 - The Development, Manufacture, Stockpiling, Acquisition or Sale of Mass-Destruction Weapons

Art. 356 - Use of Banned Means and Methods of Warfare[12]

Art 357 — Genocide - Actions aimed at the complete or partial extermination of a national, ethnic, racial, or religious group as such by killing its members, inflicting grave injuries to their health, forcible prevention of childbirth, forcible transfer of children, forcible resettlement, or by any other method of creating living conditions meant for the physical destruction of the members of this group.[13]

Art 358 — Ecocide

Art 359 — Mercenarism

Article 360 - Assaults on Persons or Institutions Enjoying International Protection'[14]

---

[10] The irony here is only on par with the Soviet Union claiming at Nuremberg that Germany's greatest crime was war of aggression. Dustin Du Cane, 'Hitler Ally Day', *Fallout* (blog), 17 September 2022, https://fallout.substack.com/p/hitler-ally-day. This author views the charge of war of aggression as a distraction when Russia and Putin personally have committed more grievous and more easily provable crimes that do not raise the 'whatabout Iraq' defence - Dustin Du Cane, 'Charge of War of Aggression in Ukraine Invasion', *Fallout*, 16 August 2022, https://fallout.substack.com/p/charge-of-war-of-aggression-in-ukraine. Ukraine as the victim however gets to choose the avenues of recourse.

[11] Lemkin drafted article 113 of the Polish Criminal Code of 1932 discussed in the other chapter.

[12] Refer to notes on Manual on International Humanitarian Law for the Armed Forces of the Russian Federation (2001) further in this chapter. FP Explainers, 'Russia "Fires" White Phosphorous Bombs in Ukraine: What Are These Deadly Munitions That "Rain down Hell"?', accessed 16 March 2023, https://www.firstpost.com/explainers/russia-ukraine-war-white-phosphorous-bombs-deadly-dangerous-munitions-rain-down-hell-12296992.html.

[13] Cited in full to underline differences with Article II of the Genocide Convention which exist in the Russian text: mental harm and physical destruction *in part* is not covered, *forcible prevention of childbirth* is not the same wording, forcible transfer of children is slightly reworded for some reason. Azeem Ibrahim, 'Moscow's Genocidal Plans in Ukraine Include Child Kidnapping', accessed 16 March 2023, https://foreignpolicy.com/2023/03/01/russia-theft-children-kidnapping-ukraine-genocide/.

[14] Also, the last article of the Russian Criminal Code. There is no prohibition against or sanction for misuse of Red Cross or Red Crescent despite the previous Soviet legislation on the subject. For comparison refer to the Ukrainian Rada, 'Criminal Code of Ukraine - Imolin' (n.d.), https://www.imolin.org/doc/amlid/Ukraine_Criminal%20Code%202001.pdf. Ukrainian law sanctions misuse of international aid symbols, as well as attacking marked objects and persons — as war crimes, art. 444-445.

Art. 356 of the Russian Criminal Code possibly, vaguely, and imprecisely (all errors in formulating criminal law) implements some Geneva and Hague Conventions. They may be additionally implemented by the other paragraphs of Chapter 34 and art. 340 which cover soldiers' duties relating to military rules.[15] So breaches of the Geneva Conventions in the form of "the cruel treatment of prisoners of war or civilians, deportation of civilian populations, plunder of national property in occupied territories, and use in a military conflict of means and methods of warfare, banned by an international treaty of the Russian Federation" are punishable. The Geneva Conventions and other treaties are not named or referred to directly. Perhaps intentionally. The Russian Criminal Code is of course not the only source of law and norms.[16"]

Applying the law

We now come to the connected issues of domestic implementation and internalisation of law within the Russian military and power structures. Law must be internalised to be applied. To internalise is to accept or absorb a process that involves a change in people's intrinsic motivation to act in accord with the law's obligations. Discussions on the 'pieces of paper' signed between states and their customs aka international law tend to concentrate on legal theory, drafting processes and case law but rarely get down to the question of how or whether the persons (soldiers and others in our case) engaging in activities are educated on that law and have 'internalised' the law. It is well and good to list the signatories of the Fourth Geneva Convention for instance and then discuss domestic legislation but that does not mean that the agents of a signatory, aka the organs and soldiers of that state, even know the contents of the Convention. To put it plainly, has a soldier been instructed as to what the laws of war are and is he likely to follow those instructions? Do his officers even know them properly? Do people at the top care about the laws of war and what the soldier knows or even does? Does a

---

[15] Tuzmukhamedov, 'The Implementation of International Humanitarian Law in the Russian Federation'. 390.

[16] Refer to international military manuals listed by International Committee of the Red Cross at ICRC, 'III. Military Manuals', in *Customary IHL - III* (Military Manuals, n.d.), https://ihl-databases.icrc.org/customary-ihl/eng/docs/src_iimima

soldier know that genocide, above all, should not be committed? Without knowledge of the law, it is difficult to always obey it, though not impossible when a law follows general moral, cultural and social conventions. The Geneva Conventions are formulated to follow accepted customs and practises between nations so avoiding a serious breach of the conventions by a soldier in a democratic liberal society should be expected even without thorough schooling and education. Unfortunately this expectation often falls apart in the grime of war. Since the later Nuremberg trials, crime of aggression was an obsession of the first international trial, legal practice is that genocide is a customary law that all nations and citizens should abide by, regardless of the treaty.

> "This is a situation that caused PFC Porter to feel appropriately angry and frustrated and to look forward to raiding a village... Potter's state of emotional turmoil against the Vietnamese people probably accounts for his [acts]."[17]

Morality and the law turn murky in situations where soldiers are scared, hungry, tired, angry, vengeful, thirsty, bored, or drunk. Or simply are life-long criminals as is the case with most Russian mercenaries. Even the elite soldiers of Western democracy can and will engage in terrible crimes despite wide-scale schooling and education with numerous allegations against and prosecutions of the 'best of the best in special forces units as well as more typical units or 'security contractors'.[18] Modern Western 'special forces', 'warriors' and 'elite soldiers' have their problems.[19] Soldiers are supposed

---

[17]. US Navy psychiatrist report on Marine leader of a murder & rape raid in Vietnam against civilians. Lieutenant Colonel Gary D. Solis and U. S. Marine Corps History and Museums Division, *Marines and Military Law in Vietnam: Trial By Fire* (CreateSpace Independent Publishing Platform, 2013). 54.

[18]. For instance, the Nisour Square massacre in Bagdad in 2007 involving Blackwater Security Consulting mercenaries. For a more ominous case of elite soldiers - Nick McKenzie, 'War Crimes Investigators Narrow Focus to Three Key Targets, Including Roberts-Smith', The Age, 19 January 2023, https://www.theage.com.au/national/war-crimes-investigators-narrow-focus-to-three-key-targets-incl uding-roberts-smith-20230118-p5cdge.html.

[19] Ryan Noordally, 'On the Toxicity of the "Warrior" Ethos " Wavell Room', 9 June 2021, https://wavellroom.com/2020/04/28/on-the-toxicity-of-the-warrior-et hos/.

to be taught the laws of war and their superiors, civilian or other, should know those laws and not give orders that force the soldier to breach them. Responsibility and the responsibility to know to go up and down the command line. The non-binding precursor to the Hague Conventions, the Oxford Manual of Law, recognised the need for 'laws to be known among all people' back in 1880. [20] However, there is nothing more ridiculous than teaching an exhausted and/or bored soldier convention articles in a classroom as if they were law students cramming for an exam and then expecting them to follow the laws of war if they have just seen their best friend shot by an unseen sniper. Or even when an insane close to elderly dictator is screaming about denazification and the wife back home is asking about a nice new Ukrainian laptop and the Russian state is blatantly engaging in national scale looting. This even regardless of the endemic systemic thievery of the organised criminal group with nuclear weapons that is the Russian state.[21] Generals, politicians and priests are thieves in the Russian state.

> "Why, it's fine. What Russian person would steal nothing? ... Well, think about it, Sofia is going to school—she will f*cking need a laptop, too." — Anon Russian wife to husband.[22]

Western militaries have varied schemes of teaching soldiers the laws of war, involving officers, lawyers, chaplains, and even civilian ethics teachers.[23] Specialised training is given to future trainers. The US has a complex system overseen by the Department of Defense which requires three-fold compliance with the law of war, Article 3 of the 1949 Geneva Conventions (Martens Clause) and the

---

[20]. Refer to previous chapter and available at 'Oxford Manual, 1880." Treaties, States Parties, and Commentaries' (1880), https://ihl-databases.icrc.org/ihl/INTRO/140%3FOpenDocument.

[21].

[22] Via Iryna Balachuk, 'Looting Russian Soldier's Wife Asks for Laptop and New Sports Clothes from Ukraine—Intercepted Calls', in *Ukrayinska Pravda*. *Ukrayinska Pravda*, 2022, https://www.pravda.com.ua/eng/news/2022/03/30/7335744/./. Intercepted calls are unverified, so pinch of salt.

[23] For references Laurie R. Blank and Gregory P. Noone, *Law of War Training: Resources for Military and Civilian Leaders* (Washington, D.C: United States Institute of Peace Press, 2013).

principles of 'military necessity, humanity, distinction, proportionality, and honor'.[24] A key element of the above policy is to implement varied training policies through three levels of training: Level A for soldiers, basic aka don't murder, steal and rape, Level B annual and deployment training for soldiers, which is conducted by lawyers or paralegals and Level C, officer training including the law of war issues for planning, aka don't put down an artillery stonk on a hospital because you have a bad feeling about it.[25] Significantly, a 'Battlefield Ethics Training Program' was implemented in 2006 following widespread reported abuse in Iraq, and when a study revealed less than 50% of US soldiers would be willing to 'snitch' on comrades for relatively minor abuses, with roughly the same percentage willing to torture captives for information.[26] At the time only half of the soldiers considered non-combatants should be treated with respect and dignity. Even the murder of innocents would only result in reporting a unit member for 55% of soldiers, 40% for Marines specifically. A quarter to a third of soldiers reported that their superiors did not make it clear that they should not abuse civilians, and a quarter reported facing ethical situations to which they were unable to respond, despite 90% (?) reporting having received training on behaviour towards non-combatants. It is also highly problematic that countries often refuse to even mention war crimes committed by their soldiers—even when prosecuted for them.[27] For instance no US Marine was ever tried for war crimes in Vietnam and this is still justified by the Department of Defense: "When members of a State's armed forces or other

---

[24] 'Dodd 2311.01, "Dod Law of War Program,"' 2 July 2020, https://www.esd.whs.mil/Portals/54/Documents/DD/issuances/dodd/231101p.pdf?ver=2020-07-02-143157-007. Department of Defense Law of War Manual, updated December 2016, see Google as hyperlink is too long.

[25] Chris Jenks, *The Efficacy of the U.S. Army's Law of War Training Program* (Lieber Institute West Point, 2020), https://lieber.westpoint.edu/efficacy-u-s-armys-law-of-war-training-program/.

[26] Refer to Office of the Surgeon. Multinational Force-Iraq.; Office of the Surgeon General (Army), Washington, DC., 'Mental Health advisery Team (MHAT) IV Operation Iraqi Freedom 05-07. Final Report', n.d., https://ntrl.ntis.gov/NTRL/dashboard/searchResults/titleDetail/PB2010103335.xhtml.

[27]

personnel violate the law of war, that State generally prosecutes those persons for offenses under ordinary domestic law or military law."[28] Not only are US soldiers protected from charges of war crimes, the protection of soldiers extends to the Pentagon refusing cooperation with the International Criminal Court [ICC] about Russian war crimes in Ukraine in fear of creating a 'precedent'.[29] This author sums up the US position as, it's only a war crime if the enemy does it and even then, it's better not to punish it, lest one day one an US soldier might be punished. 'Never again', indeed.

It is taken as a given that a US general as well as the president will know the laws of war and on genocide or at very least will have professional advisers who can try and prevent a breach or at least advise against it. In practice the role of advisers and lawyers is problematic and much has been written on how it is not how the executive follows the law but the interpretation of law follows the executive. At this point, a reader may be checking this book's cover and wondering why this essay is citing US military statistics and policies.

Unfortunately, these statistics, policies and approaches constitute a baseline when considering Russian genocide and military and political behaviour in Ukraine, especially as regards a superpower. When half of the professional soldiers of the world's greatest superpower, a law-obsessed democracy built on ideas of liberty and protection from tyranny, face serious legal and ethical issues in their pursuit of war, what hope is there for the internalisation and application of the rules and ethics of war and the ban on genocide by the badly trained, badly motivated, poverty-stricken, demoralised, abused cynical soldiers of a near fascist criminal oligarchical

---

[28] 'Dodd 2311.01, "Dod Law of War Program,"'. Also Solis and Division, *Marines and Military Law in Vietnam*. The first Australian soldier to be charged with a war crime in Australia was only charged in March 2023, Sophie Richards, 'Australia Soldier Charged with War Crimes in Afghanistan', 21 March 2023, ht tps://www.jurist.org/news/2023/03/australia-soldier-charged-with-war-crimes-in-afghanistan/.

[29] Charlie Savage, 'Pentagon Blocks Sharing Evidence of Possible Russian War Crimes With Hague Court', *The New York Times*, 8 March 2023, sec. U.S., https://www.nytimes.com/2023/03/08/us/politics/pentagon-war-crimes-hague.html.

state in a patriotic 'existential' war of 'denazification'.³⁰ Specifically, it can be argued that a statistic that soldiers say they are twice as likely to mistreat a non-combatant when angry is applicable across cultural and national boundaries. Unit casualties as well as handling bodies also increase the self-declared likelihood of mistreatment. However, a soldier that abuses civilians tends also to be a bad soldier in general. The military therefore has a self-interest in providing prevention and accountability for the abuse of the laws of war—a war criming soldier is bad at fighting.³¹ 'Bad apples' do not make good fighting soldiers.³² A brute, a liar, a thief, a rapist and a murderer do not fight well, they oppress well.

Turning suddenly back to the subject of this book and confirming Rezun's assertions re: lack of knowledge, let alone internalisation of the international laws of war, the Armed Forces of the USSR only learnt of the Geneva Conventions en masse and only in theory in 1990 via USSR Minister of Defence Order No. 75 of 1990, which promulgated the Geneva Conventions of 1949 and the two Additional Protocols of 1977 together with Guidelines for the Application of International Humanitarian Law.³³ In theory, because it's one thing to sign a treaty, another to promulgate it (publish it so the legal fiction is that it is known) and a completely different thing for

---

[30] Timothy Snyder, 'Opinion | We Should Say It. Russia Is Fascist.', *The New York Times*, 19 May 2022, sec. Opinion, https://www.nytimes.com/2022/05/19/opinion/russia-fascism-ukraine-putin.html. Lauren Sforza, 'Putin Says Ukraine War Poses Existential Threat to "Russian People"', Text, *The Hill* (blog), 26 February 2023, https://thehill.com/policy/international/3874880-putin-says-ukraine-war-poses-existential-threat-to-russian-people/.

[31] Roisin Burke, 'Troop Discipline, the Rule of Law and Mission Operational Effectiveness in Conflict-Affected States', in *Essay. In Military Self-Interest in Accountability for Core International Crimes*, ed. Morten Bergsmo and Song (Brussels: Torkel Opsahl Academic EPublisher, 2015).

[32] Kai Chi Yam et al., 'From Good Soldiers to Psychologically Entitled: Examining When and Why Citizenship Behavior Leads to Deviance', *Academy of Management Journal* 60, no. 1 (February 2017): 373–96, https://doi.org/10.5465/amj.2014.0234.

[33] "However, the guidelines offered only limited instructions about the application of codified rules of international humanitarian law", Tuzmukhamedov, 'The Implementation of International Humanitarian Law in the Russian Federation'. 394.

a soldier to internalise and respect that treaty and its provisions.[34] In 2001 a 'new' Manual on International Humanitarian Law for the Armed Forces of the Russian Federation: "...for the purpose of studying and the observance by commanders, staffs of the tactical level, as well as all servicemen of the Armed Forces of the Russian Federation of the norms of international humanitarian law in the preparation and during the conduct of hostilities.[35] A line-by-line review of this manual and its provisions are outside the scope of this book but a review suggests an attempt at conformity with the Geneva Conventions. Under this manual, military commanders are required to follow humanitarian law and personally take part in 'the dissemination of knowledge' to subordinates, with the aid of unit legal advisers.[36]

The Russian manual states that: "Liability for crimes related to violation of the norms of international humanitarian law provided for by the Criminal Code of the Russian Federation is given in Appendix 5 to this Manual."[37] This is important to note because this Manual, therefore, becomes incorporated into the Russian Criminal Code via art. 356. The manual sub-chapter: "Features of the organisation of hostilities" strongly suggests the subordination of law to the military procedure: "The rules of international humanitarian law do not change the procedure established by combat regulations, but commanders and staffs must consider the need to comply with international humanitarian law when making decisions and planning combat operations." Article 42 of the Russian Criminal

---

[34] At the time of publication, there was a 300-page handbook, which according to Tuzmukhamedov only had eight pages as practical advice.

[35] Aleksei Romanovski, trans., 'Manual on International Humanitarian Law for the Armed Forces of the Russian Federation (2002)', *International Legal Studies* 99 (2022), https://digital-commons.usnwc.edu/ils/vol99/iss1/31. in Russian and unofficial. I was not able to find the source document perhaps because some Russian law is deliberately difficult to find.

[36] Additionally, they are supposed to 'set personal examples, ensure compliance by subordinates, and bring justice' as well as aiding the ICRC.

[37] A 426-word list of violations, all of which the Russians have committed in Ukraine. 'War Crimes in the 2022 Russian Invasion of Ukraine', in *Wikipedia*. Wikimedia Foundation, 12 June 2022, https://en.wikipedia.org/wiki/War_crimes_in_the_2022_Russian_invasion_of_Ukraine.

Code foresees orders as a valid defence for crimes unless the person committing the act knows the order to be illegal. Some fragments of the humanitarian law are very 'pragmatic', i.e. allowing civilian targets to be destroyed if 'they are used by the enemy'.[38] Kriegsraison which to be fair can also be found in Western codes of conduct.[39] There are other Russian acts regulating military conduct such as the Federal Law No. 76 of 27 May 1998 on the Status of the Military Personnel (as amended to 30 December 2012), where a soldier is required to: "respect the universally recognised principles and norms of international law and international treaties of the Russian Federation."[40] The Russian Federation's Service Regulations of the Armed Forces (1993) provide a similar obligation.[41]

That is all and good about the incorporation of international law into domestic laws and acts concerning military personnel but

---

[38] The term "Holocaust by artillery" seems to have been first used in writing by Philip W. Blood, 'A Holocaust by Artillery: Russian Military Operations in Ukraine', Substack newsletter, *Fallout* (blog), 24 April 2022, https://fallout.substac
k.com/p/a-holocaust-by-artillery-russian-military-operations-in-ukraine.

[39] Scott Horton, 'Kriegsraison or Military Necessity? The Bush Administration's Wilhelmine Attitude Towards the Conduct of War', *Fordham International Law Journal* 30, no. 3 (2006), https://core.ac.uk/download/pdf/144226859.pdf. That said a captured Russian military pilot has been sentenced for bombing a civilian broadcasting centre—an act very much in line with the theory and practise of NATO attacks on 'dual-use' communication centres (France may disagree). IMI, 'Russian Pilot Who Had Bombed the Kharkiv TV Tower Sentenced to 12 Years in Prison', 3 March 2023, https://imi.org.ua/en/news/russian-pilot-who-had-bombed-the-kharkiv-tv-tower-sentenced-to-12-years-in-prison-i5117
2. 'NATO Bombing of the Radio Television of Serbia Headquarters', in *Wikipedia*, 15 January 2023, https://en.wikipedia.org/w/index.php?title=NATO_bombing_of_the_Radio_Television_of_Serbia_headquarters&oldid=1133796997.

[40] Russian Federation Parliament, 'Russian Federation - Federal Law No. 76 of 27 May 1998 on the Status of the Military Personnel (as Amended to 30 December 2012).', accessed 8 March 2023, https://www.ilo.org/dyn/natlex/natlex4.detail?p_lang=en&p_isn=93582&p_count=96861.

[41] Gavin Butler, *Russia Is Forcing Conscripts to Fight, While Ukrainians Are Desperate to Enlist* (VICE, 2022), https://www.vice.com/en/article/5dgqen/russia-conscripts-ukraine-invasion-volunteers. Ukraine has in 2023 reportedly suffered with conscription issues. 'Ukraine Finds Stepping up Mobilisation Is Not so Easy | The Economist', accessed 15 March 2023, https://www.economist.com/europe/2023/02/26/ukraine-finds-stepping-up-mobilisation-is-not-so-easy.

what about internalisation? internalisation requires both communication of laws and their acceptance by the addressee in the form of conforming to those laws. internalisation will sometimes force the addressee to act against their basic instincts, cultural norms or even orders and service regulations.

> "You go there and rape Ukrainian women, just don't tell me anything. You got me? The main thing is use protection." Anon Russian wife to husband.[42]

Internalisation is an extremely difficult process, even in the case of Western troops, who are almost always highly trained military professionals, following the virtual elimination of conscription post-Cold War. [43]

It took until 1999 for the Russian Federation's Minister of Defence to issue Order No. 333 of 29 May 1999 "On Legal Training in the Armed Forces of the Russian Federation" (with an appendix concerning specific legal training). [44] Soviet soldiers were not trained in the Geneva Conventions at all, and it took the Russian Federation time to turn to this issue. The current Minister of Defence Order No. 250, of May 5, 2021, "On Legal Training in the Armed Forces of the Russian Federation" requires a purposeful, planned and organised process of information and awareness-raising influence to form the theoretical basis of legal consciousness, improve legal culture, and also improve the legal knowledge of the

---

[42] Allegedly. Ukrinform, 'Intercept: Wife of Russian Invader Tells Husband to "Rape Ukrainian Women."', *Ukrinform. Укринформ*, 12 April 2022, https://www.ukrinform.net/rubric-ato/3455685-intercept-wife-of-russian-invader-tells-husband-to-rape-ukrainian-women.html. Sexual assault is a common war crime in Ukraine - Stefaniia Bern and Anthony Deutsch, 'Exclusive: Ukraine Accuses Russian Snipers of Abusing Child, Gang Raping Mother', *Reuters*, 14 March 2023, sec. Europe, https://www.reuters.com/world/europe/ukraine-accuses-russian-snipers-abusing-child-gang-raping-mother-2023-03-14/.

[43] Refer to David Roberts, 'Teaching the Law of Armed Conflict to Armed Forces: Personal Reflections', *International Law Studies* 82, no. 1 (31 December 2006), https://digital-commons.usnwc.edu/ils/vol82/iss1/8. 122-134 in detail.

[44] Also, requirements for military leaders to know and disseminate the law in: Russian Minister of Defense, 'Приказ Министра Обороны РФ От 29.05.1999 N 333 "О Правовом Обучении в Вооруженных Силах Российской Федерации" (Утратил Силу) | ГАРАНТ [Order of the Minister of Defense on Legal Training]' (1999), https://base.garant.ru/1356371/. In Russian.

personnel of the Armed Forces.⁴⁵ We have a flowery piece of paper requiring 'legal training' to go with the Criminal Code of the Russian Federation and its military manuals. Russia states it is a world leader in following the rules of law: "IHL norms, including the obligation of commanders to comply with its provisions and demand their strict implementation from personnel, are reflected in the Russian legal system." ⁴⁶ The quoted paper tediously lists Russian law but no mention of actual training. The Russian lawyer authors even say that what Russia does about its compliance with the law is very secret and they are not saying: "This Article has no provisions on how exactly legal reviews should be conducted and does not impose an obligation on States to make their results public, nor to provide anyone with information 4 on the subject."

Is legal training implemented in any way, let alone sufficiently to allow internalisation, considering the generally terrible level of training of Russian soldiers, especially conscripts?⁴⁷ These are the same conscripts who are too poor, which correlates with unhealthy, substance dependent and uneducated, and too intellectually limited to avoid the horrors of Russian military service. A one to two-month basic training time barely gives the Russian army time to properly beat and rape conscripts, let alone instruct them in the niceties of international humanitarian law and the laws of war. ⁴⁸ Maybe the conscripts can combine revising the Geneva

---

45 Russian text should be available in the official law database - http://publicatio n.pravo.gov.ru but is not.
46 Russian Federation, 'Working Paper of the Russian Federation National Implementation of the Guiding Principles on Emerging Technologies in the Area of Lethal Autonomous Weapons Systems', 2020, https://documents.unoda.org/wp-content/uploads/2020/09/Ru-Commentaries-on-GGE-on-LAWS-guiding -principles1.pdf.
47 Kateryna Stepanenko, Frederick W. Kagan, and Brian Babcock-Lumish, *Explainer on Russian Conscription, Reserve, and Mobilization* (Institute for the Study of War, 2022), https://www.understandingwar.org/backgrounder/explainer-ru ssian-conscription-reserve-and-mobilization.
48 "Finally, I think it is important to consider whether and how well the law is actually being accepted and implemented by the soldier in battle even if training is perfect and the gaps are all filled.," Roberts, *Teaching*, 132.

Conventions with licking their toilets clean.[49] Do we expect the laws of war to be followed by a military and government that abuses its soldiers on every level and is in breach of its laws, including sending conscripts illegally into a war?[50] Can a soldier served decade-old rations by billionaire Prigozhin, who runs his competing military, not be expected to steal chickens before his round of post-meal rape, torture and murder?[51] We have already seen that the 'best' soldiers of the West who have far better training, never suffered from dedovshchina and generally don't come from poverty-stricken deprived backgrounds, are easily capable of violating the rules of war—even according to themselves.[52] Contempt for the rules of war and violation is a natural, and psychologically understandable, state for many soldiers and one that requires immense amounts of training combined with a culture of respect for the laws of war, appropriate doctrine and respect built into the command structure to avoid. Russian soldiers are, according to internal reports, often barely capable of handling their weapons after training.[53] Russian soldiers in letters to family have a litany of complaints that exceeds even the normal level of soldierly grumbling - and some families cynically refuse to talk with POWs while

---

[49] HRW, 'The Wrongs of Passage', 29 April 2015, https://www.hrw.org/report/2004/10/19/wrongs-passage/inhuman-and-degrading-treatment-new-recruits-russian-armed-forces.

[50] Reuters, 'Russia Acknowledges Conscripts Were Part of Ukraine Operation, Some Are Pows', 9 March 2022, https://www.reuters.com/world/europe/russia-acknowledges-conscripts-were-part-ukraine-operation-some-taken-prisoner-2022-03-09/.

[51] Tony Ward, 'Military History Is Repeating for Russia under Putin's Regime of Thieves', *The Conversation*, 5 June 2022, https://theconversation.com/military-history-is-repeating-for-russia-under-putins-regime-of-thieves-181164. Postscriptum - please see my reflections at the end of this book on the now deceased Prigozhin.

[52] Jenks, *The Efficacy of the U.S. Army's Law of War Training Program*. 'Dedovshchina' is the word for hazing and abuse of junior conscripts.

[53] Marek N. Posard and Khrystyna Holynska, Marek N. Posard and Khrystyna Holynska, 'Russia's Problems with Military Professionalization', *RAND Corporation*, 21 March 2022, https://www.rand.org/blog/2022/03/russias-problems-with-military-professionalization.html.

collecting death payments.[54] Russian soldiers deprived of ammunition, shelter, training and even food, routinely beg on video, the good tsar, Putin, who as always throughout Russia history is surrounded by bad boyars, to alleviate their fate.[55] Meanwhile Russia seems to have created the equivalent of modern-day janissaries with combat losses of 'ethnic', non-ethnically Russian, troops, suffering loss rates increasing proportionally to distance from Moscow and Leningrad.[56] This all must terribly affect morale regardless of Ukrainian actions. Demoralised soldiers consequentially, without diminishing their culpability, commit war crimes. Meanwhile 'colonial' troops have throughout history been known for their, mostly encouraged, savagery.[57] The death of a comrade creates a natural revenge impulse, even for a fed, well-trained and well-equipped soldier, as shown by already discussed studies on Western troops. This is important in the context that Russia seems to be taking

---

[54] Meduza, '"I'm 21 and I Really Want to Live" Investigative Journalists at Bellingcat and the Insider Obtain Complaints Submitted to Russia's Military by Betrayed Soldiers, Their Loved Ones, and Civilians in Ukraine's Warzone', trans. Kevin Rothrock, 11 August 2022, https://meduza.io/en/feature/2022/0 8/11/i-m-21-and-i-really-want-to-live. Michael Schwirtz et al., '"This Isn't War. It's the Destruction of the Russian People by Their Own Commanders."', *The Japan Times*, 18 December 2022, https://www.japantimes.co.jp/news/2022/12 /18/world/russia-destruction-leaders/.

[55] Natalia Mamonova, 'Vladimir Putin – a Tsar without Loyal Subjects?', accessed 15 March 2023, https://www.ui.se/utrikesmagasinet/analyser/2018/april/vl adimir-putin--a-tsar-without-loyal-subjects/. Kelsey Vlamis, 'Video Shows Russian Soldiers Complaining about "incompetence" of Their Commanders and Pleading Directly to Putin for Help', Business Insider, accessed 15 March 2023, https://www.businessinsider.com/video-russian-soldiers-plead-with-p utin-complain-about-commanders-2023-3.

[56] Ministry of DefenSegoece GB [@DefenceHQ], 'The Illegal and Unprovoked Invasion of Ukraine Is Continuing.', Tweet, *Twitter*, 12 March 2023, https://twitter.com/ DefenceHQ/status/1634801422985314304.

[57] iStories, '"The Commanders Don't Give a Shit about Us" in One Russian Brigade, around 700 Soldiers Have Refused to Fight. but Their Superiors Won't Let Them Leave', 19 August 2022, https://meduza.io/en/feature/2022/08/19 /the-commanders-don-t-give-a-shit-about-us. Yousur Al-Hlou et al., 'Caught on Camera, Traced by Phone: The Russian Military Unit That Killed Dozens in Bucha', *The New York Times*, 22 December 2022, sec. Video, https://www.nytim es.com/2022/12/22/video/russia-ukraine-bucha-massacre-takeaways.html.

terrible losses, especially in areas like Bakhmut in the Donetsk area.[58] These Russians soldiers and their opponents will naturally be less inclined to show mercy or follow the law of war when thrown into a desperate meat grinder. Discipline, in the form of blind obedience, in the Russian army has and is the absolute priority over ensuring the legality, rationality and necessity of orders.[59] The military manuals and laws already discussed make this clear. An order is order. However, this discipline still manages to collapse in the face of the meat-grinder of the Donetsk fronts.[60] War crimes are also a result of collapse of basic military discipline and mutiny.

The terrible combat results shown in 2022 by even 'elite' Russian units shows a deficiency in basic areas of military training, presumably as a result of pathological and dysfunctional structural issues.[61] The beginning of this essay starts with a quote from a book that in later chapter described in detail the terrifying elite of the peak Soviet army, the Spetsnaz. They were highly trained and completely amoral, by design, specialist killers, albeit highly disciplined in the army structure. Within units' brutality was the rule,

---

58 Isobel Koshiw, 'Ukrainian and Russian Casualties Mount as Battle for Central Bakhmut Rages | Ukraine | The Guardian', *The Guardian. Guardian News and Media*, 13 March 2023, https://www.theguardian.com/world/2023/mar/13/ukrainian-and-russian-casualties-mount-as-battle-for-central-bakhmut-rages. As of time of writing, both sides are taking heavy losses and the death of comrades discourages mercy. Asami Terajima, 'Battle of Bakhmut: Ukrainian Soldiers Worry Russians Begin to "Taste Victory"', 15 March 2023, https://kyivindependent.com/national/battle-of-bakhmut-ukrainian-soldiers-worry-russians-begin-to-taste-victory.

59 Alison K. Smith, 'Drunkenness and Disorder in the Imperial Russian Army', *The Russian Review*, 16 February 2023, russ.12437, https://doi.org/10.1111/russ.12437. Viktor Suvorov, *The Liberators: My Life in the Soviet Army*, 1st American ed. (New York: W.W. Norton, 1983).

60 Nataliya Vasilyeva, '"Why Should I Fight?": How Russian Soldiers Are Mutinying in Face of "Certain Death"', *The Telegraph*, 10 March 2023, https://www.telegraph.co.uk/world-news/2023/03/10/new-russian-army-unit-sent-find-soldiers-lost-chaos-faltering/.

61 Day to day reports from Press ISW, 'Ukraine Conflict Updates." Institute for the Study of War', 15 August 2022, https://www.understandingwar.org/backgrounder/ukraine-conflict-updates. Also in Human Rights Watch, *The Wrongs*, 4. Refer to Jack Watling, 'Just How Tall Are Russian Soldiers?', *Royal United Services Institute* (blog), 11 March 2022, https://www.rusi.org/explore-our-research/publications/rusi-defence-systems/just-how-tall-are-russian-soldiers.

especially towards younger soldiers, with prison-like power structures.[62] Many sources have stated that the Russian army is only a shadow of the Red Army, especially as regards soldier quality, even among the elite troops — however the prison power structures, and brutality remain while effectiveness and discipline have disappeare[63]

So Russian elite, contract, and conscripts soldiers have issues with basic training and discipline, let alone legal training, which will be described further later on. What about Russian mercenaries? Such as those of oligarch Prigozhin's Wagner Company, an equivalent to the notorious war criminal Dirlewanger Brigade whose members even the rest of the SS despised.[64] The Dirlewanger Brigade was recruited inter alia among the most depraved of criminal (non-political) German prisoners and the Russians have openly adopted this practice as well.[65] These prisoners suffer from even

---

[62] Suvorov, *Spetsnaz: The Story behind the Soviet SAS.*
[63] For example Antony Beevor, 'Putin Doesn't Realize How Much Warfare Has Changed', *The Atlantic. Atlantic Media Company,* 7 July 2022, https://www.theatlantic.com/ideas/archive/2022/03/putin-doesnt-realize-how-much-warfare-has-changed/627600/. Or Philip W. Blood, 'A Holocaust By Artillery: Russian Military Operations in Ukraine', Substack newsletter, *Fallout* (blog), 24 April 2022, https://fallout.substack.com/p/a-holocaust-by-artillery-russian-militar y-operations-in-ukraine. Also Michael Kofman and Rob Lee, 'Not Built for Purpose: The Russian Military's Ill-Fated Force Design', *War on the Rocks,* 2 June 2022, https://warontherocks.com/2022/06/not-built-for-purpose-the-russian -militarys-ill-fated-force-design/. See Philip Blood's essay: Putin's genocide: the case of the individual perpetrator.
[64] Prigozhin is wanted by the US DOJ with a nice FBI Most Wanted Poster. James Petrila and Phil Wasielewski, 'It's Time to Designate Wagner Group as a Foreign Terrorist organisation', *Lawfare,* 1 July 2022, https://www.lawfareblog.co m/its-time-designate-wagner-group-foreign-terrorist-organisation. Verstka, '"They're Not Counting on People Making It Home" How a Prisoner's Wife Thwarted the Wagner Group's Attempt to Send Inmates to Fight in Ukraine', 18 August 2022, https://meduza.io/en/feature/2022/08/18/they-re-not-cou nting-on-people-making-it-home. Refer to Blood, *Hitler's Bandit Hunters.,* for details about Oskar Dirlewanger security actions.
[65] The Moscow Times, 'Russian Prisons, Corporations Recruit Ukraine "Volunteers" — Reports', *The Moscow Times. The Moscow Times,* 29 July 2022, https://w ww.themoscowtimes.com/2022/07/05/russian-prisons-corporations-recruit-ukraine-volunteers-reports-a78206. 'What Is Russia's Wagner Group of Mercenaries in Ukraine?', *BBC News. BBC,* 5 April 2022, https://www.bbc.com/news /world-60947877.

more terrible rates of substance abuse, congenital disorders and illiteracy than the unhealthy Russian population in general, even before the fact that a full quarter of them are likely to be convicted murderers.[66] This author doubts they have received special training in the laws of war. Any such training would also be useless considering the origin of the students. Add to that the fact that Dmitry Utkin, former GRU officer and co-founder of Wagner, is famously, purportedly, tattooed permanently with SS rank insignia.[67] Will such a man be interested in teaching his underlings the laws of war? Meanwhile, Wagner's other founder and leader, Prigozhin, has publicly condoned the execution, without trial, by sledgehammer, of a Wagner deserter.[68]

Apart from the obvious issue of the psychopathic nature, by design, composition and leadership, of a key Russian paramilitary formation, it is difficult to judge if actual formal Russian military forces at the lowest level have any actual training in the rules of law. This is despite the wide variety of domestic paper, and dated declarations and laws, however imprecise, associated with them.

---

[66] Jan Strzelecki, 'Russia behind Bars: The Peculiarities of the Russian Prison System', in *OSW Centre for Eastern Studies*, 2019, https://www.osw.waw.pl/en/publikacje/osw-commentary/2019-02-07/russia-behind-bars-peculiarities-russian-prison-system.; 'Ukraine War: Putin Allows Former Prisoners to Be Conscripted', *BBC News*, 4 November 2022, sec. Europe, https://www.bbc.com/news/world-europe-63517680.

[67] 'Dmitry Utkin', in *Wikipedia. Wikimedia Foundation*, 26 August 2022, https://en.wikipedia.org/wiki/Dmitry_Utkin.

[68] Guy Faulconbridge and Guy Faulconbridge, 'Video Shows Sledgehammer Execution of Russian Mercenary', *Reuters*, 13 November 2022, sec. Europe, https://www.reuters.com/world/europe/sledgehammer-execution-russian-mercenary-who-defected-ukraine-shown-video-2022-11-13/. The sledgehammer has become a point of honor for Prigozhin - Jerusalem Post Staff, 'Wagner's Prigozhin Gave Bloody Sledgehammer to EU for Terror Designation - The Jerusalem Post', accessed 15 March 2023, https://www.jpost.com/breaking-news/article-723234. Title says it all. Picture via Stanisław Żaryn [@StZaryn], 'Leader of the Group, Dmitry Utkin, Is Fmr. Military Officer, Russian Neo-Nazi, Described as Supporter of Nazi German SS Formation. Utkin's Career with Putin Shows Russian Hypocrisy. Moscow Falsely Accuses Others of "Neo-Nazi",and Itself Uses Services of True Fan of Fascism.2/2 Https://T.Co/Op8tt9Q5ne', Tweet, *Twitter*, 15 September 2021, https://twitter.com/StZaryn/status/1438219187470614535.

"For a number of historical, social, political, and other reasons, Russia is in a "heightened risk" zone in this respect… Without a doubt, the effectiveness of applying the laws and customs of war directly depends on the degree of personnel awareness."[69]

The Russian military does not use NCOs, professional non-commissioned officers, to the same degree as Western forces, for a variety of reasons, historical and doctrinal.[70] All aspects of military training of soldiers therefore mainly fall on officers. Russian officers themselves, in 2-3 years of training, themselves seem to receive only 10-16 (?) hours of training on international humanitarian law and the laws of conflict.[71] There were efforts to improve Russian legal training around the 2000s but information on progress since then is non-existent, at least in public, except for the usual declarations of conformance. Supposedly Russian soldiers (officers?) receive training: "Twice a year, 6–10 hours per year".[72] However junior officers in Russian service have very limited independence, freedom of command or even respect from their troops, giving them little ability to discipline their troops, even if inclined to do so and appropriately trained.[73]

Perhaps a commanding officer is not an ideal person to teach law even if thoroughly trained.[74] Knowing the law for practical purposes is not the same as teaching it.[75] Russian graduates of military

---

[69] Euphemistic use of 'heightened' here in 'Human Rights Education in Russia: Analytical Report' (Moscow: Moscow School of Human Rights, 2008). 85.

[70] Haley Britzky, 'NCOs Are the US Military's Greatest Strength - and One of Russia's Biggest Weaknesses', *Task & Purpose*, 25 March 2022, https://taskandpurpose.com/news/russia-noncomissioned-officers-us-military/. Andrew Exum, 'The Russian Military Has Descended into Inhumanity', *The Atlantic*. Atlantic Media Company, 7 April 2022, https://www.theatlantic.com/ideas/archive/2022/04/bucha-ukraine-bodies-russian-military-crimes/629485/.

[71] "At the same time, the level of skills and competencies acquired by cadets leaves much to be desired.", 'Human Rights Education in Russia: Analytical Report'. 97-98.

[72] Blank and Noone, *Law of War Training: Resources for Military and Civilian Leaders*. 34.

[73] HRW, 'The Wrongs of Passage'. 8-9.

[74] Roberts, 'Teaching the Law of Armed Conflict to Armed Forces'.126 provides an example of senior Western general 'joking' to the author that the law of conflict is all well and good, but terrorists need their legs broken.

[75] My sorry experience.

academies, a more advanced system of officer training, have, on paper, more developed academic requirements as part of interdisciplinary studies and to prepare them to teach their troops with only 8-10 hours of training. This is for advanced officer cadets, not conscripts.[76] This brings us to the state of international law on the subject, a commanding officer: "cannot use the lack of training or provision of insufficient training to undermine or defeat a finding of effective control."[77] An officer has to command responsibility for war crimes as discussed in the previous essay if his troops are untrained, along with his responsibility for not training his troops, "In other situations, however, inconsistent and improper training of troops may enable the tribunal to confirm the commander's effective control while at the same time condemning the lack of effective training." High-ranking Russian officers (above and including regimental level, >2000 troops), are supposed to be advised by qualified legal advisers as part of the fulfilment of article 82 of the 1977 Additional Protocol I to Geneva Conventions.[78] This raises the question of the post-invasion infamous Russian Battalion Tactical Groups which are supplied with their independent means of inflicting mass war crimes, aka holocaust by artillery, with organic (within the unit) formations of tube artillery and even more devastating rocket artillery. Do these units operate and target without legal support?[79] Going further, Russian commanders who have ticked the boxes of learning the laws of war in their studies should note that having received officer level training in the laws of war is an element of command responsibility– as laid down in the trial of Zlatko Aleksovski, Bosnian Croat prison commander, convicted of

---

[76] 'Human Rights Education in Russia: Analytical Report'. One academy teaches: "The question of who is guilty of provoking the war and who is its victim is the province of politicians and is irrelevant for the military."

[77] Laurie R. Blank, 'Examining the Role of Law of War Training in International Criminal Accountability', *Utah Law Review* 7, no. 4 (2017).

[78] "The High Contracting Parties at all times, and the Parties to the conflict in time of armed conflict, shall ensure that legal advisers are available, when necessary, to advise military commanders at the appropriate level on the application of the Conventions and this Protocol and on the appropriate instruction to be given to the armed forces on this subject.".

[79] Refer to Blood, 'A Holocaust by Artillery', 24 April 2022.

command responsibility for violence inflicted on detainees at Kaonik prison.[80]

Defence lawyers for high-level Russian commanders will find it difficult to explain how the paper declarations of conformance with the command, training and implementation obligations undertaken by Russia were ignored, despised and cynically violated. At this time Russian commanders, and grunt soldiers, blanket deny that Russia has committed any war crimes in Ukraine.

> "[Colonel General] Sergei Rudskoy, stated that "it is to be stressed that [the] Russian party does everything possible in order to prevent victims among civilians and does not assign targets located in towns""[81]

They will always deny that Russia, has ever, throughout history, broken those norms of law or committed genocide:

> "Russian air force planes do not strike residential districts in populated areas, in order to avoid casualties. Targets are terrorist bases, armoured vehicles and ammunition stories which are always identified by drones and always confirmed by other channels beforehand." — Russian MOD representative Major-General Igor Konashenkov.[82]

These statements already implicate the carousel of Russian commanders in Ukraine, who it seems are chosen among seasoned war criminals from the Syrian Civil War.[83] A criminal with blood on his

---

[80] Blank, 'Examining the Role of Law of War Training in International Criminal Accountability'.

[81] James Kearney, 'Russia's Airstrike Rules of Engagement Reviewed', *AOAV*, 24 March 2019, https://aoav.org.uk/2019/an-assessment-of-russias-roe.

[82] Via AOAV, 'An Assessment of Russia's Rules of Engagement, Strike Policy and Adherence to International Law - Syrian Arab Republic', *ReliefWeb* (blog), 14 March 2019, https://reliefweb.int/report/syrian-arab-republic/assessment-russia-s-rules-engagement-strike-policy-and-adherence.

[83] The New Voice of Ukraine, 'General Dvornikov "No Longer in Command" of Russian Army in Ukraine - CIT', *Yahoo! News. Yahoo!*, 3 June 2022, https://news.yahoo.com/general-dvornikov-no-longer-command-155200379.html. As of time of writing, it seems Colonel General Gerasimov, of the Gerasimov Doctrine described by Chris Bellamy elsewhere, has been handed the poison chalice. Peter Beaumont and Pjotr Sauer, 'Russia Replaces General in Charge of Ukraine War in Latest Military Shake-Up', *The Guardian. Guardian News and Media*, 11 January 2023, sec. World news, https://www.theguardian.com/world/2023/jan/11/russia-replaces-general-in-charge-of-ukraine-war-in-latest-military-shake-up.

hands is presumably more loyal to the boss because he has so much to lose—the 'made man' rule of the American Cosa Nostra except in Russian state power. The position seems to be that Russia has never broken the laws of war because it is impossible for Russia to break the laws of war. After all, Russia never breaks the laws of war.[84] Russia does therefore not even need to have a civilian casualty monitoring cell or engage with NGOs.[85] The logic leads us to the conclusion that any civilian casualty is fake news because Russia never bombs civilians, in the same way, that Russia does not fight Ukrainians, only Nazis.

> "Russian forces do not fire on civilian targets." — Dmitry Peskov, Kremlin spokesperson.[86]
> "Bucha 2.0. Nailed them! Amazing!
> Ukies did it Russians don't hit civilians if they did special op would be over 25 February" — various paraphrased Russian social media commentators.[87]

Russia already has an unhealthy obsession with the military combined with genocidal war fervour.[88] And Russia knows it never

---

[84] Kearney, 'Russia's Airstrike Rules of Engagement Reviewed'. Note the Katyń lie rearing its ugly head in Putin's Russia, Ronald H. Davidson, 'Ukraine and Genocide: A Psychological Roadmap of the Killing Grounds' (Salon. Salon.com, 16 April 2022), https://www.salon.com/2022/04/16/ukraine-and-genocide-roadmap-to-the-fields/.

[85] Kearney, 'Russia's Airstrike Rules of Engagement Reviewed'.

[86] UN, 'UN Political Affairs Chief Warns of "Utter Devastation" Facing Ukraine Cities by Russian Forces | | UN News' (United Nations. United Nations, 11 March 2022), https://news.un.org/en/story/2022/03/1113812. Also, Tomas Sniegon, 'Russia's Denial of Responsibility for Atrocities in Bucha Recalls 50 Years of Lies over the Katyn Massacre', *The Conversation*, 6 April 2022, https://theconversation.com/russias-denial-of-responsibility-for-atrocities-in-bucha-recalls-50-years-of-lies-over-the-katyn-massacre-180800.

[87] Russian Telegram comments to a Russian missile strike on a Ukrainian shopping centre - Ian Garner, "Russians on a Huge Telegram Group.," Twitter (Twitter, June 27, 2022), https://twitter.com/irgarner/status/1541446883280822278?s=20&t=VFxyGkogr2G64VCZlPxKig.

[88] Meduza, "Kids and Kalashnikovs Russia Brings pro-War Propaganda to Life at Army-2022 Expo," Meduza, August 22, 2022, https://meduza.io/en/feature/2022/08/22/kids-and-kalashnikovs. Meduza, "Daria Dugina How the Daughter of a Eurasianist Philosopher Emerged as a War Advocate in the Years before

commits any crimes, especially war crimes:

> "Russia has never done anything wrong to anyone, the world is turning against her out of pure hatred, envy and indignation" - Patriarch Kirill, billionaire and head of the Russian Orthodox Church, July 3, 2022[89]

An example of military messianic thinking would be the cover of Zavtra newspaper whose editor Aleksandr Prokhano is nowadays described as 'saying what Putin has on his mind', despite once criticizing Putin for being 'too liberal'.[90] Prozhanko wrote on April 25 2022 (Monday after Orthodox Easter), "Christ is risen, brothers! Truly risen! Fire! Fire!" with a picture of Christ, looming over a WW2 katyusha rocket launcher, AA guns, a tank and a babushka ('Babushka Z') with a Soviet flag.[91] This is more Warhammer 40K via Nazism than the politics of the 21st century - the glorification of militarism meshing with religious elements and mysticism is a key element of fascism.[92]

The messianic mission is an old theme of Russian pan-Slavism where Slavism is understood by Russians as being the Russian way,

---

Her Murder," Meduza, August 22, 2022, https://meduza.io/en/feature/2022/08/23/daria-dugina.

[89] Дмитрова Dimitrova) and Дарья, 'Patriarch Kirill: Russia Has Done Nothing Wrong to Anyone, They Attack It out of Envy - Патриарх Кирилл: Россия Не Сделала Никому Ничего Плохого, На Нее Нападают Из Зависти - Газета.Ru: Новости', *Газета.Ru*, 3 July 2022, https://m.gazeta.ru/social/news/2022/07/03/18055862.shtml. Projekt, 'New "Proekt" Investigation Uncovers Millions of Dollars in Real Estate Belonging to Patriarch Kirill and His Family Members', Meduza, accessed 15 March 2023, https://meduza.io/en/feature/2020/10/28/new-proekt-investigation-uncovers-millions-of-dollars-in-real-estate-belonging-to-patriarch-kirill-and-his-family-members.

[90] Walter Clemens, 'Putin the Risen Christ - Russia's Ultranationalist Pin-Up', *CEPA*, 10 May 2022, https://cepa.org/putin-the-risen-christ-russias-ultranationalist-pin-up/.

[91] As a blog post - Alexander Prokhanov, 'Александр Проханов: Воистину! [RISEN!]', accessed 13 March 2023, https://zavtra.ru/blogs/voistinu. The babushka is 'Babushka Z' who greeted soldiers entering her village with a Soviet flag, much to her embarrassment when they turned out to be Ukrainians - Sofia Bettiza and Svyatoslav Khomenko, 'Babushka Z: The Woman Who Became a Russian Propaganda Icon - BBC News', 15 June 2022, https://www.bbc.com/news/world-europe-61757667. For Prokhanov - Clemens, 'Putin the Risen Christ - Russia's Ultranationalist Pin-Up'.

[92] Emilio Gentile, 'Fascism as Political Religion', *Journal of Contemporary History* 25, no. 2/3 (1990): 229–51, https://www.jstor.org/stable/260731.

combining its history, invariably a history of conquest and Moscow Orthodoxy. Bizarre strands of Moscow Orthodoxy, Kissinger via Hitler Realpolitik, Russian ultra-ultra nationalism and frankly Nazi occultism combine in the political and ideological elites of Putin's Russia.[93]

> "Ukrainians need to be killed, killed, killed. I am telling you this as a professor." - Aleksandr Dugin, occultist, supposed confidante and 'philosopher', 2014 via Julia Davis.[94]

Pre-invasion there was a very worrying development in the Russian military - the Russian military and security services reintroduced politruks throughout the army to foster military patriotism (not discipline as such!) and specifically for occupation purposes.[95] Citizens of Soviet-occupied countries still shudder at the mention of the word politruk or commissar in light of their roles in red terror.[96] Politruks and commissars are war crime specialists, as in specialists in committing them alongside genocide.[97] The re-introduction of such a role may also have reduced actual military effectiveness.[98] Conscript training in international humanitarian law seems

---

[93] For a detailed look on Soviet nostalgia, Russian old imperialism and neo-imperialism, see Anton Weiss-Wendt and Nanci Adler, *The Future of the Soviet Past: The Politics of History in Putin's Russia* (Bloomington (Ind: Indiana University Press, 2021).

[94] Julia Davis, '#Putin's adviser Dugin: 'Ukrainians Need to Be Killed, Killed, Killed. I Am Telling You This as a Professor', Tweet, *Twitter*, 13 June 2022, https://twitter.com/JuliaDavisNews/status/477282526537334784.

[95] Andrew Osborn, 'In Soviet Echo, Putin Gives Russian Army a Political Wing', 31 July 2018, https://www.reuters.com/article/us-russia-military-politics-idUSKBN1KL1VA. Ray C. Finch, *Ensuring the Political Loyalty of the Russian Soldier* (Army University Press, 2020), https://www.armyupress.army.mil/Journals/Military-Review/English-Edition-Archives/July-August-2020/Finch-Russian-Political-Loyalty.

[96] Robert Service, *Spies and Commissars: Bolshevik Russia and the West*, 1. publ (London: Macmillan, 2011). or Norman M. Naimark, *The Russians in Germany: A History of the Soviet Zone of Occupation, 1945 - 1949*, 3 printing (Cambridge, Mass: Belknap Press, 1997).

[97] Institute of National Remembrance, *The Destruction of the Polish Elite Operation AB-Katyn* (Warsaw, 2009), https://edukacja.ipn.gov.pl/download/210/406836/OperationABKATYNENG.pdf. All of the commisars.

[98] Jason Gresh, 'Professionalism and Politics in the Russian Military', no. 67 (2021).

to have been recently folded into 'military-political- training with 6 hours of training as compared to 66 hours of what must be described as lies, myths and indoctrination of 'patriotic education, military history of Russia, traditions of the army and navy, days of Russian military glory' (!).[99] These same politruks may be tasked with 'military-legal work'.[100]

The idea of great Russian, rodina, military glory is deeply embedded within the Russian military itself. At the end of August 2022, a Russian paratrooper, Pavel Filatyev, samizdated his terrible account of the Ukraine war in ZOV, named after the labelling of 'special operation' invasion vehicles.[101] This is not a dissident screed or the Russian All Quiet on the Western Front. His main complaints are about how Russia treats its soldiers, how Russia is betraying its glorious army and how he is disappointed with the war as it is going. Along the way, he repeats many catchphrases of Russian propaganda, including tales of Ukrainian torture of Russian POWs via castration, something which Russian soldiers have engaged in as well as the European Union actually attacking the rodina - something which only a powerful army can protect against.

> "But the most terrible and the most important institution of the state is the army! There is no one country created without an army! An army is a country!" — Alexander Filyatev

This is a professional, contract, soldier who decided to desert but

---

[99] Finch, *Ensuring the Political Loyalty of the Russian Soldier*. During this war Russia has introduced compulsory 'Russian glory' studies for all undergrad students.UWN Correspondent, 'Compulsory Russian Statehood Course for All Undergrads', University World News, accessed 15 March 2023, https://www.universityworldnews.com/post.php?story=20221216145937536.

[100] Mikhail Sukhorukjov, 'Замполиты-Политруки, Но Уж Точно Не Комиссары. Часть 3 [Political Officers, Political Instructors, but Certainly Not Commissars. Part 3', *Topwar.Ru*. Topwar.Ru, 7 January 2019, https://topwar.ru/152102-zampolity-politruki-no-uzh-tochno-ne-komissary-chast-3.html.

[101] Dustin Du Cane, 'The Paratrooper - I'm Just a Poor Boy from a Poor Family." The Paratrooper', *Fallout* (blog), 19 August 2022, https://fallout.substack.com/p/the-paratrooper-im-just-a-poor-boy.Links to original samizdat and translation in the article.

even as a deserter he continues to deny Russian war crimes.[102] He despises his superiors but shares their denials of Russian atrocities which he must have witnessed, and there are hints of that within the text. The viewpoints in ZOV are not Solzhenitsyn, they're reminiscent of the worst trashy post-WW1 German proto-Nazi fronterlebnis literature.[103] Here corruption amidst Putin's elites replaces Jews, Communists and Socialists of that junk variety of literature, but the pure glorious abused military that is the soul of the nation is the core of the nation theme is exactly the same. This is the road to a form of efficient military fascism, as espoused by the Wehrmacht, even more dangerous than Putin's kleptocratic imperialist and inherently corrupt fascism.[104] Filatyev's stories, which seem heavily edited but contain references to torture and violence against civilians, confirm the terrible state of the Russian military. Soldiers' rights, enshrined in Russian 'law', are routinely abused. Russian military law is a facade that only exists to repress and oppress soldiers. How can we expect these brutalised soldiers to respect the rights of POWs and civilians?[105] Chillingly, Russian (and Ukrainian) soldiers are experiencing their own Kampfzeit (time of struggle) which will radicalise some, as war always does with veterans.[106] Radicals care little for law at home or at the front.

---

[102] As a counterpoint: 'Russian Soldier Confessed to Murdering Civilians in the Kyiv Region', MIL.IN.UA, 15 August 2022, https://mil.in.ua/en/news/russian-soldier-confessed-to-murdering-civilians-in-the-kyiv-region/. and Ekaterina Fomina, '"I Confess to All the Crimes": A Russian Soldier Admits to Executing a Civilian and Denounces His Commanders', *OCCRP*, 18 August 2022, https://www.occrp.org/en/investigations/i-confess-to-all-the-crimes-a-russian-soldier-admits-to-executing-a-civilian-and-denounces-his-commanders.

[103] David Redles, 'The Nazi Old Guard: Identity Formation During Apocalyptic Times', *Nova Religio-Journal of Alternative and Emergent Religions* 14 (1 August 2010): 24–44, https://doi.org/10.1525/nr.2010.14.1.24.

[104] Peter Dickinson, 'Putin Admits Ukraine Invasion Is an Imperial War to "Return" Russian Land', *Atlantic Council*, 10 June 2022, https://www.atlanticcouncil.org/blogs/ukrainealert/putin-admits-ukraine-invasion-is-an-imperial-war-to-return-russian-land/.

[105] Similar stories of dissatisfaction, casual war-crimes and low soldier morale are propagating throughout social media as of time of editing.

[106] Jasper Craven et al., 'How the Military Turns Troops Into Extremists', *The New Republic*, 4 February 2021, https://newrepublic.com/article/161121/military-veterans-extremism. Kathleen Belew, *Bring the War Home: The White Power*

Regardless of individual soldier's actions at the front or behind it, it seems that Russia, as a state, has taken to publicly mass murdering Ukrainian POWs. Just after a particularly gruesome story of the torture and murder of a Ukrainian POW broke in autumn 2022, Russia upped the ante with a deadly explosion a prison camp in Olenivka.[107] There are theories that the murder was to cover up the torture of these POWs in the light of the revelation of torture.[108] This would not be the first or last case of Russia murdering POWs.[109] Protection of POWs dates back to the Hague Convention (II) with Respect to the Laws and Customs of War on Land and its annex: Regulations concerning the Laws and Customs of War on Land of 1899. The torture of Ukrainian POWs, let alone murder, is in the direct purview of the ICC as war crimes under art. 8 par. 2 of the Rome Statute, Russian Security Council veto or no veto. Even if Russia hadn't actually murdered its prisoners, though it did, Geneva law requires moving soldiers out of range of combat, which disrupts the Russian lie that Ukraine killed its own prisoners with an unlikely strike of such precision that it would make US drone services proud.[110] Pictures of the site show only one small hut with a hole in its roof, the surroundings completely untouched - a Russian-planted bomb is a more likely explanation.

Movement and Paramilitary America (Cambridge, MA: Harvard University Press, 2018).

[107] Brendan Cole, 'Video of Russian Soldier Allegedly Castrating Ukraine POW Sparks Outrage', *Newsweek*, 29 July 2022, https://www.newsweek.com/russia-ukraine-castrate-torture-video-1728988.

[108] Michael Schwirtz et al., 'Ukraine Builds a Case That Killing of P.o.w.s Was a Russian War Crime', *The New York Times*. *The New York Times*, 3 August 2022, https://www.nytimes.com/2022/08/03/world/europe/russia-ukraine-prisoners-killed.html.

[109] Dan Peleschuk, 'An Infamous Russian Rebel Admits to Killing Ukrainian Pows: Report." An Infamous Russian Rebel Admits to Killing Ukrainian POWs: Report', n.d., https://theworld.org/stories/infamous-russian-rebel-admits-killing-ukrainian-pows-report.

[110] ICRC, 'International Committee of the Red Cross. "Prisoners of War: What You Need to Know', 19 August 2022, https://www.icrc.org/en/document/prisoners-war-what-you-need-know. Convention (III) relative to the Treatment of Prisoners of War. Geneva, 12 August 1949, article 23 in particular.

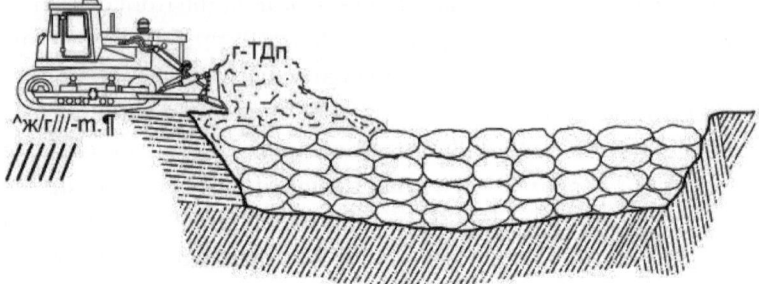

Figure 1 - The sacks are body bags - via Russian manual on mass grave building applicable from February 2022 (!) — innocent or preparatory? Via Julia Davis, , Tweet, *Twitter*, 3 April 2022, accessed 30 April 2022, https://twitter.com/JuliaDavis News/status/1510444406792503301., with link to https://allgosts.ru/13/200/gost_r_42.7.01-2021.pdf. The date of publication is February 2022—despite the file name. The title is the ominous "Civil defense. Urgent burial of corpses in wartime and peacetime. General requirements"

Figure 2 - Ukrainian sniper, identified as Tymofiy Mykolayovych Shadura, murdered on video from which this still is taken distributed by Wagner Company social media and MFA of Ukraine UA [@MFA_Ukraine], Tweet, *Twitter*, 6 March 2023, accessed 10 March 2023, https://twitter.com/MFA_Ukraine/status/1632798249361842176. 'Slava Ukraini' means Glory to Ukraine. Static picture via Ukrainian government media.

Russia's Wagner mercenaries meanwhile seem to have engaged in personally summarily executing Ukrainian troops, as with the case of the Ukrainian soldier murdered on video—in a striking loop back to Goran Jelisić, the Serbian convict turned police-man, who murdered a Bosnian on video, certain of impunity.[111] 'Never again' means little if potential perpetrators don't know or care.

Chillingly Russia's narrative on Azov Regiment prisoners belonging to a criminal and terrorist organisation (which Wagner is, while the Azov Regiment is a formal part of the military) may be an attempt to utilise the flawed US justification for not giving Taliban fighters prisoner of war status during and now after the war in Afghanistan.[112] Russia has at every step in it legal justifications for war and its copied the arguments used by the USA in previous wars.[113] The linkage between the Taliban and Al-Qaida and 9/11 took Taliban soldiers outside of the protection of the Geneva Conventions, Dugin daughter's death might serve the same in sham trials.[114] The legal nonsense used against the Taliban can be used by Russia while having their mafia underlings in pseudo-separatist states carry out executions on 'Ukrainian Nazis'.[115] A complicit lawyer can find a terrible and flawed excuse for any atrocity - that does not mean it stops being an atrocity or that the law is flawed. John Bolton and Donald Rumsfeld have a sorry legal and political legacy which will cripple and distort international law for decades as Russia has grown from neo-con apprentice to rodina master of the dark

---

[111] See the author's other chapter.
[112] Lauri Linnamäe, '1/5 Second Look: "Azov Batallion ID" Presented by FSB', *Twitter*, 22 August 2022, https://twitter.com/IssandJumal/status/1561781504975540225.
[113] Michael N. Schmitt, *Russia's 'Special Military Operation' and the (Claimed) Right of Self-Defense* (Lieber Institute West Point, 2022), https://lieber.westpoint.edu/russia-special-military-operation-claimed-right-self-defense/.
[114] Meduza, 'Zelensky Threatens to Refuse Negotiations with Russia If "Trial" of Pows Is Held in Mariupol', 22 August 2022, https://meduza.io/en/news/2022/08/22/zelensky-threatens-to-refuse-negotiations-with-russia-if-trial-of-pows-is-held-in-mariupol.
[115] Silvia Borelli, 'Casting Light on the Legal Black Hole: International Law and Detentions Abroad in the "War on Terror."', *International Review of the Red Cross* 87, no. 857 (2005): 39–68, https://doi.org/10.1017/s1816383100181184.

international pseudo-legal arts.[116] Whatabout is a flawed weapon based on a fallacy but it is as effective at the UN as it is on Twitter.[117] Russia's real political magick might be its abuse of international humanitarian law and the UN process. That said Guantanamo's horrors are nothing compared to those of Russian camps, from which Ukrainian soldiers return, if lucky and exchanged, starved and crippled, looking as if they had been liberated from the death wing of Dachau.[118] Waterboarding is preferable to a bullet or lead pipe beating.

Memory in law

As a direct result of the Ukrainian war and in a panic after the unexpected wave of Western sanctions and flooding of media, traditional and new, with evidence of Russian aggression, genocide and crimes, the Russian state reacted in the only way it could, and it is now in 2023 illegal to accuse the Russian Federation of committing war crimes under these wonderful transparency and light provisions of the Russian Criminal Code:

> "Article 207³. - Public dissemination of deliberately false information about the use of the Armed Forces of the Russian Federation
> Article 280³. Public actions aimed at discrediting the use of the Armed Forces of the Russian Federation in order to protect the interests of the Russian Federation and its citizens, maintain international peace and security"[119]

---

[116] John R. Bolton, 'The Risks and the Weaknesses of the International Criminal Court from America's Perspective', *The International Criminal Court*, 2017, 459–76, https://doi.org/10.4324/9781351146401-18.

[117] On the subject of the Soviet Russian origin of the technique - 'Whataboutism', *The Economist*, 31 January 2008, https://www.economist.com/europe/2008/01/31/whataboutism.

[118] 'Released Ukrainian Prisoner of War Reveals Torment at the Hands of Russians', Sky News, accessed 23 March 2023, https://news.sky.com/story/released-ukrainian-prisoner-of-war-reveals-torment-at-the-hands-of-russians-12709287.

[119] Russian Federation Parliament, 'Federal Law No. 32-FZ of March 4, 2022 "On Amendments to the Criminal Code of the Russian Federation and Articles 31 and 151 of the Code of Criminal Procedure of the Russian Federation' (n.d.), http://ips.pravo.gov.ru:8080/default.aspx?pn=0001202203040007 in Russian.

This follows up on a widely reported amendment to the Criminal Code in 2014, Article 354.1. which masquerades to be about Nazism but the text mostly deals with slandering the rodina and in practice is exclusively used to target critics of Russian history - saying that the rodina committed a war crime or genocide, like say at Katyn or in Ukraine is slandering the rodina and its veterans.[120] Investigating genocide is a criminal activity in the glorious rodina.[121] The jingoistic golden glow of nostalgia ensures war crimes will be perpetrated and never investigated. The state has declared itself innocent of crimes — via law. This is the vicious 19th-century state sovereignty that Rafael Lemkin and Hersch Lauterpacht worked to limit. A country that makes illegal a discussion of abuse of international law and war crimes is a country whose international humanitarian laws exist only on paper.[122]

> "I, a military serviceman from military unit 51460, guards private first class, Frolkin Daniel Andreevich, confess to all the crimes I committed in Andriivka, to shooting civilians, stealing from civilians, taking their phones,"
> — Daniel Frolkin, Russian soldier of the 64th Motor Rifle Brigade[123]

This author mentioned earlier that no US Marine has been charged with war crimes in Vietnam, as such, obviously to avoid the embarrassment of such a charge and possible command responsibility for not preventing the war crime or neglecting training on the law of conflict. Russia goes a step forward; a soldier who confessed to killing civilians in Ukraine was charged with and sentenced for

---

[120] TASS, 'Ban on Putting Soviet Union, Nazi Germany on Same Footing Submitted to State Duma', *TASS*, 5 May 2021, https://tass.com/politics/1286677. Also, Francine Hirsch, 'Putin's Memory Laws Set the Stage for His War in Ukraine', *Lawfare*, 28 February 2022, https://www.lawfareblog.com/putins-memory-laws-set-stage-his-war-ukraine

[121] History of human rights abuse: 'FIDH Releases Mini Documentary on "Crimes Against History" as Russia Reoffends', International Federation for Human Rights, accessed +13 March 2023, https://www.fidh.org/en/region/europe-central-asia/russia/fidh-releases-a-mini-documentary-on-crimes-against-history-as-russia.

[122] A fuller look on Russian mythology, see Anton Weiss-Wendt, *Putin's Russia and the Falsification of History: Reasserting Control Over the Past* (London: Bloomsbury Academic, 2022).

[123] Fomina, '"I Confess to All the Crimes": A Russian Soldier Admits to Executing a Civilian and Denounces His Commanders'.

spreading 'fake news'.[124] Not for genocidal murder or war crimes, but for confessing to them. Officially a Russian soldier has never committed war crimes, even when he confesses to them.

Obviously 'justice' in Russia is highly selective. Even calling Putin's special operation a war is a crime.[125] Except when Putin or Kremlin genocide journalists Solovyov and Simonyan do it.[126]

The thread of humanitarian law, 'patriotism' and military training and practice have come together in 2022 in the perverse hanging noose of Putin's Russian laws. As Hirsch states in a blog post, "Putin and Pushkov like the Nuremberg verdict for a simple reason: It blames Nazi Germany alone for certain Soviet-German crimes against peace." and sets the stage for future expansion.[127]

In summary, the Russian military has internalised the laws of war to the degree to be able to competently cite appropriate treaties and domestic and customary law which also strips them of the ability to claim ignorance of those laws. Officers and leaders have a responsibility to instruct their soldiers in humanitarian law. Officers and leaders also bear responsibility for permitting, not just ordering war crimes. Russia claims implementation and instruction of international law, even though there is little evidence of instruction, except declarations and implementation is difficult to find, even in Russian sources. Criticism of Russia, including accusations of

---

[124] Pjotr Sauer, 'Russian Soldier Who Confessed to Killing Ukrainian Civilian Jailed over "Fake News"', *The Guardian. Guardian News and Media*, 16 March 2023, sec. World news, https://www.theguardian.com/world/2023/mar/16/russian-soldier-confessed-killing-ukrainian-civilian-jailed-fake-news-daniil-frolkin.

[125] 'Russia Sends Official to Prison for 7 Years for Anti-War Comment', *Bloomberg.Com*, 8 July 2022, https://www.bloomberg.com/news/articles/2022-07-08/russia-sends-official-to-prison-for-7-years-for-anti-war-comment.

[126] Alia Slisco, 'Putin Faces Push to Be Investigated and Jailed for Calling Conflict "War"', Newsweek, 22 December 2022, https://www.newsweek.com/russia-president-vladimir-putin-faces-calls-investigated-jailed-calling-ukraine-conflict-war-1769190. Isabel Von Brugen, 'Russia Finally Admits It's Fighting "War" in Ukraine as Facade Cracks', Newsweek, 6 October 2022, https://www.newsweek.com/russia-war-ukraine-state-tv-vladimir-solovyov-putin-ally-1749352; Thomas Kika, 'Russian State TV Admits "War" and "Special Military Operation" Are the Same', accessed 17 March 2023, https://www.newsweek.com/russian-state-tv-admits-war-special-military-operation-are-same-1777368.

[127] Hirsch, 'Putin's Memory Laws Set the Stage for His War in Ukraine'.

committing war crimes is however a crime. Russia, its soldiers, and its authorities have not internalised the laws of war. Russia despises the law. I noted in the previous essay that Russia has appropriated World War Two and subsumed the genocidal murder of Jews, above all, into its narrative of the Great Patriotic War. Russia's laws make this narrative impossible to question. Part of the reason why Russia is committing genocide in Ukraine now is because of its approach to law, history, and historical memory which involves never confronting its genocidal past - including the Holodomor.[128] The rodina is always right. Russia is proud of starting the most terrible war in history in alliance with the Nazis.[129]

---

[128] Dickinson, 'Putin Admits Ukraine Invasion Is an Imperial War to "Return" Russian Land'.

[129] This author has avoided using bold in this text except for this one singular example of utter evil, equivalency and historical fraud.

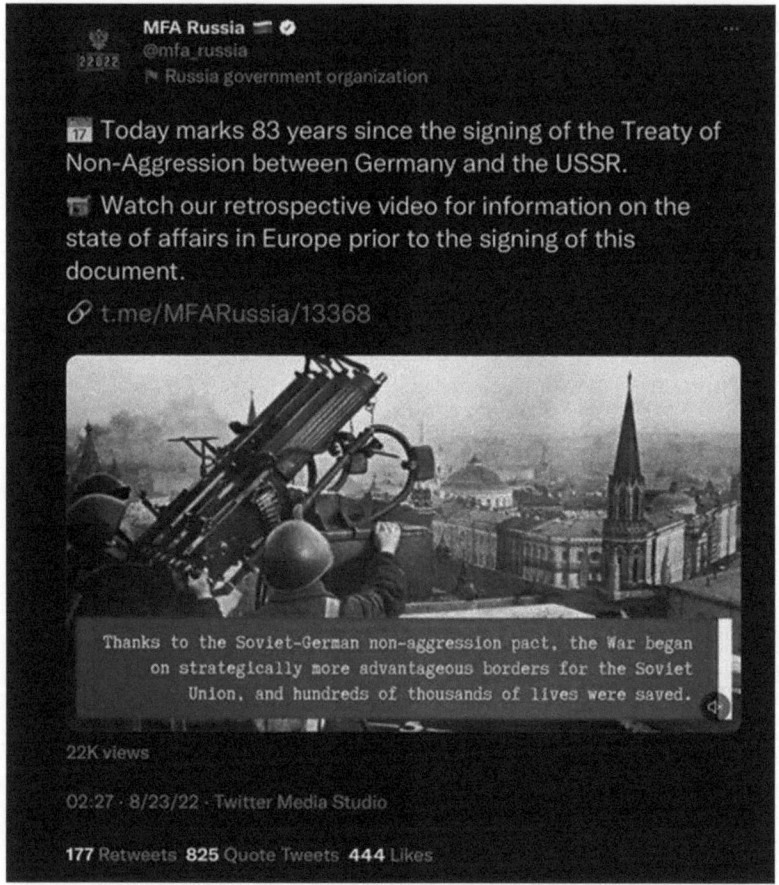

Figure 3 - Russian Foreign Ministry tweet - via Twitter. Content on Twitter - MFA of Russia RU [@mfa_russia], 'Today Marks 83 Years since the Signing of the Treaty of Non-Aggression between Germany and the USSR.', Tweet, *Twitter*, 23 August 2022, https://twitter.com/mfa_russia/status/1561963305320779776. Hopefully will be deleted eventually.

Currently, the rodina is threatened with genocide by the Ukrainians, it, therefore, must genocide Little Russia first. As Russian pundits demand genocide every day and night on Russian tv, even Russian diplomats take to demanding war crimes and genocide.[130]

---

[130] Alexey Kovalev, 'Russia's Brutal Honesty Has Destroyed the West's Appeasers', *Foreign Policy*, 12 August 2022, https://foreignpolicy.com/2022/08/12/russia-ukraine-war-crimes-genocide-appeasement-mearsheimer-putin/.

Mikhail Ulyanov ✓
@Amb_Ulyanov
⚑ Russia government official

No mercy to the Ukrainian population!

Володимир Зеленський ✓ @Zelen... · 3h
⚑ Ukraine government official

I highly appreciate another 🇺🇸 military aid package in the amount of $775 million. Thank you @POTUS for this decision! We have taken another important step to defeat the aggressor. 🇺🇦 will be free!

Figure 4 - The Russian ambassador to the UK threatening Ukraine's population with genocide - via Twitter. Deleted by Kovalev quickly but preserved for posterity. Refer to Dustin Du Cane, 'Blue Tick Shields Drunk Genocidal Ambassador.', *Fallout*, 20 August 2022, https://fallout.substack.com/p/twitter-doesnt-react-so-russian-ambassador.

Now that might have been a discombobulated tweet referring to the Ukrainian government having no mercy for its population but we can suspect it is a statement made in vino veritas from the Ambassador's subconscious. We can call it proof of genocidal intent for the purposes of the Genocide Convention. Maybe he was trying to upstage the Russian Embassy in the UK who called for executing Ukrainian POWs. These chapters have covered Lemkin's and Nikitchenko's opinions on propaganda being the precursor to atrocities. Lemkin wrote the first law banning speech calling for aggressive war - and the Russian Criminal Code also criminalises incitement of hatred (art. 282). Does that matter for Russian ambassadors? Russian ambassadors and officials as a group probably even fall under the definition of an extremist under art. 282.1 of the Russian Criminal Code.[131]

---

[131] "Creation of an extremist community, that is, of an organised group of persons for the preparation or for the performance, with the motives of the ideological, political, racial, national or religious hatred or enmity, as well as on the motives of hatred or enmity towards any one social group…"

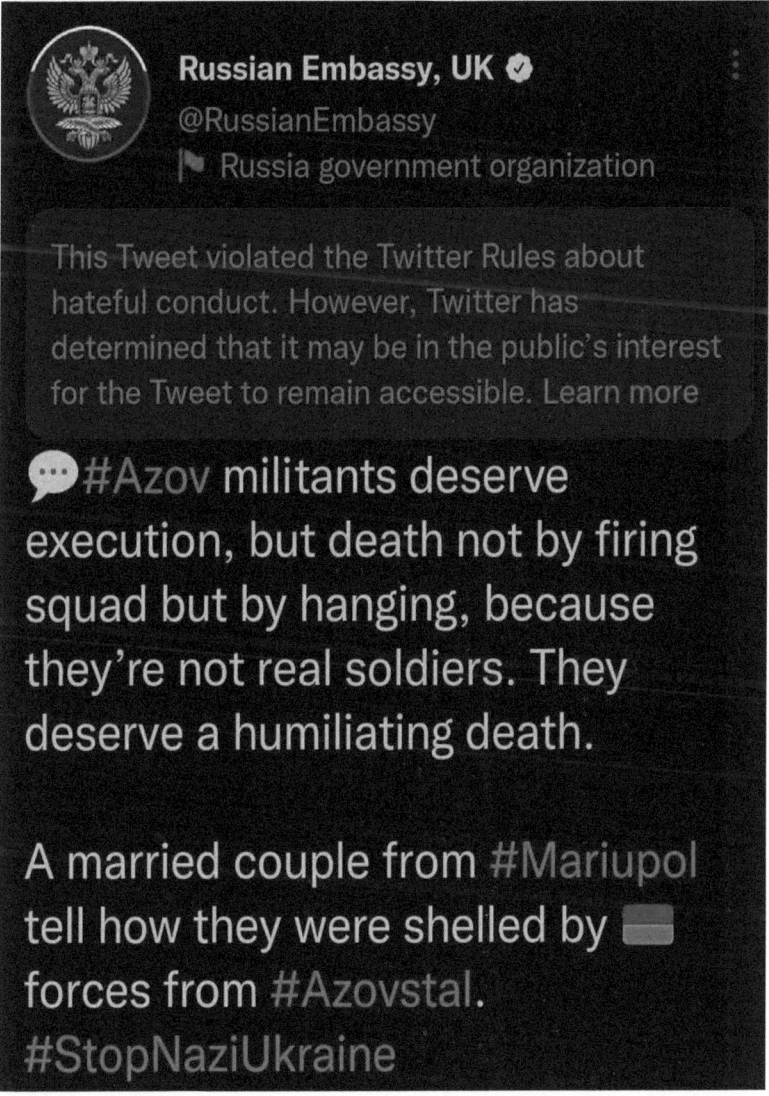

Figure 5 - 'A married couple' but almost certainly actually a prompted statement. Content on Twitter, hopefully will be deleted eventually - Russian Embassy, UK [@RussianEmbassy], Tweet, *Twitter*, 29 July 2022, accessed 30 July 202, https://twitter.com/RussianEmbassy/status/1553093117712162828.[132]

---

[132] Refer to Dustin Du Cane, 'Russian Embassy Demands War Crimes, Twitter Doesn't Mind', *Fallout* (blog), 14 August 2022,

A faux quote or even a true quote can be incitement depending on context. The context here is Russia running a genocidal war.[133]

> "Yesterday I sent my letter of resignation to the competent authorities: lawyers can defend more or less questionable causes. But it has become impossible to represent in forums dedicated to the application of the law a country that so cynically despises it." — Alain Pellet, Counsel for Russia before the ICJ and other international tribunals until 23 February 2022.[134]

Alain Pellet is an internationally recognised and renowned lawyer. Pellet's perhaps belated (the invasion and annexation of Crimea would have been a good time) resignation just before the invasion was fortuitous in light of subsequent events.

The theme of these two essays has been to show that Russia is a state with no respect for international humanitarian law, whose representatives promote, deny and represent genocide, war crimes and crimes against humanity. The allegation of at least 65.000 recorded war crimes in Ukraine as of time of writing shows the brutality prevalent in this war. This exceeds the scope of the post-Yugoslavia war by a magnitude and its next comparison will be the Second World War.[135]

Existential war is genocide war.[136] War framed by media as existential must become genocidal. A soldier is told kill or be killed, children and women are also the enemies and naturally the laws of

---

https://fallout.substack.com/p/russian-embassy-demands-war-crimes.

[133] Kristina Hook, 'Why Russia's War in Ukraine Is a Genocide', *Foreign Affairs*, 22 August 2022, https://www.foreignaffairs.com/ukraine/why-russias-war-ukraine-genocide.

[134] Alain Pellet, 'Open Letter to My Russian Friends: Ukraine Is Not Crimea', *EJIL*, 3 March 2022, https://www.ejiltalk.org/open-letter-to-my-russian-friends-ukraine-is-not-crimea/.

[135] Amanda Macias, 'Ukraine Russia War: 65,000 War Crimes Committed, Prosecutor General Says', accessed 15 March 2023, https://www.cnbc.com/2023/02/01/ukraine-russia-war-65000-war-crimes-committed-prosecutor-general-says.html.

[136] Julia Davis, 'Russia Genocidal State Media Justify Ukraine War Crimes - CEPA', accessed 15 March 2023, https://cepa.org/article/morality-shouldnt-get-in-the-way-russias-genocidal-state-media/. Randall L. Bytwerk, 'Goebbels' 1943 Speech on Total War', n.d., https://research.calvin.edu/german-propaganda-archive/goeb36.htm.

war go out of the window like one of Putin's critics. A soldier's callousness grows not only from the horrors and stress of war but also from the 'writings and pronouncements of journalists and politicians', the endless rhetoric of genocidal hatred from Russian pundits makes them almost as guilty of war crimes as the soldiers acting on their incitements.[137] Solovyov, quoted at the beginning of this essay, with his tv shows that put the Orwellian 'Two Minutes Hate', to shame for timidity, is right to fear future justice:[138]

> "A hideous ecstasy of fear and vindictiveness, a desire to kill, to torture, to smash faces in with a sledgehammer, seemed to flow through the whole group of people like an electric current, turning one even against one's will into a grimacing, screaming lunatic.[139]" – Nineteen Eighty Four [Author's underlining]
>
> "Let me tell you that if we manage to lose, the Hague – whether real or hypothetical – will even come for the street cleaner sweeping the cobblestones behind the Kremlin." –Russian propagandist Margarita Simonyan, head editor of RT on Evening With Vladimir Solovyov, November 29th 2022[140]

Many volumes can and will be written about the calls for genocide that spew daily from Russian state tv. Never in human history have such calls be made so openly and clearly, even during the Rwanda genocide with its infamous Radio Télévision Libre des Mille Collines.[141] The Nazis never made their murderous intentions so clear, even when Goebbels at the Sportpalast or Adolf Hitler Mein Kampf came close to naming extermination as their final solution. Despite Russian law on the subject of inciting genocide or war of

---

[137] Solis and Division, *Marines and Military Law in Vietnam*. 138, citing Guenter Lewy, *America in Vietnam* (Oxford: Oxford Univ. Pr, 1980).

[138] 'Two Minutes Hate', in *Wikipedia*, 2 March 2023, https://en.wikipedia.org/w/index.php?title=Two_Minutes_Hate&oldid=1142516678.

[139] George Orwell, Thomas Pynchon, and Peter Davison, *Nineteen Eighty-Four*, Penguin Modern Classics (London New York, NY: Penguin Books, 2003).

[140] Via Julia Davis, 'Putin Cronies Resort to Begging on Live TV Over War Failures', *The Daily Beast*, 4 December 2022, sec. world, https://www.thedailybeast.com/russian-propagandists-make-desperate-pleas-over-ukraine-war-failures-on-state-tv.

[141] For literal daily examples see RMM, 'Russian Media Monitor - YouTube', accessed 16 March 2023, https://www.youtube.com/@russianmediamonitor.

aggression, such Russian murder journalists and genocide pundits are not punished or censured, with exceptions that prove the rule.[142]

We have seen that Russia has a military history and tradition that is deeply connected with international humanitarian law - mostly in a negative aspect via its soldiers, but with a few positive contributions to law and jurisprudence. We see that Russia's foot soldiers believe in glorious rodina, even if they object to a badly run war. Those foot soldiers deny the obvious war crimes being committed as do their commanders and their priests. Russia's masters of international law go into genocidal rants on Twitter, thankfully its foreign lawyers refuse to represent it further. Russia is destroying Ukraine with artillery and tanks while simultaneously destroying the foundations of international humanitarian law. A genocide on Ukraine, its people and the protections against genocide. The chain of responsibility goes from the soldier culpably ignorant or ignoring the laws of war, to the general who ordered a crime or didn't teach the soldier, to diplomats spewing cover for Russian genocide by claiming self-defence against genocide, up to Putin declaring genocidal Orthodox jihad 'special operation' on Ukrainian 'Nazis', i.e. those who refuse to be good Little Russians.[143] And finally we can be certain that win or lose, Russophobia is and will be blamed by Russians in the future for this special murder operation, not Russia's nor Russians' actions.[144]

---

[142] Andrew Roth, 'Russian TV Presenter Accused of Inciting Genocide in Ukraine', *The Guardian. Guardian News and Media*, 24 October 2022, sec. World news, https://www.theguardian.com/world/2022/oct/24/russian-tv-presenter-anton-krasovsky-accused-of-inciting-genocide-in-ukraine.

[143] Lorenzo Tondo and Pjotr Sauer, 'The 4-Metre-Wide Board Detailing the Entire Russian Military Chain of Command in Ukraine', *The Guardian. Guardian News and Media*, 14 March 2023, sec. World news, https://www.theguardian.com/world/2023/mar/14/the-4-metre-wide-board-detailing-the-entire-russian-military-chain-of-command-in-ukraine.

[144] UN Press, '"Russophobia" Term Used to Justify Moscow's War Crimes in Ukraine, Historian Tells Security Council | UN Press', accessed 15 March 2023, https://press.un.org/en/2023/sc15226.doc.htm. UN Press.

9. REALKRIEG IN WARTIME

Philip W. Blood

We, the audience, bear witness to a Shakespearean tragedy in the actions of Putin, a man who appears to stride confidently along a path he believes is his destiny. He embodies an historical caricature, the last political soldier in a long and ignoble tradition of ideological criminality. He wields history as both a political tool and a weapon to maintain his grip on power.

In casting himself as the new Tsar (Caesar) of the Russian empire, Putin's war has unfolded into a complex narrative, much like the sub-plots of a Shakespearean play. Like *Macbeth*, Putin's imagination is darkly cruel; he has courted popularity through brute masculinity and Caesar-like authoritarianism. He has cultivated a mafia-capitalist elite, imposed regimentation upon the masses, all while binding them together with the sentimental nostalgia of a fabricated Russo-Soviet past.

In the landscape of contemporary Russian politics, there is no middle ground, only extremes characterize the regime. Regardless of whether Putin's war against Ukraine truly began in 2014, it represents an imperial project that has been in the making for over two decades. If Putin's ambition is to recreate a new Rome in Europe, the devastation of Mariupol serves as his unmistakable Carthaginian warning. In the words of Shakespeare's *Julius Caesar*, 'War gives the right to the conquerors to impose any condition they please upon the vanquished,' a principle that has since defined victor's justice and serves as the cornerstone of Putin's strategy.

The Russian genocide is a chilling endeavour, involving the enslavement of children and the mechanized destruction of Ukraine, reducing a modern nation to the remnants of archaeology. These are the hallmarks of an ancient form of conquest revived for modern imperial warfare. While Putin maintains the strategic upper hand, the 'new' Russian empire falters, akin to an intoxicated

Falstaff, stumbling through each day, surviving on the dwindling reputation of its past glory. The question looms: can Putin be dislodged from his firm grip on strategic control of the war?

One of the significant cultural shifts brought to light by Putin's invasion pertains to war reporting and its influence on democratic processes. The tradition of war reporting had long been shaped by correspondents on the frontlines or strategic analysts working away from the battlefield. During World War II, these reporters were joined by historians and social scientists who delved into the experiences of soldiers under the intense stress of warfare.

Since the end of the Cold War, and especially with advancements in telecommunications, notably mobile phones, on-the-ground war reporters had gained prominence. Reporting on modern conflicts had bifurcated, with one aspect focusing on pure military matters such as weapon effectiveness, operational performance, and manoeuvre warfare, while the other emphasized humanitarian concerns like morality, human suffering, war crimes, and genocide. This division in reporting became the norm as both sides in a conflict sought global coverage for their messages and propaganda.

Putin, with the suddenness of his invasion and the constant shifts in the Russian government's reporting, exposed the limitations of both types of reporting. Western reporters found themselves heavily reliant on Ukrainian sources for information, effectively turning the reporting into a one-sided account of the war. This generated profound uncertainties within the various cultures of Western security. It's possible that Putin's cyber warriors had planned or anticipated this outcome. As a result, established defence policies became obsolete, forcing NATO to assume the role of a passive observer, as exemplified by Britain's counterinsurgency doctrine and America's pursuit of breathing space.

Many European nations, caught off guard, lacked a coherent strategy, operational plan, or the necessary forces for resolute defence. Meanwhile, social media reverberated with a cacophony of claims, historical analogies, and predictions of an imminent Ukrainian victory. Even by autumn, hopes of a Ukrainian offensive victory were being propagated by experts and pundits alike. These events underscore the severe repercussions for democratic societies when they receive inadequate advice on security or defence matters, raising questions about the failure of predictive analysis.

The deficiency in predictive strategic analyses had already become evident prior to Putin's invasion. These failed predictions could be traced back to the politics of strategic thinking that emerged after the end of the Cold War, alongside the commercialization of strategy. Furthermore, the limitations of military history as a predictive tool were swiftly exposed. Analysts often immersed themselves in Clausewitz's theories of war, yet these maxims, while instructive, proved insufficient in explaining the realities of modern warfare, terrorism, or conflicts driven by aspirations for great power status.

For instance, the events in former Yugoslavia illustrated the inadequacies of Clausewitzian orthodoxy when applied by ineffective Western political leadership and NATO's flawed strategic methods. However, since 2008, there has been a notable cultural shift in Western strategic thinking. The power elites within the military-industrial complex have grown less confident in resorting to military force, while their governments have implemented disjointed defence policies. Confusing budget expenditure levels with military effectiveness became a common pitfall. By 2022, nearly all Western military forces found themselves in varying states of inadequacy. This was partly a response to the growing societal weariness of prolonged conflicts.

To encapsulate the evolving fluctuations in policies and the widening gap from the realities of warfare, I introduced the term *RealKrieg*. Just as *Realpolitik* once denoted realism and pragmatism in politics, *Realkrieg* represents the illusions associated with war in the realm of national defence. *Realkrieg* characterizes the surrealism within political discourse concerning defence and security, along with the peculiar self-deception that meticulous budget management equates to military effectiveness. Within six months of the war's onset, Western politicians had lost touch with the nature of modern warfare, resorting to slogans to mask leadership failures.

Putin treated Western leaders as mere paper tigers, and they responded accordingly. *Realkrieg* became deeply ingrained in the public consciousness as journalists, military experts, and pundits issued statements, made assumptions, and, more gravely, predicted Russia's defeat. The conclusion drawn is that the West may have won the Cold War, but the advent of social media played a significant part in undermining the peace. This essay examines how social media has shaped the narratives of the war.

Ripping yarns: culture wars and gaming strategy

Strategic myopia is the west's security malaise that has been socialised into public discourse. There were always reservations in democratic nations about free opinion in a time of war. In Putin's war, social media has become a platform for mass engagement. Social media is compulsive but also encourages a false empowerment. Questionable commentaries by news pundits and unsound opinions from the shoals of military 'experts' have come to define the Western interpretation of Putin's war. Governments and politicians have eagerly adopted this content to shape their statements to meet popular opinions. During the Gulf War of 1990, several leading military historians had complained about the lack of serious media exposure, but the same cannot be written of Putin's war.[1] Since February 2022, 'experts' and pundits have used social media to present some of the most outlandish interpretations and fantasies of war ever presented to the media in the history of warfare. The predictions about Putin have verged on the hysterical. Some of the wildest theories about the Russian Army have imagined the use of the wrong vehicle tyres, the absence of artillery shells and a poor logistics system. At the six-month stage, the war raged despite social media fantasies. Some of the most experienced military historians and renowned masters of war studies have maintained a constant flow of one-sided rhetoric and predictions from when the war will end (since February 2022) to how Ukraine had already won (since March 2022) and why the Russian Army was useless (a constant

---

[1] Ian Stewart and Susan L. Carruthers (eds), *War, Culture and the Media: Representations of the Military in 20th Century Britain* (London: Fairleigh Dickinson University Press, 1996).

since long before the war). Little or no regard has been given over to sound strategic analysis of Putin's war aims. This stands in stark contrast to the Cold War analyses and even the flawed methodologies that set the doctrines for the War on Terror. The consequences of these predictions have been to remove the war from the headlines

One like-minded group of Twitter activists included: Trent Telenko (@TrentTelenko), a retired US Department of Defense official[2]; Phillips O'Brien (aka Twitter handle @PhillipsPOBrien) a professor of strategic studies; Eliot Cohen (aka @EliotACohen), a US defence spokesperson; and former US Army General Mark Hertling (@MarkHertling). Several are known for their hawkish opinions about the global projection of American military power, and Cohen's support for Ukraine has been described by Hannah Gurman as his re-fighting the Iraq War through the Ukrainians.[3] There was a typical post of this content on 3 March, when Telenko wrote a thread about Russia's poor vehicle maintenance that featured a theory about tyres. This thread received a remarkable level of popular attention at the time, but the reality of the war cut short its durability.[4] Despite Telenko's efforts to revamp his thread, it was unsustainable since the war had progressed beyond his level of reasoning. O'Brien, who has been much more prolific, has focused on logistics. On 30 March, he posted a thread that is pinned to his Twitter profile: '[S]ome people have asked for a summary of my views on war (why my analysis of the Ukraine war has been so pointed), so I thought I would make this thread with reference to my research (where possible free or library access material).' He described his views as 'profoundly boring'. He announced that 'war is a struggle of communication' and claimed that all 'focus bravery/cowardice of destruction/tragedy while compelling as a human story, tells us

---

[2] Trent Telenko (@TrentTelenko), tweet, 30 April 2022, https://twitter.com/TrentTelenko/status/1520452865684295680 (accessed 16 September 2022).

[3] *Rambo III, Counterinsurgency, & Ukraine w/ Hannah R. Gurman/New FBI Documents on 9/11 & Saudi Arabia w/ Branko Marcetic*, 2022, https://open.spotify.com/episode/557Ni0MuubPxM64TmpGbhQ.

[4] Trent Telenko (@TrentTelenko), tweet, 3 March 2022, https://twitter.com/trenttelenko/status/1499164245250002944 (accessed 14 September 2022).

nothing about why wars are won and lost'. To establish his credentials as an expert on Putin's war, O'Brien presented his book How the War Was Won (2015), with two pages on the Eastern Front, his uncritical biography of an American admiral,[5] and a general comment about the value of management and organisational studies to reinforce his argument, but without clarification.[6]

On 10 May, O'Brien posted: 'Russians are falling back on their "doctrine", which is to blast an area with artillery before sending in artillery. Ukrainians, however, still have mobility, and now much more long-range capability, and basically the Russians can't advance much at all because of these.'[7] The next day, he claimed the Russians were running out of precision missiles.[8] On 29 May, he posted: 'My guess is that the Russians are simply running out of front-line combat vehicles in that area (and much of Ukraine). Was interesting to see that the Pentagon on 26 May said they calculated Russian tank losses at approx. 1000.'[9] On 5 June, O'Brien responded to a thread about the condition of Russian tanks: 'Sort of looks like Jed Clampett [a reference to the Beverly Hillbillies TV show from the 1960s] fitted out a tank to go to Hollywood, and then you realise this tank was designed the exact same year the Beverly Hillbillies first aired.'[10] In July, O'Brien tweeted: 'What we see is Russia getting increasingly weaker and relying on older systems. There [sic] tanks, APCs, missiles, etc, are all degrading as they try to make up losses/wastage by bringing older systems into operation.'[11] A

---

5 Phillips Payson O'Brien, *The Second Most Powerful Man in the World* (London: E. P. Dutton, 2020).
6 Phillips O'Brien (@PhillipsPOBrien), tweet, 20 March 2022, https://threadreaderapp.com/thread/1505563536403091464.html (accessed 16 September 2022).
7 Phillips O'Brien (@PhillipsPOBrien), tweet, 10 May 2022, https://twitter.com/phillipspobrien/status/1523913361674706944 (accessed 16 September 2022).
8 Phillips O'Brien (@PhillipsPOBrien), tweet, 11 May 2022, https://twitter.com/phillipspobrien/status/1524281890932412416 (accessed 16 September 2022).
9 Phillips O'Brien (@PhillipsPOBrien), tweet, 29 May 2022, https://twitter.com/phillipspobrien/status/1530828716410130432 (accessed 16 September 2022).
10 Phillips O'Brien (@PhillipsPOBrien), tweet, 5 June 2022, https://twitter.com/phillipspobrien/status/1533530338500165632 (accessed 16 September 2022).
11 Phillips O'Brien (@PhillipsPOBrien), tweet, 3 July 2022, https://twitter.com/phillipspobrien/status/1543491101063086081 (accessed 16 September 2022).

summation or reflection, depending upon one's viewpoint, was posted on 3 August 2022: 'But also, something is different in this war than we thought. It will take some serious reflection when it's over. A lot of things are happening here, from the inability of Russia to control the air, the failure of its offensive abilities, the power of Ukrainian defensive firepower.' A short while later, he added: 'I wonder if the Ukrainians are setting them up by talking the offensive up so much to make the Russians send masses of forces there, and then cut the logistics line.'[12] O'Brien's North Atlantic compass has no bearing to the Eastern Front 1941–4 or Ukraine since 2014. His content has not explained Putin's motives, which run counter to the usual narratives in management and organisational behaviour studies.

Members of the armed forces community, retired and serving, have also presented less than comprehensible analyses of the war. Mick Ryan (@WarintheFuture) has been a regular exponent of the militarised tweet/thread. His book *War Transformed* (2022) is drawn from his experience as a senior officer in the Australian Army. The book is typically Clausewitzian, with that 'gung-ho' golden thread common to most military-based narratives, but his ideas and opinions about modern war are insightful. He has a grasp and vision of modern war that engages with advanced technology. However, in his threads and posts on Twitter, he has focused entirely on Ukraine and has expressed little interest in what the Russians are doing, except following the common opinion that Putin is losing. Mark Hertling, a retired former commander of US Army Europe, did present an article comparing the Russian and Ukrainian armies in April 2022.[13] Hertling had the experience to draw a balanced analysis of the opposing forces, but his ideas drifted as the anecdotes began to rise. The West's military assessment of the Russian

---

[12] Phillips O'Brien (@PhillipsPOBrien), tweet, 3 August 2022, https://twitter.com/phillipspobrien/status/1554896157868007424 (accessed 16 September 2022).

[13] Mark Hertling, 'I Commanded U.S. Army Europe: Here's What I Saw in the Russian and Ukrainian Armies', The Bulwark, 11 April 2022, https://www.thebulwark.com/i-commanded-u-s-army-europe-heres-what-i-saw-in-the-russia
n-and-ukrainian-armies (accessed 16 September 2022).

military establishment as a 'Spartan order and parade ground antics' had not prevented the Russian forces from operating on a 3,000-kilometre front, with multiple lodgements, massive firepower, and rising numbers of war crimes.

Another group of experts congregated from the UK Ministry of Defence, the Royal United Services Institute, and the schools of British military education. The track record of this grouping had been exposed in the War on Terror when several soldiers and scholars claimed the insurgencies in Iraq and Afghanistan could be defeated. Claims of an 'intellectual insurgency' exposed the deeply uncritical analysis in favour of institutionalised dogma.[14] The allied powers were losing the war, but these experts were arguing it was winnable. A decade later, they began publishing new narratives claiming that they knew all along it was never winnable.[15] This accumulation of failed rationales was reshaped for social media, in the expectation that the pre-social media age was long forgotten, and old theories of counterinsurgency were durable. On radio, television and social media, British military experts and pundits decided it was going to be a counterinsurgency conflict. So far, 2022 has been like Iraq 2003–9 all over again.

Lawrence Freedman (@LawDavF) has been prominent on social media. Freedman is one of Britain's leading exponents of war studies and has published widely on defence, security, and war. However, his overall presence in Putin's war has been one-sided in favour of Ukraine. He has shown little interest in why Putin went to war or his strategic goals. The sense of his tweets can be seen in a post from 25 March, when Freedman delved into small unit combat action: 'The long column was stuck. No point in attacking it when it wasn't moving. Better to concentrate on columns that were moving. Where things remain murky is scale and success of Ukrainian counterattacks. Just because we don't know everything doesn't

---

[14] The collected essays under 'Intellectual Insurgency', *The Royal United Services Institute Journal* 154, no. 3 (June 2009).

[15] Theo Farrell, *Unwinnable: Britain's War in Afghanistan* (London: Penguin, 2017).

mean we don't know anything.'[16] On 2 April, he wrote: 'It depends on the course of the war. Unless Russian forces can sort themselves out then the Russian elite at some point will have to confront the possibility of an even greater military humiliation.'[17] In April, he wrote: 'Ukrainians have not played down their civilian casualties, and I don't think they deliberately play down their military. This has been an asymmetric conflict so far in strategy and tactics.'[18] On 16 April, he posted: 'I don't think we're close to a "world war". I doubt if Russia wants a war with US either. So, the issue is whether nukes will be used, which by itself does not = WW3 — although it would take us into a new and dangerous time.'[19] On 30 April, he wrote: 'I think we are talking ourselves into an unnecessary crisis here posing a choice for Putin between having to back down and an absurd nuclear war. He has a very clear red line — no direct interference by NATO — which is being respected.'[20] On 24 August, he published an article, 'Constantly Operating Factors: Stalin's Lessons for Putin'.[21] Like O'Brien, Freedman has presented his books — The Future of War (2017) and Command (2022) — to frame his viewpoints of the war. O'Brien and Freedman have not expressed any inkling that they comprehend what Putin expects from this war. Like most senior defence analysts, they have struggled to explain the reasons for genocide or the war crimes.

In Britain, one of the foremost media platforms to showcase both politicians and expert opinions about the war is LBC, a twenty-four-hour talk radio show. On 21 March 2022, at the height of the

---

[16] Lawrence Freedman (@LawDavF), tweet, 25 March 2022, https://twitter.com/1 awdavf/status/1507348049768685573 (accessed 16 September 2022).

[17] Lawrence Freedman (@LawDavF), tweet, 1 April 2022, https://twitter.com/la wdavf/status/1510022189864607753 (accessed 16 September 2022).

[18] Lawrence Freedman (@LawDavF), tweet, 16 April 2022, https://twitter.com/la wdavf/status/1515457610249650186 16 September 2022).

[19] Lawrence Freedman (@LawDavF), tweet, 16 April 2022, https://twitter.com/la wdavf/status/1515249597693796353? (accessed 16 September 2022).

[20] Lawrence Freedman (@LawDavF), tweet, 30 April 2022, https://twitter.com/la wdavf/status/1520462167903985664 (accessed 16 September 2022).

[21] Lawrence Freedman, 'Constantly Operating Factors: Stalin's Lessons for Putin', Substack, 24 August 2022, https://samf.substack.com/p/constantly-operating -factors?utm_source=twitter&sd=pf (accessed 16 September 2022).

media frenzy early in the war, James O'Brien asked his talk show audience to contemplate: 'Why are we not fighting back when it comes to Russia's invasion of Ukraine?' Not to be confused with Phillips O'Brien, James O'Brien tries to appear original in his phone-in show but relies on the news headlines or social media trends to set out his daily agenda. He also refreshes his threads by crossing themes, for example in his talk about Ukraine O'Brien opened with a diatribe about Brexit, the problems of the Johnson government and corruption. He then referred to Russia's forced civilian deportations and mass abductions from Mariupol. He kept referring to genocide because he claimed it was mentioned in The Times newspaper. War crimes, genocide and forced deportations are going on today, 'of course Grozny was a war crime', which he added as an afterthought. 'The word genocide is appearing in British newspapers in our lifetime, to describe something that is happening in a country that borders Poland.' O'Brien exclaimed:

> "This is Europe in 2022 and we're seeing words that we haven't seen in eighty years, routinely appearing in newspapers, about a war that is unfolding, in a country that neighbours the EU member country that sends more friends, neighbours, lovers, family members, colleagues, to this country than any other in the world."

In a despairing tone, he stated: "I want something to fill the space that is currently occupied by impotence and confusion, and right now I will take almost anything. His final appeal before opening the phone lines to the public was: '[W]hy aren't we fighting back?"[22]

British media-driven 'conversations' around 9 May 2022 became fixated on Russia's forthcoming commemorations of the Great Patriotic War and parades in Moscow. On 28 April 2022, Ben Wallace, the UK defence minister, joined Nick Ferrari on his LBC talk show. Wallace referred to Putin: 'I think he will try to move from his "special operation". He's been rolling the pitch, laying the ground for being able to say "look this is now a war against Nazis, and what I need is more people. I need more Russian cannon

---

[22] James O'Brien, 'Why Are We Not Fighting Back When It Comes to Russia's Invasion of Ukraine?', LBC, 21 March 2022, https://podcasts.apple.com/gb/podcast/james-obrien-the-whole-show/id1460121501 (accessed 16 September 2022).

fodder."' He speculated that Putin 'is probably going to declare on this May Day that "we are now at war with the world's Nazis, and we need to mass mobilise the Russian people"'. Wallace claimed the introduction of Russian reserves would be Putin's admission of defeat, and declared he wasn't concerned by Putin's threat to use nuclear missiles.[23] Regardless of Wallace's expertise as a former soldier, his assessments of Putin's war were shambolic as shown by subsequent events. A few days later, on 2 May, Matthew Wright hosted a series of experts to amplify the Ferrari–Wallace dialogue. Robert Fox, a defence correspondent for the Evening Standard, opened his comments by saying that 'Putin is a wind-bag.' He claimed Putin had to say something on 9 May because the Russian Army was an enormous military machine that was 'rotten', 'corrupt' and 'failing'. However, he was cautious enough to warn NATO not to make any foolish claims about being at war with Russia. The next guest was Dr Chris Parry, who in reference to 9 May claimed, 'if Putin succeeds in the south, Putin will freeze the conflict and declare victory'. He then added the counter: 'If no success he will continue to huff n' puff. He's a big bad wolf.' This was a strange and contradictory assessment by an 'expert'. Similar in sentiment and parsimonious in content was Freedman's tweet of 10 May: 'Latest post on the significance of 9 May and a lacklustre parade without a major announcement from Putin. A Victory Parade Without Victories.'[24] Parry's hawkish reached another low, when he posted a tweet in October 2022, attached to an article in The Times, that implied RAF pilots serving in China should be 'shamed and shunned.' [25] Sky News subsequently revealed the pilots had been ordered to instructed Chinese pilots by the Ministry of Defence. [26]

---

[23] '"We Outgun Him": Defence Sec "Not Rattled" by Putin's Nuke Threat of "Lightning" Strikes', LBC, 28 April 2022, https://www.lbc.co.uk/news/russia-war-ukraine-ben-wallace-lightning-strikes (accessed 16 September 2022).

[24] Lawrence Freedman (@LawDavF), tweet, 10 May 2022, https://twitter.com/lawdavf/status/1523984970422882307 (accessed 16 September 2022).

[25] Chris Parry (@DrChrisParry), tweet, 18 October 2022, https://twitter.com/DrChrisParry/status/1582239057366564864 (accessed 30 October 2022).

[26] Deborah Haynes (@haynesdeborah), tweet, 28 October 2022, https://twitter.com/haynesdeborah/status/1586061609335721987 (accessed 30 October 2022).

There was a similar theme across US media reporting at that time.

The public callers into the shows, across the entire period from March to May, reflected the mounting confusion among the British public. This was entirely caused by the streams of mind-numbing fantasies and predictions of the war by experts. The public's comments included comparisons between the Russian genocide and the Nazi Holocaust. There was a consensus that the conditions in Ukraine were worsening and that 'Putin was just another Hitler.' Some public callers wanted to draw the line under the war, to somehow limit the fighting to the Ukraine or Poland's frontier. James O'Brien had compared Putin's and Boris Johnson's behaviour before the law, claiming that they had pushed against legality but had not broken any laws, hence the deep feeling of helplessness expressed by many people. NATO received considerable criticism for failing to respond to Russian aggression, and Joe Biden, the American president, was accused of cowardice. There were analogies to other wars and references to the ubiquitous war drama, as in The Band of Brothers (1999), in seeking to contextualise the war. There was a general sense that that the war had to be contained, while no nation was prepared to stand up against the genocide. These talks are always punctuated by commercial adverts for 'happy meals' or legal advisers, generating a surreal tone of genocide and consumerism. In thirty minutes, callers drifted between the massive despondency of nuclear war to the extensive cases of Russian corruption and intervention in Western governments. Since there was little difference between the public callers to Ferrari and Wright and the public callers to James O'Brien's, raises questions over the rationality of the West's strategic thinking in the public mindset.

Then change happened. There was a sudden shift of reporting from the Financial Times. The war had not gone the way of the experts, and newspapers restored investigative journalism. Paraphrasing the words of a Ukrainian soldier, Tyson, a drone operator, the Financial Times journalists wrote:

> [S]ix months into Russia's all-out assault on Ukraine, what Tyson sees worries him. Both sides are at a stalemate across much of the 2,400km front line and Russian forces are entrenching themselves for the winter ahead. 'All day long, they dig, and they dig, and they dig ... the enemy has learned fast,' he

said with a tone of respect.

The operator continued: '"[W]hat we saw in the beginning, and what we are seeing now—it's the difference between night and day."'[27] The journalists have finally caught up and surpassed the experts and pundits. On the same day (24 August 2022), Mick Ryan posted a thread that referred to an article about the Ukrainian Army's ability to adapt to the changing conditions of the war.[28] The troubling feature of these kinds of articles is not that they address a specific military theme but that they seem to ignore previous posts and content. Six days before, Ryan was claiming the defensive form of war had returned as a 'pivotal moment in military history', a rhetorical observation might ask - when did it fade from military history?[29] In a previous tweet, he had claimed that predicting war was impossible,[30] but that had seemed no barrier to his constant predictions. The Western public has struggled to comprehend the war, and this has been a serious outcome of false war analyses and predictions. The illogical word of politicians has been a constant in history, but the failings of the experts is more troubling and illustrates deep structural flaws within Western strategic doctrine. This is a striking summation that also summarises Putin's dismissive attitude towards the West.

The Anaconda Plan One Year On

On 24 March 2022, I wrote a paper that suggested Putin's strategy was an 'Anaconda Plan'. This was not an endorsement of the Russian way of war, but an objective assessment based upon generally

---

[27] Mehul Srivastava et al., 'Six Months of War in Ukraine: "The Enemy Learned Fast"', *Financial Times*, 24 August 2022.

[28] Mick Ryan, 'How Ukraine Is Winning in the Adaptation Battle against Russia', Engelsberg Ideas, 24 August 2022, https://engelsbergideas.com/essays/how-ukraine-is-winning-in-the-adaptation-battle-against-russia (accessed 16 September 2022).

[29] Mick Ryan (@WarintheFuture), tweet, 26 August 2022, https://twitter.com/warinthefuture/status/1562980930574172162 (accessed 16 September 2022).

[30] Mick Ryan (@WarintheFuture), tweet, 20 August 2022, https://twitter.com/warinthefuture/status/1561108570724536320 (accessed 16 September 2022).

known facts. I vehemently reject Putin's genocidal ambitions and the threat he represents to European culture. However, strategic analysis doesn't require tank-spotting level information to identify trends and patterns. The Russians have never once relinquished strategic control since this war began. They have repeatedly lost battles and suffered serious casualties, but they retain the strategic hold over the direction of the war. Since August, professionals in the USA and Europe have made repeated claims that have highlighted the Ukrainian predicament. The supply of weapons has enabled the Ukrainian Army to keep fighting, but the army has lost sight of strategy. Holding on, across all fronts and for every grain of sacred earth causes a reverse attrition. Ukraine has adopted a static punch-for-punch fight and consequently this has caused a depletion of troops and military reserves. To compensate for the losses, Ukraine has requested even more advanced weapons. It should be acknowledged that western weaponry has caused casualties to Russian forces but have failed to stem the rain of shells and missiles that are depleting Ukraine's industrial infrastructure. Has anyone considered when will Ukraine's military-industrial complex break and what are the implications for the west?

Putin's Anaconda plan is not strangling Ukraine, while ground forces penetrate the strategic avenues of the country. Instead, Putin is using mass to smother Ukraine. Mass of troops, masses of equipment and long fronts have stretched Ukrainian defenders. This inflicts slower destruction, but also heightens the genocidal impact of the war on Ukraine's population. As the depletion of infrastructure is intensified, at some point Ukrainian society will break if this onslaught continues. The longer this kind of war continues the deeper the destruction and the scale of human catastrophe. General Sherman's march in 1864 cut a trail of destruction that is still recalled in the southern historical memory. Putin's artillery has flattened villages and towns, and devastated cities—this is now fixed in memory, possibly forever. The scale of destruction is reaching total war levels and the war is far from over. Russia has continued to escalate the destruction and has shown neither mercy nor any intention of settling for anything less than Ukraine's extermination. Genocide is a word easily spoken but less well understood in its gravity. The destruction of Ukrainian people, culture, society, and memory will not stop with Ukrainians. Russia has become a train of violence without end. Poland is a likely target, as is Sweden. Firing missiles from Belarus, the Russians have used the forests on the frontier to amplify the threat of extreme violence westwards.

Putin's audacity is sustaining the Russian war effort. He has transformed Russia and he did this through his former KGB authority. At one time the KGB was the secret police organisation of the Soviet Union. After 1989 the reforms and changes led to the corporate takeover of the state by the security police. Today, the Federal Security Service (FSB) is a corporate secret police state that has a controlling interest over the Russian empire. The old KGB roots are still visible, especially in Putin who was trained as a guardian of the Soviet Union but now behaves as the godfather of Russia. Putin has different faces for different audiences, like a KGB handler, but his plans never waiver.

Since 2014, he has exploited his intelligence and security expertise to colonise the west from within. At the same time, he has exploited his long-term low-level conflicts to sustain his powerbase at home. He has bought and intimidated western leaders and politicians. Putin's methods have played all sides against the centre, financing both left and right political parties. This has muddied all political debates since Brexit and beyond COVID. Through these methods he has been able to undermine western security. However, Russian colonisation through intelligence and security has been a long-term process that began decades ago, and the consequences are only emerging from this war.

Putin has sent paid assassins to murder and rampage overseas. He leveraged political-economic control over western strategic energy supply rendering nations like Germany compliant. He drowned the City of London (*Londongrad*) in filthy money and regardless of sanctions the funds have continued to flow. He also arranged friendships with dubious national leaders to bend European Union regulations to breaking point. In other partnerships, his 'friends' have served the plan to block NATO expansion (Ukraine). His 'associates' have tried to cut the sinews of Ukraine's war. The Russian sphere of influence remains extensive regardless of western economic sanctions and political pressure. By February 2022, Putin held the pulse of western security and decided the patient was suitably anaesthetised to go to war. Early in the war the western opinion-makers were pushing all kinds of unrealistic assessments — Russia would collapse through logistics, the tyres were wrong, and the never-ending expectations that 'tomorrow' was Russia's demise. The Russian silence at the start enabled Ukraine to appear to gain the upper hand in the propaganda war. It has proven hollow — positive propaganda has backfired. All the claims of Russian failures have persuaded the Europeans that long-term war is not their problem.

Let's not have any illusions about the West's penchant for *Realkrieg* — which is a reluctance for war while making warlike noises. Putin has exploited this western credo. His threats have intimidated western decision-makers into limiting the supply of conventional weapons to Ukraine. This intimidation has benefits. Past arguments over contributions to NATO, has shifted to who has supplied Ukraine 'with the mostest'. Scrutiny reveals they are derisory amounts of arms and technologically advanced weapons systems. Profits are high but so are Ukrainian losses — USA and NATO should re-examine that ratio because it looks to all the world that the west fiddles the books while Ukraine burns. The supplies have forced Ukraine from a sound strategic response to the war and into stop-gap battlefield management. Holding the front at all costs, retaining lost ground at all costs, are honourable operational decisions but are limiting Ukraine's strategic options. Ideas of giving up ground for a better strategic position are heckled as cowardly or defeatist, which takes us back to why positive propaganda has become a curse to Ukraine's warfighting. Ukraine has acquired the defender's dilemma, even after fighting serious defensive battles, the lines have barely changed. But Ukrainian exhaustion is beginning to show, and the Russians have not retreated but on the contrary are getting stronger.

Neutralising the west has been Putin's most significant strategic success that hangs over the war zone. NATO should have immediately imposed an air-exclusion zone when Putin's troops crossed the frontier — on the grounds of sphere of influence.

Western *Realkrieg* failed against Putin's KGB style of command-and-control culture in modern war. This is a serious failure, confirmed within days when a former British general claimed NATO had been defeated. Putin had learned from the experience of NATO's intervention during the Civil War in former Yugoslavia. By forcing a restriction on NATO air power, he has been able to rain mechanised genocide on Ukraine without any interference. Unable to counter the Russian artillery, Ukraine is in an unsustainable strategic position. Helpless to counter this level of destruction, it has had a withering effect on morale. It's also noticeable that Ukrainian's soldiery is ageing, in their 40s and 50s. Major Vadim Khodak, of the 4th Tank Brigade, assigned to learn about British tanks, is 57 years old. To apply an appropriate Second World War comparison, Michael Wittmann, an SS tank officer, was 30 when he was killed in combat. Even the bravest fighters wilt under endless bombardment and the civilians suffer serious psychological problems. These are the lessons of modern war; a lesson Russia has factored into its way of war.[31]

NATO cannot regain the initiative without causing an escalation of the war and thus *Realkrieg* bungles along. There is no value in NATO promises of air power to protect member states, especially when territories are in danger of falling or being outflanked. Russia's strategic options increase daily as does China and Russia's other allies. NATO isn't even consoling the western public that has remained resolutely reluctant to go to war. Since the end of the Cold War, Yugoslavia, Rwanda, Iraq, and Afghanistan have taught Europeans that being allied to America is not entirely a secure option. America predictably thought of America first and decided NATO was not going to be involved. This suited NATO which had long given up strategic thinking and is home to petty careerism—another faceless and unaccountable institution. Europeans, as in 1968 and 1956, are forced to watch as Ukraine is bombarded into rubble and millions of refugees' flood across Europe's borders.

Nations that were already burdened with caring for the victims

---

[31] Dmitri (@wartranslated), tweet, 13 February 2023, https://twitter.com/wartranslated/status/1625255755606552601 (accessed 30 April 2023).

of the failed war on terror once again faced another human catastrophe. The torrid collapse of Afghanistan, abandoned by America, was another tiresome replay of America's failed imperialism like Vietnam in 1975. Always half in-half out, Biden didn't want Putin's war but has played the hawk to out-trump Trump. Meanwhile a small nation is struggling with a trickle of weapons, which suits Biden's America but is a long-term disaster for Europeans. Slowly, very slowly, the truth will out over the reasons for western sluggishness toward the war. On 15 February 2023, Ben Wallace the UK's Defence Minister, tried to defend the appalling condition of Britain's armed forces. This has come after a year of thuggish jingoism from the wholly populist Johnson government that abandoned a barely coherent defence policy for a failed doctrine of counterinsurgency (COIN dogma). Since then, several governments have tried to formulate a coherent policy while offering a few old and unreliable tanks. We now know that 12 tanks reflect the wholesale failure of UK defence policy under long-term Conservative governance.

Back in 2012, in a BBC documentary, Lord Guthrie, the former chief of staff, warned Britain was running dangerously close to a 'critical mass' in defence and that one day 'the risks might catch us out.' The Strategic Defence Review was a disaster, said Max Hastings, and Britain is losing all notion of 'grown up armed forces'. Hastings added that future governments required better judgement over selecting wars. Guthrie and Hasting predictions can now be seen as a withering indictment of British defence today. The British are betwixt n' between nostalgia or past wars and the realities of modern defence policy. In 2016 Britain abandoned Europe but has yet to formulate a serious defence policy. The Conservative government has rendered post-Brexit Britain defenceless, relying on NATO and the USA to pick up the slack. Alarmingly, no one seems surprised or appears to care for the political ramifications, such are the scale of socio-economic problems in UK. This is a 1940 moment—who are the Guilty Men? Thus, one year into this war and the UK public can see the utter foolhardiness of a popular government that has spouted torrid jingoism, but without the firepower to back it up. Europeans have fared little better, although civil-military relations and the military-industrial complexes in Europe have been more coherent in expenditure and effectiveness. Europeans have avoided defence committees on weapons requirements that in Britain have led to catastrophic failure. German Leopards are wanted, whereas the British Ajax is a financial disaster and wanted by nobody. European naval fleets have avoided the absurdity of aircraft carriers without aircraft or weak air defences. Often forgotten in the calculations of European defence is France, which remains Europe's nuclear power. Altogether this sets the added dimension of a framework for a European Army. Indeed, given the disasters of western security, a European Army represents the best solution for united Europe's long-term defence against Russia.

Being first to suggest Putin had gone to war with a genocidal intent was the outcome of decades of research into extreme war. There was also that moment of horrible realisation that Putin was replicating atomised wastelands with conventional artillery. The tubes were pointing at civilian communities. Having researched security warfare, where there are few rules or laws, fewer logistics or big war, and less care for civilians, genocidal war was not difficult to identify as logical for the corporate Russian way of war. In this context, Putin's methods are not unpredictable. Putin's war has followed patterns even though he attempts to hide them. Security warfare has featured in smallish wars since 1900, with mixed results but a large part of its strategic value lay in bluff. When genocide was practised against primitive peoples, it was done so to render them pacified very quickly to save on national resources. The Russians are attempting to teach the west a brutal lesson by the application of security warfare in Europe. Putin's armies are delivering total destruction with low grade arms, a poorly trained soldiery and less than average field command. It's also a strange story of a second-hand army defying western military orthodoxy. If the West confronted him, would his bluff collapse — this is the strategic question of the war.

The hard hand of war is devious. Putin, for all his assumed faults as a warlord, has shown no signs of losing control. His command, communication and control have barely faltered. His commanders have been forced to face responsibility for failure before the nation. The generals and the armies have been bound to the body politic through the military order, through political control and through religion. This is an extreme form of civil-security relations, where the national army is subsumed as the corporate arm of war for a security state. Russian media voices all manner of threats against the west and Ukraine, while Putin remains resolute. This constitutes orchestrated dramatic war-making, and the war has given Putin time to perfect his script knowing full well the west remains confused and undecided.

The Anaconda plan is also being indirectly fuelled by western *Realkrieg*—endless conferences and the drip-drip-drip of weapons to Ukraine, but how long can this last? What is the breaking point? For Ukraine, there is every reason to carry on fighting, which is a lesson from the Nazi Holocaust. However, if the rain of shells continues unabated, at some point Ukraine will lose its viability, as both a self-sustaining state, and as an independent nation. All the faith in the ability to achieve 1:5 or 1:10 kill ratios is fading against common-sense analysis and the realities of war. Both sides are suffering attrition losses, long-term this is unsustainable, but Ukraine has most to lose. The early predictions of Russian collapse or Putin's demise lacked the credibility of comprehending his legacy or the growing determination of Russians to win. Thus, analysts have continued to believe Russia was a busted flush against Russia's history of an imperial destiny, not always manifest but unmercifully brutal.

Genocide is the determining factor in this war. Russia's annihilation warfare was formulated in the 1990s when the 'new' Red Army generals realised winning at any cost was politically rewarding in Putin's corporate security state. Destroying cities is Putin's trademark if 'pushed' into prosecuting war. Once committed to war, the scale of destruction is always disproportionate. This war of annihilation is not a departure, as many observers have assumed, but a stage in the process of rebuilding/restoring the old Soviet borders/Soviet greatness. Putin's negative propaganda has created a new Russian identity of national pride, he's sealed a partnership with the past, and has not only weaponised nostalgia, but fuelled it with wartime sentiment. Recently a statue of Stalin was unveiled in Stalingrad (3 February 2023). This has longer-term meaning: even if Putin were removed, his legacy is the higher national calling for all the inheritors of his crown. Putin's legacy is the national mission that demands Ukraine must be destroyed and Russia to become great again. Russia's destiny has become Putin's legacy. Thus, the west confronts a serious dilemma: a general reluctance for war and without a credible strategic dogma just as war became global.

The western quandary

Social media has created an echo chamber for mass individualism. The ramifications from telecommunications in the past were confined to a national level, but today globalisation has been facilitated by new technologies. At the same time, in the last decade, a new politics has emerged that has been trying to stall the slow drift toward the dystopia caused by artificial intelligence. However, the COVID pandemic, financial uncertainty, wars and conflicts, and the increasing natural catastrophes caused by global warming have rendered governments impotent. The West today is on the cusp of a technical revolution, driven by artificial intelligence, that will have the power to disarm armies and undermine governments.

Strategic thinking and telecommunications are about to face the whirlwind of change sowing confusion in conventional armies. A newer politics is emerging that is casting aside all forms of political rationality. The collective western response to Putin's invasion has revealed how far down the road society and social media has already travelled toward future dystopia. The old Churchillian order of Atlantic security has unravelled and can no longer protect western societies. Russia has been confronting both change and dystopia, since 1992, and Putin's regime thrives on chaos and confusion. This has not undermined Putin's retention of the strategic initiative in this war. This should be a painful lesson for western societies, but governments have successfully deflected all discussion on this subject. The west watches as the unthinkable has unravelled in Ukraine, hoping Russia will lose, but utterly failing to engage in any discourse about sustainable security in the event of a Russian victory. Meanwhile Russia is trashing the Ukraine, as it did in Syria and Chechnya, annihilating the country's viability as a normal state.

REFLECTIONS

Final summaries and individual conclusions:

Philip W. Blood

Things fall apart. The concept of things falling apart has been ingrained in post-modern societies for decades, with Russia's systematic dismantling of Ukraine serving as a stark example. This ongoing conflict has left countless refugees as long-term casualties, reduced cities, and communities to rubble, and tragically resulted in genocide. Ukraine faces an existential struggle for its long-term survival as a modern state. Images of this war paint a dystopian reality on our screens, reminiscent of the once-fictional film *Children of Men* (2006) which now seems like an ominous blueprint for our future.

The fear of global infertility and aging societies underpins Putin's war aims, bl

urring the line between film fantasy and grim reality. In the 1980s, the original *Mad Max* film trilogy reflected similar dystopian fears of a post-nuclear war world, and once again, the dread of nuclear apocalypse looms. Gloom and doom have been constants in Western culture, from Oswald Spengler's *The Decline of the West* (1918) to H.G. Wells' *The Shape of Things to Come* (1933). More recently, scholars have delved into the looming global environmental apocalypse.[1] Despite these concerns, many still underestimate the impact of a distant war. Many people still blindly assume we have nothing to fear from a war so far away.

Predictably, nothing fell apart faster than post-modern Soviet structures. On 26 April 1986, Chernobyl nuclear power station, in Ukraine, suffered a catastrophic explosion. By July 1988, the Soviets justice system began a show trial against senior officials of the plant,

---

[1] Justin G.Edwards, Rune Graulund, and Johan Höglund (ed.), *Dark Scenes from Damaged Earth: The Gothic Anthropocene*, (Minneapolis: University of Minnesota Press, 2022).

blaming them for failing to follow set procedures, but all nuclear power plants were modernised to prevent a repeat of Chernobyl. Within three years of the disaster, the Soviet Union's political authority was failing. The Red Army was forced to withdraw from Afghanistan, the Berlin Wall collapsed. In August 1991 the first steps were taken to unseat Gorbachev. In December 1991 Ukraine and Belarus announced independence, a few weeks later the Soviet Union dissolved. Decades later Gorbachev claimed Chernobyl led to the collapse of the Soviet Union. The estimated human cost of the disaster ranged from 4,000 (UN estimates) to 60,000 deaths or more from other sources, and more than 4,000,000 people were directly affected by the fallout of radiation. Regardless of the actual numbers of casualties, the fear of radiation remains constant across western society as is the concern for environmental devastation.[2]

Then in February-March 2022, Russian forces began military operations in the Chernobyl region. Whether it was deliberate act on Putin's part to awaken European fears over radiation, or was a genuine error, is open to speculation. The breach into the exclusion zone attracted the leading observers from the UN and Europe's green politics. The first was Rafael Grossi in April 2022, he led an 'assistance and support' mission for the International Atomic Energy Agency (IAEA).[3] Then European politics entered the story when Greenpeace Germany decided to carry out an investigation to test the claims of Grossi's IAEA report that the radiation levels were 'normal'. The Russian soldiers had dug trenches and Greenpeace Germany tested the levels of radiation in the soil. They found harmful levels of 'gamma radiation' much higher than normal and were concerned that the IAEA was being unduly influenced by the Russian nuclear power agency.[4] However, it would be a mistake to

---

[2] Clive Ponting, *A New Green History*, (New York: Penguin Books, 2007).

[3] 'UN Nuclear Watchdog to Head Mission to Chernobyl as Russians Withdraw from Site | Ukraine | The Guardian', accessed 3 August 2023, https://www.theguardian.com/world/2022/apr/01/russians-fled-chernobyl-with-radiation-sickness-says-ukraine-as-iaea-investigates?CMP=Share_iOSApp_Other.

[4] 'Greenpeace Investigation Challenges Nuclear Agency on Chornobyl Radiation Levels', Greenpeace International, accessed 3 August 2023, https://www.green

assume the European press had been stirred about the Chernobyl disaster because of this war.

A cursory glance through newspaper and social media archives reveals a story that never went away. There was authoritative reporting across decades with deep concerns for general health and safety. Opposition to nuclear war, concerns for nuclear safety and fear of radiation have been constants in European politics since 1945. Hence why Putin's threat to unleash 'satanic' nuclear missiles was received with disgust, while Russian soldiers digging trenches within the exclusion zone was treated with incredulity. Since the war there have been growing threats to sources of energy supplies and the environment. While interest in nuclear power has increased, concerns over safety have remained constant. It is within the parameters of these issues regarding the politics of energy that Europe must formulate a strategic doctrine.

War has no true winners, as collateral damage takes a toll on all sides. Putin's war underscores the need for a comprehensive European defence strategy. Moreover, European society requires a new epistemology of war that acknowledges its destructive potential in the postmodern world. Traditional military history and strategic thinking have lost relevance, and we must address the evolving nature of conflict in the twenty-first century. Today, war has resurfaced in European society, entangled with new forms of barbarism and post-industrial genocide. The study of war and society stands at a crossroads, no longer adequately addressing the complexities of conflict in the digital age. Our societies confront uncertain futures, unprepared and without robust governance.

As we navigate this precarious path, shaped by advanced technology, the threat of dystopia, and the lessons of *Children of Men*, our cultural resilience remains a pressing concern for the future of the West. In this grim tapestry of war and dystopia, the lessons of history are stark. As Europe confronts a new era of uncertainty, it's clear that the time for innovation and a fresh strategic doctrine has arrived. The spectre of war, shaped by digitalization, artificial

---

peace.org/international/press-release/54762/greenpeace-investigation-challenges-nuclear-agency-on-chornobyl-radiation-levels/.

intelligence, and global complexities, demands a new epistemology — one that doesn't dwell in the shadows of the past. While the future may hold challenges reminiscent of dystopian fiction, our immediate concern must be the preservation of our cultural resilience.

Dustin Du Cane

When we started writing this book last year, I didn't think the day would come, at least before the end of the war, perhaps never, that Putin would have an international arrest warrant looming over his head. No global issue, except global warming and perhaps nuclear proliferation, is as politically fraught as holding the leaders of nations accountable for international crimes. For instance, the West is weary of accusing even its ideological enemies of the crime of genocide, for a spectrum of reasons ranging from fear of being accused of minimising the Holocaust as a type of genocide, despite Lemkin doing so and which he was accused of, to the Responsibility to Protect resolution which nobody expected would be invoked only two decades later against a nuclear power, to decrepit German Ostpolitik and finally the US Pentagon's personal offense at the existence of the International Criminal Court. The Global South, correctly to some degree, sees international justice as selective, especially selecting brown people without nuclear weapons. What about Iraq when you decry the invasion of Ukraine? Gordon Brown's refusal to engage with the elephant in the room, his role as a very powerful number two in the British government, during the sordid preparation and conduct of war against Iraq, is a great propaganda gift. Perhaps Brown should have left this campaigning on a trial for crime of aggression to Ukrainians. Rogue states like Russia and Iran obviously decry international justice using the language of the Global South and the Pentagon. Meanwhile China, the actual only superpower competing with the US, treats international law as a tool of expansion and empire-building, as skilfully as the Soviet Union, but not Russia, did.

However, Putin, the supposed master of 5-dimensional chess,

is simply a chimeric chaotic bully who doesn't respect or even understand red lines. It's possible to fudge genocide, war crimes and most atrocities. But parading kidnapped Ukrainian children on tv, personally praising their kidnapping, and rewarding the kidnapper in chief on television, crossed a line that even the West can't ignore—even as it mostly tries not to name the (quiet) genocide of Ukrainians via knife, bullet, rocket and artillery. It ironic and appropriate that the war crime Putin is accused of takes the same form in practise as one of the types of genocide—the only difference, though perhaps a vital one, is genocidal intent. Importantly however it can be labelled a war crime, not the powerful genocide word… A difference of intent, not action, that Putin is blatantly personally responsible for. Hitler never publicly pinned medals on Himmler congratulating him for killing all the Jews, though he congratulated him in private and promoted him publicly. There was always a layer of deniability. But Putin is too stupid, too crass, too brutish, too KGB to understand what red lines are for the West. Putin also doesn't also understand the consequences of ignoring his own so-called red lines, threatening a series of terrible consequences if the West supported Ukraine, if the West sent weapons, if the West sent tanks, if Crimea was attacked, if Ukraine reconquered Kherson. Putin spent too much time dealing with US, British and German diplomats, corrupt politicians, and venal businessmen, engaging in their dirty realpolitik horse-trading, atrocity winking, and façade building and thought he would always act with impunity. Germany wants trade, the US wants to concentrate on China and Russia owns London - it never can go wrong. But the Hague with a Polish chief judge (Lemkin would presumably be proud!) and British chief prosecutor finally acted with a degree of independence and courage impossible to understand for a graduate of a Leningrad pseudo-law course which simply served as an apprenticeship to the KGB.

It was and is also rank stupidity for Putin to allow his court jesters daily rant about genocide and war crimes that they want committed, on tv and social media. Putin's diplomats are out of control on Twitter and even former president Medvedev manages to drunkenly implicate himself and his master regularly on social media. Goebbels would have been aghast out how the message was out of control. The Reich propaganda minister was laser focused on keeping media from saying out loud what everybody knew was happening, in order to preserve personal and state deniability. There is no veneer of deniability about Russian intent.

Adding to clear intent, almost every crime in the Rome Statute establishing the International Criminal Court, ranging from the types of genocide, including deportation of children, to war crimes such as targeting civilians indiscriminately or discriminately, to crimes against humanity has been committed in Ukraine by Putin, his generals, and his soldiers, since 2014, not just 2022. I told friends in February 2022 that now the West would see people who look like them, next door to them, getting the same brutal treatment at Russian hands, as the people of Syria and Chechnya. This was another mistake that Putin made. Long used to his brutality in countries far away of which we know little, to quote Chamberlain, being ignored, Putin let loose the same dogs of war he had blooded in Syria. Except the Ukrainians had tanks, artillery, and planes. Ukrainian men and women fought back and meanwhile their families, as refugees streaming to Europe across friendly borders brought news of atrocities which couldn't be dismissed as those of Afghans, Syrians, and Africans. Ukrainians speak English, Polish, and German, they don't have the accents that post 2001 signalled terrorist thanks to the West's brown people war. It's fair to despair at the racism those war brought, it's unfair to complain about for instance Poles welcoming people who speak a similar language, look almost like them, and often have family ties, more warmly than the equally desperate, needy and traumatised refugees from the Middle East, victims of dictators and climate change. Putin went to war with people who had old friends and who quickly made new ones. I foresaw that Ukrainians would be warmly welcomed to Poland, there was already a quiet but huge diaspora in Poland. I have been in relationships with Ukrainians who speak better Polish than me and I'm writing these words in a bar run by a Ukrainian, with a Ukrainian cleaning lady and texting with my best friend who married a Ukrainian and adopted her son. All of these Ukrainians were in Poland before the war. Old ties are reviving. I'm surprised there hasn't been a stronger nationalist push-back, but I have seen examples of nationalist scum trying to provoke hatred between the nations. On both sides.

Speaking of nationalist scum, another elephant in the room is Stefan Bandera. On January 2, 2023, the Ukrainian parliament decided to celebrate his birth, with a picture of the commanding general of the Ukrainian army sitting under his portrait. This caused shock waves to which the Ukrainian seemed oblivious before committing this incredible *faux pas*. As Eugene Finkel, genocide historian, stated on Twitter that day: "Appalling. Bandera would have hated a democratic, liberal Ukraine. He would be the first in line to assassinate its Jewish president." There exists a myth of Bandera which Finkel described as being a cartoon figure in Ukrainian memory. However, Banderas was a fascist, genocidal anti-Semite, and genocidal hater of Poles as well as a Nazi collaborator. Bandera's falling out with his masters over Ukrainian independence was an argument among bandits, not an act of political heroism. The rehabilitation of Nazi collaborators, including those of the Baltic and Ukrainian SS is piggy-backing natural revulsion at Russian genocide. Fighting and opposing the Russians or Soviets however does not make you good or a friend- a lesson the Americans ignore and have ignored forever. The enemy of my enemy is not my friend. I will not accept being told on social media that Bandera's legacy could 'perhaps' be re-examined after war. No, it's Ukrainians pulling him out, mostly innocent because of the cartoon image, but still offensively, during the war—as I found perusing an Ukrainian market in Lviv where pictures of Bandera snuggled next to those of rabbis. Something Bandera hopefully despairs of in hell. The surviving fascists who were in Azov before 2014 are still fascists until proven otherwise. War rarely deradicalizes soldiers, even when they're shooting now at the people, they used to mosh with at white power concerts.

I visited Lviv in February 2023. I found a plaque to Hersh Lauterpacht near the market where black & red Ukrainian Insurgent Army (UPA) memorabilia caused me to shiver. I saw the street where my grandmother lived, in her mixed Polish-Ukrainian family that Bandera's UPA would have crucified like a hundred thousand others. I went through two mild power cuts. I saw people determined but tired. It didn't feel like home, but it did a little. A week later a pro-Ukrainian booster declaimed Ukraine as the synonym of Ukrainness on Twitter. Well perhaps it is now, now that the previously dominant population-wise Poles and Jews were ethnically cleansed.

These are paradoxical, at first glance and perhaps irrelevant thoughts in a book mostly about Russian atrocity and above all genocide. Poles and Ukrainians are friends. Both sides need however to look at their past. Something the Russians are incapable of doing. Don't be Russian.

Those are my thoughts arising from researching and writing my essays. I'd write Svala Ukraini but the origin and usage of that phrase prevents me, so Long Live Free and Democratic Ukraine. Putin, the Russian state, Russian society and active and passive Russians, individually, bear sole and joint responsibility for this war.

I take some satisfaction writing these final lines in 2023 that I can now call Prigozhin a war criminal without being sued. A dead war criminal.[5] His imminent death was a prediction I publicly made back in March 2023, a while before his mutiny and obviously before the hot-take analysts got to work talking on Foreign Affairs piece about the imminent collapse of Putin's regime.[6] Sometimes I despair at the analysts and think tank pundits who often seem to have less insight than a Moscow taxi driver. Throughout the summer I also thought of Chris Bellamy's and Dennis Showalter's descriptions of the battle of Kursk in 1943 as Ukraine bled and died inching onto Russian barbed wire, though of course in 2023 the neo-Nazis

---

[5] My comments on him and his friends are available elsewhere, including at www.fallout.substack.com.
[6] Dustin Du Cane [@DustinDuCane], Tweet, *Twitter*, 25 June 2023, https://twitter.com/DustinDuCane/status/1672911750746763268 and Dustin Du Cane [@DustinDuCane], 'Which Prigozhin Falls out of a Window First?', Tweet, *Twitter*, 27 March 2023, https://twitter.com/DustinDuCane/status/1640443356944670734.

are defending from liberation.⁷

It feels surreal writing this final sentence looking on two young Ukrainian women, not necessarily refugees but perhaps, talking in Russian, in a Warsaw park café, n Bucha they would be dead after sexual assault.

Chris Bellamy

In January 2022, Professor Mark Galeotti, a noted Russia-watcher, and scholar, based in London, published a book called The Weaponisation of Everything: A Field Guide to the New Way of War. ⁸ It encapsulates many of the aspects of 'non-linear warfare' outlined in earlier essays in this book. The sub- title 'a field guide' is clever as the 'field' is now life, the universe and everything Mark Galeotti's book explains how 'non-linear warfare' includes global geopolitics, business, and trans-national crime, 'buying friends and influencing people' — notably the Chinese investment in bases abroad and developing countries, life in general, law, information, and general culture ('soft power').

In the first year the conflict expanded geographically, but not as much as many had feared. Conventional military operations remained confined to Ukrainian territory. However, in addition to the Black Sea blockade hampering grain, oil and fertiliser exports to the rest of the world, on 26 September 2022, a series of clandestine bombings and subsequent underwater gas leaks occurred on the Nord Stream 1 and Nord stream 2 natural gas pipelines under the Baltic Sea off Denmark. Both pipelines had been built to transport natural gas from Russia to Germany, and were majority owned by the Russian majority state gas company Gazprom. The

---

[7] Dennis E. Showalter, *Armor and Blood: The Battle of Kursk, the Turning Point of World War II*, First edition (New York: Random House, 2013). Bellamy, *Absolute War*.

[8] Mark Galeotti, *The Weaponisation of Everything: A Field Guide to the New Way of War*. (Yale: Yale University Press, 2022). Professor Galeotti is based at the School of Slavonic and East European Studies (SSEES), University of London, the Royal United Services Institute (RUSI) and various Universities around the world.

perpetrators' identities and motives behind what was clearly the sabotage remain debated.

Prior to the leaks, the pipelines had not been operating due to disputes between Russia and the European Union following the Russian invasion but were filled with natural gas. On 26 September at 02:03 local time (CEST), an explosion was detected originating from Nord Stream 2; a pressure drop in the pipeline was reported and natural gas began escaping to the surface southeast of the Danish Island of Bornholm. Seventeen hours later, the same occurred to Nord Stream 1, resulting in three separate leaks northeast of Bornholm. All three affected pipes were rendered inoperable; one of the two Nord Stream 2 pipes remained operable and is thus ready to deliver gas through Nord Stream 2. The leaks occurred one day before Poland and Norway opened the Baltic Pipe running through Denmark, bringing gas to Germany rather than from Russia. Therefore, the sabotage, whoever was responsible, reflects a wider economic conflict between Russia and the EU.

A further and related expansion of the conflict south-eastward, into the Caspian Sea, manifested itself in January 2023. As noted in earlier essays Russia was running out of ammunition (as was Ukraine). On 8 March Sky News reported that Iran had supplied large quantities of bullets, rockets, and mortar shells to Russia for use in the conflict. Like many states in the Middle East, Iran is primarily equipped with Russian designed ordnance and by January 2023 Iran started supplying Russia's deficiency in ammunition while challenging its perceived opponents in the west. The deliveries had reportedly been made by two Russian-flagged cargo ships that travelled from Iran to the Russian port of Astrakhan on the Caspian Sea.

The two ships, the Musa Jalil, and the Begey, were reported at the Iranian port of Amirabad, north-east of Sari on the southeastern shore of the Caspian, on 9 January 2023 and both appeared to have left on 10 January. The Iranian cargo may have included about 100 million rounds of Small Arms ammunition, 300,000 shells and 10,000 flak jackets and helmets. However, some experts suggested this estimate was a bit high. Having left Amirabad, the ships stopped off Turkmenistan on 12 January for two days and arrived at the Russian port of Astrakhan on 27 January. They left there on 2 February.⁹

In the Black Sea the 22 July 2022 Grain Initiative (BSG) to safeguard oil and grain supplies beyond the theatre of war was renewed in November 2022 for 120 days. It was due to expire on 25 March 2023 but on 13 March the Russians agreed a further two-month extension. Ominously, however, any further extension would be subject to preconditions. By 17 March 2023 UNODC inspectors have helped to clear over 1600 vessels bringing over 24.9 million metric tons of grains and foodstuffs to the wider world. Nearly 21 per cent had gone to Low and Lower-Income countries, including 44 per cent of wheat exports, while the World Food Programme had transported over 481,000 metric tonnes of wheat grain from Ukrainian ports intended for the hungriest in Afghanistan, Ethiopia, Somalia, and Yemen.

Additionally, by helping food exports reach global supply chains, the BSGI had helped to lower prices, reducing financial burdens on consumers worldwide.¹⁰

As shown in previous essayss, the initial Russian plan to decapitate Ukraine by a swift seizure of the capital failed. It might be seen at best, as a costly example of 'reconnaissance by battle'. The battle of Kyiv lasted from 25 February 2022 to 2 April 2022 and ended with the withdrawal of Russian forces. Russian efforts switched to the Donbas where Russia already had a foothold and where the Russian focus remained for the rest of the war's first year. In September Putin declared the annexation of the four oblasti of Luhansk, Donetsk, Zaporizhzhya and Kherson. The Russians did not control any of them entirely and lost the capital of one — Kherson — in November. By then Russia had lost half of the full extent of Ukrainian territory captured in the earlier phases of the war. The

---

9 'Iran's Alleged Ammunition for Russia's War in Ukraine: The Secret Journey of the Cargo Ships Accused of Supplying Invasion | World News | Sky News', accessed 3 August 2023, https://news.sky.com/story/irans-alleged-ammunition-for-russias-war-in-ukraine-the-secret-journey-of-the-cargo-ships-accused-of-supplying-invasion-12828039.

10 'Black Sea Grain Initiative Extended on Deadline Day | UN News', accessed 3 August 2023, https://news.un.org/en/story/2023/03/1134762.

front moved very little between November and March 2023, in part because of the winter weather and the rasputitsa— 'season of bad roads'—in autumn and spring.

The fighting in the east came to focus on the unlikely town of Bakhmut. It was strategically insignificant but proved useful to Ukraine as a 'meat grinder' to fix Russian and pro-Russian forces. Like Verdun in 1915-16. The main Russian assault towards the city started on 1 August after Russian forces advanced from Popasna following a Ukrainian withdrawal from that front. The main assault force primarily consisted of mercenaries from the Russian paramilitary organization, supported by regular Russian troops and separatist forces from the Donetsk and Lugansk Peoples' Republics.

Casualties in these battles have been terrible. Neither Ukraine nor Russia has issued detailed figures and any figures are likely to be underestimates. 'Casualties' are, in any case, problematic and complicated. Some are killed instantly. Some are mortally wounded and die of wounds later. Some are badly wounded and disabled for life, so cannot return to any form of military service but may be of further use to the war effort, such as sergeant Kalashnikov. Some are less badly wounded and may recover and be sent to back to the war. Under the traditional norms of war, prisoners-of-war (PoWs) are hors de combat, disarmed and detained until hostilities are ended. However, the practice of PoW exchanges, which goes back hundreds of years, complicates that. The Russians, with their commendably precise approach to such matters, differentiate between 'irrecoverable losses' and others. The former includes killed, PoWs and missing.[11]

Ukraine said an average of 824 Russian soldiers were dying every day in February 2023, and while those figures cannot be independently verified, the general analysis was supported by the U.K. government, which estimated in February 2023 that Russia has suffered between 175,000 and 200,000 casualties during its war in Ukraine, including 40,000 to 60,000 killed.

---

[11] Krivosheyev, G F, trans. Christine Barnard, *Soviet Casualties and Combat Losses in the Twentieth Century*. Russian original 1993 (Greenhill books, Stackpole, PA, 1997, Digitized by the University of Michigan 2009).

The British intelligence services estimated that Russia's private Wagner Group, which has sent a large number of mercenaries, including convicts recruited from prisons to the front lines in Ukraine, has taken losses at a rate of up to 50 percent

For perspective, the then-Soviet Union lost a total of 15,000 troops Irrecoverable losses) during the entirety of its 10-year conflict in Afghanistan between 1979 and 1989.12 In December, an adviser to Ukrainian President Volodymyr Zelenskyy said as many as 13,000 Ukrainian troops had been killed since the start of the war, CBS News partner network BBC News reported.13

The Wagner Group, which has played a major, possibly the major role in the Battle for Bakhmut is of particular interest. As noted, mercenaries from Private Military Companies PMCs) are expendable and deniable. But it goes further. On 10 March 2023 a source — Alex Kochkarov — now based in London - tweeted extracts from a document found on a Russian soldier killed in action (KIA), containing some unusual information. Russian soldiers had been told to remove unit insignia from their uniforms and that

> 'In case of incidents (traffic incidents, servicemen under influence of alcohol/drugs, injuries or fatalities among civilians, etc.) identify yourself as a Wagner PMC combatant.'14

Could it be, therefore, that reports of the preponderance of the Wagner Group in the Bakhmut area might themselves be the result of disinformation and that if anything goes wrong the Russian Army does not have to take the blame?

In analysing the Russian military performance in the first year of the full-scale war, there is an extraordinary anomaly in Russian command structure and arrangements. Historically, the Russians

---

12   Ibid.
13   'One Year of Russia's War in Ukraine, by the Numbers - CBS News', accessed 3 August 2023, https://www.cbsnews.com/news/ukraine-war-news-russia-invasion-by-the-numbers/.
14   Alex Kokcharov [@AlexKokcharov], '6. In Case of Incidents (Traffic Incidents, Servicemen under Influence of Alcohol/Drugs, Injuries or Fatalities among Civilians, Etc.) Identify Yourself as a Wagner PMC Combatant. 4/x', Tweet, *Twitter*, 10 March 2023, https://twitter.com/AlexKokcharov/status/1634195053676580467.

have been good at high-level command, although there were cases in the Great Patriotic War where, for example, Rokossovskiy, commanding a front (army group) resented the intrusion of representatives of Stavka, the Supreme High Command.[15] In the 2022 Ukrainian operation there was at first no single military leader for all Russian forces in theatre. On 10 April 2022, General Aleksandr Dvornikov (1961–), a veteran of operations in Syria, known as 'The Butcher of Aleppo', was apparently placed in charge of military operations in Ukraine, although he did not have a formal title. Before his appointment, he had been one of several in charge of the various fronts.[16]

On 3 June 2022, it was reported, citing Russian soldiers, that Dvornikov had been replaced by Colonel General Gennady Zhidko in command of the invasion. However, on 5 June the Ukrainian governor of Luhansk oblast', Serhiy Haidal, said Dvornikov was still in command and had been given until 10 June by his superiors to complete the operation to capture Severodonetsk. On 25 June, it was reported that Dvornikov had been dismissed from his post.[17] He was replaced by another Syria veteran, Col Gen Gennady Zhidko (1965-) Having assumed the position in May, Zhidko was transferred a month later to be head of the Eastern Military District, and Gen Sergey Surovikin (1966-) was publicly announced to have taken the position on 8 October. His appointment was announced hours after the attack on the Crimean Bridge. Although there were earlier reports that Dvornikov and Zhidko had effectively held this post, it was the first time an overall Commander-in-Chief had been formally confirmed. Surovikin's first day at work saw Ukraine hit by a wave of Russian missile attacks — the biggest

---

[15] Bellamy, *Absolute War*, pp. 574-73.
[16] Doha Madani, Courtney Kube and Alexander Smith, 'Russia Appoints General with Cruel History to Oversee Ukraine Offensive', NBC News, 10 April 2022, https://www.nbcnews.com/news/world/russia-appoints-general-cruel-history-oversee-ukraine-offensive-rcna23784 (accessed 12 August 2022).
[17] '"Butcher of Aleppo" Sacked as Vladimir Putin Shakes Up Russian Top Command Again', *The Telegraph*, 25 June 2022, https://www.telegraph.co.uk/world-news/2022/06/25/russia-shakes-up-top-command-ex-syria-war-general-sacked (accessed 12 August 2022).

in months.

Later, on 11 January 2023, Putin took the extraordinary step of replacing Surovikin with Valeriy Gerasimov himself as C-in-C in Ukraine.[18] In the articles signed by Gerasimov in February 2023 he had said the non-linear phase would be 80 percent of the war and the last fifth - four to one — would be linear. Putin had been promised a swift victory in maybe ten days. On 11 January 2023 the war was in its 321st day. It had been Gerasimov's concept so now Putin put him in charge in Ukraine to sort it out.

Given the combination of sea, land, and air forces it seems strange it took Putin so long to appoint an overall theatre commander. Initially the four main groupings, based on Military Districts, seemed not to be operating in a coordinated fashion. Only when the Russians had suffered severe setbacks, in April, was an overall commander appointed and even then, his position was more of a primus inter pares. Maybe Putin feared that, had the invasion gone to plan and resulted in a swift and spectacular victory, its perceived commander would have represented a Caesar-like figure

Combined with the dominance of long-range artillery and missiles, and the massive expenditure of ammunition resulting in shell shortage, the first year of the war very much resembles the Western Front in World War One. The failed assault on Kyiv resembles the German aim to achieve a knock-out blow in the Schlieffen Plan. That was replaced by a long-drawn-out war of attrition. At sea and in the air new technologies, notably drones and drone-boats, radically altered the nature of war, as aircraft and submarines had between 1914 and 1918.

The art of war is, like any visual art, a blend of imagination, ambition, and physical and mental effort. The materials may change, from the pigments used for cave paintings to the pixels that make up electronic images, but the artist must make the most of what is to hand. The basic principles of perspective, composition

---

[18] 'Russia Appoints Top Soldier Gerasimov to Oversee Ukraine Campaign | Reuters', accessed 3 August 2023, https://www.reuters.com/world/europe/russia-appoints-gerasimov-top-commander-ukraine-2023-01-11/.

and balancing colours remain largely constant. So it has been in the first year of the war still largely confined to Ukraine.

Roger Cirillo

Genocidal war is in Europe is now a dilemma for the West. Vladimir Putin's decision to invade Ukraine in February 2022 may well bring about Armageddon, the end of the world as we know it. Whether this will happen through nuclear war or in the dystopia of the forever war will matter little to history. If humanity survives, the leaders of Europe must break with the past and their long-held reluctance towards defence. Europe must acquire an army, which must project a strong defensive posture, but with a mailed fist, in its fighting power, to back up its threat potential. Much of the old Cold War rhetoric is still functioning and extending NATO membership to countries outside of the original NATO perimeter is dangerous.

NATO membership does not offer security for the eastern European countries, if Russia only sees threats from their existence under an Article 5 umbrella and the push forward of modern long-range weapons to the Russian border.

Putin's military response, though morally regrettable, was also a miscalculation in force projection, lacking the full weight needed to rapidly crumble his opponent. NATO's proxy participation with drones, satellite surveillance and a Niagara of munitions and weapons has held back a decisive thrust, but those mistakes have potentially been removed by a completely regenerated and repositioned Russian force, poised around the battered remnants of Ukraine's forces as this is being written.

Fighting a proxy war by NATO is both dangerous and unjustified. European nationalism and expansionism of any state has no place in NATO, nor will it be supported by the bulk of the Western populace. The political leaders of the 1930s created the conditions for the Second World War. It should be remembered that the populations suffer the consequences of any decision to wage war. This is the unvarnished lesson of our history.

Acceptance of neutrality is not defeat except for those in NATO who believe that Russia must be an enemy. As neither NATO nor Russia want to escalate to a nuclear response, and Western Europe's military is neither fit nor willing to engage Russia in a conventional ground war, the continued hammering of each other in Ukraine has past reached a genocidal situation for the victims of the war, the Ukrainian people, whose own government refused to relent based on NATO's assurances and military aid, and the western powers whose funding and equipment has prolonged the war indecisively for those they claim to help.

Russia refuses to accept a NATO power on its border. This is an unalterable military fact, not a political one. This has been repeated constantly in many forums since the 1990's. Russia has not been militarily defeated nor appreciably damaged militarily or economically despite the active information war of claims made by the United States and Great Britain and the Zelensky government. This war parallels the great war of claims made by the United States during the final years of the Vietnam War. As military stalemate and defeat is not possible as a NATO alternative, a transfer of political oversight from NATO to the EU or perhaps a different security construct accommodating neutrality and UN oversight for the Eastern Countries is called for. An extension of Article 5 to Ukraine will not save its position, but it will spark a general war.

Russia has both adapted and regenerated her armed forces and can and inevitably will destroy Ukraine's military. Russia does not want a military occupation of an unfriendly nation but most likely will accept a neutral status for the areas in question. If moralists claim genocide for the Russians, so too, they must consider as genocidal the prolonging of a war that they have neither the stomach nor intent to fight to its final military conclusion with its own forces. This is as much a moral and reprehensible policy, as the original policies on both sides created the situation in the first place. It is genocidal to provide the means to fight interminably with no possible military conclusion.

The military stalemate created between the Warsaw Pact and NATO in the 1980's seems both improbable and far more deadly today in the Ukraine war, in 2023. Russia has chosen not to use it full might to change this. How long this will eventuate is both a moral and a military decision that can only be decided by the Ukrainians and not their NATO supporters, who have no legal or political agreement to guarantee Ukraine's safety.

***ibidem**.eu*